UNIVERSITY OF CAMBRIDGE
DEPARTMENT OF APPLIED ECONOMICS

MONOGRAPH 23

# THE ECONOMIC IMPACT OF THE PATENT SYSTEM

UNIVERSITY OF CAMBRIDGE
DEPARTMENT OF APPLIED ECONOMICS

*Monographs*

This series consists of investigations conducted by members of the Department's staff and others working in direct collaboration with the Department.

The Department of Applied Economics assumes no responsibility for the views expressed in the Monographs published under its auspices.

The following Monographs are still in print.

# THE ECONOMIC IMPACT OF THE PATENT SYSTEM

## A STUDY OF THE BRITISH EXPERIENCE

**C. T. TAYLOR**

*Deputy Director, Department of Applied Economics*
*Cambridge*

*and*

**Z. A. SILBERSTON**

*Official Fellow, Nuffield College, Oxford*

CAMBRIDGE
AT THE UNIVERSITY PRESS
1973

Published by the Syndics of the Cambridge University Press
Bentley House, 200 Euston Road, London NW1 2DB
American Branch: 32 East 57th Street, New York, N.Y.10022

© Cambridge University Press 1973

Library of Congress Catalogue Card Number: 73–77173

ISBN: 0 521 20255 8

Printed in Great Britain
at the University Printing House, Cambridge
(Brooke Crutchley, University Printer)

# CONTENTS

# LIST OF TABLES AND FIGURES

[ ix ]

# PREFACE

Research on the patent system has been carried out at the Department of Applied Economics for a number of years. This volume presents the results of about three years' work on the basic economic effects of the system, and is a sequel to an earlier volume on the law and administration of the system.

The research for this study has been undertaken by Christopher Taylor, under the general direction of Aubrey Silberston. Although we share full joint responsibility for all the arguments and findings presented, and for the general shape of the work, the detailed planning and execution was carried out primarily by the former. We have however been in regular consultation throughout the work and the book, while being mainly the former's handiwork, is in important respects the fruit of a long period of harmonious cooperation and exchange of views and ideas between us.

Although she did not remain with us long enough to be involved in the main industrial research, Miss J. M. Bradley was engaged on the early stages of the work. She participated in planning the study and contributed a comprehensive survey of the American literature, on which we rely heavily in the first section of Chapter 3.

Our thanks are due firstly to the Social Science Research Council for its generous support in financing the research.

We owe next an especially large debt of gratitude to the companies which cooperated in the industrial inquiry that forms the backbone of our study. Some forty-four industrial firms supplied information and participated in discussions and judgments in the course of this inquiry. We offer our particular thanks to all the patent and licensing managers and other patent specialists in these firms who bore the brunt of our requests for help. We were unfailingly impressed by their constructive and detached approach to the problems discussed and by their skill and knowledge in their professional fields. A number went very far beyond the call of duty in digging out material, explaining the quirks of the system, discussing its more problematical and subtle effects and commenting (often in considerable detail, often critically, but always helpfully) on drafts and re-drafts of the parts of the book submitted to them. Without their interest and help the study would have been very much poorer. It would clearly be inappropriate to mention individuals here, much as we are tempted to do so; the names of the companies involved are listed in Annex 1 of Appendix B (page 377).

At the same time we emphasise that, while particular results of the inquiry were in many cases the outcome of a joint exercise in which the industrial respondents usually played an important part, final responsibility for all assessments of economic effects lies with us. It cannot be safely assumed that those whom we consulted in industry are always in agreement with our findings; most would have reservations of a major or minor sort on certain parts of our conclusions. Furthermore any inaccuracies or errors of fact that remain in the text are solely our responsibility.

We received valuable help on special aspects of the study from a number of public bodies and other organisations. Principal among these were the National Research Development Corporation and the Institute of Patentees and Inventors, with officials of both of which we had meetings. Parts of the book were shown to officials of the Patent Office and the Office of the Registrar of Restrictive Trading Agreements, and valuable comments were received. However, it must be stressed that we retain absolute and sole responsibility for our accounts of the law and administration of the system, and for opinions relating thereto.

' In a project of this sort, it would obviously be impossible to list all the persons who have helped and stimulated us in various phases of the work, or all the written sources that have influenced our thinking. (Full references to the latter are given where appropriate in the text.) In some instances our debt will be readily apparent – as, for instance, to the Banks Committee on the Patent System (of which one of us was a member), and to its Report. However, we are particularly anxious to acknowledge the help of colleagues and friends in the Department of Applied Economics, and of visitors to the Department who are interested in this field. In particular our thanks are due to the Director, Mr W. A. H. Godley, for his forbearance in allowing the first author to pursue the later stages of the work at a time when other Department duties and research have had a claim on him; to Professor W. B. Reddaway, who has provided general encouragement, as well as commenting in his usual penetrating way on drafts of Chapters 9 and 10; and to Professor O. J. Firestone of Ottawa University, Professor E. Hope of the Norwegian Business School, Bergen, and Mr C. Lindstrom, of the University of Umeå, Sweden, for helpful discussions. Finally we gratefully acknowledge the work done on the study by the Department's staff, particularly Mrs Judy Bottrell, who helped to launch and keep a check on the industrial inquiry; Miss Pat Seaby, who produced working tables of data from the inquiry; the computing staff under Miss Marion Clarke, who undertook computations needed for Chapter 4; and the typing staff under Mrs Lilian Silk, who dealt with innumerable (and barely legible) drafts with unfailing patience and good humour; and to Mrs Joyce Leverett and Mrs Nola Pegram, who also did valuable work in preparing the final manuscript.

*Cambridge*                                                     C.T.T.
*Oxford*                                                          Z.A.S.
*August 1972*

# PART I

---

# THE BACKGROUND

# 1. INTRODUCTION AND OUTLINE OF THE PATENT SYSTEM

## A. INTRODUCTION TO THE STUDY

The present study was designed to be the second part of a two-volume work on the patent system. The first volume dealt with the history, law and administration of the system in the U.K.,[1] but could do little more in the space that was left than mention some of the economic issues and offer some fairly aggregated data on patent applications, grants, oppositions, etc. It was promised at the time that a second study would follow and would concentrate on the economic impact of the system. This volume is an attempt to fulfil that promise.

Although intended as a sequel to the earlier book, the present study has emerged as a fully self-contained work that should make sense on its own to a reader primarily interested in economic questions. For that reason, some matters already covered at length in Volume 1 are explained again here very briefly, mainly in the opening chapter. However, a reader requiring a thorough treatment of legal and administrative questions should look to Volume 1 and to the various specialist legal works cited there.

The aim of the present study is to assess the principal economic consequences (if any) of the sort of patent system that currently exists in the U.K. and most other developed countries outside the Communist sphere. It should be stressed at the outset that the work is concerned with fundamentals, i.e. the principal economic benefits and costs that follow from having a system by which inventors are permitted on certain conditions to monopolise their inventions in the field of manufacture for about 16 years after applying for patents on them. Doubtless, one could spend much time investigating the implications of modifications in the length of the patent term or in the ease or difficulty of obtaining patents, but that is not our main purpose, although we do devote some attention to these matters in the course of the study. In our view, the critical feature of the patent system is the legal monopoly that it confers and we are primarily interested in the economic implications of this feature.

Our intention to concentrate on fundamental economic questions was strengthened by the knowledge that the detailed amendment of the U.K. system was considered with extreme thoroughness by the recent

[1] Klaus Boehm in collaboration with Aubrey Silberston, *The British Patent System: 1. Administration* (Cambridge University Press, 1967).

Banks Committee (of which one of us was a member) and was dealt with very fully in its Report.[1] While the Committee felt able to make a number of recommendations concerning the modification of the British system, given its existence, their affirmation of the fundamental value of the system was somewhat guarded and they admitted that there is little information concerning the essential value of patents on which a proper judgment can be formed (page 10). It seemed to us that we could contribute best by attempting to obtain the information necessary for such a judgment. In doing so, we had no alternative but to take the British system as we found it, 'warts and all'; we could not of course anticipate what changes would be made in it as a result of the Banks Report, although a number (if none radical) doubtless will be made.

With this in mind we set out to investigate the following central question: how would the U.K. economy be affected if the *monopoly* element in the patent system were absent (i.e., if inventors could obtain patents much as they do at present, but could not refuse *bona fide* applications for licences on them, as they can under the existing system)? It was considered that this question was preferable to the more extreme issue of what would happen if no recognisable patent system were in existence. The latter would be more difficult to analyse, would depart too far from actual experience and would add little to our understanding of the critical features of the system gained from the less extreme (but still fairly radical) alternative chosen.

Conceivably, three main aspects of economic activity could be significantly affected, namely: the rate and direction of inventive and innovative activity; the disclosure and spread of new technology; and the degree of competition between suppliers of patented products or users of patented processes. There might be others, but these seem to be the most important types of activities that could be *directly* affected. Our chief efforts are therefore devoted to the assessment of the impact on these three.

Admittedly, a complete answer to the question would require our net to be cast wider. Thus it might be argued that the impact of patents on the distribution of income between inventors (or shareholders of research-based firms) and other classes should be a subject for investigation. While we recognise that this could be an important issue, we felt that we could not deal with it centrally in the present study, although our results do shed some light on it.

Again, it might be argued that a full assessment should incorporate not merely the impact of patent monopolies on inventive activity but also the impact of that activity on, for example, the growth of industrial

---

[1] *The British Patent System*, Report of the Committee to Examine the Patent System (Banks Committee) (London, H.M.S.O., July 1970).

productivity. While some attention is devoted to wider impacts of this sort, we were obliged by limitations on space and time to concentrate on the main *direct* consequences of the system, as outlined above. This in itself proved to be a far from straightforward exercise.

One unavoidable source of complication is that the patent system is essentially an international institution with many international ramifications. Although Volume I was able to deal almost exclusively with the 'British' patent system, it became evident at an early stage of work for this study that the economic implications of overseas patenting and licensing by British firms could not be safely ignored. The impact of patents on British industry might depend very much on whether patent monopolies were available overseas as well as at home and we accordingly felt it necessary to consider the broader question of international patenting and licensing, although this inevitably contributed to the difficulties of the investigation.

In view of the complexity of the subject and the scarcity of published data, particularly on licensing, we decided to undertake an intensive industrial inquiry in which firms with an interest in the patent system could give information and help assess 'effects'. This seemed the best way of investigating the impact of the system on broad sections of British industry. Moreover, it is with *industry* that we are chiefly concerned, since the great bulk of formal efforts to improve technology and introduce new products in our economy take the form of research and development by industrial firms. We do not neglect the small inventor and the 'very small' firm, but feel it right to concentrate our main attention on 'R & D' by firms of large or at least moderate size. Accordingly, the central part of our investigations consists of an intensive industrial inquiry involving some forty (mainly large) firms and providing the data and assessments on which our results are principally based.

In the assessment of such a complex phenomenon as patents, it would be a mistake to imagine that adequate results can be obtained using a single method of analysis. Some authors have attempted to rely solely on regression analysis, but have invariably obtained rather inconclusive and sometimes misleading results. We do our best within the space available to draw attention to the pitfalls attending too general or purely statistical an approach. Throughout our investigation such slogans as 'appearances are deceptive', 'mere numbers are meaningless' and 'generalisations are dangerous' were repeatedly brought home to us. We were nevertheless convinced of the desirability of obtaining and analysing aggregative data, and collected as much as seemed possible and useful, given our resources and objectives.

Other authors have relied entirely on the more particular type of

approach found in case studies, but these on their own can be as misleading as 'macro-quantitative' methods. In fact, we adopted both
types of approach where they seemed fruitful and our industrial inquiry
is something of an amalgam of both, consisting as it does of a framework
of data on patents, licences, R & D expenditure, etc., within which a
series of judgments about effects is developed.

*Plan of the study*

Part I deals with matters of an introductory or background character
and is intended to give perspective of various sorts. Chapter 1 contains
a sketch of the law and administration of the patent system and is
followed by chapters on the principal issues as portrayed in economic
theory, a brief review of previous empirical literature in which patents
figure prominently, and a 'bird's eye' view of R & D and patent
activity in the U.K. drawn from published data. The last section of
Chapter 4 describes a rather simple statistical attempt to correlate
'R & D intensity' with productivity growth in U.K. industry, based
mainly on official data.

Part II is essentially a report of our industrial inquiry. Chapter 5
describes the inquiry briefly. Chapter 6 summarises what we learned
about the role of industrial patent departments and Chapter 7 deals
with the main features of licensing seen through the eyes of industrial
firms. The central part of the research is contained in Chapters 8 and 9.
Chapter 8 presents the principal figures on patents, licences, royalties,
R & D and sales obtained by category of production and concludes
with an exercise comparing actual with 'commercially reasonable'
rates of royalty. Chapter 9 sets out the principal estimates of effects
reached in the course of our discussions with firms and attempts to
quantify them where possible. This chapter contains what can be
regarded as the key results of the study. (Details of the conduct and
coverage of the inquiry, including the questionnaire forms and covering
notes, are given in Appendix B at the end of the book.)

We are only too aware that the analysis contained in Chapters 8
and 9 is sometimes highly condensed and that much is left to be taken
'on faith' by the readers. In an attempt to corroborate and amplify
some of the main results described there, it was decided to supplement
Part II with a series of detailed studies of the impact of the patent system
on particular industries and inventions. Lack of time and space
unfortunately compelled us to limit ourselves to three industries which
have been traditionally thought of as having a high stake in the patent
system – pharmaceuticals, basic chemicals and electronics – and studies
of these are presented in Part III. In each case, we discuss the industry

as a whole and examine a major patented innovation as an illustration of our main points. Part III ends with a chapter on the small inventor and the very small firm.

Finally, Chapter 14 reviews our principal findings in relation to the 'standard alternative' of worldwide, thoroughgoing, compulsory licensing and discusses effects in comparison with other alternatives, including unilateral operation of compulsory licensing in the U.K. Although this chapter is intended mainly as a summary of the principal arguments and results, some new material on the development of nylon and Terylene and the float glass process is introduced for purposes of illustration. The chapter concludes with some suggestions for policy with regard to the U.K. patent system.

### B. PRINCIPLES OF PATENTING

Any worthwhile study of the economic issues surrounding the patent system requires some understanding of the principles of patent law and the basic features of patent systems. We aim in the remainder of this chapter to give the minimum information necessary for that purpose, with particular reference to the U.K. Since this ground has already been covered in detail in Volume I, rigour and completeness will generally be sacrificed for brevity. The reader is, however, warned that the patent law is a specialist subject whose intricacies can puzzle the inexpert – as the present authors have sometimes found to their cost – while a bare account of law and institutions cannot convey a proper idea of the practical working of the system. We shall accordingly try to outline the practice as well as the principles of the system, especially where this has an important bearing on the economic issues.

Readers who wish to go into the subject of law and administration more deeply should consult Volume I and, for a thorough discussion of the system and possible reforms, the Banks Report. Those who have already done so or who are otherwise knowledgeable about the patent system can probably skip the next two sections of this chapter.

A patent is an official document that confers proprietorship of an invention on the recipient (or 'patentee'). It is granted by an official of State (in the U.K., the Comptroller-General of Patents) in accordance with patent law and is enforceable in the courts. Grant of a patent is preceded by examination of applications by the patenting authority (the Patent Office in the U.K.), but the final responsibility for validating or invalidating a patent lies with the courts.

The fundamental principle behind patents is that the Crown awards

exclusive control over an invention for a fixed number of years (16 in
the U.K.) to the individual who first discloses the invention within
its territory, disclosure meaning publication in a form prescribed by the
patenting authority. In most systems, a patent is granted to whichever
applicant is first to submit a detailed description ('specification')
of the invention, provided he can go on to satisfy the patent authority
and if necessary the courts regarding certain conditions laid down by
patent law.[1] The main conditions for a valid patent in U.K. law can be
summarised as follows:

(i) The invention must be described fully and precisely, and the
patentee clearly identified. The U.K. law requires that the description must be adequate to enable an expert in the field (someone
'skilled in the art') to implement it.

The principle here is that the Crown will confer the privilege of a
patent only if it receives for publication in exchange a description of an
invention that is fully workable without further assistance from the
patentee. This objective can readily be achieved in case of a rather
straightforward invention, but is less likely to be so in cases where much
highly specialised experience and judgment is involved of the sort that
only emerges in the course of implementing an invention. This sort
of information (which we henceforth call 'technical know-how') is
seldom written into patent specifications, either because it depends
heavily on things that are not themselves inventions in the sense of the
patent law, or because it is too cumbersome to warrant the effort of
writing down, or because it arises too late for incorporation in the
specification.[2]

Nevertheless numerous inventions depending substantially for their
implementation on unpatented know-how *are* patented and this
represents a departure in practice from the law's intention.

Patent specifications must include, in addition to a detailed description, a statement of claim by the applicant regarding the scope of the
monopoly he seeks over his invention. The claim is usually of a relatively
broad nature, its purpose being to identify the range of products or
processes that the patentee claims to monopolise. It therefore commonly
covers variations of the invention referred to in the detailed specification. While the patentee obviously has an interest in claiming as wide a
monopoly as possible, he has also to consider that the broader his
claim, the more likely it is to be challenged and the more vulnerable

---

[1] *1949 Patents Act* (12, 13 and 14 Geo. 6. Ch. 87). Not all these conditions are applied by the
Patent Office in the course of granting patents; some are left to be decided either in proceedings for opposition or revocation before the Comptroller, or by the courts in the
event of a patent dispute reaching them.
[2] For this reason, 'know-how' may be regarded in a loose sense as non-patented technical
information.

it is likely to be. Accordingly a judicious balance has to be struck when drawing up a claim between its scope and its credibility.

A U.K. patent on an invention made in the U.K. can only be awarded to the true inventor or his assignee. In the case of inventions originating overseas, the law at present states that whoever first introduces the knowledge into this country will be regarded as the inventor. Under the Paris (Industrial Property) Convention, of which the major patenting nations are members, the date of first filing in a convention country can be used (for a period of 12 months) as evidence of priority for purposes of filing in other convention countries. Thus a foreign inventor has a 12-month period of grace in which to file in the U.K.[1] This privilege is reciprocal for British inventors filing overseas.

The logic behind the principle of confining patent awards to the inventors concerned is that the Crown seeks to encourage not simply disclosure of inventions but *invention* itself. More will be said about this in the next chapter.

(ii) The invention must be 'a manner of manufacture', as laid down by law and interpreted by the courts.

The interpretation of 'manner of manufacture' seems in effect to be fairly broad, embracing all objects that are man-made together with methods of making them, and, to some extent, uses for them. Processes can be patented provided they lead to a product, while uses can be patented if they are uses in manufacture, but not if they are uses in human consumption. Thus the use of a substance as a catalyst or weed-killer can be patented, but not as a human medicine or foodstuff. The only way in which a new food or drug may be protected is to patent it as a new chemical product. Although claims in a patent on a new substance cannot extend to the substance when found in its natural state, methods of mining and agriculture may be patentable. As a special case of the latter, it was established in a famous decision of the U.K. Divisional Court in 1962 that certain types of animal treatments may be patentable.[2]

Methods of organising a firm or distributing its products are not

---

[1] The Banks Committee have recommended that 'absolute novelty' be adopted in the U.K. as the relevant criterion for awarding a patent. (This is in line with the Strasbourg Convention, Article I.) If so, the criterion of 'first to introduce' would be abandoned. See Banks Committee, pp. 71–2.

[2] *R. v. P.A.T. ex parte Swift and Co.*, (*1962*) *R.P.C. 37*. This decision was of particular importance to the administration of the U.K. patent system because it ruled that it is not the function of the Comptroller or the Patents Appeal Tribunal to decide finally whether an alleged manner of new manufacture is actually patentable. The Patent Office should refuse only applications which 'on no reasonable view could be said to be within the ambit of the Act'. The significance of this decision is discussed in the Banks Report, pp. 62–6. The Committee recommended (page 66) that the Act should be amended to include agricultural and horticultural processes as patentable, and to exclude methods of veterinary treatment.

patentable. Sets of technical instructions or mathematical methods are not in themselves patentable; they must attach to some specific manufacturing process. There is some doubt in the U.K. as in most other countries as to the patentability of computer programs other than those designed for specific manufacturing uses. Neither the law nor the courts have yet dealt with this point, although there seems to be a consensus among patent practitioners that computer 'software' is not in general patentable, a view that has been somewhat qualified by recent Patent Office policy.[1]

The principle remains that an invention can be patented only to the extent that it has a particular application in what economists normally think of as 'production'. Naturally the boundary between what is and what is not patentable is sometimes fairly arbitrary and in some cases seems to reflect what can be feasibly administered. Thus a compelling reason for not making computer programs patentable is doubtlesss the sheer volume of programming expertise that would have to be diverted to patent matters, in industry as well as in the Patent Office.

(iii) The invention as claimed must be novel, i.e., not anticipated by any previous publication or use ('prior art') in the U.K. (Prior disclosure or use overseas do not invalidate the patent.)

The principle here is that nothing can be patented which is already in the 'public domain'; the Crown is unwilling to award anyone control over an invention that is already publicly available. At the very least, the Crown must avoid granting a patent monopoly on something for which a monopoly has already been granted.

There is seldom much scope for doubt as to whether one invention anticipates another, even when the former is not patented, except in the occasional instances where concurrent applications contain similar claims. The latter are the subject of quite complex legal provisions, but the principle at present laid down is that a patent is not valid if its claims are anticipated in another (on which a patent has been granted) with an earlier priority date (date of filing), notwithstanding that this was published after the priority date of the later application.[2]

The relatively undemanding test for novelty prescribed in the 1949 Act has been much criticised on the ground *inter alia* that a valid U.K. patent may be obtained on an invention which, although previously unknown in the U.K., has been published or implemented overseas. The recommendation of the Banks Committee in favour of 'absolute novelty' would, if adopted, require the extension of the U.K. novelty

---

[1] For a discussion of the patenting of computer programs, see Banks Report, Ch. 17.
[2] The Banks Committee has recommended that this test, known as the 'prior claim' approach, should be replaced by a more stringent test – the 'whole contents' approach. See Banks Report, Ch. 10.

criteria to include prior disclosure (including oral disclosure) or use overseas as a ground for invalidating a U.K. patent.[1] This step (if modelled on the definition of absolute novelty in the Strasbourg Convention) would also require that prior *secret* use in the U.K. would no longer be a ground for denying the novelty of an invention. At present, prior secret use of an invention in the U.K. may lead to revocation of the patent and may be an admissable ground for defence against a charge of patent infringement. If absolute novelty on the lines of the Strasbourg Convention is adopted, some new provision to protect the interests of a person (other than the patentee) who has made substantial preparations to use an invention, but who has not actually commenced operations at the date of the patent, will probably be needed.[2]

(iv) The invention as claimed must be genuinely inventive, i.e. it must not be obvious, as judged with reference both to what has gone before in the U.K. as prior art and, presumably, to common knowledge.

The principle at stake here, of course, is that the Crown will not award control of an alleged invention which it judges to be commonly accessible through being obvious. The question of whether an invention is genuinely inventive within the meaning of patent law is very much a matter of judgment. In the British system, the issue is left entirely for settlement in proceedings for revocation of a patent, either before the Comptroller or in the courts.

The preceding conditions are applied fully in the U.K. only when a patent, having been granted, is officially contested by a third party, and only in the courts are all the conditions applied to their fullest possible extent. Thus the procedure for granting patents falls far short of strict conformity to the conditions for a valid patent laid down in law. This is so partly for economic reasons.[3] The resources available for patent administration are limited, and, given the existence of a patent system, it is in the interest of both the public and the inventor that patents should be granted with reasonable speed. Yet proper assessment of the claims attaching to a technical discovery is likely to be a difficult and laborious procedure requiring a great deal of scientific knowledge and judicial skill. Unless patents as granted by the patenting authority are largely immune from challenge by outsiders – which is

[1] Banks Report, pp. 69–72.    [2] *Ibid.*, p. 73.
[3] However, it has also been argued that examination for obviousness might lead to the refusal of applications by the Patent Office which might well be held by the courts to have inventive merit. The Banks Committee did not accept this argument, and was impressed by the widespread desire in industry for refusal of applications that clearly have no inventive merit. The Committee accordingly recommended the introduction by the Patent Office of an examination for obviousness. (Banks Report, pp. 37–9.)

rare outside socialist countries – a compromise has to be made between speed and 'quality' of patents and this entails either a narrowing down of the examination procedure or selectivity in examining applications. The British system leans towards the former approach, employing selectivity only in the sense that the difficult issue of obviousness is left to opposition and revocation actions in the Patent Office and the courts in the relatively few cases that reach them.

### C.    BRITISH PATENT ADMINISTRATION

The official institutions of the British patent system are the Patent Office, headed by the Comptroller and staffed by patent examiners and supporting staff; the Patents Appeal Tribunal, which hears appeals against decisions of the Comptroller, and 'the Court', namely a High Court judge appointed to hear patent actions. Patent applications are almost invariably drawn up by patent agents, members of a highly specialised profession who act as intermediaries between applicants and the Patent Office. In order to be acceptable to the Comptroller, patent agents must be properly qualified in accordance with the strict examination and training requirements of the Chartered Institute of Patent Agents, and must be registered with the Institute.[1]

The work of examining patent applications is extremely skilled and specialised. The Patent Office employs upwards of 500 examiners, all of whom are science or engineering graduates, with executive and clerical staff of another 600 persons, some of whom staff the Designs and Trade Mark Branches of the Office. In 1968, about 48,800 complete specifications were filed (approximately 70 per cent of which originated outside the U.K.) and about 43,000 patents were sealed (granted).[2] The total number of U.K. patents in force at the end of 1968 was nearly 224,000.[3]

The work of the Patent Office is broadly self-supporting through fees charged for processing patent applications (which typically amount to about £20 per patent) and annual renewal fees, which are first payable at the end of the fourth year of a patent's life, rising from £6 to £30 for the final year. (The fees are revised from time to time.) Total receipts from patent fees were some £3¼ million in 1968.[4]

---

[1] This may be no mean achievement. One patent agent in our industrial inquiry said that, having obtained a Cambridge 'first' in electrical engineering, he proceeded to fail the Chartered Institute finals at the first attempt, and only passed narrowly at the second.

[2] *86th Report of the Comptroller-General of Patents, 1968*, Appendix D. Figures are given here for 1968 because this was the year chosen for our industrial inquiry. The figure for complete specifications filed in 1971 was about 48,200. (See Comptroller's Report, 1971.)

[3] *Ibid.*, 1968, Appendix E. The figure for end-1971 was about 239,000.

[4] *Ibid.*, Appendix B. Patent fees received in 1971 were £4·9 million.

The Patent Office vets all applications quite rigorously for adequacy of description and patentability as a 'manner of manufacture' (conditions (i) and (ii) above), but confines its assessment of novelty to a search of British patent specifications published within the preceding 50 years. No test for inventive step is made. In the course of the examination procedure, the applicant will be given an opportunity to amend his specification if necessary and considerable correspondence may take place between the examiner and the applicant's patent agent. This interchange is prone in many cases to be long-drawn-out and it has been necessary to set an overall time limit of $2\frac{3}{4}$ years between date of filing a full-scale (i.e., complete) specification and satisfaction of the examiner's requirements, after which the specification is published if the patent application is accepted for grant. Most applications take from $1\frac{1}{2}$ to $2\frac{1}{2}$ years before publication.

For a period of 3 months between publication and grant, and for a further period of 12 months after grant, third parties may contest the patent before the Comptroller. In such 'opposition' proceedings the conditions for patentability are applied more fully than in the patent examination. Evidence is admitted and assessments are made on both novelty and obviousness with reference to all prior publication and use in the U.K. However, at this stage as earlier, the benefit of doubt is given to the applicant. Thus, for example, a successful opponent has to show that the invention in question *clearly* involves no inventive step, whereas when a patent is contested in court the word 'clearly' is omitted. The wording here is significant and has much to do with the fact that opposition is seldom advised under the British system. Less than 2 per cent of applications that survive examination are opposed before the Patent Office, and the majority of these are upheld, if sometimes in amended form.[1] Very few oppositions result in refusal of the application (before grant) or, in the case of 'belated opposition', revocation (after grant), although a fair proportion (about 30 per cent) lead to the relinquishing of the patent application.

Although the process of opposition or revocation in the Patent Office takes time (a typical case may last two years from the start of opposition to a decision), actual hearings before the Comptroller (or a 'hearing officer' i.e., a senior patent examiner) are much less elaborate than court hearings and are generally over in a day. For this reason, they are much preferred by industrialists to full-scale actions in the courts.[2]

---

[1] Some 670 oppositions and applications for revocation were lodged before the Comptroller in 1968 (and 490 in 1971).

[2] The Banks Committee, impressed by arguments in favour of the 'robust justice' available at the Patent Office, has recommended that the period for applications for revocation before the Comptroller should be extended to cover the life of a patent. (Banks Report, pp. 51–3.)

As with examination, decisions in opposition proceedings are subject to appeal to a High Court judge sitting as the Patents Appeal Tribunal, and there is a limited further right of appeal to the Court of Appeal. Of the 96 appeals against opposition and revocation decisions heard by the Patents Appeal Tribunal in 1968, only 27 were allowed, the rest being withdrawn or dismissed.[1]

Although the Patent Office has complete authority over the granting of patents and the determination of oppositions, a patent once granted can only be said to be entirely valid if it is upheld by judicial pronounce-ment in the Court, for it is only then that the patentability conditions outlined earlier are applied with their full rigour, together with a number of additional ones such as inutility and false representation. Grounds for revoking or amending a patent at this stage are extremely broad, including for example prior use of the invention in the U.K., whether public or secret, other than for purely experimental purposes by someone to whom the patentee communicated his invention in confidence. Moreover, the Court does not entertain the same degree of presumption in favour of the patentee as in proceedings before the Comptroller.

In view of the fact that all British patents as granted are at least technically open to question, it may on the face of it appear surprising that very few patent disputes actually reach the Court (49 being reported in 1968 and 39 in 1971). One reason for this is undoubtedly the time and expense involved in court hearings, which in turn reflect the complexity of patent issues. But a more basic reason is that the most effective remedy available to third parties against a weak patent is to infringe the patent rather than petition the courts for its revocation. Indeed, the testing of patents in the British system, as in most other patent systems, is very largely *unofficial*, in that it is conducted almost entirely by infringement and counter-infringement, leading, where economically significant patents are involved, to negotiations 'behind the scenes' rather than a trial in court.

This aspect of patent systems has led one noted legal authority to describe use of the patent system as a game of bluff in which large companies bargain with one another on the basis of highly speculative patent positions.[2] While this observation is doubtless exaggerated, there is a certain amount of truth in it. Most patent practitioners would

[1] Comptroller's Report, 1968, p. 7. There were 88 appeals in 1971, of which 30 were allowed.
[2] T. A. Blanco-White, *Patents for Inventions* (3rd Edition, London: Stevens, 1962) pp. 7–8. In a section on the relative ineffectiveness of patents, the author comments: 'In relation to major inventions it works well enough as a system for collecting and disseminating technical information, but as a system for encouraging the making and commercial use of inventions it is defective, and tends even to degenerate into a game of bluff, part of business politics rather than productive industry.' (Page 8.)

freely admit that there are many U.K. patents in force that would probably not be upheld if tested in court, or at least would only survive with amendment. This uncertainty about the status of patents seems inevitable in any system where patents are granted with only partial assessment by the patenting authority, although it is less prominent in the British system than in 'deferred examination' systems where no patent applications are examined until a specific request is made for examination, or in 'registration' systems where all official assessment of patents is left to the courts.

While uncertainty as to the status of patents is a feature of patent systems that an economist cannot ignore, it would be wrong to give the impression that it is a dominant feature. There exist numerous uncontested patents in active use whose validity is not effectively in doubt, while it is probable that few economically significant patents of doubtful validity survive for long without being challenged, unofficially through infringement if not officially. The vast majority of 'doubtful' patents that do survive untested and uninfringed are probably either of negligible economic importance or ones whose vulnerability could easily be rectified by minor amendments.

### D.   THE NATURE OF THE PATENT MONOPOLY

Formally speaking, a patentee acquires the right, enforceable at law, to decide who shall and who shall not use his patented invention. He retains this right for 16 years provided he pays the renewal fees, and in some cases he may secure an extension if he can convince the Court that there has been 'inadequate remuneration' or loss due to war. Cases of extension have been very few outside immediate post-war experience, when a considerable number of 'war loss' extensions were granted.

The patentee's legal monopoly over his invention is limited in several quite different senses. Firstly, as we have seen, his monopoly claims are subject to amendment or revocation by the courts in respect of defects which were not detected prior to grant. Even though legal action remains no more than a background possibility for most patentees, the use they make of patents will be governed by the likely outcome of such action, should it take place.

Secondly, where the invention is a development of an earlier invention, the patentee may have to obtain a licence and pay royalties to the earlier patentee.

Thirdly, the patentee's rights are limited by patent law, quite apart from the question of the validity of his patent. Thus, in most patent systems the patentee is required to *work* his invention, either on his own account or by licensing another to use it, if he wishes to retain his monopoly. The provision in the U.K. Patents Act (Section 37) is that the Comptroller may, after three years from the sealing of the patent, grant any applicant a 'compulsory licence' if he can demonstrate that a patented invention is not being commercially worked 'to the fullest possible extent that is reasonably practicable' in the U.K. Other grounds for granting a compulsory licence include failure to meet U.K. demand on reasonable terms, hindering the commercial use of the invention in the U.K. by importing the patented article, hindering the efficient working of any other patented invention in the U.K., or unfairly prejudicing the establishment of any commercial activity in the U.K. However, much is left to the judgment of the Comptroller, both as to what is reasonable commercial use and as to what are reasonable terms for a licence.

This provision is clearly designed to prevent unfair exploitation of his monopoly by the patentee, and in particular the suppression of the invention in the U.K. (Thus, working of a U.K. patent requires that the invention be operated *within* the U.K.; it is not sufficient to meet the market by importing the patented article.) The allowance of three years before compulsory licences may be granted is intended to give the patentee a fair opportunity to work his patent, and the Comptroller has discretion to allow more time to commence working.

Applications for compulsory licences under these provisions are in fact extremely rare. In the ten years 1959–68 16 applications were filed, two were allowed, one was refused and the remainder were withdrawn (with several still pending). The two appeals to the Patent Appeals Tribunal were dismissed.[1]

Reasons for the slight use of Section 37 will be discussed in later chapters. It should, however, be emphasised here that lack of activity under this Section does *not necessarily* mean that its provisions have no effect. Just as interested third parties are likely to infringe a patent that they believe to be invalid, so the threat of a compulsory licence application may induce the granting of a voluntary licence when the patent is being exploited unfairly. In neither case should it be assumed that lack of official activity indicates that legal conditions and checks on a patentee are ineffectual, at least as far as they purport to go.

It should perhaps be noted that there is, of course, no legal compulsion for a patentee to work a patent that he does not wish to monopolise. Indeed, the majority of patents are probably never worked at all in the sense of the Act, although many of these may be of some 'defensive' value to the patentee, as will be explained later.

---

[1] Comptroller's Report, 1968. Since 1968, a further 9 have been filed, three refused, and two withdrawn. Two further appeals to the P.A.T. have been dismissed.

It is significant that patent monopolies cannot be referred as such to the Monopolies Commission. However, the Patents Act (Sections 40 (3) and (4)) provides that the Board of Trade (now Department of Trade and Industry) may refer patent situations brought to light in the course of Monopolies investigations to Parliament, which may declare them against the public interest. They are then subject to compulsory licence upon decision of the Comptroller. The provisions are cumbersome and have never in fact been used.[1]

The U.K. patent law provides special limitations on patent monopolies in the field of foods and medicines (and also surgical and curative devices). Under Section 41 of the Act, the Comptroller must grant compulsory licences on such patents to any applicant, unless he sees 'good reasons' for not doing so. The principle here is that new drugs and medicines may be vital to consumers and are therefore particularly prone to exploitation by a monopolist. The Comptroller is consequently obliged by law to grant licences for these items on what he deems reasonable terms if any are requested, unless the patentee can show compelling reasons for not doing so. Case law has established that one such reason could be the applicant's unsuitability to hold a licence, while the Act clearly implies that another reason could be the inability of the patentee to make a reasonable return from his invention if it were licensed to others.

Activity under Section 41 has been on the whole fairly slight since its introduction in 1949, apart from a notable flurry in 1963–4, when 23 of the 41 applications made between 1958 and 1968 were filed, and a further flurry in 1969–70, when a further 22 applications were filed.[2] Of the total of 64 applications filed under this Section to the end of 1971, 14 have been allowed, the rest being refused (8) or withdrawn (31), with 11 still pending at the end of 1971. Of 13 appeals to the Patents Appeal Tribunal, three were withdrawn and the rest dismissed. This record poses some interesting questions which will be dealt with in Chapter 10 on the pharmaceutical industry.[3]

A final legal limitation on a patentee's right to monopolise his invention in the U.K. is found in the provision that patented inventions may be used by Government departments at their immediate discretion for the 'services of the Crown', terms being fixed later either by agreement or by the Court. The relevant Section (46) of the Act does not

---

[1] See Volume 1, p. 115, and Banks Report, pp. 151–2. In the recent Roche Products case, the Department has taken the (so far as we know) unprecedented course (on 12 April 1973) of ordering the patentee to reduce prices of patented items – the order to be confirmed by Parliament.

[2] Comptroller's Report, 1968, p. 8, and 1971, p. 9.

[3] The Banks Committee has recommended the repeal of Section 41. (Banks Report, page 119.)

define services of the Crown, except to say that they include meeting the defence requirements of foreign governments in accordance with U.K. treaty obligations. It does, however, state that Crown use does not include *sale* of patented items or authorisation of others to sell them. The principle behind Section 46 is that the Goverment may exercise the Crown's concurrent rights in patents in order to authorise use of patented goods and processes where a duty is laid on a Minister (e.g., to provide a hospital service), although it may not itself exploit the patented inventions for commercial gain.[1] The significance of this provision has greatly increased with the growth of the economic role of some Government departments since the war, in particular the Ministry of Health. The right of the latter to purchase drugs from the cheapest source for the national hospital service irrespective of patents has had important implications for the pharmaceutical industry, and was unsuccessfully contested in the courts by the Pfizer Corporation in 1965.[2] More recently the Sainsbury Committee, set up in 1965 to consider the relationship of the pharmaceutical industry and the National Health Service, recommended the extension of Section 46 to cover the general medical and pharmaceutical (i.e. general practitioner) services of the Health Service. This was enacted in the *Health Service and Public Health Act 1968*, thereby greatly increasing the Minister's reserve powers in this field.

While it is true that Section 46 cannot be invoked in respect of other than services of the Crown (and does not extend, for example, to the operations of nationalised industries, except for this purpose), the Section has become an important feature of the British patent system. There is no exact counterpart among world systems (apart from a few in Commonwealth countries that have adopted this type of provision).[3] Consideration will be given in later chapters to its economic impact, especially on the electronics industry, which so far is the one most widely affected, and on the pharmaceutical industry, in relation to which dramatic use of the Section was made in the early 1960s.

Apart from the foregoing limitations, a patentee has exclusive right 'to make, use, exercise and vend' his patented invention in the U.K. As the sole proprietor, he may utilise the invention himself, assign it to another or authorise others to use it by granting them licences. The advantages of licensing as opposed to assignment are that more than one licence can be granted if desired, and licensing enables the patentee to retain control over the invention and stipulate conditions regarding its use.

[1] See Banks Report, pp. 120–1.
[2] Volume 1, p. 122. See also Chapter 10 below, pp. 236–7.
[3] However, some other countries, like the U.S.A., achieve a similar result for public interest fields without having Section 46-style provisions in their patent legislation.

*Licences*

Basically, a patent licence is a document giving the parties, particulars of the patent, duration of the licence and the conditions and payments involved. A licence may be 'exclusive', 'sole' or 'plain'. An exclusive licence grants rights under the patent to the licensee alone, while a sole licence retains these rights for the licensor as well. A plain licence contains no exclusivity provision of any sort.

In practice, a licence may be anything from a simple letter of intent to an elaborate formal contract containing many clauses and occupying 20–30 typewritten pages. In some cases a 'licence' is merely a small part of (or attachment to) a larger agreement for the exchange of technical information, which may refer to patents briefly or in no more than a general way. There is some question as to whether an agreement of this sort is best thought of as a 'licence agreement' or a 'know-how agreement'. Our practice throughout the study has been to treat all agreements that refer in some definite and explicit way to existing or future patents, whether individually or collectively, as *patent licence agreements*; we have treated other agreements relating essentially to technical knowledge as 'pure know-how agreements', even though they may contain a brief reference to possible future patents, or to patents that have expired. Inevitably, differentiation between licence and pure know-how agreements is sometimes a matter of judgment, and in our industrial inquiry the final distinction was left to respondents themselves.

The terms and conditions found in licence agreements vary a great deal with circumstances, but certain kinds tend to recur. Thus it frequently happens that the licensee's market is confined to a particular territory, a common pattern being that the licensor reserves the home market for himself and divides overseas markets between various licensees. The licensee is usually restricted to particular uses of the invention. Some licences permit only *sale* of a patented item, while others permit both manufacture and sale. The licensee frequently has to observe quality standards for the patented item or process, and he may also be required to observe minimum (first-hand) selling prices on patented goods or goods produced by a patented process. The period of the patent licence may be shorter than that of the patent (but not longer, although the part of the agreement relating to know-how, if separate, may relate to a longer period), and there may be clauses covering renegotiation of the licence. The licensee is generally forbidden to sub-license or divulge associated know-how to third parties. Clauses governing the type and extent of know-how to be exchanged are likely where significant know-how is involved.[1]

[1] A detailed discussion of the content of licence agreements can be found in Chapter 7.

Apart from stipulating that a patentee may not restrict a licensee regarding sources of supply of goods not covered by his patent (Section 57), the patent law is silent on what are reasonable terms and conditions for a licence. Provided he steers clear of the provisions regarding abuse of monopoly (Sections 37–40 and 57), there is nothing official to prevent a patentee from imposing severe conditions for a licence – unless he is a producer of foods or medicines, or a Government supplier.

Patent licences are explicitly exempt from the provisions of U.K. restrictive practices legislation. However, if the licence agreement contains restrictions relating to goods or processes that are not patented, it is registrable and the restrictions in question may be declared illegal if they are found to be against the public interest.[1] Thus the monopoly powers of a patentee, including his right to license patented products or processes on restrictive terms, are not limited by legislation on monopolies or restrictive practices – in so far as the restrictions are confined to those products or processes. On the other hand, a patentee is not permitted to fix *resale* prices for output produced or sold under licence. (See *Resale Prices Act 1964*, Section 1(2).) Some special problems relating to the legality of restrictive provisions in licence agreements are discussed in Chapter 7, pp. 130–4.

It should be added that, on entry into the Common Market, patent licences involving U.K. firms will become subject, like all types of agreements for the licensing of commercial property rights, to the competition rules of the E.E.C. The significance of these E.E.C. provisions is briefly discussed in Chapter 7, page 135.

### Infringements and disputes

Of the quarter of a million or so patents currently in force in the U.K., only a minority (probably somewhere between a fifth and a third) are actually worked. This amounts nevertheless to a large number of patented inventions in active use – certainly tens of thousands – and these will be found mainly in the hands of major manufacturing companies. It is difficult to estimate what proportion of those in active use are habitually infringed. More will be said about this in later chapters, but we can observe here that it is rather unlikely that a 'strong' (i.e., substantially valid) patent of appreciable commercial importance will be consciously infringed against the wishes of the patentee. As we shall see, patentees in some circumstances have good reasons for tolerating infringement, while a fair amount of unconscious infringement undoubtedly occurs. But a manufacturer will not consciously infringe if he believes the patent to be substantially valid and utilised

[1] *Restrictive Trade Practices Act 1956*, Section 8 (4).

legitimately, and if he knows the patentee to be on his guard against infringements. The possibility of being stopped from infringing and the likely consequences in terms of disruption and 'loss of face' are too serious to warrant much risk-taking where strong patents are involved.

Naturally, the picture is entirely different in cases of decidedly 'weak' (substantially invalid) patents. It is safe to say that most weak patents of appreciable commercial importance will sooner or later be infringed and that the patentee will be reluctant to tackle the infringer for fear of having the weakness of his patent exposed.

There remain a considerable number of patent claims the validity of which is largely a matter of opinion, and it is in this area that most patent disagreements and disputes arise, either in the Patent Office or in the courts. In fact, active disputes are likely to emerge only where the patents are important and where the arguments of the parties concerning validity are fairly evenly balanced.

Initiative for enforcing a patent rests exclusively with the patentee, who is responsible for detecting infringements and bringing them to the infringer's attention. There is a strict rule (Section 65) that the patentee may not threaten legal action without the possibility of incurring severe counter-measures (including damages if the threats prove to be groundless) – the main purpose of which is to prevent patentees threatening the customers of alleged infringers without pursuing the primary infringer. In practice, a polite letter pointing out the existence of the patent carries the implication that the patentee will sue if the infringement continues. There are undoubtedly many cases in which such a letter is quite effective in suppressing an infringement.

If the infringer is persistent, the patentee may consider whether he wishes to offer a licence. Many incipient disputes are settled through licence negotiations at an early stage, the terms of the licence reflecting the bargaining strengths of the parties. But if the patentee is reluctant to license on terms acceptable to the licensee, he may have recourse to legal action by suing for infringement and seeking an injunction to restrain the infringement. The invariable legal response of an infringer who wishes to pursue the contest is to petition for revocation of the patent.

As stated earlier, the great majority of patent disputes never reach the stage of legal action but are settled through negotiation. Of those that do reach the stage at which official legal steps are taken, very few go beyond the pre-trial stage, the usual outcome being settlement before a court hearing, possibly with the help of an unofficial arbitrator from the legal profession. Settlements of this nature may well take several years to reach – especially in complicated cases – but they do not typically involve large legal costs.[1] Such settlements almost invariably involve a licence and possibly damages as well.

One reason why very few patent disputes reach the courts is that the scope for a compromise settlement in such cases is usually quite large, for few disputes will have reached this stage unless both parties have tenable arguments to put forward. A second reason is that the pressures to settle become increasingly strong after commencement of legal steps. Legal costs escalate considerably once a writ has been served, while there is usually a long delay between the serving of a writ and the court hearing. If the case proceeds to the Court of Appeal and then to the House of Lords, several more years will probably pass and the legal costs for each party may exceed £100,000. But apart from the costs and time involved in litigation, both parties to a dispute are likely to wish to avoid a trial. The defendant often has little to gain and much to lose thereby, for at best the patent will be found invalid, which is merely a confirmation of the circumstances prevailing at the outset from his point of view, while at worst he will be subject to an injunction and damages. The plaintiff will in most cases offer a licence on some terms, as he can seldom expect to obtain a complete ban on the use of the invention in a dispute that has reached a court hearing.[2] Only when the economic stakes are exceptionally high – or where strong personal animosity is involved – will disputes be taken to trial.

The rarity of patent infringement actions in the courts should not of course be taken as an indication that patentees seldom attempt to exploit their rights or that patents are seldom resisted by third parties. As we have seen, really strong patents either do not require explicit enforcement or can be enforced with minimal pressure, while patents of more debatable quality lead, if infringed, to licensing negotiations of a more or less unofficial character, with both parties reluctant to invoke the official machinery of the patent system. Most disputes take place behind the scenes in company patent departments and conference rooms. The Comptroller and the courts are a last resort in the relatively small minority of disputes that are both intractable and of outstanding economic importance to the protagonists.

*Conclusions*

It appears from this opening review of the patent system that a patent in most areas of invention is, potentially at least, a valuable monopoly instrument for someone who wishes to operate the invention on a commercial scale. A strong patent in the hands of an industrial firm can normally be readily enforced (although this may be more difficult

---

[1] Volume I, p. 96.      [2] *Ibid.*, p. 97.

for the 'small man') and its use is not subject to the usual legal restraints that apply in the U.K. against monopoly and restrictive practices. The most important legal limitation on a patentee's rights is probably the ability of the Government to use the invention, whether the patentee agrees or not, for the services of the Crown, but this is important only in areas where the Government is itself a major purchaser of the patented goods (e.g., nowadays, mainly in the military field) or in the special area of medicines. Patents of suspect validity are of course less effective as protective devices but in circumstances where contesting a patent is time-consuming, expensive and uncertain, even the flimsiest patent on a commercial product or process may have some protective value, especially in the hands of a large industrial company.

Needless to say, the economic significance of patent monopolies may vary considerably. Even a cast-iron patent may be of little commercial value to its owner if competitors have ready access to close substitutes for the invention concerned. Moreover, even where patents are capable of creating valuable commercial monopolies, it does not necessarily follow that they will be used for this purpose, or that they constitute the critical protective element in the situation. Finally, it does not at all follow that even where patents are an effective device in creating or sustaining a commercial monopoly, this is necessarily undesirable from society's economic viewpoint. This question is of course one of the most important with which we shall be concerned in this book.

# 2. THE GENERAL ECONOMIC ISSUES

Before proceeding to examine the evidence concerning the impact of the patent system in detail, it seems useful to consider first of all the general economic issues from an *a priori* standpoint, and this is done in the present chapter. We follow this in the next chapter with a brief stock-taking of the main comments and findings of those economists who have attempted a serious investigation of the subject. One of the advantages of such a review is that it induces one to think more closely about the problems of assessing the patent system and, in particular, to establish exactly what, as an economist, one is trying to discover about the system.

## A. THE BASIC ARGUMENT

It is probably fair to say that anyone with a background in economic theory is inclined to approach the patent system with a feeling of distrust. This antipathy springs from the association of monopoly with inefficiency and unfair exploitation that comes from orthodox economic analysis, but it is reinforced by the economist's idea that existing inventions, like all forms of knowledge, are 'free goods' (i.e., goods whose stock is not diminished by use). Thus an invention, once made, can be regarded as a non-wasting asset whose use involves no additional economic cost, beyond costs of communication and learning.[1] (It might be countered that an invention may depreciate through obsolescence, but since this is not a cost to the economy as a whole, we can ignore it here.) It is a well-established principle of welfare economics that the net economic benefit derived by society from such goods is normally maximised if no charge is levied or other hindrance put on their use. An invention is similar in kind to the much-cited Hotelling's bridge which, once built, should ideally be freely available for public use (except for charges to cover maintenance, for which there is no parallel in the case of an invention).[2]

---

[1] K. J. Arrow, 'Welfare Economics and Inventive Activity' in *The Rate and Direction of Inventive Activity*, National Bureau of Economic Research (Princeton, 1962) pp. 617–18.

[2] F. Machlup, *An Economic Review of the Patent System*, Study No. 15 of the U.S. Senate Subcommittee on Patents, Trademarks and Copyrights, 85th Congress, 2nd Session (U.S. Government Printing Office, 1958).

If inventions fell like manna from heaven, there would clearly be no economic justification for monopolising them or controlling access to them in any way – at least in a simple world where the implementation of inventions was a relatively costless activity. Indeed, one can argue on economic grounds that inventions of the sort that occur spontaneously, as pure 'flashes of insight' should ideally command no price – beyond a payment to the inventor to cover his publication costs. However, most inventions in the real world do have an appreciable cost in terms of economic resources. If decisions to allocate resources between invention and other activities are based essentially on assessment by the prospective inventor of private costs and gains (i.e., those accruing to him), then the inventor should receive at least part of the return from his invention. Furthermore if, as we assume, inventions are sold in a market, there will be a correct 'price' for an invention which will at the margin be exactly equal to its cost, including a minimum return necessary to induce the inventor to make the effort. Anything in excess of this will unnecessarily restrict access to the invention; anything less will depress the level of inventive activity below the economically desirable level.

The real difficulty arises because many inventions, like other types of knowledge, are not simply 'free' goods: they are to a large extent 'public' goods as well. That is to say, the returns from many inventions cannot be appropriated by their inventors without special safeguards, because once they have been implemented or otherwise disclosed they can, in the absence of protection of some form or other, be freely copied by others. If so, there is little incentive for an individual or firm to invest resources in inventive activity, even where the prospective return to the community as a whole may be very large. (Indeed there is likely to be a *disincentive*, since copyists would obtain the invention without incurring any of the attendant costs, and would then be in a superior economic position to the inventor.) It is therefore argued that, in the absence of a patent system, there tends to be too little invention. Patents are a device whereby a prospective inventor can be fairly sure of appropriating at least part of the return from whatever inventions he makes, and their primary justification on economic grounds is as a necessary incentive to inventive activity.

Several important points can be made in conjunction with the above argument, even at this simple level. The first is that patents as we know them can be defended on the above lines only within the framework of a private enterprise economy, and not otherwise. Thus patent monopolies can be justified where invention (and the application of inventions) is carried on according to the criteria of a market economy; they obviously have no place in a

socialist economy,[1] and can have relevance to inventive work undertaken on behalf of governments or for academic purposes in a 'mixed'
economy only if commercial considerations influence the latter.
Implicit in any defence of patent monopolies is thus the view that
a substantial amount of inventive effort can and should be undertaken
by the private sector of the economy.

The second point is that patents can be justified on the above lines
only in so far as invention involves a deliberate (calculated) commitment of resources beforehand. As has already been suggested, it can
hardly be argued that prospective patent protection can have any
direct effect on the generation of 'bright ideas' – except in so far as
these emerge through 'serendipity'.[2] On the other hand, if bright ideas
are costly to implement, it can be argued that patents are capable of
encouraging the application of inventions that may not themselves be
dependent on the system. We shall return to the question of the
application of inventions shortly.

Thirdly, the argument in its fullest sense applies only to inventions
that are vulnerable to being copied, once disclosed or implemented.
As noted in Chapter 1, many inventions are patented whose implementation requires substantial know-how not contained in the patent
(and, it should be added, not easily obtainable by observation of the
patentee's operations or product). In extreme cases of this sort (i.e.,
where know-how is crucial) it cannot truly be argued that the patent
system provides effective monopoly protection to the inventor, for if
the patent without the know-how is virtually useless to a potential
competitor, the inventor effectively controls the invention by controlling
the emission of know-how. In such cases the most that can be claimed
for the patent system is that it encourages the *publication* of descriptions
of inventions that might otherwise not be published; it cannot logically
be argued that it has any stimulating impact on invention or implementation of inventions whose essential know-how can be kept secret.

There will of course be many inventions that fall between the extremes of complete dependence and non-dependence on secret know-
how. In these cases patents may have some protective value and may
therefore be a factor in encouraging invention.

There will moreover be many inventions that involve little special
know-how but nevertheless cannot be copied instantly or with ease
because of other factors – e.g., routine problems associated with the

---

[1] Socialist countries have adopted the device of State awards for inventors, paid out of public
funds and based on an assessment of the returns from the invention, up to a (fairly modest)
fixed maximum. The inventions then become State property. As we shall argue later, this
type of system is suitable only in an economy where decisions regarding the development
and implementation of major inventions are in public hands.
[2] Machlup, pp. 51–2.

introduction of new products or processes (re-tooling, modification of plant and equipment, etc.). Where technology is moving rapidly and the life of new products or processes is short, the 'head start' obtainable by the inventor through these factors may be quite adequate to deter copyists, and patent protection may become a minor consideration – especially where industrial application of the invention is a relatively complicated matter.

### Invention and innovation

The argument thus far has been confined to pure 'invention'. While this emphasis may have been appropriate in times when industrial technology was simpler than it is today, the argument must clearly be broadened to take account of the huge resources that are nowadays devoted to the application of inventions in industry. It has indeed been claimed that the proper modern justification for the patent system is that it stimulates technological development and, in addition, investment in large production ventures that advanced technology is alleged to require.[1]

A few definitions seem to be called for here. We follow Kuznets in using *invention* to mean the creation of 'potential' new products or processes, i.e., designs, specifications or models that embody the essential working principles of useful technological discoveries.[2] An invention is thus something that can be patented, but it does not include the engineering work needed to convert an invention into an economically viable operation.

We understand *applied research* to mean the organised pursuit of inventions by firms, individuals or institutions, together with scientific work on consolidating or extending inventions. We distinguish this type of research from *pure research* – the disinterested pursuit of scientific knowledge without a specific technological objective in view. We follow Schmookler in preferring this term to 'basic' research on the ground that much basic (i.e., fundamental) research in industry is done with a fairly definite technological end in view.[3]

We think it best to use *innovation* as a general term to refer to the whole process of converting inventions into full-scale productive operations, including investment in new plant and equipment for the purpose. *Development* is then the formal pursuit of innovation, comprising mainly engineering work on getting inventions to the stage of an

---

[1] This point was recognised by the Swan Committee in 1946 and stressed by the recent Banks Committee. See *Second Interim Report of the Departmental Committee on the Patents and Designs Acts 1946*. (Cmd. 6789) para. 9 and Banks Report, para. 56.

[2] S. Kuznets, 'Inventive Activity: Problems of Definition and Measurement' in *The Rate and Direction of Inventive Activity*, pp. 20–4.

[3] J. Schmookler, 'Comment' on Kuznets in *The Rate and Direction of Inventive Activity*, pp. 43–6.

economic prototype or pilot plant, but not including the investment necessary for full-scale production. It is important not to overlook the latter, however, and we will refer to it, for want of a better term, as *innovatory investment.*

Admittedly, it is sometimes hard to draw a line between, say, 'research' and 'development' in the real world and more will be said about this and about the actual process of innovation in industry in later chapters. The point we wish to make here is that the deliberate pursuit of innovation and, above all, the engineering work of developing new products and processes is nowadays an extremely important and highly organised activity in a number of industries, and it is the impact of the patent system on this activity that will occupy much of our attention in future chapters. It is necessary to recognise at this stage that a patent may be capable of protecting, not merely an invention *per se,* but new products or processes developed from that invention. Whereas patents have traditionally been thought of as a device for protecting inventions, they are nowadays better regarded as a means of protecting novel technological ventures.

Naturally both the degree of protection and the corresponding incentive to innovation that a patent is capable of providing will vary with the strength of the link between the invention and the product or process to which it applies. A valid patent on a complete machine is likely to have much more protective value than one on a minor component of the machine, for it will be easier for competitors to find a substitute for the latter than for the former. According to most industrialists, patents of the former type are nowadays relatively few and far between, as only rarely are machines of an entirely novel character introduced. It is nevertheless still possible to conceive of entire new industries being based on patented inventions and being therefore dependent in a fundamental way on the patent system. In less extreme examples it is reasonable to think that patents may have a significant influence on the proportion of resources devoted to research and development and the proportion of investment that is innovatory in character.

B.   IMPACT OF THE SYSTEM IN MORE DETAIL

The indiscriminate promotion of innovation is obviously not a defensible economic objective from any point of view, except possibly that of those who earn their living as professional inventors or research workers. Implicit in any proper economic defence of the patent system is that it encourages broadly the 'right' amounts and types of innovation, i.e., the right allocation of resources between different types of invention and innovation, and between these and other activities in the economy. Critics of the system have pointed out a number of possible ways in which patents may encourage a misallocation of resources. One possibility is that by enabling innovating firms to earn monopoly profits the system draws resources away from routine types of production and may ultimately result in an excessive expansion of innovation at the expense of conventional consumption and investment activities.[1] Another possibility, stressed by Sir Arnold Plant, a prominent critic of patents in the 1930s, is that the system tends to divert effort quite arbitrarily from non-patentable to patentable inventions and furthermore, that it encourages wasteful research devoted to the circumvention of existing patents (an activity known in industry as 'designing around').[2] Others argue that such duplication of research may on balance be beneficial since it leads to the thorough exploration of viable alternatives in important new technical fields, and in any case such waste as does occur can be regarded as an unavoidable cost of technical progress, along with the undesirable monopoly elements in the system.

These are obviously highly complex issues on which rational discussion unaided by facts is likely to be inconclusive. Those who support the system believe that patents offer about the right degree of protection to inventors and innovating firms, inducing them to undertake investments that are capable of yielding at least 'normal' profits plus an allowance for the extra risk involved in innovation, but discouraging them from attempting to charge very much more than this for licences or patent-based products. Those against believe, on the whole, that patents offer an unwarrantable degree of protection to innovators and that they take advantage of this to make large monopoly profits and restrict production. If so, the rest of the economy may be ultimately worse off through having patents than it would be without them.

It is fortunately no part of our task in the present study to pronounce on what is a 'normal' rate of return, or a proper target rate of return, on invention and innovation. It is nevertheless interesting to consider some implications of the patent system in this regard. The period of a patent monopoly is 16 years, but in reality the maximum effective period of protection is nearer 15 years, since few patentees bother with enforcement of their rights where infringements commence less than one year from the expiry of the patent. In most cases, the actual period of protection is even shorter, for patents (if granted) take effect from the date of filing the complete specification, whereas it is normally some

[1] Machlup, *An Economic Review of the Patent System*, pp. 46–9.
[2] A. Plant, 'The Economic Theory Concerning Patents for Inventions', *Economica*, new series, Vol. 1 (1934) p. 45.

time after this before the innovation begins to earn income. (Patent applications typically occur at some time during the development phase, but before the commitment of large innovatory expenditures. For example, there is likely to be a delay of at least three years between the patenting and marketing of a new drug, and this reduces the actual period of a patent monopoly in this field to about 12 years.)

Accordingly, patents cannot provide much inducement for firms to undertake projects with long 'pay-off' periods – say, 12 years or more – however strong the temporary monopoly they offer. This appears on the surface to give more than adequate time by prevailing industrial standards, even in the case of an elaborate and complex innovation that takes, say, 3–5 years between the start of the intensive development effort and the commencement of earnings. The available evidence suggests that industrialists tend to avoid major R & D projects with pay-off periods of much more than 5 years (calculated from the first commitment of major development expenditures) and have a strong preference for an even more rapid pay-off.[1] On the other hand, it can probably be argued that industrialists adopt unduly conservative criteria from the point of view of the community when it comes to assessing R & D projects. Thus they probably discount the future more heavily than might be thought desirable by the community as a whole (hence having an undue preference for minor innovations with short development periods); they tend to ignore external (spillover) benefits of R & D elsewhere in the economy; and, as a special instance of the latter, they do not count company taxes as part of the return to their investment.

Moreover, it must be remembered that invention and innovation is on average a much more risky activity than routine manufacturing. For every invention that succeeds commercially there will be many more that fail. Where organised research and development by industrial firms is concerned, and where firms cannot predict which of a number of potential inventions will be successful, they must pursue large development programmes in order to be reasonably sure of getting the one or two that will succeed. Accordingly the research costs of all the associated unsuccessful inventions should properly be included with the R & D costs of a successful venture for the purposes of calculating a meaningful pay-off period or rate of return, and this will lengthen the true pay-off period for such projects beyond that usually cited.

Thus, on reflection, it appears that an official patent term of 16 years may be quite reasonable in the sense that it implies a maximum pay-off period for 'patent-based' innovations of roughly 10–12 years.

---

[1] The evidence is admittedly scanty, and relates mainly to U.S. industry. See, for example, E. Mansfield, *The Economics of Technological Change* (Longmans, 1969) pp. 65–6.

Moreover, it can be shown that if rates of return are calculated on a discounted cash flow basis, as increasingly adopted for major project selection by industrial firms, even an appreciable lengthening of the patent term would have a relatively small impact on the 'marginal' project undertaken on the basis of patent protection. If, for illustration, the minimum acceptable D.C.F. rate of return on new R & D projects is taken to be 15 per cent, a patent-based project with an earning life of 12 years (corresponding to the present legal patent term of 16 years) would require annual profits (after tax but before depreciation) of about £18½ per £100 of initial outlay in order to be selected. By comparison, annual profits for a similar project with an earning life of 16 years (corresponding to a patent term of 20 years, as proposed by the Council of Europe and recommended for the U.K. by the Banks Committee)[1] would have to be about £17 in order to qualify – very little lower. On the other hand, annual profits of a project with an earning life of only eight years (corresponding to a patent term of 12 years) would require to be at least £22½, showing that a reduction in the patent term would have a heavier impact than an increase of equal absolute size.

For these reasons it can be argued that the length of the official patent term may well be about right in so far as it affects the selection of R & D projects at the margin, although it is recognised that projects with exceptionally long development phases or in exceptionally speculative areas of technology could conceivably be under-rated as a result of the present term. By the same reasoning, it can be argued that the present system, in theory at least, appears to be indulgent to projects or areas of innovation that are distinctly better-than-marginal, e.g., those that involve, if the R & D is protected from copyists, a much shorter pay-off period than 10 years. It is possible in such cases that the use of patents to monopolise or rigidly control the spread of new products with potentially large markets or of new processes with wide cost-saving implications could be both extremely profitable to the monopolist and extremely costly to the rest of the economy.

Ideally, a patent system would deal with this either by adopting patent terms of various lengths to suit the circumstances of particular cases, or more directly by specifying the maximum profits (including licence fees) that patentees can earn from patented inventions. However, as we shall see later in connection with licence fees, such refinements raise difficult practical problems of measurement and administration. The question therefore remains whether, given the impossibility of an ideal system, the economy as a whole is 'better off' or not from having the present patent system, even allowing for cases where large

[1] Banks Report, Ch. 11.

profits are obtained from the exploitation of patents. The answer to this question must largely depend on whether or not individuals and firms affected by the system behave in the manner of monopolists and competitors assumed by orthodox economic theory, and above all on the willingness and ability of innovating firms to exploit the full restrictive potentialities of the system.

*A simple model –* ı

A theoretical example may help to clarify the issues. Consider an industry where there are a number of firms in competition with one another, each selling a somewhat differentiated product but all using the same processes and facing substantially similar cost conditions. The number of firms could be large or small, but it is fairly stable, for although market shares are moderately responsive to price variations the firms normally refrain from direct price competition because of the likelihood of retaliation by their immediate rivals.

Suppose that one firm stumbles (at zero or minimal cost) on a major process improvement that, if adopted, would bring about a net reduction in routine production costs of £x per unit. (Alternatively, the firm might purchase the improvement from a private inventor.) Suppose further that the development cost to the innovating firm (including any cost of purchase involved) is £Y, a non-recurring outlay which is a substantial investment expenditure by the standards of the individual firm, but smaller than the estimated future cost savings of the industry, suitably discounted. Suppose finally that the improvement, once developed and implemented, can be copied by other firms without incurring very much development expenditure (i.e., no significant part of the fully-developed improvement can be kept secret, once it has been industrially launched).

In these circumstances the firm in question will think twice about exploiting the invention solely on its own account without protection, for if it attempted to do so and if the other firms behaved like stereotyped competitors they would at once copy the improvement without incurring much of the development costs, thereby obtaining a competitive advantage over the innovating firm. The larger Y is in relation to the prospective cost-savings of the individual firm and the more prone the other firms are to 'pirate' the improvement, the less likely is the innovation to take place, despite its undoubted profitability on wider economic grounds. On the other hand, if the other firms are disposed to refrain from copying for some reason, or if they can be prevented from doing so, the innovation will probably be adopted.

If the innovating firm has a (valid) patent on the improvement, it may consider licensing it to the other firms. This will be profitable in the circumstances depicted, for under competitive conditions the other firms can be induced to pay a royalty of something approaching £x per unit of output and, as we have seen, the discounted cost savings of the industry exceed £Y. (Firms will not of course pay more than £x, for at that level the existing process is preferable.) The more competitive is the industry, the more nearly will the royalty approach £x. In the extreme case, the licensor will be able to appropriate the entire cost saving for 15 years, leaving little during that time for the other firms or for the industry's customers.[1]

One point to notice in this illustration is that the licensor cannot charge more for licences than the cost reductions they make possible, for otherwise he will not sell licences. Quite simply, the patentee cannot appropriate more than the total benefit from his invention. Accordingly, in the circumstances depicted (i.e., where there is licensing between willing parties), the economy as a whole must be better off through having a patent system. The function of the system is to introduce a market for the invention, enabling a proper test of the economic value of the invention to be made, whereas in its absence there would be no such test and the innovation would not be undertaken.

From the consumer's point of view, a preferable solution would be one in which the licence royalty was just sufficient to cover the development cost (i.e., lower than the 'competitive' level of £x), for then prices would fall and there would be some increase in output. Nevertheless, failing this solution, the rest of the economy could presumably share in the benefit in a 'second best' way through taxation of the licensor's profits.

### A simple model – ii

We now consider what happens in our hypothetical example if the innovating firm decides to exploit the (patented) invention on its own account while at the same time refusing licences to others. The firm is likely to proceed by developing and implementing the invention and may take advantage of the reduction in routine production costs to lower prices just sufficiently to put pressure on competitors. The latters' profits will suffer and, if the innovating firm persists in its course, they will either be compelled to leave the industry or become vulnerable targets for takeover, while the former will be poised to buy them up on the strength of its superior technology and, in due course, mounting profits. Logically the process will continue until the innovating

---

[1] Where cost reductions are very substantial in relation to price, it may pay the licensor to charge less than the unit cost reduction, so leaving some benefit for others. See Arrow in *The Rate and Direction of Inventive Activity*, pp. 619–22.

firm has become a complete or virtual monopolist in the market. When this status has been achieved the way is then clear for the firm to behave as a profit-maximising monopolist, raising prices above the level that would prevail in a competitive market and reducing output below the competitive level. It is quite conceivable that the industry's prices would ultimately be higher, and output lower, than those existing before the innovation. In this case (especially in the absence of substantial taxes on the monopolist's profits), it can be argued that the rest of the economy would be better off if there were no patent system.

A *priori* reasoning suggests that where patents are used to create a monopoly the outcome in any particular case will depend, other things being equal, on the size of the cost reduction and the potential degree of monopoly implicit in the demand for the product or range of products affected by the patent. It can be shown on certain highly simplified assumptions that, given the elasticity of demand for the product and provided the cost reduction associated with the patented innovation represents an appreciable advantage over competitors, the likelihood of the patentee's prices being ultimately higher (once he gains a monopoly) than those prevailing before the innovation is larger the smaller the cost reduction involved.[1] In broad terms, this means that a policy of granting patent monopolies over innovations will probably be justifiable on economic grounds where large productivity increases follow from an innovation, but may not be so in cases where the productivity gains are only moderate. It also suggests that patents on any given technological improvement are more likely to be justifiable where there are close substitutes for the patented product in consumption or use than where the product concerned is unique.

[1] In the example referred to, let the initial (pre-invention) price of the product in long-run competitive equilibrium be $p$ and the numerical value of elasticity of demand for the product in general (as opposed to that of any particular firm) be $e$. In these conditions, both average and marginal costs per unit of product, including an allowance for 'normal' profits, approximate to $p$. If the reduction in marginal costs resulting from the invention is $x$ per unit at the pre-invention level of output, the post-invention level of marginal costs at that output will be approximately $p-x$. If $p-x$ exceeds the level of marginal revenue implied by the industry's demand curve at pre-invention output $\left(\text{i.e., if } p-x > p\left(1-\dfrac{1}{e}\right)\right.$ or, more simply, if $\dfrac{x}{p} < \dfrac{1}{e}\Big)$, a profit-maximising monopolist taking over control of the entire industry would reduce output and raise price. Alternatively, if $\dfrac{x}{p} > \dfrac{1}{e}$, output would be increased and price reduced, while if $\dfrac{x}{p} = \dfrac{1}{e}$, price and output would be unchanged (the monopolist's profit being $x$ per unit). Clearly, at any given level of $e$, the likelihood that consumers will benefit from a patented innovation increases with $\dfrac{x}{p}$, and, for any given level of $\dfrac{x}{p}$, increases with $e$.

Several points are worth noting in connection with the case we have been discussing. Firstly, the essence of this case is that patents are used to create a position of market domination which would otherwise be difficult to achieve, because the natural economic forces are not such as to give any one firm an overwhelming market advantage. Secondly, the compulsory licensing provisions of the Patents Act, which might be thought to provide some safeguard against the harmful exploitation of patent monopolies, are wholly inadequate to deal with the situation. Thus the patentee can honestly show at all stages of the takeover process that he is 'working the invention' and 'meeting the market' within the vague meaning of these terms.

One possible flaw in our chain of reasoning (apart from the basic assumption that the innovation transforms a competitive industry into a monopoly) is the question of what happens when the patent expires. If there are genuinely no natural cost advantages in being 'large', apart from those associated with the *development* of the innovation, and if the improved process becomes accessible to all firms once the patent expires, will not other firms move into the industry at this stage, attracted by the monopolist's profits? (We assume the takeover process to be completed before the expiry of the patent.) If so, it is hard to conceive of any case in which the economy will not ultimately be better off through having patents, despite a possible interim period of high profits and restricted output. However, we can easily imagine a number of quite plausible reasons why the ultimate revival of competition might never happen. Thus, we could invoke the well-known reluctance of even quite powerful outsiders to join battle with a well-established dominant firm, especially in 'high technology' fields. More explicitly, three convincing reasons suggest themselves.

Firstly, it seems likely in many situations that a major process innovation, once adopted, would affect production costs in such a way that the optimal plant becomes large in relation to the total market. (This is not the same thing as saying that the development costs of the new process are large, which is the only assumption about firm size we have made so far, but it seems plausible that the two assumptions should go together.) If so, new entrants will be deterred by their inability to match the large incumbent's costs.

A second possibility is that the patentee may be able to prolong his patent protection through 'patents of addition' which, as the name implies, are follow-up patents to an initial master patent. In some cases these can make imitation of a basic invention difficult even after its patent expires, if seldom absolutely impossible.

The third possibility is really a variation of the second. It is that new processes and products in many fields of technology, once introduced, evolve more or less continuously – possibly for many years after their first adoption. Once the basic principles are established (and patented), the evolution may well be more in the field of informal knowledge than formal research – although that may be important too. After a period of fifteen years an active firm is likely to have built up such a lead in terms of (unpatented) know-how that this can, if kept secret, provide an effective barrier to entry even though the patents themselves are moribund.

## Conclusions

We consequently conclude that patents are capable of being used to create powerful and self-perpetuating monopolies and that these can in some circumstances be exploited in such a way that the cost of the monopoly to the rest of the economy outweighs the benefit of having the patent-based technology. It is equally possible to conceive of circumstances in which patents monopolies operate to the benefit of the economy as a whole. Whether the utilisation of patents actually results in a net benefit or net loss to the economy in particular cases, and indeed whether patents have any appreciable impact on economic activity, will depend on a variety of factors, among which the following seem to be foremost: the validity of the patents concerned; the extent to which innovations are based squarely on patents; the vulnerability of innovations to copying by outsiders, and in particular the extent to which secret know-how provides an effective protection; the presence or absence of barriers to competition other than patents; the extent to which patentees actually behave like conventional monopolists and the extent to which other firms behave like conventional competitors; the size of cost reductions or product improvements associated with the innovation; and the size of the market involved and the price elasticity of demand for the patented product (which in turn will reflect the availability of substitutes). These factors will determine the size of the total potential economic gain from an innovation, its dependence on prospective patent protection and the degree to which the spread of the innovation is actually restricted by patents. The economy as a whole must clearly gain from patents where an important invention is adopted essentially on the strength of patent protection, and where the innovating firm has a liberal policy with regard to licensing or internal implementation of the innovation; it must clearly lose where patents are used to create or sustain a rigid monopoly over an invention that would have been introduced in the absence of patents.

Without extensive knowledge of what actually happens, it is impossible to judge which set of circumstances is likely to predominate in the real world, since these are not questions on which *a priori* economic reasoning alone can contribute very much. The most we can say from a preliminary consideration of the issues is that there can be no general presumption in theory that a patent system of the sort that we have in the U.K. is either advantageous or disadvantageous to the economy as a whole. This conclusion is of course similar to those reached by most economic theorists in recent times and is very much in line with the agnostic position taken by Professor Machlup at the end of his review.[1] It reflects not so much a deficiency in economic theory as the almost total absence of information about patenting and licensing in practice with which economists have hitherto had to contend.

[1] Machlup, *An Economic Review of the Patent System*, pp. 76–80.

# 3. PREVIOUS RESEARCH FINDINGS

While modern economic research has not altogether ignored patents, there have been very few sustained attempts to investigate the impact of the patent system in detail, although a great deal of qualitative discussion has continued to take place on the subject and a special subcommittee of the U.S. Senate has commissioned a series of studies on it. In this chapter we shall first comment briefly on the literature on market structure and innovation, which involves patents without considering them as a central issue, and then look at the few extended attempts that have been made to investigate the impact of the patent system head-on.

## A. MARKET STRUCTURE AND INNOVATION

Patents have figured directly in several contributions to the extensive economic literature on market structure and innovation, in which American authors have been especially prolific.[1] The literature is essentially concerned with the impact of monopoly and firm size on technical progress, and patents are used in some empirical investigations as a measure of inventive activity, a determinant of technical progress.

The author primarily associated with the use of patents as an index of inventive output is Professor Schmookler, who has shown that patent activity in various industries and at various times is correlated with the pressure of demand for products, and has argued from this that the rate of technical progress is responsive to changing economic conditions as well as to the underlying advance of scientific knowledge.[2]

---

[1] For a useful review, see D. F. Turner and O. E. Williamson, 'Market Structure in Relation to Technical and Organisational Innovation', a paper prepared for the International Conference on Monopolies, Mergers and Restrictive Practices held at King's College, Cambridge, 23–6 September 1969. We have relied heavily on a substantial unpublished summary of the literature produced in conjunction with our own study, viz., J. M. Bradley, 'A Survey of the Literature on the Effects of Firm Size and Market Structure on Research and Innovation', (unpublished research paper of the Department of Applied Economics, 1968).

[2] J. Schmookler, *Invention and Economic Growth* (Cambridge, Mass.: Harvard University Press, 1966). A study of British experience has recently been undertaken on somewhat similar lines. Using data on U.K. patents covering more than a century, it finds a lagged

Although numbers of patents are, when used with caution, an acceptable if very rough indicator of inventive activity for some purposes, we are doubtful about using them in a statistical analysis of firm size and inventive output designed to examine the impact of market structure or size of firm on technological performance. A number of such studies have been done, of which probably the best-known is the one by Scherer in 1965.[1] Briefly, Scherer's approach is to correlate number of patents issued to a firm with size of firm (measured by sales or net assets) for a sample of 448 U.S. manufacturing firms drawn from the 'Fortune 500' list. A moderate degree of correlation between these variables ($R^2 = 0.42$) is found for the sample as a whole, and quite strong correlations for some industries considered on their own, especially electrical equipment and communications ($R^2 = 0.90$), transportation equipment ($R^2 = 0.82$), stone, clay and glass ($R^2 = 0.79$) and rubber products ($R^2 = 0.78$). This is taken to reflect 'the response of inventive output to the overall pull of demand' on the Schmookler pattern (page 1099). Relationships between patents and sales are then examined more closely using nonlinear regression equations to see whether patents per dollar of sales increase with firm size. No such pattern emerges and indeed the tendency in most industries is for the patent/sales ratio to decline as firm size increases.

A number of further possible relationships between patent/sales ratios and various measures of market power – including base year profitability and liquid asset ratios – are also tested, but no marked positive association between patent activity and market power emerges. These results are alleged by Scherer to disprove the Schumpeterian idea that larger or more monopolistic firms tend to have superior inventive efficiency (p. 1122).

The essence of our doubt about using patent data in this type of analysis is that individual patents are likely to vary enormously in their economic significance, and this variation may not be random as between firms of different size. Scherer himself admits that his results would be questionable if propensity to patent were inversely correlated with firm size, but doubts that this is the case (pp. 1110–12). However, there seem to be powerful *a priori* reasons for expecting that it will be true, of which the following appear particularly persuasive. Firstly, it seems likely that large firms may patent less per unit of R & D (or sales) than smaller firms in the same field, because the formers' R & D

correlation but in the reverse direction – i.e., variations in investment in the U.K. appear to *follow* those in patent activity, rather than preceding them, as Schmookler's results suggested. See J. Higgins, 'Invention and Economic Growth' (unpublished research paper of the Department of Applied Economics, 1971).
[1] F. M. Scherer, 'Firm Size, Market Structure, Opportunity and Output of Patented Inventions', *American Economic Review*, Vol. LV (1965) p. 1097.

programmes include a higher proportion of non-patentable work – such as 'development' – involving few basic inventive ideas but a great deal of engineering or organisational effort. Secondly, large firms seem on the whole likely to tackle R & D projects which are technically more complex than those tackled by small firms, and which therefore require larger inputs per patentable invention for technical reasons. Scherer recognises the latter possibility, but doubts that 'system inventions' generate fewer patents per unit of input than less complex ones.

Inevitably the issue can be solved only by resort to the facts. Scherer himself finds evidence of diminishing returns in the response of patent activity to R & D inputs, firm sales being kept constant, but is not convinced by it (pp. 1112–13, especially equation (7)). As a by-product of our industrial inquiry, some information was obtained on patent propensity by size of 'research division' of participating firms. The details can be found in Chapter 8, pages 146–51, especially Table 8.2, and are discussed more fully there. We believe that these data are superior to those used by Scherer in that they are obtained directly from responding firms, and relate where appropriate to divisions of firms rather than entire enterprises. This reduces the distortion that can arise when data from firms which have substantial operations in several different technical areas are utilised. Briefly, our conclusion is that there is a strong tendency for patent propensity to decline sharply with size of R & D 'division' in two of the three major industrial fields examined. (However, it is also found that 'development' does not account for a higher proportion of R & D in large as compared with medium-sized firms – see Table 8.3 – but the data there are much cruder than those in Table 8.2.)

In short, while recognising that patents are a convenient if rough indicator of inventive output for some purposes, we nevertheless feel that their use in the type of regression analysis referred to could well be misleading.

Other attempts to correlate inventive output with standard indicators of firm size, industrial concentration, etc. have adopted alternative measures of inventiveness. The most favoured appears to be R & D expenditure, as used for example by J. S. Worley (*Journal of Political Economy*, April 1961), but a potentially more fruitful approach has been attempted which counts major recorded inventions in selected fields and weights them in accordance with some more or less arbitrary index of economic importance. The best-known example of the latter is probably the paper by E. Mansfield (*Journal of Political Economy*, December 1963), which examined inventions in iron and steel, petroleum refining and coal using this method. All, or almost all, reach the conclusion that there is no clear correlation between available measures of inventive efficiency and size of firm in particular fields.

While these approaches seem procedurally sounder than those relying on patent data, we feel that they are subject to certain criticisms of a conceptual kind. The first is that they make no allowance for the likely fact that, in many if not all science-based industries, R & D projects undertaken by large firms are very different in character from those undertaken by medium-sized firms and, *a fortiori*, by small firms. They are not necessarily more 'valuable' or of a higher technical quality, but they are larger and more complex, owing primarily to large technical indivisibilities in some kinds of projects. It is hardly realistic to ask whether an industry consisting of a large number of small (uncoordinated) firms is likely to be more efficient than a highly concentrated industry when it comes to developing and introducing, say, computers or jet aircraft or telephone systems, or even a new synthetic fibre: the choice does not exist.

The second criticism is that none of the studies which have come to our attention seem to make adequate allowance for the existence of economies of scale in the *use* of R & D results. The fact that large companies in some industries have relatively low propensities to invent or patent in relation to sales may reflect their ability to spread fixed R & D costs over very large outputs, rather than deficiencies in their technical progressiveness, although these may exist. Studies that utilise R & D/sales ratios or some variant as indicators of inventiveness seem often to overlook this factor, and we know of none that manages to take full account of it in their results, although some (e.g., several studies by Minasian, one of which is discussed in Chapter 4, Section C) have tried.

More will be said on these points in Chapter 8, which deals with the evidence on R & D arising from our inquiry. To sum up, we have doubts about some of the main findings produced by the literature on market structure and inventiveness. The empirical results so far have been rather inconclusive and occasionally misleading, and we wonder whether the authors have always been attacking the right questions. For example, more attention should perhaps be devoted to the idea, frequently expressed by industrialists, that many types of innovation which are essential to modern economic development can be effectively carried out only by very large organisations. (The development of plastics and electronic computers, well documented by Freeman,[1] are leading examples.) In such fields, it is argued, small firms may make a valuable – and in some fields an indispensable – contribution, but they

[1] C. Freeman, 'The Plastics Industry', *National Institute Economic Review* (Nov. 1963) and 'Research and Development in Electronic Capital Goods', *Ibid.* (Nov. 1965).

tend to specialise in particular types of research or narrow phases in the innovation process; they are not thought to be practical alternatives to large organisations in a range of science-based industries and if this is true the question of a statistical relation between size and technological efficiency in these cases would not be relevant. If one accepts this view, the real question in such cases is whether it is worth suffering the disadvantages that may go with large monopoly-wielding corporations in order to obtain the technical advantages that, short of nationalisation, only they can achieve. The issue is, in some respects, analogous to the one that we are tackling in relation to patent monopolies in the present study.

### The small inventor

Before leaving this area of the literature, we should mention the work of Jewkes, Sawers and Stillerman on the sources of invention.[1] This study examines a number of major inventions of the modern industrial era and assesses their causes and the conditions under which they have taken place. A principal finding is that the sources of invention have been very diverse and that independent inventors and small firms were responsible for a significant proportion of the inventions examined. The policy conclusion is that a wise government will keep open all the various sources of invention, and in particular will give encouragement to the small inventor. These conclusions are compatible both with the findings by Scherer and others of the absence of a statistical association between firm size and inventive efficiency, and with the view referred to above that small firms may have a special role to play in 'high technology' industries.

It is perhaps significant that Jewkes and his colleagues do not appear to think that the patent system has much effect on the rate of invention in large-scale industry, for at no stage in their discussion of industrial R & D or in the supporting case studies do they even raise the question. They do however strongly suggest that patents are an important stimulus to the small inventor:

'One conclusion can be put forward immediately with confidence. So long as the survival of the individual inventor is not utterly despaired of (and the evidence of the preceding chapters suggests that there is no need to do this) and so long as nothing better can be suggested for the purpose, there is a very strong case for retention of the patent system.'[2]

The authors go on to admit that the patent system has many drawbacks – in particular that it operates by restricting the use of

[1] J. Jewkes, D. Sawers and R. Stillerman, *The Sources of Invention* (2nd ed., MacMillan, 1969).
[2] Jewkes et al., *The Sources of Invention*, p. 187.

information – but they argue that 'for the individual inventor or the small producer struggling to market a new idea, the patent right is crucially important'.[1]

This view of the patent system as being valuable mainly for the small inventor is not necessarily at variance with our emphasis on the role of patents as a possible inducement to organised industrial innovation. It is quite conceivable that patents could be a powerful stimulating influence on individual inventors and small firms as well as larger firms, and this possibility is considered in our study (see Chapter 13). However, while we do not ignore the small inventor, we devote most of our attention to the impact of the system on large-scale industrial innovation. Since small inventors rarely if ever take charge of the commercial development of their inventions in the modern era, as is confirmed by Jewkes,[2] it seems essential to study the operations of major industrial companies if real light is to be shed on the problem.

Few of course would go so far as to argue that the monopoly element in patents is of no interest to private inventors. Clearly the payment that an inventor can expect for his patent will depend very much on whether he is offering something that an innovating company can monopolise. For this reason, we imagine that the enthusiasm shown by Jewkes for Professor Polanyi's proposal some years ago that patent monopolies be replaced by a system of inventors' awards payable out of public funds, with unrestricted access for all prospective users of the invention, might not be shared by the inventors themselves.[3]

B.  IMPACT OF PATENTS

Turning now to the research studies that have had the patent system as their main subject, we start with the series of studies commissioned by the Patents Subcommittee of the U.S. Senate.[4] Several of these deserve special attention, although their empirical content is for the most part relatively limited. Among them, in addition to the study by Machlup mentioned earlier (Study No. 15), are those by Frost (No. 2), Vernon (No. 5) and Melman (No. 11). More recently, a substantial study by Gilfillan has been published for the Joint Economic Committee of

[1] *Ibid.*, p. 188.
[2] Although about half the inventions studied by Jewkes originated partly or wholly with small inventors, their commercial development was in virtually all cases undertaken by large business organisations to whom the relevant patents had been assigned or licences granted.
[3] M. Polanyi, 'Patent Reform', *Review of Economic Studies*, Vol. XI (1943–4) p. 61.
[4] U.S. Senate Subcommittee on Patents, Trademarks and Copyrights, 85th Congress, 1st and 2nd Sessions, *Study of United States Patent System* (U.S. Government Printing Office, 1957 and 1958).

the U.S. Congress, and merits consideration for its sheer size and scope.[1]

These documents contain much useful information of various sorts about the U.S. patent system, and they discuss the issues at considerable length. However, while the authors often display impressive experience and grasp of their field, their studies all suffer from a lack of systematic quantitative data on crucial matters and they are compelled to make judgments on the basis of highly partial evidence. All are aware of this deficiency, and Vernon in particular draws attention to it:

> Policy toward the international patent system turns heavily on an appraisal of its economic impact, and much of the data needed in order to consider the impact objectively is lacking or inadequate. Although information exists with respect to the system, its value is limited because of its subjective and impressionistic nature or because of the unrepresentative character of the situation it covers.[2]

It is therefore hardly to be expected that the principal views of these authors should closely coincide, although one is hardly prepared for the variation in opinions offered. Thus, for example, Frost, a practising patent attorney and professor of law, is strongly convinced that patents provide an important incentive to research and development and to competition in the development of new technology, and cites an impressive list of cases in support, without being able to do much more than assert flatly that patent protection had an effect in each case. More convincingly, he argues that the likelihood of harmful monopolies occurring in the U.S.A. through the accumulation of large patent holdings is small, because of the active enforcement of anti-trust legislation in that economy.

By contrast, Vernon, an economist who has made a number of contributions in the field of international investment and trade, is sceptical about the incentive effect of patents on research and believes strongly that cross-licensing between international companies operates to restrain international trade. He concludes in favour of an extension of compulsory licensing on a selective basis (p. 35).

A yet more derogatory view of the patent system is taken by Gilfillan, who makes the most serious attempt of all these writers to deal quantitatively with the subject, and yet fails to justify adequately his sweeping indictments of the system and proposals for reform. His presentation of a series of rough indicators of American inventive activity since 1880, while debatable in some respects, introduces a welcome sense of perspective and demonstrates that, by any standards, American

---

[1] S. C. Gilfillan, *Invention and the Patent System*, a study for the U.S. Congress Joint Economic Committee, 88th Congress, 2nd Session (U.S. Government Printing Office, 1964).

[2] R. Vernon, Study No. 5 for the Senate Subcommittee, p. 5.

inventive output has increased enormously in the intervening period (possibly one hundredfold), while patenting activity has risen merely threefold. Furthermore, his estimates of financial support for inventive activity, including pure research, R & D, etc., by various sources in the U.S.A. are revealing:

> Attempting to measure in Chapter 9 the various sources of support for invention, and for the researches in physics, chemistry, and such sciences that are indispensable and largely inseparable bases for modern invention, we find the Federal Government supports 61% of these, including 15% through tax benefits, highly organized industry 31%, small companies and unorganized inventors 2%, patent pooling 3·7%, Compulsory Licence, Sales of Know-how, Suggestion Systems, Foundations, and Universities, each about ½%, and the remainder in smaller contributions from State governments, Professional societies, Trade Associations, and Awards.[1]

These estimates are well documented and they are interesting in showing the dominant role of the Federal Government as a source of funds for U.S. invention, and the insignificance of the small inventor in this respect. (We shall consider the corresponding picture for the U.K. in the next chapter.) On the other hand, Gilfillan's disparaging assessment of the patent system as giving no encouragement to basic invention and too much to 'minor improvements and gadgets' is very lacking in systematic evidence. Similarly his proposal that the system should be reformed by providing preferential patent grants for cooperative research done in expanded semi-public trade associations, membership and support of which would be obligatory for all industrial firms, is highly speculative to say the least.

Some useful analysis of the patent activity of U.S. firms has stemmed from the valuable data produced by Federico for the U.S. Senate Subcommittee.[2] It is now reasonably well established that ownership of U.S. patents became somewhat more concentrated in the hands of large corporations in the period 1939–55 compared with the inter-war period, that the concentration has not increased much in the last decade, and that the prevailing concentration of patent ownership is much lower than that for net assets or R & D expenditure.[3] While this information is of great interest so far as it goes, more research would be needed before reliable deductions could be made regarding the impact of patents on industrial concentration and similar questions.

[1] Gilfillan, *Invention and the Patent System*, p. 8.
[2] P. J. Federico, *Distribution of Patents Issued to Corporations, 1939–55*, Study No. 3 of the Subcommittee on Patents etc., *loc. cit.*
[3] D. S. Watson and M. A. Holman, 'The Concentration of Patent Ownership in Corporations', *Journal of Industrial Economics* (April 1970) pp. 112–17.

*Patent utilisation study*

The high level of interest in the patent system and associated matters in the U.S.A. has led to the foundation of the Patent, Trademark and Copyright Research Institute at the George Washington University. This organisation has published through its journal[1] a stream of specialist research material on every aspect of patents, including the economic impact of the system. Most notable for our purposes are the reports of the Institute's *Patent Utilisation Study*.[2] This study was undertaken as a preliminary basis for the Institute's long-term programme of assessment of the patent system, and is of particular interest to us because its main questions are in some respects close to those that we tackle in our own study. While we have reservations about the methodology of the Institute's study, we do not doubt that its general strategy – i.e., the survey of attitudes of industrial patentees – is a useful one. Since the study's findings are of considerable interest, we shall outline them here.

The method adopted for the survey was to select at random from official patent listings a sample of 1,220 patents issued in 1938, 1948 and 1952, amounting to some 2 per cent of all U.S. patents outstanding at the date of the study. Questionnaires were mailed to the assignees requesting a series of judgments relating to the sampled patents, and 600 responses were obtained, virtually all of which were from industrial firms. Some interviews were undertaken in the course of the study, but the great majority of those responding were apparently not interviewed.

Of the many interesting results that emerge, the following particularly stand out. Three-quarters of the 600 patents for which replies were obtained were claimed to have some measurable economic value for the assignee. Of the total, 57 per cent were 'used' or 'about to be used', 11 per cent were alleged to have 'other benefits' (mainly the remoter possibility of use), and 7 per cent (not including those in the above categories) were licensed to others. Unfortunately, no explanation of 'use' was found in the papers cited, but we presume that it means 'worked at some time in the assignee's own processes or products'. The authors are clearly impressed by this finding, which they feel disproves the prevailing contention in the literature that a rather small proportion of all patents issued – possibly 10 per cent according to Machlup – is actually used in industry.

[1] *IDEA, The Patent, Trademark and Copyright Journal of Research and Education* (P.T.C. Foundation, Washington D.C.).

[2] See B. S. Sanders, J. Rossman and L. J. Harris, 'The Economic Impact of Patents', *IDEA*, Vol. 2, No. 3 (Sept. 1958) pp. 340–62 and 'Attitudes of Assignees Towards Patented Inventions', *Ibid.*, Vol. 2, No. 4 (December 1958) pp. 463–504.

It should be noted that the authors ignore lapsed patents. This could be an important omission, for many patents issued in the selected years must have lapsed by the time of the Institute's study and these might contain a relatively high proportion that were never really used. Thus the Institute is covering a different 'population' from that referred to by Machlup, and this could account for part at least of the apparent discrepancy between them. Nevertheless, the proportion of outstanding patents said to be of measurable economic value is high – much higher than the Banks Committee Report or our own study would suggest[1] – and if this is true it would certainly cast a new light on the patent system. As it turns out, the Institute's efforts to establish the size and nature of the alleged benefits are not very convincing.

The study examines the claims regarding the value of patents by inviting respondents to say whether the alleged benefits accrued through increased sales or reduced production costs, and to grade the effects in accordance with whether they were 'slight', 'moderate', etc. It is reported that, of the 30 per cent of sampled patents that were in 'current use', the great majority were judged by firms to yield 'slight' or 'moderate' benefits, mainly through sales increases, and to a lesser extent through cost reductions. (The minority were said to yield losses.) It is not easy to discern the basis for these judgments, but apparently respondents made 'informed guesses' as to the net effect on their profits of inventions covered by the sampled patents, including costs of making and applying the inventions. Some respondents (about 60) went so far as to offer dollar estimates of these net benefits; for patents in current use, net gains averaged $600,000 per patent yielding gains, while net losses averaged $88,000 per loss-making patent.

These results are intriguing, but it is important to be aware of their limitations. Firstly they are, as the authors admit, wholly unverified guesses in the vast majority of cases. While we do not object to the technique of inquiry in principle, and indeed we rely quite heavily on it in our own study, great care should be exercised in the process. It does not appear that enough care was taken in this aspect of the Institute's study, so far as we can tell from the reports cited. Thus, no corroborative evidence of any sort is offered for the guesses and the researchers do not appear to have assessed them or participated in them in most cases, merely accepting the mailed returns without query. This seems a serious shortcoming and greatly detracts from the credibility of the results. Rough estimates *may* be adequate for an investigation of this

[1] The Banks Committee estimates the proportion 'in commercial production' of all patents in force at about 30 per cent, on the basis of a mailed questionnaire (see Banks Report, Appendix G(b)). Our own estimate, relating to the proportion of all patents granted which are renewed for their complete term, is one-fifth to one-quarter (see Chapter 6, page 97).

sort, but there is a good chance that some will not be. (This is especially likely to be so where a single patent is being assessed, for its effects may be quite indistinguishable from those of others, if complex products or processes are involved.) In any case, it is absolutely crucial in such an exercise that the researcher should be able to discuss the basis of the estimate with the respondent, familiarise himself with the technical and commercial background, and in important cases share responsibility for the judgments reached. This does not appear to have been done in the study under review.

One unfortunate consequence is that the authors can offer no explanation of the manner in which the impact on sales or production costs comes about, the products or processes affected, the markets involved, etc. Neither are they able at this stage to explain how patents enter the picture. However, at another point in the exercise, a useful attempt is made to assess how far patent protection was instrumental in persuading firms to proceed with the commercial exploitation of patented inventions. It is reported that of the 448 replies received on this question (including, confusingly, replies on patents not 'in use' as well as those 'in use'), 70 per cent of respondents said that they would have gone ahead with the commercial development even had they not obtained a patent. The corresponding proportion for replies relating to patents in use, which are said by the authors to be more reliable than those for patents not in use, is 84 per cent. The authors point out that the replies to this question were (not surprisingly) much hedged about by qualifications, and that in a substantial portion of cases the respondents may have been saying that the question had no bearing on their situation (i.e., because the patent was not commercially exploited) rather than that patents had no stimulating effect. At all events, the meaning of the replies is rather unclear; there is moreover no indication of the importance in terms of alleged economic benefits of the cases where patents were said to be a factor in decision-making. As elsewhere the authors are hampered by their inability to verify and interpret replies.

While this study has several admirable features – in particular its genuine concern to unearth the relevant facts and to obtain rough estimates of some crucial orders of magnitude – its findings seem open to considerable doubt. The failure of the researchers to explore in detail the returns on their questionnaires and to provide much corroboration or logical support for the results is a serious drawback. Apart from these deficiencies, reliance on the scientific sampling of a 'population' of individual patents seems misplaced in a study in this field, bearing in mind the object of the exercise. Admittedly, this technique may be appropriate if one is trying to discover, for instance, what proportions of patents are worked, although bias presumably occurs in the response if, as seems likely, respondents tend to be firms with a relatively large stake in the system. But while questions of this type may be of interest to those who are concerned with the efficient working of the system (and who may wish to assess the amount of 'wasteful' patenting that takes place), they do not themselves go very far in answering the fundamental issues that concern us. It seems likely that it is either the exceptional 'basic' patent, or the large accumulation of possibly quite minor patents in a single holding, that are capable of influencing the behaviour of firms. If so, a sampling exercise that is devoted to discovering the characteristics of the average or 'representative' patent will probably fail to capture the true impact of the system, whatever it may be.

### Cost–benefit approach

A second and totally different study appearing in the Institute's journal also merits attention here. It was published as an example of the 'cost-effectiveness approach' to evaluation of the patent system.[1] Again we do not feel that the analysis fully bears out the conclusions claimed by the authors, but the study is nonetheless instructive in that it constitutes the only serious effort to assess the impact of patents by macro-quantitative statistical methods that we know of.

The main interest for us lies in the authors' attempt to demonstrate that there is a link between a firm's propensity to patent and the subsequent growth of its sales. The reasoning behind this hypothesis is not made perfectly clear, but the idea seems to be that prospective patent protection induces firms to undertake more R & D, and more investment, than otherwise, and firms with a high level of patent activity in relation to sales are therefore likely to grow faster than others.

The approach was to correlate growth in sales, 1955–65 (adjusted for mergers, etc.) with propensity to patent (ratio of patents in force to sales in 1955) for 375 major U.S. firms in 15 industries, using a contingency table approach. It was found (page 363) that in 12 of the 15 industries examined, the combined sales growth of firms with an above-average propensity to patent in their industry exceeded that of firms with below-average patent propensity, sometimes quite substantially. The exceptions, surprisingly, are drugs, electrical machinery and farm machinery. It was also found that the proportion of firms tending to support the hypothesis (i.e., those combining above-average patent propensity and above-average sales growth, together with those combining below-average patent propensity with below-average sales

[1] R. F. Dale and J. K. Huntoon, 'A Cost–Benefit Study of the Domestic and international Patent Systems', *IDEA*, Vol. 11, No. 3 (Fall 1967) pp. 351–406.

growth) exceeded 50 per cent in 12 (but not the same 12 as in the previous result) of the 15 industries (page 365) – a result that probably could not arise by chance, according to the test of significance used.

The authors are understandably worried by the apparently negative relationships between growth and patent propensity found in drugs and in electrical and farm machinery. In both of the latter two industries the relationship was found to be due to the influence of a few large firms and became positive when firms were given equal weight in the analysis, but this was not so in the important case of drugs. The authors are obliged to conclude in this case: 'The problem cannot be resolved within the scope of the study and perhaps not at all. Suffice it to say that the statistics point toward drug industry growth not being supported by patents' (page 371).

The possibility was admitted that the general association found between patent propensity and growth of firms could well be a reflection of more basic influences – in particular those of corporate size and R & D effort – and various attempts were made to bring these factors into the analysis. Again using contingency tables, the authors show that 'large' firms did not in general grow significantly more or less than 'small' ones in the same industries and conclude from this that 'size did not account for the patent-growth relationships in the sample' (page 366). Their efforts to utilise R & D expenditure in a similar exercise were unfortunately hampered by the fact that published R & D data were available for only 174 of the 375 firms initially included, while in four of the 15 industries the resulting samples were too small to be useful and had to be discarded, thus reducing the overall sample to 157 firms. The contingency table analysis for these firms showed a positive, but not statistically significant, correlation between R & D effort (R & D expenditure as a percentage of sales in 1955) and sales growth for firms in the same industries, and a very slightly higher correlation between patent propensity and sales growth (significant at the 10 per cent level – page 368).

The authors remark: 'An arbitrary but seemingly reasonable conclusion from the foregoing was that the relationship between patent propensity and sales growth may be accounted for about equally by patents and by R & D' (page 369). This observation is puzzling, in that it implies that R & D and patent activity are separate explanatory factors, whereas ordinary reasoning would seem to suggest that they are really different manifestations of the same basic activity of industrial innovation.

The contingency table approach is supplemented by a series of multiple regressions in which sales growth for each firm is regressed on numbers of patents in force, together with various combinations of indicators of firm size and R & D expenditure. Although correlation coefficients for these regressions are generally quite high, the results of particular interest to us do not appear very convincing. As the authors point out, in several industries the small numbers of firms (hardly more than 10 in some cases) coupled with highly-skewed size distributions result essentially in two-point regressions, so that high values of $R^2$ in these cases should usually be discounted. Furthermore, the partial regression coefficients of sales growth on patents (purporting to measure the impact of inter-firm variations in patent propensity on sales growth in particular industries) sometimes differ quite substantially between different 'models' – especially where R & D in one of two alternative versions enters the equation (Table 5). Moreover, although the relevant regression coefficients are often significant at the 30 per cent level, this is frequently not so where R & D is included as a separate independent variable. (Table 5, models 1, 4 and 5.)

Finally, there is the awkward fact that the partial regression coefficients of patent propensity on sales growth emerge as negative (sometimes significantly so) in four or five of the industries analysed, depending on the precise set of variables used. (Drugs, electrical machinery, farm machinery and soaps and cosmetics are notable offenders.)

Thus, while the study does suggest that there is an association of some sort between a firm's patent propensity and its subsequent sales growth, other things being equal, it is, as might be expected, a rather weak and irregular one on the statistical evidence presented. More especially, the 'perverse' conclusion for drugs is surely unacceptable, and casts doubt on the remainder of the exercise. There is accordingly real doubt as to whether the hypothesis of a *causal* relation between propensity to patent and sales growth is indeed 'on reasonably solid ground', as the authors claim. The evidence of neither the contingency tables nor the regression analysis seems persuasive on this. One is left with the feeling that much of what the authors wish to attribute to patents is really a reflection of more basic influences. They do not dispose of the likely possibility that the more rapidly growing firms in research-based industrial fields in the U.S.A. achieve success because they are more technically progressive (and therefore, do more R & D and patent more) than their less active rivals. In this process, patents do not *necessarily* contribute a separate stimulus either to research or sales growth. They may indeed do so, but the answer to that complex and difficult question is not revealed in the study under discussion.

The authors finally attempt to translate the alleged impact of patents on sales growth into national economic benefits. Briefly, their suggestion is that, if the average patent in active use increases a firm's sales by $x per annum, the annual economic benefit to the nation in money terms

from having patents is $x times the number of patents in active use –
not counting any effects on sales in previous years. Quite apart from
our objections to the statistical part of the study, we find this reasoning
quite unacceptable. To swallow it, it would be necessary to believe that
additional sales by firms with a high patent propensity are largely the
result of increases in their productivity or in their employment of
hitherto unused resources. This might be so in some cases, but equally
plausibly the sales increases of high-patent firms might be largely at the
expense of their less patent-conscious rivals (as a result of the exercise
by the former of patent monopolies). Without a great deal of study it is
impossible to judge the relative importance of these effects, and therefore quite wrong to regard the value of patent-inspired sales increases
as net benefits to the national economy on a dollar for dollar basis.

## Conclusions

This review of the empirical literature involving patents suggests that
there are some serious unsolved research problems in the field; we are
particularly impressed with the limitations of conventional statistical
approaches for measuring the impact of the system. So far as we can
judge, researchers in the patent field have not overcome these problems,
partly because of inadequate data, partly because of the very real
difficulties of quantitative analysis in this area, and partly because they
have not got to grips with the logic of the underlying situation. We are
consequently not much nearer a reliable evaluation of the patent
system than the highly agnostic position reached by economic theorists,
although much of interest can be learned from the research work that
has been done.

## Postscript – a Canadian study

Professor Firestone's study of the Canadian patent system unfortunately
reached us too late for proper discussion in this chapter.[1] It is manifestly a substantial and informative piece of work which requires attention by any serious student of the subject. However, although there is a
great deal of material in it which is of interest to our study, and on
which notes can usefully be compared, its relevance to the role of
patents in the British economy is limited because of the very special
situation that exists in Canada. There some 94 per cent of patents are
issued to foreigners, reflecting the dominant position of American-
originating technology in Canadian industry (page 319). In this
respect, Canada finds itself more in the position of a less-developed
economy tending to import technology than of a highly-industrialised

[1] O. J. Firestone, *Economic Implications of Patents* (University of Ottawa Press, 1971).

economy like the U.K., where 30 per cent of patents originate domestically. It is therefore very understandable that the patent system should
be found on balance to operate against the interests of the Canadian
economy – tending to reduce competition, limit manufactured exports
and facilitate foreign control of Canadian industry, while offering
relatively little compensation in terms of faster technological progress
(pages 320–1).

It would certainly be unwise to apply these judgments to the British
situation, as Professor Firestone would doubtless agree. Moreover,
the study is concerned, quite properly in view of its terms of reference,
with the impact of the Canadian patent system, taking as given the
existence of patent systems elsewhere. Its conclusions might well differ
if, for example, the existence of patent systems in the U.S.A., the U.K.
and other major technology-generating economies were also in question.

# 4. U.K. INDUSTRIAL RESEARCH AND DEVELOPMENT IN PERSPECTIVE

While published information on R & D, patents, etc. does not provide anything like a complete basis for measuring the impact of the patent system, it does offer a convenient starting point for the investigation. Thus, it enables one to see which are the areas of economic activity where formal inventive effort is concentrated, and whether these are also areas where patent activity tends to appear. We shall look at these questions in Sections A and B below, without attempting to infer any causation between patent activity and research.

The impact of inventive effort on technological progress is of course highly relevant to an economic assessment of the patent system. Economists are beginning to devote serious attention to this relationship, but they have so far managed to produce little clear indication of its precise nature and size and it remains one of the important unsolved questions confronting investigators in this general field. We ourselves did not feel that we could tackle such a large and complicated question as a principal target of our industrial inquiry and it is dealt with there only in so far as we investigate the impact of patent protection on production of a research-intensive kind. We were nevertheless reluctant to abandon all direct approaches to the problem, and it did seem worth trying to produce a tentative answer with the aid of available industry data. While this material is far from ideal, it did respond to some attempts at refinement and statistical analysis, and we present the results of the exercise in Section C.

## A. THE OVERALL PICTURE

As far as can be calculated, annual expenditure on 'formal' invention and innovation in the U.K. amounts to something under three per cent of the gross national product. The great bulk of this consists of 'scientific research and development' undertaken by firms, research associations, nationalised industries, government research establishments and universities. This expenditure has been estimated officially, with the help of sample surveys, to be in the order of just under £1 thousand million in 1967–8, as shown in Table 4.1.

TABLE 4.1. *Scientific research and development in the U.K., 1967–8 (£m)*

| Sector | As source of funds[a] | As user of funds |
|---|---|---|
| Government | 493 | 239 |
| Universities, etc. | 6 | 75 |
| Public corporations | 45 | 42 |
| Research associations[b] | 1 | 13 |
| Private industry[c] | 360 | 570 |
| Overseas | 30[d] | — |
| Other | 28[e] | 24[f] |
| Total | 962 | 962 |

NOTES:

[a] Payments for royalties and licence fees are not attributed to the paying sector as source of funds unless regarded by the user as an external source of finance for R & D, which seems rare; if so, they are attributed to 'other'.

[b] Mainly industrial research associations.

[c] R & D budgets of firms with 25 or more employees.

[d] Payments for research contracts, grants and subscriptions from overseas, mainly to private industry, including payments from overseas subsidiaries and parent companies. Licence fees and royalties from overseas are not included.

[e] Payments to industry, Government and universities from individuals and from sale of patents, licences and equipment, etc.; and may include some payments from industry for contract research.

[f] Payments to individuals, very small firms, private research organisations and societies, mainly by Government as research grants.

SOURCE: Department of Education and Science/Ministry of Technology, *Statistics of Science and Technology* 1970.

These figures relate to what might be called 'organised' research and development of a scientific and technical nature, including pure research but not market or economic research. They do not include activity undertaken by self-employed or part-time inventors or by very small firms from their own funds – on which we shall say more in a moment. Neither do they include inventive activity of an 'informal' (i.e., unplanned) nature such as occurs as a by-product of routine technical work, problem-solving by management, etc. Although such informal activity may be quite costly in relation to associated effort put in on routine work, no way of measuring it has yet been devised, and no estimate is offered here. Fortunately this is not a serious omission from the viewpoint of our present study, as informal inventive activity, being essentially unplanned, is not likely to be sensitive in any direct way to inducements offered by the patent system.

So far as we know, no estimate has ever been made of the self-financed inventive activity of the small inventor (individuals and very small firms), at least in the U.K. We are therefore obliged to fall back on a rough calculation of the following sort. Assuming that the great bulk of self-supported invention by very small firms is in the manufacturing field, and that these firms spend the same amount per employee on their research and development on average as do larger ones, we can estimate that very small firms spent about £34 million on R & D in 1967–8, i.e. 6 per cent of the amount spent by larger manufacturing firms (6 per cent being the approximate ratio of employment between the two groups[1]).[2]

It is rather harder to assess the inventive effort of self-employed inventors, and yet this is something we should not ignore since, according to Jewkes,[3] about 32 per cent of applications for British patents came from private inventors in 1955. (The share has declined steadily for many years and in 1968 was possibly about 25 per cent.) Furthermore, we have been told by the National Research Development Corporation, one of whose functions is to develop inventions originating outside industry, that over one thousand inventions were submitted to it in 1967–8 by individuals, although very few of these had much economic value. Clearly a significant inventive effort is involved, even if the effort is not always very successful, and even allowing for the fact that very few private inventors finance the *development* of their inventions, which is the phase of the work where industry spends heavily. If we assume that about half the British patents granted to private inventors originated in the U.K. (i.e. a higher proportion than that of U.K.-originating patents to all British patents, reflecting the tendency of private inventors to patent on a smaller scale overseas than do companies), we can estimate that roughly 30 per cent (approximately 8,000) of U.K.-originating applications in 1968 were attributable to private inventors. It is hard to express this in terms of expenditure on invention, but we may perhaps be fairly near a reasonable *maximum* figure if we assume that private inventors contribute only to the *research* phase of their inventions, and that they do so on the same scale per patent as does industry. Multiplying total (current) research

[1] Board of Trade, *Census of Production* 1963, Summary Table 1.
[2] The recent Department of Trade and Industry survey for the Bolton Committee has estimated the share of 'small firms' (those with up to 200 employees) in all industrial R & D at 4 per cent. This suggests that our guess here is on the high side. See Chapter 13, page 316.
[3] Jewkes *et al.*, *The Sources of Invention*, p. 89.

expenditure in 1967–8 per patent applied for by British industry in 1968 (about £7,500) by the estimated number of patent applications attributed to private inventors, we arrive at roughly £60 million for the 'expenditure' of private inventors.[1]

£7,500 per patent application may seem rather a high figure, especially if we accept Gilfillan's argument that most patented inventions are of the 'gadget' variety, but it must be remembered that it includes the work of inventors who were 'unsuccessful' in the year in question, as well as those who applied for patents.

If these estimates are accepted, we may say that very small firms and private inventors spent (from all sources) up to about £100 million in round figures on their own inventive activity in 1967–8. If we deduct from this the £24 million or so financed externally through grants, awards, contractual payments, etc. already shown in Table 4.1, we arrive at a reasonable maximum estimate of about £75 million for the 'small' inventor to be added to the expenditure shown in that table, giving an amended total for all 'formal' R & D of about £1,040 million.

At about 7 per cent of this total, our estimate for the small inventor is considerably larger than Gilfillan's estimate for the U.S.A. mentioned earlier (page 45), – which was based on an entirely different set of calculations. This may be at least partly due to the fact that ours is a maximum estimate, whereas Gilfillan seems to be concerned to minimise the importance of the small inventor in his assessment of the American picture.

Several interesting points may be noted from the orders of magnitude we have mentioned so far. Firstly, it seems clear that by any standard formal invention and innovation absorbs a very small slice of our national resources: three per cent is hardly an impressive share of current production to devote to the formal improvement of science and technology.[2] Secondly, the Government emerges as the main source of funds for these activities, although industry (private and public) is not far behind. Thirdly, industry emerges by a wide margin as the predominant agent for the work, accounting as it does for 60 per cent of the total. Fourthly, the portion of the R & D effort that is potentially sensitive to patent protection is very much less than the whole. If, as seems reasonable, we eliminate work financed by Government and

---

[1] A large part of this 'expenditure' is likely to be 'notional' (not included in G.N.P.), since the earnings of many private inventors probably fall far short of the true economic cost of the work done.

[2] However, the U.K. spends more in relation to G.N.P. than any other non-Communist country with the exception of the U.S.A. See OECD, *The Overall Level and Structure of R & D Efforts in OECD Member Countries* (Study 1 for the International Statistical Year for Research and Development; Paris, 1967), Table 2.

universities, on the ground that this is probably not very much influenced by commercial considerations, we are left with some £540 million (i.e., £1,040 million minus £499 million) financed by industry, 'overseas', and small inventors. However we should perhaps also deduct from this the finance provided by industry, etc. to Government and universities (some £29 million[1]), in the belief that this is likely to be principally for pure research, and therefore also not much influenced by prospective patent protection. If so, we come down to a figure of some £510 million, or just under half the national R & D effort, as being potentially responsive to the influence of patents, and thus of interest to us in the present study.

### B.   R & D AND PATENTING IN INDUSTRY

In the remainder of this chapter we shall concentrate on R & D in industry, which, as we have seen, constitutes the bulk of the national R & D effort financed from commercial sources. However, we do not wish to overlook the contribution of the small inventor, and we shall return to that question in Chapter 13.

The industrial distribution of R & D expenditure in the U.K. is shown in Table 4.2, which ranks industries in order of column (4). The first point to note is that virtually all reported industrial R & D occurs in manufacturing, so we can quite safely confine our attention to those industries.

Column (1) shows the approximate total sums spent on industrial R & D from all sources, but since the view taken in our study is that Government support for R & D is not likely to be much influenced by patent protection, we are more concerned here with *commercially-financed* R & D. As virtually all industry's finance from non-commercial sources comes from the Government, we may obtain a reasonably adequate figure by deducting Government-financed from total expenditure, which is done in column (2).[2]

It can be seen by comparing columns (1) and (2) that Government support is particularly important in aircraft (where about four-fifths of the total is financed through Government contributions, mainly

[1] Dept. of Education and Science/Ministry Technology, *Statistics of Science and Technology* 1970, Table 4.
[2] Admittedly, a good deal of industrial R & D done under Government contract has commercial applications, and in some important cases the Government provides support for 'commercial' ventures – such as 'Concorde' or I.C.I.'s basic work on computers – but the point remains that this support is not motivated by the commercial criteria normally adopted by industrial firms, and is thus not likely to be affected by the question of patent protection, although follow-up development financed by the firms themselves may well be.

TABLE 4.2. *R & D and net output, by industry, 1967–8*[a]

| | (1) R & D expenditure 1967–8 (£m) | (1A) Proportion spent on 'development'[b] (%) | (2) R & D expenditure less funds from Government 1967–8 (£m) | (%) | (3) Net output 1968 (£m) | (4) Commercial R & D ratio (2)÷(3) (%) |
|---|---|---|---|---|---|---|
| Petroleum products | 11·1 | 39 | 11·0 | 2·6 | 103 | 10·7 |
| Electrical engineering | 153·2 | 78 | 103·7 | 24·1 | 1,403 | 7·4 |
| Aircraft | 163·6 | 95 | 32·6 | 7·6 | 490 | 6·7 |
| Chemicals and coal products | 77·0 | 52 | 75·0 | 17·4 | 1,468 | 5·1 |
| Motor vehicles | 45·6 | 83 | 44·7 | 10·4 | 1,091 | 4·1 |
| Scientific instruments | 13·8 | 72 | 11·2 | 2·6 | 278 | 4·0 |
| Railway equipment | 1·8 | 53 | 1·8 | 0·4 | 57 | 3·2 |
| Mechanical engineering | 62·3 | 74 | 51·1 | 11·9 | 2,064 | 2·5 |
| Rubber and products | 5·8 | 50 | 5·8 | 1·3 | 264 | 2·2 |
| Non-ferrous metals | 6·7 | 52 | 6·4 | 1·5 | 305 | 2·1 |
| Iron and steel | 14·2 | 52 | 13·7 | 3·2 | 793 | 1·7 |
| Bricks, pottery, glass etc. | 10·2 | 54 | 9·9 | 2·3 | 610 | 1·6 |
| Textiles, man-made fibres | 12·1 | 53 | 11·7 | 2·7 | 1,104 | 1·1 |
| Food, drink, tobacco | 19·6 | 49 | 19·4 | 4·5 | 2,002 | 1·0 |
| Other manufactures | 3·4 | 67 | 3·4 | 0·8 | 359 | 1·0 |
| Metal products n.e.s. | 7·2 | 71 | 6·9 | 1·6 | 999 | 0·7 |
| Ships, marine engineering | 2·7 | 47 | 1·5 | 0·3 | 286 | 0·5 |
| Wood and paper products etc. | 8·9 | 68 | 8·7 | 2·0 | 1,735 | 0·5 |
| Clothing, footwear, leather | 1·3 | 66 | 1·2 | 0·3 | 601 | 0·2 |
| All manufacturing | 620·6 | 75 | 420·3 | 97·6 | 16,012 | 2·6 |
| Other industries | 10·8 | 65 | 10·1 | 2·3 | 4,419[c] | 0·2 |
| Total | 631·4 | 75 | 430·5 | 100 | 20,431 | 2·1 |

NOTES:

[a] 'Industry' comprises private industry, public corporations and research associations. R & D relates to work carried out within, or financed by, industry. The latter includes R & D done for industry by universities and government research establishments.

[b] These shares are based on *current* expenditure, which comprises nearly 90 per cent of total R & D expenditure.

[c] Net output of construction and public utilities; mining and quarrying are not included.

SOURCES:

(1) and (2) Department of Education and Science/Ministry of Technology, *Statistics of Science and Technology* 1970. (3) *Census of Production* 1968 (preliminary results).

under defence contracts), while electrical engineering (mainly electronics) and mechanical engineering (mainly industrial plant, much of which is supplied under Government contract in the power generation field) also benefit substantially from Government help.

As it turns out, the principal concentrations of commercially-financed R & D occur in the electrical and mechanical engineering industries, in chemicals and allied products, and in motor vehicles. Each of these accounts for more than 10 per cent of the industrial total, their combined share being nearly two-thirds.

*R & D and net output*

By calculating the ratio of commercially-financed R & D to net output, we obtain (column (4)) a rough indicator of the degree to which various industries 'rely' on such R & D. This is of special concern to us, since it is reasonable to think that industries with a high 'commercial research ratio' will be ones that have a keen interest in methods of protecting the commercial fruits of their research (of which patents are one). As might be expected, the chemical and engineering industry groups appear highest on the list (with ships and marine engineering a notable exception). Despite its heavy reliance on Government support, aircraft comes third. This is a reflection of the outstandingly high ratio of total R & D to net output in the aerospace industries, a state of affairs which makes these industries an awkward special case, as we shall see in Section C.

Although the figures in Table 4.2 are adequate for our present purposes, they should be treated with a certain amount of caution. For one thing, the 'product groups' for which information on R & D is collected do not always precisely match the Standard Industrial Classification on which net output is based, although they are pretty close. Furthermore, some firms with diverse operations may have difficulty in dividing their R & D between 'product groups' in a meaningful way. There are, moreover, anomalies of a special kind in certain groups, e.g., petroleum products, where British R & D helps to support essentially international operations, including exploration and crude oil production. A figure that relates British R & D to net output in the U.K. clearly overstates the 'research intensity' of the petroleum products industry. (Nevertheless the proper ratio is undoubtedly high, and would probably place petroleum products near the top of the table.) In other industries, a reverse type of anomaly may apply, in that British research ratios may be unduly low because the leading firms are subsidiaries of foreign parents and therefore tend to rely heavily on foreign R & D. Electronics in particular may reflect this type of anomaly.

In another sense, the figures may be affected by the arbitrariness of the distinction between R & D and other functions of a business. The official survey instructions on this (which we followed in our own inquiry) are to class as *development* all work 'directed to the introduction or improvement of specific products or applications, up to and including the prototype or pilot plant stage'.[1] Specifically excluded are 'routine testing and analysis, operational research, market research and work study, trial production runs, design costs to meet changes of fashion or style, and all legal and administrative work in connection with patent applications, records and litigation'. Nevertheless, the dividing line is sometimes hard to draw, especially in such industries as aircraft, where frequent design modifications of a more or less fundamental sort are made in the course of routine production, and in heavy engineering, where much industrial plant is custom-built.

The division between *research* and *development* is probably less difficult to draw in most fields, as these activities are usually fairly distinct, even though they frequently take place in the same establishment. Research is generally distinguishable in practice as being work directed to the discovery of the *principles* of a new product or process, including the construction of small-scale mock-ups or working models, while development comprises the conversion of principles, formulae or models into saleable products or commercially-viable processes. Examination of the official data shows that, as might be expected, industries that do most R & D tend to be ones that do most development. Nevertheless, there appears to be no very strong tendency for the ratio of research to development to be high or low in industries that rely relatively heavily on R & D in proportion to net output. Thus while it can be calculated from column (1A) that industries in the top half of Table 4.2 have on average a slightly higher ratio of 'D' to 'R' than those in the lower half, there are several significant exceptions (e.g. petroleum products, chemicals).

### Patent activity, by industry

Our next task is to fit patents into the broad industrial picture. Unfortunately, we are hindered by the lack of an appropriate up-to-date classification of published patent data. Ideally, we should like to have numbers of total patents in force and new patents granted by industry, but there is no detailed information for patents in force, while the data reported by the Patent Office on new patents, although adequate for some purposes, are classified in a way that does not fit at all closely

---

[1] Board of Trade Census Office, 'Inquiry into Expenditure on Scientific Research and Development' (Questionnaire), p. 6. The instructions further state: 'The guiding line... is the presence or absence of an element of novelty or innovation'.

with the Standard Industrial Classification on which the rest of our industry data are based. (In particular, it is impossible to obtain a satisfactory division between mechanical engineering and other industries.) We accordingly have no alternative but to rely on the data, classified according to the S.I.C., that were produced for our own earlier volume.[1] These figures only go as far as 1960, but we did not feel it necessary to undertake the considerable labour of updating them for the present study. Thus, although the level of patent activity in relation to R & D varies somewhat over time, the figures for 1960 enable one to see the broad differences between industries, which is our main object here (Table 4.3).

The patent classification in Table 4.3, it should be noted, refers to the subject matter of a patent, which does not always coincide with its industry of origin. This may lead to inconsistencies – as, for instance, when a patent on a piece of textile machinery invented by a machinery producer is classified in textiles rather than mechanical engineering. Although this type of anomaly probably does not very seriously distort the allocation of patents between broad groups of industries, it may well affect the relation between patents and other orders of magnitude in particular industries. Thus the ratios in columns (2) and (3) should be viewed with caution.

It appears from Table 4.3 that nearly three-quarters of all new patents in manufacturing accepted for grant by the British Patent Office in 1960 were for inventions in the fields of chemicals and allied products and electrical and mechanical engineering (including scientific instruments and 'metal goods n.e.s.'). No other industry group is prominent in the manufacturing total. (We should add that new patents on inventions outside the field of manufacturing, which are not shown in the table, account for only about 3 per cent of the overall total.)

Column (2) is intended to show in a rough way the degree of an industry's involvement with the patent system. Thus patent activity in 1960 is shown as a ratio of net output (a measure of the size of an industry) in 1958, there being a time lag of $2\frac{1}{2}$ years between application and acceptance in most cases. Nor surprisingly, the chemical and engineering (mechanical and electrical) industries head the list by a wide margin. They are followed by a broad category – 'other manufacturing', which in this table includes rubber products as well as plastics products, toys and baby carriages. The ratios in the remaining industry groups are below the average for all manufactures, reflecting the high concentration of patent activity in the chemical and engineering fields. It is noteworthy that the vehicle and aerospace industries together show only 3 new patents per £ million of net output, which

---

[1] Vol. 1, page 176. See also pp. 142–5 for an account of the derivation of this data.

TABLE 4.3. *New patents in manufacturing, by industry, 1960*[a]

| | (1) New patents 1960[b] No. | (%) | (2) New patents, 1960, per £m of net output, 1958 | (3) New patents, 1960, per £10,000 of R & D expenditure, 1958 | (4) Royalty receipts 1963 £m | (%) |
|---|---|---|---|---|---|---|
| Chemicals, etc. ⎫ Petroleum products ⎭ | 9,000 | 21 | 12·2 | 2·1 | 8·1 | 23 |
| Mechanical engineering ⎫ Electrical engineering ⎬ Scientific instruments ⎭ | 21,890 | 52 | 10·0 | 2·1 | 9·5 | 27 |
| Other manufacturing | 1,330 | 3 | 5·8 | 3·2 | 1·0 | 3 |
| Bricks, pottery, glass, etc. | 1,180 | 3 | 4·0 | 3·7 | 0·4 | 1 |
| Aircraft ⎫ Motor vehicles ⎬ Railway equipment ⎭ | 2,390 | 6 | 2·9 | 0·2 | 3·7 | 10 |
| Metal manufacture | 1,860 | 4 | 2·7 | 2·3 | 1·0 | 3 |
| Textiles, man-made fibres ⎫ Clothing, footwear, leather ⎭ | 2,310 | 6 | 2·4 | 2·7 | 7·3 | 20 |
| Wood and paper products | 1,190 | 3 | 1·5 | 6·0 | 0·7[c] | 2 |
| Ships and marine engineering | 300 | ½ | 1·3 | 1·3 | 0·1 | ½ |
| Food, drink, tobacco | 520 | 1 | 0·6 | 0·9 | 3·9 | 11 |
| All manufactures | 41,970 | 100 | 5·3 | 1·4 | 35·7 | 100 |

NOTES:
[a] Net output of these industries in 1958 totalled £7,851 m, and R & D expenditure £297 m.
[b] References to British patent acceptances, including foreign- as well as U.K.-originating patents, which were about half the total in 1960. This figure generally exceeds new patent grants by a small percentage.
[c] Not including publishers' royalties.

SOURCES:
(1) Volume 1, p. 176.
(2) and (3) See Appendix A, page 366.
(4) *Census of Production* 1963, summary table 9.

suggests that these industries are not in general highly 'patent conscious' in the way that many branches of the chemical and engineering industries are.

Column (3) presents an attempt using the published data to measure what might be termed the 'patent propensity' of particular industries (i.e., the ratio of new patents generated per unit of R & D expenditure). Unfortunately, the estimates here are subject to considerable shortcomings – in addition to the inconsistencies in data classification mentioned above. Firstly, the figures for patents include those originating outside industry (i.e., those attributable to small inventors). These probably accounted for about one-quarter of all U.K. acceptances in 1960, with sharp differences between fields (see Chapter 13, page 315). Secondly, the figures also include patents originating overseas (including some from small inventors); these comprised about one-half of U.K. acceptances in 1960, according to official data. A proper measure of patent activity in U.K. manufacturing would exclude these classes, but unfortunately the published data do not make the necessary distinctions by industry. (One of the aims of our industrial inquiry is to remedy this deficiency, at least in the fields covered.)

Accordingly, the estimates in Table 4.3 provide no more than a very rough guide to patent propensities in particular industries. Nevertheless it seems safe to note one or two salient points, namely: the degree of variation between different fields appears to be quite large, and not at all related to 'research-intensity'. Thus none of the fields showing the highest patent propensities – wood and paper products, bricks, pottery, glass etc., 'other manufacturing' and textiles, etc. – appears in the top half of Table 4.2. Furthermore one or two major fields in which R & D is important in both absolute and relative senses, especially aircraft and motor vehicles, appear to have extremely low patent propensities. This may not be unconnected with the fact that 'development' comprises a relatively high proportion of R & D effort in these fields, but there are doubtless other explanations as well.

Speaking generally, there appear to be three main reasons for variations in patent propensity between different fields. There is firstly variation in the 'fruitfulness' of R & D effort, which in turn reflects primarily the differing technical circumstances of different industries (or 'technical opportunity' as some writers have called it). In this respect, it may seem somewhat odd that wood and paper products and building materials should have high patent propensities; one possible explanation is that these industries are unusually selective spenders on R & D, and that their effort is limited to certain 'progressive' areas (e.g., printing machinery or float glass manufacture) where research has been outstandingly successful. Secondly, variation occurs in the suitability of R & D results for patenting. Thus one explanation of the very low rate of patenting in vehicles is probably that a great many of the advances made in this field come about through design modifications, on which strong patents are notoriously hard to obtain. Thirdly, variation occurs in the 'pressure' to patent, i.e. the pressure on firms to use patents as a device for monopolising their innovations. This pressure is likely to be highest in fields where innovations can easily be copied and where the innovator is in keen competition, actual or potential, with other suppliers. The pharmaceutical industry is a clear example of this type of situation.

These are questions to which we shall devote more attention in later chapters. The main conclusion here is that the propensity to patent seems fairly high in the engineering and chemical fields, with the suggestion that it is also high in 'sophisticated' areas of general manufacturing and processing (e.g., glass-making technology, ceramics, plastics goods, synthetic fibres and associated textile processing, rubber products, etc.), but very low in 'assembly' and design-oriented industries. Unfortunately the crudeness of the published information and the anomalies in classification mentioned earlier prevent us from being more precise than this.

The final column of Table 4.3 shows gross royalty receipts reported by firms in the various industry groups. These figures are derived from the 1963 Census of Production, which is the only available official source of royalty information in the necessary detail; they relate to all types of current payments received for the use of patents, trademarks, manufacturing rights, etc., including lump sums as well as running royalties, and including payments for know-how. As such, they should not be strictly regarded as income from patents, although in most industries this is probably a substantial component. We nevertheless include them as a very rough indicator of the areas of industry that are particularly active in patent licensing. The use of figures for 1963 in our table is not wholly inappropriate, since there is generally a substantial time lag between granting and licensing of patents; it thus seems fair to compare the distribution of royalty income with that of patent activity in an earlier period.

It appears from column (4) that the chemical and engineering industry groups account for about half the total of manufacturing royalties, which accords very loosely with the pattern of patent activity in column (1). Several other industries show up as royalty earners, notable textiles, food, drink and tobacco, and vehicles. Inspection of the original data reveals that man-made fibres and textile finishing are the areas of textiles concerned, while tobacco accounts for the bulk of payments in its group. (Royalties for the use of trademarks etc. are probably an important item there.) Aircraft and motors account for most of the royalty payments in the vehicles group; these could well be for know-how rights rather than use of patents. Royalties in the remaining industries are all relatively small, with non-ferrous metals (part of metal manufacture) comprising the largest single earner among them.

A further point that emerges in connection with the royalty figures is that they are extremely small in relation to the net output of the industries concerned. (In chemicals and petroleum products royalties

3

are of the order of three-quarters of one per cent of net output in 1963.) On the other hand, they are not always small in relation to R & D expenditure. Thus in chemicals and petroleum products royalties amount to just under one-tenth of R & D in 1958, while in textiles they exceed R & D, in 1963 as well as in 1958. As we shall see later, royalties constitute an important return on R & D for some technologically active firms, although R & D is seldom undertaken for the purpose of obtaining royalties.

The information summarised in this section shows that commercially-financed R & D and patenting and licensing activity are fairly heavily concentrated in the fields of chemicals and allied products, electrical engineering and mechanical engineering. These are clearly the areas of industry which our study must examine in detail. Moreover the figures suggest that the aircraft industry, despite its high research ratio, should be avoided on account of the overwhelming role of the Government as a source of finance, while motor vehicles seem a poor candidate because of the low level of patent activity. In a choice of industries to put alongside chemicals and engineering, petroleum products recommends itself through having a high ratio of commercially-financed R & D to net output and through its link with petroleum chemicals, which seems a particularly important field for study. Finally textiles, including as it does the critical area of man-made fibres and accounting for substantial royalty earnings, seems a suitable area for attention. These five industry groups account together for roughly 80 per cent of patenting, 70 per cent of royalties, and 60 per cent of commercially-financed R & D in British manufacturing industry.

### C.   R & D AND PRODUCTIVITY

We now pause to examine a question that goes far beyond the patent system while being highly relevant to an economic assessment of it – namely the link between R & D and something which we may loosely call productivity. Clearly, if patents do influence R & D effort, it would be convenient if we could generalise about their implications in terms of effects on productivity.

The simple form of the idea we wish to consider is that, broadly speaking, there is a tendency for industries or firms that do a lot of R & D to have a higher rate of growth of productivity than those that do little. The reasoning is as follows: there are certain fields of production that are by their nature highly responsive to R & D, in the sense that if R & D is applied on or above a certain minimum (absolute) scale, it sooner or later gives rise to 'superior' products or processes; there are other fields that are not at all responsive in this way, where no amount of R & D effort will raise productivity by very much, and yet others that are moderately responsive. Industrialists have a rough notion of which lines are likely to be responsive, and plan their R & D accordingly. The successful areas flourish, the unsuccessful ones die, and a loose pattern of correspondence between R & D effort and productivity growth emerges; indeed the former may be said to be a cause of the latter.

Some economists have taken this idea further by suggesting that there is in many, if not most, industries a fairly close functional relationship between R & D inputs and productivity. While we are inclined to be sceptical about this approach, it is a potentially attractive one and merits some attention here.

Briefly, the suggestion is that R & D should be viewed as an input into the production process whose impact is to shift the production function upwards in a fairly regular and predictable way.[1] This does not of course rule out the possibility that productivity may depend on other things as well, and ideally the approach seeks to introduce other determinants, such as R & D inputs in other (technologically-related) lines, the general state of the technological arts, etc.[2] It is recognised that the exact nature of the relation will vary from one line to another, depending on 'technological opportunity', but the implicit view seems to be that important general similarities will hold between lines (such as diminishing marginal returns to R & D when it is increased beyond 'optimum' levels).

Unfortunately, serious problems arise when attempts are made to test the link between R & D and productivity in the real world. For one thing, the conceptual approach suggests that the *level* of productivity in any line depends on past as well as present R & D, on the ground that R & D results are in the nature of investments whose impact is cumulative, although subject to depreciation on account of obsolescence.[3] It then follows that the rate of growth of productivity is a function of past as well as present R & D inputs (with a lag to allow for the time that elapses in applying R & D). Thus a thoroughgoing attempt to measure the impact of R & D should incorporate *past* R & D, probably with a time lag, and this is likely to present data and estimation problems for the researcher.

Secondly, the idea of a stable functional relation between R & D and productivity is obviously questionable in fields where the scientific

[1] J. R. Minasian, 'The Economics of Research and Development', in *The Rate and Direction of Inventive Activity* (N.B.E.R. 1962) pp. 98–103.
[2] E. Mansfield, *Industrial Research and Technical Innovation: An Econometric Analysis* (London: Longmans, 1969) Ch. 4.
[3] *Ibid.*, p. 66.

foundation for technology is either not established or changing rapidly. There are industries whose technology has been revolutionised through some basic (and possibly quite cheap) discovery, while retaining their superficial characteristics unchanged; the introduction of synthetic fibres in the man-made fibres industry is a case in point. The task of predicting productivity movements from R & D inputs in such industries is likely to be extremely hazardous, especially if long-term predictions are attempted. For similar reasons the approach seems quite unsuitable for the assessment of pure research; most exponents would probably agree that it is best confined to research and development of a distinctly 'applied' kind.

Thirdly, although the approach usually refers to 'output' of a constant quality, it is acknowledged that the impact of R & D may come about through the introduction of new or radically modified products, superior to the old in customer appeal and for that reason not comparable with them. Conceptually this problem can be handled by giving output a quality as well as a quantity dimension and treating new products as improvements in quality, but the practical problems of placing new products with old on a 'quality index' are difficult and have yet to be overcome.

Fourthly, it is now fairly well established by economic research that productivity in many lines is positively related to output, in a dynamic if not in a static sense.[1] Any attempt to assess the link between R & D and productivity that does not somehow take account of this seems likely to arrive at misleading results.

Connected with this is a further set of difficulties that may confuse the picture; viz., the wide differences in demand conditions that attach to different types of production. If, as seems plausible, the most rapid increases in demand for manufactured goods in an industrial economy tend to occur in technologically novel (high research) lines, either because the products are improved or because their prices fall, and if productivity growth is associated with increases in scale, there will appear to be a correlation between R & D and productivity growth that is at least partly bogus. This possibility means that any statistical findings must be interpreted with the greatest care.

Finally, it is more than probable that in some important fields the impact of technological progress occurs, not in the industries generating the change (by doing the R & D), but at other stages of production. The more pervasive the impact of an industry's R & D throughout the rest of the economy, the less likely is an analysis that ignores the inter-industry impact of R & D to produce a reliable evaluation of the impact of R & D on *overall* productivity. And yet the problems of

[1] W. E. G. Salter, *Productivity and Technical Change* (C.U.P., 1960) Chs. IX and X.

incorporating inter-industry effects into a statistical analysis are severe; as far as we know, no exponent has yet succeeded in doing so, although several have pointed out their existence.

For these and other reasons, the task of assessing the impact of R & D activity on productivity has proved to be a difficult one and few extended attempts have been made to tackle it. One of the earliest and most interesting of these is contained in the paper by Minasian referred to above. Since the latter's findings are relevant to our present question, we shall outline them here.

Minasian starts with the general proposition that '...the greater the research and development expenditure [by a firm],...the greater is the subsequent rate of growth in the productivity of the firm' (p. 100). He proceeds to test this by investigating the association between the annual rate of growth of productivity and 'research intensity' in 18 U.S. chemical firms for the period 1947–56, both variables being in real terms. The $r^2$ for the sample is found to be 0·67, suggesting that about two-thirds of the variation in productivity growth between firms is explained by research intensity. The degree of correlation is much reduced when shorter periods are used, owing (the author says) to the greater influence of abnormal years and erratic changes in prices, capacity utilisation, etc., but is improved if a lag is introduced. The correlations are not greatly affected by alternative measures of research intensity, output, etc. and survive the introduction of further explanatory variables such as profitability, fixed investment and increases in firm size. The simple regression coefficient of productivity growth on R & D intensity comes out at about 0·25 (although it varies appreciably with the precise periods, etc., used) – which suggests that an increase in R & D intensity of $R$ per cent is associated with an addition to annual productivity growth of about $R/4$ per cent.

Minasian's results are, of course, open to criticism. Thus, the sample is small and possibly biased in a number of ways; the measures of the variables are rough and depend on special assumptions about the nature of production functions; R & D in the remoter past is not explicitly included; no attempt is made to distinguish the impact on productivity of 'external' research; and no allowance is made for the impact of R & D via new products. Furthermore the measure adopted for 'research intensity' (the ratio of real R & D expenditures by a firm to an index of its total inputs) seems far from ideal in this particular exercise. The author's reason for adopting this measure is to 'standardise the firms for the effects of scale', but it is doubtful whether he fully achieves this, at least with reference to R & D effort. If, as he appears to assume, the research cost (in absolute terms) of a given increase in productivity is the same for different products and different scales of output in the chemical field, a measure of R & D deflated by inputs would seem to distort the true research effort of different firms, especially if they are of very different sizes. If, on the other hand, the amount of R & D needed by a firm to achieve a given increase in productivity increases with the extent of diversification in the firm, and if large firms tend to be more diversified than small, the use of Minasian's measure would seem more justified.

It is nevertheless hard to avoid the suggestion of a fairly strong relationship between R & D and productivity growth among the chemical firms examined, although one may have doubts about the stability of the functional relationship that Minasian has in mind. We would prefer to remain with the simpler idea that there is a tendency for 'high' R & D effort to give rise to 'high' productivity growth, and Minasian's results certainly seem consistent with this. At all events, it is this modest version of the idea that we wish to explore below in the context of U.K. manufacturing.

### *Some results for U.K. manufacturing*

Data on productivity growth and R & D effort for 26 manufacturing industries are summarised in Table 4.4 (see page 71), industries being ranked in order of column (4). Figures in this table were derived from the larger table in Appendix A at the end of the book, which gives details of sources, etc. The industrial breakdown is as fine as is permitted by recent official information on R & D expenditure.

The first four columns are index numbers comparing the average of the two years 1963 and 1968 with the average of 1958 and 1963.[1] (Averages were chosen in an attempt to reduce the type of irregular movement found by Minasian.) All are in real terms, the values of net output and capital stock being expressed in constant prices. The productivity index was derived thus:

$$P = \frac{Q}{L(W) + K(1 - W)}$$

where $P$, $Q$, $L$ and $K$ are index numbers of productivity, net output, labour and gross fixed capital stock in an industry for the stated period, and $W$ is the share of labour income (including employers' contributions to national insurance, pensions, fringe benefits, etc.) in the industry's net output in 1963. It is, then, a total productivity index in which inputs of labour and capital are combined, using their shares in net output in the middle of the period as weights. Although it is admittedly a fairly crude measure of productivity growth it does make

---

[1] The exercise is limited to these years because it relies heavily on detailed census of production data.

TABLE 4.4. *R & D ratios and productivity growth, U.K. manufacturing industries*

| Industry | (1)<br>Net output (at constant prices) | (2)<br>Employ-ment | (3)<br>Gross fixed capital stock (at constant replace-ment cost) | (4)<br>'Total' produc-tivity | (5)<br>R & D/ net output 1958–63[a] |
|---|---|---|---|---|---|
| | Index numbers 1963–8[a]<br>(1958–63[a] = 100) | | | | % |
| 1. Man-made fibres | 191 | 109 | 129 | 156 | 10·6 |
| 2. Domestic electric appliances | 222 | 122 | 110 | 136 | 7·1 |
| 3. Rubber products | 152 | 109 | 125 | 131 | 2·7 |
| 4. Plastics | 177 | 135 | 139 | 130 | 10·3 |
| 5. Petroleum products | 159 | 95 | 138 | 129 | 16·6 |
| 6. Pharmaceuticals | 152 | 114 | 129 | 127 | 7·2 |
| 7. Other electrical products[b] | 135 | 108 | 110 | 124 | 6·4 |
| 8. Aircraft | 118 | 91 | 117 | 119 | 38·0 |
| 9. Electrical machinery and generating | 112 | 92 | 110 | 117 | 7·6 |
| 10. Other chemical products[c] | 133 | 94 | 128 | 116 | 6·4 |
| 11. Motor vehicles | 137 | 117 | 127 | 115 | 3·9 |
| 12. Electronics and telecomm. | 152 | 117 | 156 | 114 | 16·6 |
| 13. Bricks, pottery, glass etc. | 128 | 101 | 133 | 111 | 1·7 |
| 14. Mechanical engineering | 124 | 104 | 123 | 111 | 2·7 |
| 15. Clothing and footwear | 109 | 95 | 105 | 111 | 0·3 |
| 16. Other textiles[d] | 104 | 90 | 101 | 110 | 0·2 |
| 17. Paper, printing | 123 | 107 | 120 | 109 | 0·3 |
| 18. Timber, furniture | 117 | 104 | 119 | 107 | 0·5 |
| 19. Scientific instruments | 140 | 121 | 144 | 105 | 6·6 |
| 20. Iron and steel | 111 | 98 | 124 | 102 | 1·4 |
| 21. Other manufacturing[e] | 131 | 122 | 137 | 102 | 1·4 |
| 22. Railway equipment | 68 | 61 | 103 | 102 | 1·5 |
| 23. Non-ferrous metals | 113 | 104 | 127 | 100 | 2·2 |
| 24. Food, drink, tobacco | 115 | 106 | 124 | 99 | 0·9 |
| 25. Metal products, n.e.s. | 111 | 109 | 117 | 98 | 1·0 |
| 26. Ships and marine engineering | 82 | 80 | 108 | 93 | 1·4 |
| All manufacturing | 121 | 102 | 121 | 109 | 4·0 |

NOTES:

[a] Averages of two years.
[b] Electrical engineering *less* electronics and telecommunications, electrical machinery and generating, and domestic appliances.
[c] Chemical and coal products *less* pharmaceuticals and plastics.
[d] Textiles *less* man-made fibres.
[e] Mainly n.e.s.

See Appendix A for basic data and detailed notes on these figures. For other explanations, see text.

rough allowance for capital inputs and we believe it is quite adequate for the present exercise, bearing in mind the deficiencies in the data used.

The derivation of the data is described in Appendix A, but it should be emphasised here that some of the methods used to obtain figures in the desired industry detail were extremely rough and ready. Moreover, there are serious theoretical as well as practical objections to the use of capital stock data, as many economists have pointed out. We are aware of these objections, but felt it desirable on balance to include a measure of capital inputs in this particular exercise.[1] The use of gross rather than net figures for fixed assets was unavoidable, but it is in any case debatable whether net figures would be preferable as a measure of capital inputs. It seems reasonable to think that the 'services' flow of capital is roughly measured by the gross figures, provided disposals are deleted and assuming plant and equipment are maintained in effective working order.

It may well be that our capital stock indices tend to understate somewhat the true movement in capital inputs over the period. While it is generally accepted that a time series of gross fixed assets will give a reasonable approximation of the true movement in capital capacity if net extensions occur steadily through time and if fixed assets wear out at a constant rate on average, this will not be true if, for instance, plant and equipment tend to become more durable, for then the proportion of gross investment needed for replacement tends to fall and the true rate of additions to capacity progressively exceeds the rate of growth shown by gross fixed assets. Furthermore, if 'concealed' quality improvements occur in plant and equipment, as seems likely, this will tend to mean that conventional capital goods price deflators of the sort used to convert growth of fixed assets to real terms are too large. While both these types of deficiency are probably present in our figures, we have no readily available way of correcting for them. Nevertheless, the figures as they stand are probably adequate for our present purpose, which does not demand a high order of accuracy.

---

[1] Most economists would probably agree that new plant and equipment contribute to output via the technical progress they embody as well as through the mechanisation they represent; it might therefore be thought improper to regard fixed assets as a determinant of output which is entirely independent of R & D inputs. While we accept this general argument, we would defend our present procedure by pointing out that the R & D 'embodied' in new capital equipment is incurred in the industry that supplies the equipment, not the industry that uses it. Provided it is understood that our exercise here attempts to measure merely the effect of R & D on productivity *within the industry that performs it*, it seems right to treat fixed investment as a separate source of productivity gains in the industry that uses it. A more ambitious exercise would perhaps have attempted to attribute productivity gains from use of new capital equipment among the industries that develop and supply the equipment, but this was beyond the scope of the present analysis.

Column (5) of Table 4.4 gives ratios of R & D expenditure to net output (average of 1958 and 1963) in the various industries, and is intended to represent the 'intensity' of R & D in each. It might be objected that, like Minasian's estimates of research intensity, these are subject to distortion owing to differences in the scale of associated outputs. We would argue, however, that such distortions are minimised when one is dealing with industry groups, for the R & D costs of procuring a given increase in an industry's productivity are probably not independent of the scale or diversity of its output. Moreover, it would be very hard to defend the use of absolute R & D expenditures by each industry as the relevant measure here, and estimates of R & D per firm are scarcely more meaningful.

One advantage of using R & D ratios is that they allow to some extent for the influence of past R & D, since they do not vary enormously in particular industries through time. Nevertheless, they do vary somewhat, as Appendix A indicates, and it therefore seemed desirable to introduce a time lag into the exercise (i.e., to compare 'initial' R & D ratios with subsequent productivity movements).

Inspection of columns (4) and (5) suggests that there does indeed appear to be some tendency for industries with rapid productivity growth to have high R & D ratios, although there are exceptions (e.g., rubber products, electronics and telecommunications, and scientific instruments). In order to get a better idea of this pattern, we plotted column (4) against column (5) on a scatter diagram (Fig. 1). The latter excludes aircraft, which is an extreme case of an industry that does a large amount of development in the course of 'routine' production activities, the development being directed mainly at improvements in design and performance that are not likely to be reflected in our index of net output. The industry consequently fell so far outside the 'scatter' of other industries that it seemed best to exclude it here.

Fig. 1 shows that there is a relatively large concentration of industries with low R & D ratios and, in most cases, modest productivity growth roughly equal to, or somewhat below, the (weighted) average for all manufacturing (nine per cent), while eight of the remaining ten industries with 'high' R & D ratios display comparatively high rates of productivity growth. This picture is quite consistent with the view that R & D is one of a number of factors 'explaining' productivity growth, its influence tending to show clearly only when it is administered in fairly large doses.

This interpretation is supported by the least squares regression line fitted to the data. The slope of this line is positive and suggests that a variation of 1 percentage point in the R & D ratio from one industry to another is associated with a corresponding variation in the productivity

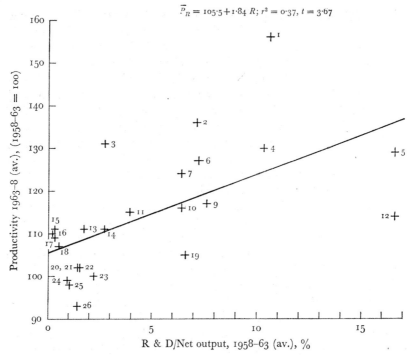

Fig. 1    R & D ratios and productivity movements in 25 manufacturing industries

index of nearly 2 percentage points in the five year period under consideration;[1] however, the degree of correlation is rather weak (only about 37 per cent of the total variation in P being explained by R)[2] and the amount of residual variation is uncomfortably large.

Further inspection of Table 4.4 suggests, as might be expected, that there is some tendency for industries with the fastest productivity growth to have a relatively rapid growth of net output, and Fig. 1 supports this. (Thus industries lying well above the least-squares line – e.g. man-made fibres (1) and domestic electrical appliances (2) – have rapid growth of net output, while those with falls in net output – railway equipment (22) and ships and marine engineering (26) – are both well below the line.) We clearly need to allow for the association between output growth and productivity growth if we are to identify the influence of R & D on the latter more closely.

The scatter diagram of productivity growth on net output growth for the 25 industries (Fig. 2) confirms the suggestion of a fairly strong positive association between them. The $r^2$ for the linear correlation is

[1] Equivalent to variation in average annual productivity growth of 0·35 per cent.
[2] Nevertheless, the t-value of 3·7 suggests that the correlation is unlikely to arise by chance.

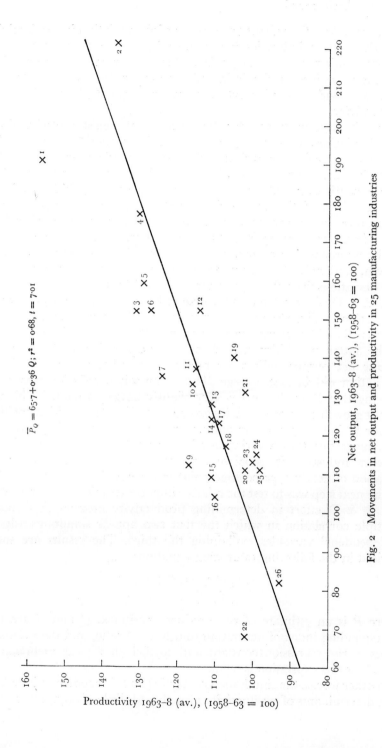

Fig. 2   Movements in net output and productivity in 25 manufacturing industries

0·68, suggesting that about 70 per cent of the variation in productivity growth between industries is explained by differences in net output growth, while the regression coefficient suggests that a difference of 10 percentage points in the index of net output between industries is associated with one of nearly 4 percentage points in the index of productivity.

At this stage we encounter doubts about the existence of a direct causal relationship between R & D and productivity growth, for inspection of Fig. 2 shows that while some industries that lie above the regression line (e.g. man-made fibres (1), petroleum products (5), pharmaceuticals (6), other electrical products (7), electrical machinery and generating (9)) have relatively high R & D ratios, a number of others (e.g., rubber products (3), clothing, footwear and leather (15) and railway equipment (22)) have low ratios. This casts some doubt on the existence of a clear-cut link between R & D and productivity growth, and indeed we have to consider the possibility not merely that deviations from the least squares line in Fig. 2 reflect other factors than R & D effort, which is of course to be expected, but also that the correlation in Fig. 1 may be essentially the reflection of an association between R & D effort and net output growth.

The latter possibility was checked by regressing R & D ratios against net output indices for our 25 industries, and a significant association did in fact emerge. The $r^2$ for this correlation was 0·38, showing that R & D effort is very slightly better correlated with net output growth than productivity growth. The simple regression coefficient for R & D effort on net output growth was 0·09 (with a $t$-ratio of 3·9), suggesting that a variation of 10 percentage points in the latter between industries is associated, on average, with a corresponding variation of nearly 1 percentage point in their R & D ratios.

The next step was to test the relative importance of net output growth and R & D effort in determining productivity movements through multiple correlation in which the first two appear simultaneously as 'independent' variables explaining the third. The results are summarised in the following estimating equation:

$$\hat{P} = 69\cdot8 + 0\cdot32Q + 0\cdot49R$$
$$(7\cdot8) \quad (0\cdot07) \quad (0\cdot46)$$

where $\hat{P}$ is an estimate of the productivity index, $Q$ and $R$ are the corresponding index of net output and R & D ratio, and the standard errors of the regression constant and coefficients appear in brackets. The $r^2$ for this expression is 0·69.

In other words, the simultaneous use of $Q$ and $R$ together as independent determinants of productivity growth adds little if anything to the simple correlation of $P$ on $Q$. Moreover, while the regression coefficient for $Q$ remains little changed and significant, that for $R$ is much reduced and acquires such a large standard error that it entirely ceases to be significant.

How should these findings be interpreted? The first conclusion is that the apparently direct association between R & D effort and productivity growth in Fig. 1 does not really stand up to analysis. Much of the influence that R & D appears to have on productivity growth is in fact 'borrowed' from net output growth, which appears from the various measures of association ($r^2$) we calculated to be much more powerfully correlated with productivity growth than is R & D effort. The possibility is not of course ruled out that there may be some direct relationship between R & D effort and productivity growth, but the multiple correlation results suggest that this is both quite small and very erratic.[1]

More tentatively, our results support the view that there is a moderate and significant *indirect* link between R & D and productivity growth. This may be explained, partly at least, by the idea mentioned earlier that demand and output tend to grow relatively rapidly in technologically novel lines of production (hence the association between R & D effort and net output growth), and that growth in output governs the rate at which productivity can grow, through its influence on the rate of introduction of new products and techniques and on the realisation of economies of scale. This seems especially plausible in fields where R & D is directed at the improvements in *products* (particularly capital equipment) rather than *processes*. Examples of these are electronics and telecommunications and scientific instruments, both of which are 'science-based' (with high R & D ratios) but lie well below the regression line in Fig. 2. Since these industries, or at any rate their research-intensive areas, produce mainly capital goods, it seems probable that the productivity benefits that result from their R & D tend to be realised in industries that they supply rather than in their own operations.

Furthermore, the existence of a positive, if very poorly specified, regression coefficient for $R$ does give slight support to the view that R & D has a direct impact on productivity in addition to its impact via

---

[1] The size of the coefficients in the equation on page 76 might seem to suggest that $P$ is more responsive to $R$ than $Q$. But quite apart from the large standard error of $R$'s coefficient, this is a mistaken impression; it fails to take account of the fact that, because of the different units in which they are expressed, the same unit change in $Q$ and $R$ implies a much smaller proportionate change in $Q$ than in $R$. (Hence for example a variation of $P$ from 110 to 112 as between industries is associated on average with a proportionate difference of about 5 per cent in $Q$, $R$ being the same in each, or an approximate doubling of $R$, $Q$ being the same in each.)

net output growth, and observations for industries where 'process' research is known to be heavy (e.g., petroleum products and man-made fibres, both of which lie well above the least-squares line in Fig. 2) bear this out. Moreover Minasian's results for chemicals, refined as they are to allow for changes in scale of output of individual firms, do support this relationship.

It would clearly be unwise to attempt to be more categorical than this, bearing in mind the manifest shortcomings of the exercise. Imperfections in the data and index numbers are quite capable of explaining a good deal of variation in the industrial observations at our disposal, but equally important, if not more so, may be differences in the technical and economic circumstances of individual industries. It is hardly necessary to point out, for instance, that the impact of economies of scale (unrelated to technical progress) differs considerably from one industry to another, and that the scope for productivity improvement through means other than formal R & D (e.g., work study, market and economic research, rationalisation of industrial structure, etc.) differs greatly between industries. It would need a far more detailed and extensive statistical exercise than our simple effort here to bring these to light.

# PART II

---

## THE INDUSTRIAL INQUIRY

# 5. THE INDUSTRIAL INQUIRY: PROBLEMS AND METHOD OF APPROACH

Enough has been said in the opening chapters to underline the need to be explicit about what one is trying to discover in connection with the patent system. It should therefore be stated that our primary object in the present study is to assess the principal economic effects of having a patent system of *roughly* the sort that we know in the U.K. – namely, a system that offers more or less valid legal monopolies for a fixed term of about 15–20 years to genuine inventors and innovators in a wide field of production. We are not much concerned here with administrative and legal aspects of the system, as this ground has been covered in Volume 1, nor with the implications of adjustments to the system that do not affect its basic character, as these have been examined fully by the Banks Committee. We are dealing here with fundamentals, so far as we can, and we hope to shed enough light on these to judge the economic desirability of retaining a patent system on the existing lines.

## A. THE INDUSTRIAL INQUIRY

In view of the meagre nature of published data on patenting and licensing activity it was evident from the beginning that we would have to undertake a special inquiry in order to provide the basic quantitative information for the study. Most debates on the subject have been seriously hampered by lack of detailed figures and it seemed to be our first priority to try to remedy this. It was also pretty clear, in view of the complexity of some of the problems and the unsuitability of aggregative statistical techniques for dealing with them, that the inquiry would have to be in depth in order to build up a sufficiently detailed picture of the system to warrant judgments about its impact.

With these considerations in mind we decided that the inquiry should concentrate on a limited number of industrial companies in a selection of manufacturing industries. Our particular concern with industry reflects the fact that it is within industry that the bulk of resources for invention and innovation of a commercially-oriented kind (i.e., the kind likely to be responsive to patent protection) are committed. The great majority of all patents of any economic significance are nowadays issued or assigned to industrial organisations – or to bodies such as the

National Research Development Corporation, whose main function is to act as an intermediary between the private or academic inventor, or the inventor in Government research establishments, and industry. Virtually all licensing of any consequence involves industrial companies. The lion's share of development of inventions for commercial purposes and virtually all the follow-up effort on their production and marketing is carried out by major industrial companies. In our view the economic impact of the patent system must essentially be judged with reference to what happens in industry.

### *Main features of the inquiry*

A full description of our industrial inquiry will be found in Appendix B, but it may be helpful if its main features are summarised here. We initially selected for examination five broad industry classes – chemicals and allied (including pharmaceuticals), oil refining, electrical engineering (including electronics), mechanical engineering, and man-made fibres.[1] The classes chosen include most of the industries that invest heavily in organised research and development, with the exception of aircraft, where the Government makes a dominant contribution to the financing of these activities. Inevitably some non-research-intensive fields are also covered, since a number of firms in the inquiry reported data for more than one field. The number of industries was governed by the number of companies we felt we could tackle, given our resources (i.e., about 50), and the need to have a reasonable number in each class.

The inquiry did not attempt to obtain a representative sample of companies in the industries concerned, much less to compile a comprehensive census of patents, licences, etc. Our twin aims were: to cover a substantial proportion of patenting and invention in our chosen fields, which on the whole we managed to achieve, largely because the bulk of these activities tends to be concentrated in the hands of the largest companies; and to investigate in detail a variety of different industrial situations, including both some in which patents might be expected to have a relatively important influence, and others in which they might not. By selecting industry classes which included most of the ones with high potential impact we felt we could insure against the danger of ignoring important effects of the system. At the same time, we did not want to swing the pendulum too far in favour of the system, and so we included some companies that were active in R & D but professed to have little interest in patents – on the principle that it is

---

[1] In the event, it did not prove possible to include detailed information on oil refining in our tables, because of data problems.

sometimes as revealing to consider reasons for the absence of a thing as for its presence.

The procedure adopted was to present interested firms with a fairly extensive set of data requirements (see Form A, reproduced in Annex 2 to Appendix B), at the same time inviting them to complete as many items as they reasonably could. Form A relates exclusively to information of a factual sort (sales, R & D expenditure, patents, licences, royalties, etc.). Because most of the data would have to be extracted with some difficulty from company records, it was decided to confine the request for figures to 1968, except for one or two items for which a run of years seemed desirable. The data supplied were then used as a basis for assessing the effects of the patent system, on the lines of a comparative approach to be described more fully in due course. This was done by means of interview sessions with officials of the companies concerned, during which they were asked to assess the impact of the existing patent system in their major markets and product lines. This part of the inquiry consisted essentially of an exercise in informed estimation and guesswork in which the officials concerned were invited to participate. In this way it was possible to explain the nature of the exercise to them, and to question them closely on their replies.

Detailed explanations of the questions asked will accompany our presentation of results. However, interested readers will find the formal set of questions in Form B (also reproduced in Appendix B), which was used as the framework for interview discussions. This Form contains questions on policy and on 'effects'; it differs from Form A in that it seeks judgments rather than facts.

Of the 44 companies that agreed to participate, 30 managed to supply the bulk of the data required in Form A.[1] For the remainder, we had to be content with one or more interviews, supplemented by documentary information from various sources, ranging from annual accounts to technical papers, licensing brochures, etc. In all these cases we were able to obtain reasonably reliable figures for certain key items, as well as fairly full policy impressions and estimates of effects in Form B.

### Technical problems

Undoubtedly our difficulties in the inquiry were increased by our desire to obtain some data by category of production within industries. While appreciating that it might create problems for diversified companies, we adhered to this course because we wanted to explore the wide

---

[1] The companies are listed in Annex 1 of Appendix B, page 377. The numbers are reduced by one if I.C.I. Fibres is counted as part of the main I.C.I. Group, as happens in some of our tables.

variations in patenting and licensing activity that appear to exist between different types of production, frequently within the operations of a single firm. While we were not able to go as far as we would have liked in sub-dividing the data in this way, we feel that the effort was worthwhile and that it emphasises the pitfalls of generalising on patent matters, even when describing the policy of a single firm. Where possible in the forthcoming chapters we shall distinguish between the (fairly broad) categories of production for which we managed to obtain separate data, although this task is often hampered by problems of matching and disclosure.

Problems of an entirely different sort were caused by the need to fit international companies into the inquiry. In some of the areas of British industry that we set out to cover, major technological contributions have been made by companies that are subsidiaries of foreign (mainly American) parents. It obviously made sense to invite participation by them, and several are included in the inquiry.

Two types of problems arise, the first being the severely practical but nevertheless highly inconvenient fact that in many such cases the relevant records are kept overseas by the parent company and group policy on these matters is largely administered from abroad. Fortunately, these cases are usually (but not always) ones where the U.K. operations are fairly 'junior', and omissions were never crippling.

The second problem relates to the coverage and interpretation of data supplied by the international companies that were able to help. For instance, it is frequently the practice of an international group that has an important manufacturing operation in the U.K. to assign all its U.K. patents to the U.K. subsidiary, receiving in turn all the subsidiary's American patents (if the parent is American). This is done largely for convenience in processing applications, renewals, etc. In such cases it was necessary to decide whether the U.K. subsidiary should report for *all* patents assigned to it, or merely for those arising from R & D work in the U.K. There is unfortunately something to be said for both procedures. If one is interested in assessing the impact of patents on British invention, it is patents arising from the latter that seem more relevant, but if one is trying to judge the impact on British *sales*, it is the wider figure that seems preferable. We usually resolved the dilemma by asking on Form A for 'U.K.-originating' patents (with, if possible, some idea of the group total for U.K.) and on Form B for the impact on 'patent-based' production, including production based on foreign-originating patents.

A number of other problems arose over the handling of international companies, particularly in connection with licensing and licence payments. We shall point these out where appropriate either in the detailed account of our findings, or in Appendix B.

B.    SELECTION OF A 'YARDSTICK'

As several commentators have observed, an intelligible assessment of
the patent system requires that one should have a fairly definite notion
of what might be put in its place. When measuring effects, it matters
a lot whether one has in mind an alternative state of affairs in which
there is no patent system of any sort or a situation in which a patent
system exists but with major modifications. As will be explained, we
found it advisable in our inquiry to adopt the latter rather than the
former alternative as a yardstick for comparative purposes.

The various constraints that confronted us at the outset of the study
led us to think that we should confine our attention, at least initially,
to the British patent system and to its effects on the British economy.
We felt we could not keep the work within manageable proportions if
we tried to examine foreign systems and economies as well. This need to
limit the scope of the inquiry, together with our basic wish to examine
the fundamentals, rather than the marginal features of the system,
might seem to suggest that we should choose an alternative situation in
which there were no British patent system, all foreign systems being
unchanged. However, as we came closer to grips with the study, it
became clear that a rather more subtle yardstick would be preferable
for purposes of analysis.

*A compulsory licensing system*

It seemed to us firstly that, as economists, we should be essentially
concerned with the monopoly element of the system, for it is from this
that the interesting and problematic economic issues arise. We felt
secondly that it would be extremely hard to envisage the impact of a
situation in the U.K. in which no legal provision whatsoever were
made for the encouragement, identification and publication of inventions. (This was subsequently confirmed in discussions with industrialists, many of whom found it difficult to imagine such a radically
changed situation.)

We thought, finally, that complete abandonment of the patent system
in a country like the U.K. was too remote a possibility to be of much
practical interest. We consequently decided that we should not spend
a lot of time pursuing an extreme comparison of this sort.

On the other hand, it is relatively easy to think of situations in which
patent systems akin to the British one operate quite normally, while
lacking the traditional monopoly element for some industries or areas of
invention. As observed in Chapter 1, this situation holds at the moment
in the case of pharmaceuticals in the U.K. by virtue of Section 41

of the Patents Act, although in this instance the provision seems until very recently to have had little real force.

The monopoly element in patents is enshrined in the right of the patentee to refuse to permit others to use an invention that he wishes to work himself. Inevitably much of the value of patents is removed if this right can be over-ruled, as happens for instance if the patent authorities are empowered to grant compulsory licences. A 'compulsory licensing system' would be one in which all inventions would be patentable in the normal way, but subject at an early stage after grant to compulsory licensing on terms mutually agreeable to the parties or, failing that, fixed by the patent authority, acting as arbitrator.

We accordingly decided to adopt a compulsory licensing system as the relevant yardstick for assessing the impact of the British patent system. It should at once be stressed that this implies no prejudice on our part concerning the relative merits of conventional patent systems and compulsory licensing systems.[1] The choice of the latter as an alternative to the present system is merely a device to enable us to concentrate our attention on the element of the system which we consider most important. It has the distinct practical advantage that it represents a much less radical departure from the present system than, say, having either no patents at all or a system of minor awards for inventors. For that reason, it proved far easier to handle in the industrial inquiry than the more extreme alternatives mentioned.

The type of compulsory licensing system we have in mind is one in which the grant of licences by the patent authority would be more or less automatic. We do not envisage that applicants would need to show suitability for a licence, or to go through elaborate quasi-legal proceedings about terms, as is in practice the case under the present Section 41 in the U.K., despite the presumption in law that a serious applicant will receive a licence. In our imaginary system, the Comptroller (or some newly created officer under him) would award whatever licence payment seemed to be commercially reasonable upon careful but summary consideration of the case, and would do no more than satisfy himself that the applicant was a responsible person or firm. Inevitably there is some room for debate as to what a 'reasonable commercial' payment would turn out to be in particular cases, but we proceeded in

---

[1] At the same time, compulsory licensing represents in some commentators' minds a workable and even an inevitable reform in traditional patent systems. Thus, for example, one economist writes: '...The use of the compulsory licensing device by the U.S. courts must be recognised as a significant new factor in conditioning the future position of the United States with respect to intergovernment patent agreements.' He also refers to the increasing frequency with which decrees in U.S. anti-trust cases oblige the defendants to grant compulsory licences under the U.S. patents. (See R. Vernon, Study No. 5 for the U.S. Senate Subcommittee on Patents, Trademarks and Copyrights, pp. 4–5.)

the expectation that fairly predictable patterns of royalties, etc. emerge for licences of various standard kinds, and in various fields. In fact, our preliminary research suggested that industrial patenting and licensing specialists typically have fairly clear ideas of 'standard' terms for licences in their fields, and this greatly facilitated the use of our compulsory licensing alternative as a method of analysis.

It is necessary to distinguish the type of 'strong' compulsory licensing system adopted as our standard alternative from systems that contain relatively weak or partial compulsory licensing provisions (e.g., provisions that apply only to obvious and blatant abuse of patents monopolies, such as those of Section 37 of the U.K. Patents Act). In the following pages, the term 'thoroughgoing' compulsory licensing is used to mean a system where all patentees normally expect to have to grant compulsory licences, if applied for, on terms that would be judged 'commercially reasonable' by an independent arbitrator such as the Comptroller. Of course, the precise implications of such a system raise numerous interesting points, discussion of which will be resumed at the appropriate stage (see especially Chapter 9, Section A).

### *The broader alternative*

In the early stages of the study an important consideration arose which convinced us that we should not in practice hope to confine our attention exclusively to the system as it operates in the U.K. It became apparent in our preliminary discussions that, for many British firms, much of the impact of patents is felt in their overseas business and in their dealings with overseas concerns. For these firms, the consequences of major changes in the British system alone would be very different from those of similar changes in other major patent systems of the world as well. To ignore patenting and licensing overseas would therefore mean presenting a very incomplete picture of the impact of the patent system in general. We had somehow to face the fact that the patent system is in many respects an international institution; as such, its total impact is probably very much more than the sum of the individual impacts of all national systems considered on their own.

For this reason, we felt obliged to set our sights as far as we could on assessing the consequences of changes in the *international* patent system – while still devoting our main attention to effects on the U.K. economy. More precisely, our central concern became the effects on invention, competition and the spread of technology within U.K. industry of a switch from existing patent systems to 'thoroughgoing' compulsory licensing in the economies of the major industrial nations. For the practical purposes of the inquiry, such an enlargement of the issues was not always necessary: for some companies, particularly smaller ones, it was quite sufficient to concentrate mainly on the British system. In general, however, consideration of the broader alternative proved more instructive and fruitful than the narrower question of a change in the British system, the rest remaining unchanged.

Although our inquiry concentrated mainly on the compulsory licensing alternative, we did not feel that we should entirely ignore more drastic changes. We therefore explore briefly in Chapter 14 (Section B) the implications both of having no patent system (or virtually none) anywhere in the world, and of having no system in the U.K., the rest being unchanged. But for reasons given above we do not dwell very long on these rather remote possibilities.

### Relevance of our findings

It should finally be said that we set out to investigate the impact of the patent system on British industry *as it is today*. While being prepared to admit that the influence of patents may well be greatest in an era of basic industrial discovery such as existed in the nineteenth and early twentieth centuries, we nevertheless are not doing a historical study, and we would not claim that our findings are necessarily applicable to earlier years. Our study is concerned with an industrial period that has been devoted mainly to the evolution of second- and third-generation technologies, i.e., an age of technological refinement and improvement rather than basic discovery. While we have investigated as many instances of the development of new or infant technologies as came our way in the study, these are nowadays fairly rare and should not be overemphasised if a balanced view of the whole field is required. Moreover, while we did during our investigations inquire as far as we could into the antecedents of present-day situations, this was to obtain a proper understanding of the latter, rather than to delve into the past for its own sake.

# 6. PATENTING AND LICENSING IN PRACTICE: THE INDUSTRIAL PATENT DEPARTMENT

This is the first of three chapters dealing with the main facts about patenting and licensing that emerged from our industrial inquiry. Although some selection and interpretation of material is necessary, the object in these chapters is to give information that does not involve us in major judgments – even though it may depend to some extent on bold estimation by people in companies who were faced with the job of summarising unwieldy records of patents, licence agreements, etc. This factual material will be used in later chapters as a foundation for assessing the impact of the patent system, so far as is possible, and that part of the exercise will inevitably incorporate important judgments, estimates and opinions that were arrived at in the course of the inquiry.

A start is made in this chapter with matters on which generalisation seems easiest – namely, the organisation and functions of industrial patent and licensing departments and selected aspects of patenting, licensing, etc. as seen through their eyes.[1] While a certain amount of detail of this sort is helpful to an understanding of what follows, the account is not intended to be comprehensive; it rather aims to bring out the features that seem to have economic significance.

It should be pointed out that we shall be referring mainly to the fields of industry covered by our inquiry – namely the chemical and engineering fields, broadly defined. Our observations may apply fairly generally to other fields, but this is not necessarily the case except where it is stated to be so.

## A. SIZE AND ORGANISATION

The degree to which patenting in a company is put on a formal basis naturally depends on the scale of patent activity that the company generates. Four successive stages of organisation may be distinguished. The first and probably by far the most common in industry as a whole is the stage at which no distinct arrangements for dealing with patents exist at all. Responsibility for patenting matters in such situations is generally assumed by a company's chief engineer or chemist, or possibly by its technical or research director, who will probably also take charge of licensing matters. He is likely to have no special staff for the purpose,

[1] The relevant part of our questionnaire is principally Form A, Section II (see page 386).

although he may call on regular help from a junior engineer or scientist, who thus acquires familiarity with patenting matters, and from the company solicitor, who assists with the legal aspects of licensing. The professional work of drafting patent specifications and processing applications will be put out to one or more firms of patent agents which have experience in the relevant field – and possibly a long-standing association with their client.

Arrangements of this *ad hoc* sort seem capable of handling up to about half a dozen patent applications and a handful of licence agreements per year, but not much more. If the activity extends beyond this, pressure emerges for a patent specialist within the company. Such a person may be termed 'patent officer', or perhaps 'patent consultant', and his staff will probably be very small. He is likely to be fairly senior graduate engineer or scientist but seldom a qualified patent agent. As in the *ad hoc* stage, all professional patent work will be handled by outside patent agents, while routine work on licensing will probably be dealt with by the company's legal department, if it has one. The patent officer may well take chief responsibility for licensing, and will probably advise senior management on licensing policy, negotiations, etc. Arrangements of this sort can probably handle up to two dozen or so U.K. patent applications per year and a similar number of foreign applications.

The types of minimal patent organisation described above are by no means confined to small or even medium-sized companies. They are quite common among large engineering companies (say, those with annual sales exceeding £40 million or so), although most chemical companies of medium or larger size (say, those with annual sales exceeding £15 million or so) are likely to have more elaborate arrangements, as indeed are most companies in any technological field that spend much more than £1 million annually on R & D.

Table 6.1 gives some idea of the sizes of patent departments in our sample, together with two other key orders of magnitude – new U.K. patents obtained annually and annual sales in the U.K. The eight companies here with minimal or very small patent and licensing organisations (0–5 persons) had annual sales in the U.K. ranging from somewhat under £10 million in 1968 to over £60 million, the average being £27 million. The others all had more elaborate organisations; they include some medium-sized firms, but most are groups of companies with group sales in the U.K. exceeding £40 million.

The middle two tows in the table contain what can be thought of as the typical or standard 'fully-fledged' patent departments in our sample. The size range here is quite large, and we have accordingly divided these departments into smaller and larger (standard) categories.

TABLE 6.1. *Size of patent and licensing departments, new U.K. patents and U.K. sales, 1968*

| Size of patent department[a] (full-time employees) | Number of companies | New U.K. patents granted[b] (average, 1966–8) | U.K. sales (£m, 1968) | New patents per £m of sales |
|---|---|---|---|---|
| 0–5 | 8 | 71 | 217 | 0·3 |
| 6–15 | 9 | 244 | 364 | 0·7 |
| 16–35 | 7 | 712 | 807 | 0·9 |
| Over 35 | 3 | 828 | 523 | 1·6 |
| Total | 27 | 1,855 | 1,911 | 1·0 |

NOTES:
The data here relates to our 'main sample' (see Annex 1 of Appendix B, page 377), except that the oil companies are excluded because of data difficulties. Here, I.C.I. Fibres is included with I.C.I. as one 'company'.

An effort was made to obtain mutually consistent figures for employees, patents etc. (E.g. where groupwide sales and patents were reported, allowance was made for groupwide patent and licensing employees – including 'local' as well as 'headquarters' staffs.)
[a] Includes employees engaged essentially on licensing and associated work, whether within the patent department or in a separate licensing department.
[b] Includes some 330 patents arising from R & D done by overseas affiliates of reporting groups, responsibility for obtaining patents on which rests largely with the U.K. department. Annual averages are given in order to allow for large variations reported in a number of cases. An industrial breakdown of the total appears in Table 6.3, page 103.

The typical industrial patent department is normally headed by an official who is a fully-qualified patent agent as well as being a graduate engineer or scientist. He will probably be assisted by a number of other scientific graduates, some of whom are likely to be patent agents or training to become so, together with supporting secretarial and clerical staff. A good deal of professional work on drafting etc. will probably be done within the department, although some may well be placed outside – especially work on foreign applications, which are necessarily processed through foreign agents.

In the case of a group of companies there will normally be a central patent department located at the group's administrative headquarters. This will usually be supplemented by individuals or small units in each of the group's main R & D and production subsidiaries, branches or establishments. The latter are likely to be scientists or engineers who handle patenting work as part of their normal routine, but in larger subsidiaries etc. they may be patent specialists; in most cases an important part of their function is to act as liaison with the central patent department. (Estimates of local patent specialists are included in the figures of employees in Table 6.1.)

The head of the typical patent department will normally have the status of a specialist middle manager responsible to the group's technical or research director, although in some patent-conscious companies he is clearly a more important figure. He may be in charge of licensing as well as patents, but if licensing activity is carried out on an appreciable scale (say, with more than three or four dozen active agreements), there is likely to be a separate licensing specialist – probably a graduate with legal training. The latter may function within either the patent or the legal department, but if licensing activity is substantial he may acquire separate status as a licensing manager with his own department, staff, etc.

The typical industrial patent department will usually handle several dozen U.K. applications annually (of which a number may be abandoned before completion), together with perhaps three times as many foreign applications. It will have on its books anything from a hundred to several hundred active U.K. patents.

The fourth and final stage of patent organisation might be termed the 'super' patent department. The three departments in the over-35 size class of Table 6.1 fall into this category, as perhaps do one or two of the slightly smaller ones. While there are not many more than a large handful of these departments throughout British industry, they probably account for a substantial amount of patent activity. Assuming that our inquiry covered about one-third of patents granted to all super patent departments in the U.K., and that roughly 12,000 new U.K. patents per annum were granted to U.K. residents in 1966–8 (as implied by figures in recent Comptroller's Reports), it appears that the very largest patent departments accounted for about one-fifth of all U.K. patent activity in this period – not including U.K. patents awarded to non-residents.

The total staff of the super patent department may number upwards of fifty, including secretarial and clerical staff. All professional patent work will be carried out within the department, except the sort that needs to be done by foreign agents. In addition there is likely to be a fully-fledged licensing department. Patenting and licensing activity combined may occupy something approaching a hundred graduates in the very largest organisations, either as patent agents, scientific or technical assistants or legal specialists. Annual applications for U.K. patents will probably run into several hundreds for such organisations, with foreign applications perhaps five times that number or more. Active licences may also run into several hundreds.

While size and R & D effort obviously have an influence on the extent of a company's patent activity, it is not easy to be more precise at this stage of the argument. One fact that does not emerge in the table is the considerable diversity in 'patent intensity' between firms. Thus although (as the table suggests) there is an overall tendency for firms with larger patent departments to obtain more patents per unit of sales than those with smaller departments, there is great diversity between departments of approximately equal size. (For example, the ratio of new U.K. patents per £ million of sales in 1968 ranged for individual companies in our sample from a small fraction to about seven patents, with three-quarters of firms falling within the range 0·2 to 1·5.) Similarly, considerable diversity exists in ratios of new patents to R & D effort and even to measures of patenting effort itself. We shall return to these quantitative comparisons in due course.

B.    FUNCTIONS

*Obtaining patents*

Apart from dealing with specialist questions, such as the exact scope of monopoly claims, which can have important commercial implications, the patent manager's chief responsibility in connection with applying for patents is to exercise discretion over what is patented. Two main types of problems arise. There is firstly the task of identifying all the firm's inventions that are patentable, which involves examining the work of R & D and technical departments, an activity which most patent specialists take seriously, as we shall see later. There is secondly the question of how far to go in patenting what is patentable. We found a fair amount of variation in views and attitudes on this, and we shall discuss the question with respect to different industries in later chapters. However, it can be said here that patent managers almost always exercise some discretion on the matter.

The question is somewhat complicated by the difference between filing *provisional* and *complete* specifications. We found it a fairly common procedure that companies file provisional specifications on most things that are patentable, on the ground that they thereby obtain a priority date at negligible cost (£1 per application plus a small amount of drafting and clerical work), without divulging any secrets. (Provisional, like complete, specifications, are treated as confidential by the Patent Office until acceptance of the application, and are not divulged if the application is abandoned before that stage.) Only two companies in our inquiry said that they did not bother to file provisional applications: in most cases, provisionals are taken out as soon as there is anything to patent.

Within 12 months of filing a U.K. provisional application, a decision must be made on whether to complete it and, if so, whether to file overseas and where. It is in this period that serious consideration usually occurs on whether to go ahead with particular applications. In most of the companies we visited, discretion over patenting policy appeared to be shared more or less equally between the patent manager and other middle management in the departments of the business most affected by its patents. Most companies fell mid-way between two extremes which may be described as follows: in one, decisions on how much to patent and in which countries rest essentially with the firm's principal production or sales managers most concerned, the managing directors of manufacturing subsidiaries, etc.; this conforms to the case in which the patent department has the status of a 'service' department. At the other extreme, discretion rests essentially with the patent manager, and in this case the patent department has a status which is more akin to that of an operating department. Companies were usually closer to the first than the second pattern, but some, especially in the chemical field, inclined towards the latter.

One point that did emerge fairly clearly from the inquiry is that decisions on what is patented are seldom a matter for *top-level* management. Unlike licensing questions, decisions on patent applications rarely if ever reach the board of a company. The most that senior management does in this regard is to guide policy in the broadest possible way, which may commonly amount to no more than an informal understanding – a philosophy or 'atmosphere' which communicates itself to the patent manager indirectly – although in some cases there are standing instructions relating to general policy.

It is known from official figures that some 70–5 per cent of all U.K. provisional applications are completed.[1] The experience of companies in our sample was that 82 per cent of provisionals in 1965[2] were completed, which suggests that there is less wastage among industrial applications than among those from small inventors. There appears to be a certain amount of variation in wastage between industries, oil and chemicals having the lowest completion rate (78 per cent) and electrical engineering the highest (86 per cent).

The main reason given in our inquiry for not completing applications, apart from the trouble and cost involved in obtaining, renewing and policing patents, was failure of the 'inventions' concerned to live up to expectations. The clearest examples of this type are found in industries that put a lot of effort into synthesising new chemical compounds – e.g., for drugs, weedkillers, additives, catalysts, etc. The tendency in these fields is to rush through provisional applications for

---

[1] Vol. I, p. 77.    [2] Some companies reported for 1966.

every new compound in the hope that some will respond to analysis and turn out to have commercial uses. Inevitably a large proportion fails to respond and is discarded. While examples of unsuccessful inventions and researchers losing interest can be found in all fields, the relatively high rate of wastage found in the chemical industries is probably explained in part by the high incidence of 'speculative' discoveries in these fields.

A further reason given for the abandonment of applications was the discovery of 'prior art' after intensive appraisal by the patent department. More often than not, however, this leads to the amendment of specifications rather than to their abandonment.

It is perhaps significant that companies seldom appear to abandon applications on the ground that, after consideration, they are reluctant to reveal the details of an invention by patenting it. Even those that have a liberal policy towards filing provisionals did not mention preference for secrecy as a reason for wastage. A number of explanations are possible. Firstly, some companies (but probably not many) exercise a measure of selectivity before the filing of provisionals. Secondly, it happens quite frequently that technical information which is essential to the most efficient operation of an invention on a large industrial scale is not divulged in a patent specification. This may be because the specification is drafted so as to avoid disclosing a vital piece of knowledge, or it may reflect the fact that the information is not known when the time for putting the specification into order is reached. In other cases the information is simply too cumbersome to put into a specification, as, for instance, when the details of a process vary greatly with the local conditions under which it operates, the purpose for which it is used, etc.[1] Thirdly, the advantages of obtaining patent protection

---

[1] The majority of patent specialists to whom we talked agreed that it is not infrequently possible, where an invention entails important new technical expertise, for a patent specification to fulfil the requirements that the best method of working the invention be disclosed, and that the description should be adequate to enable the invention to be worked by someone 'skilled in the art', while at the same time not divulging all information, know-how, etc. necessary to what is eventually the optimal working of the relevant product or process on an industrial scale. This applied especially in the engineering and bulk chemical industries, where critical operating skill and experience are likely to be acquired in developing a mass-production process, often well after the stage of filing complete specifications. Others maintained that less than full disclosure is not advisable in their fields, since this may mean sacrificing part of the patent protection which would otherwise be available. Responses of this type tended to occur in fields where invention usually involves relatively little new manufacturing know-how, e.g. pharmaceuticals and electronics. Nevertheless, one patent specialist in a pharmaceutical firm commented as follows:

'It is rare for the complete [specification] to contain a really full and adequate disclosure for commercial operations but this is not because of secretiveness. Rather it is an inevitable result of the "first to file" system. Under this, it is essential to obtain an early priority date and invariably commercial exploitation will not take place for three or four years, and in the pharmaceutical field often five to ten years later.'

of some sort on an invention – in terms of controlling access to the invention or, more commonly, of licensing it to others – are almost invariably considered to outweigh the associated disadvantages, i.e., the partial sacrifice of secrecy involved (although there are notable exceptions). We received this impression quite strongly from most, if not quite all, firms in our inquiry. It seems to be a widespread presumption held not only by patent specialists, as might be expected, but also by other management spokesmen in the various industries covered by our investigation.

### Renewals

British patents are renewable (upon payment of fees) for the first time at the end of four years after filing the complete specification, and annually thereafter until expiry. The patent department deals with renewals, usually by means of a regular screening process in which managements of operating departments are consulted. Thus, the marketing department will probably be consulted on whether a particular product patent is helping sales, while production departments will advise on whether particular process patents are being used, or are likely to be used. Responsibility for decisions seems to be shared about equally between patent specialists and management in the operating departments most closely concerned.

Most companies appear to follow a policy of renewing patents more or less automatically for their fifth year, on the ground that '...if we took the trouble to get a patent, it seems foolish to abandon it so soon after grant'.[1] This is confirmed by the returns on our forms, for of 2,140 U.K. patents reported as being due for renewal for the first time in 1968, 86 per cent were actually renewed, there being no significant difference in the practice of different industries. However, renewals in later years are normally considered more critically, as is indicated by Table 6.2, which gives details for patents granted since 1954 for which the necessary (published) information is available. The table suggests that the process of abandoning patents of a given vintage proceeds at an increasing proportionate rate from the fifth to the sixteenth year, at which time rather less than one-fifth survive. An interesting point is that the process of reduction after the fourth year occurs at a surprisingly regular rate; there appears to be no critical year of their life in which patents are abandoned relatively heavily.

It is reasonable to assume that the patents that survive for their full term comprise the ones of significant value to their owners, and this

---

[1] Because of processing delays, few U.K. patents are nowadays granted much less than two years after filing the complete specification, with the result that most become renewable for the first time two years after grant or less.

TABLE 6.2. *Rates of renewal of U.K. patents*

| Year of renewal | Proportion renewed of all patents granted in: | | | |
| | 1954 – 17,985 (%) | 1955 – 20,630 (%) | 1956–7 (av.) – 22,572[a] (%) | 1957–8 (av.) – 21,868[a] (%) |
|---|---|---|---|---|
| 5th | 85 | 83 | 83 | 88 |
| 6th | 77 | 73 | 76 | 83 |
| 7th | 68 | 65 | 68 | 74 |
| 8th | 60 | 57 | 61 | 67 |
| 9th | 53 | 51 | 55 | 60 |
| 10th | 47 | 45 | 48 | 52 |
| 11th | 41 | 39 | 42 | 45 |
| 12th | 36 | 35 | 37 | 39 |
| 13th | 32 | 30 | 32 | 32 |
| 14th | 28 | 26 | 27 | 30 |
| 15th | 24 | 22 | 23 | 25 |
| 16th | 18 | 17 | 18 | 19 |

NOTES:

It is assumed here that patents were granted on average approximately 2 years after filing the complete specification; thus a patent is assumed to be renewable for the first time (and to qualify for a '5th year' renewal fee) on average 2 years after grant.

[a] Two-year averages of grants (and associated renewals) were adopted so as to allow for the effect on processing times of unusually large fluctuations in patent activity during these years.

SOURCE: Calculated from data in Comptroller-General's Reports.

was confirmed by responses to our inquiry. The proportions that survive thus long seem to be fairly constant, as is shown in the table, which indicates that roughly one-fifth to one-quarter of U.K. patents are kept alive for essentially their full effective term (i.e., for their fifteenth year). This is an interesting result and tends to bear out what was discovered by the Banks Committee, as noted earlier (page 47 above).

Companies invariably told us that they are more selective in their approach to renewing their foreign patents than their U.K. patents. The main reason given was that renewal fees and other costs of operating and enforcing patents are usually appreciably higher overseas. The proportions of foreign patents in British hands that survive to any given maturity are accordingly much lower than for the corresponding U.K. patents – possibly something in the region of one-quarter to one-half of the percentages given in Table 6.2.

*'Oppositions'*

Although not a major activity, opposition under Section 14 and applications to the Comptroller for revocation under Section 33 of the Patents Act are a matter for the patent specialist, who must keep abreast of published specifications and be prepared to consider possible grounds for opposition when his company's interests – or those of its customers – are materially affected. Responses to our inquiry confirmed that while many major firms do become involved in opposition proceedings from time to time, the actual number of oppositions filed is very small in relation to the total number of patents applied for or granted, as was observed in Chapter 1 (pp. 13–14). Thus while about half of the companies in our sample sustained 'oppositions' to their patents (pre- or post-grant) in the two-year period 1967–8, the actual number of oppositions they reported – 86 – was small in relation to the number of U.K. patents they applied for – approximately 2,200 per year in 1965–6. The rate of opposition in our sample was quite high in relation to the rate implied in the Comptroller-General's reports (about 2 per cent), the incidence in our inquiry being highest in mechanical engineering (roughly 5 per cent of annual applications), moderately high in oil and chemicals ($3\frac{1}{2}$ per cent), and low in electrical engineering (about $\frac{1}{2}$ per cent).

Reasons given for the generally low level of oppositions may be summarised as follows. Where a patent can be shown to be on very shaky ground, the mere suggestion of opposition to an applicant is likely to be sufficient to persuade him to withdraw, without the action being entered. Where a patent is clearly on strong ground, it is highly doubtful that a patent expert would venture to oppose, however much he might wish to do so. Only where the arguments regarding inventive step, etc. are relatively evenly balanced are oppositions likely to be seriously considered, and even then experienced patent agents are likely to be cautious in selecting targets. This is because the chances of substantial success in opposition are generally felt to be poor unless the grounds are strong, because the benefit of any doubt in hearings before the Comptroller is usually given to the applicant, as explained in Chapter 1.

As a result, oppositions are normally entered only when the arguments against the patent are judged to be fairly strong, and in fact the record of decisions tends to bear this out. Thus, in only 40 of the 86 oppositions reported in our inquiry did the patent under attack survive substantially unscathed, and in a few of these the opponent was granted a licence as a result of his opposition. (The latter step may or may not represent a defeat for the patentee. In some cases the patentee was anxious to grant licences, while in others he was reluctant to do so and the outcome represented a compromise with the opponent.) The other 46 oppositions resulted in either substantial amendment of the patent (20), withdrawal or refusal of the specification pre-grant (24), or revocation (2), so that the chances of success on this evidence seem about even. Figures in the Comptroller's Reports suggest that this experience is fairly typical of the overall picture.

As was argued in our opening chapter, the low rate of opposition in the U.K. should not be interpreted to mean that industry is apathetic on the question of patents. In some cases, companies with the necessary resources and interests at stake prefer to oppose overseas, before one of the patent offices that apply more rigorous criteria than the British Office. The strictest authority is usually held to be the West German one, and for that reason the rate of oppositions in West Germany is higher than in the U.K.[1] Far more commonly, however, a company that confidently doubts the validity of another's patent will simply ignore it, infringing if necessary and leaving to the patentee the onus of bringing about a dispute that may eventually reach the courts, so invoking the prospect of a rigorous test which even a substantially valid patent may not survive unscathed.

### Infringements

It follows from what was said in the previous section that the suppression of infringements may be an important responsibility for the industrial patent manager, at least in industries that have a major stake in patents. While the onus is on staff 'in the field' to detect them in the first instance, the patent department has the task of checking infringements and bringing them to the infringer's attention if it is felt desirable to do so. Where an infringement is thought to be serious and the infringer persists, which he is likely to do if he is unable to withdraw from production or adopt alternatives without loss, he may be offered a licence and if so the matter becomes one of negotiating terms for a licence rather than a problem for the patent specialist. Nevertheless, the patent manager is likely to be consulted in difficult or important licence negotiations, especially where litigation exists as a

---

[1] This is perhaps an oversimplification of the situation. One company patent agent commented:

'For historical reasons arising from the form of the German Law, it is almost a traditional pastime for German companies to oppose one another in the patent courts. Various commercial advantages can be obtained by use of the opposition procedures including, in certain instances, discovery of various documents and long delay of the grant of the patent. In fact frequently grant of the patent only occurs late into its normal life and probably after expiry of its useful life. However, this is really a misuse of the patent system and the German system of oppositions is generally disliked by all concerned.'

background possibility, for his expert judgment is needed on the strength of the patent arguments available to the two parties and on the probable outcome of a court action. And if resort is eventually made to legal action the patent department, as well as the firm's legal specialists, will again be principally involved.

More broadly, the patent manager is likely to have some influence on his company's general policy with regard to infringements. Our inquiry revealed that wide variations of policy are to be found between companies, ranging from complete indifference to all infringements to tenacious suppression of them. While the main cause of such policy variations must be sought in differences in the role and impact of patents in different industries and types of production, as we shall show in subsequent chapters, the temperament and business outlook of the patent manager also seems to play a part, as well as the attitude adopted by senior management.

In a similar way, a company's policy with regard to infringing others' patents varies both with industrial circumstances and with the philosophy of individuals involved, and generalisations are difficult. In industries where patents are enforced rather carefully, the patent manager is responsible for keeping in touch with his company's plans for new products and processes to see whether anything is proposed that seems likely to fall within the scope of another's patents. When cases of this sort crop up, he brings them to management's attention and advises whether a licence should be sought.

If he is to be in a position to give timely warning of infringement, the patent manager must be well-informed about the patent situation in the fields in which his company operates. For this purpose, and also to facilitate the internal appraisal for patentability of new ideas and improvements, patent departments typically maintain fairly extensive records of patents in their major fields, with the main facts of scope, ownership, expiry, etc. The usual practice is to update these continuously by utilising one of the recognised patent abstract services, such as that supplied by the Derwent Publishing Company. The 'standard' patent department will probably have an elaborate card-indexed filing system for this purpose, which may extend to technical literature as well as references to U.K. patent specifications and those of other major industrial countries in the fields where the company has an interest. Some of the largest departments have gone so far as to incorporate patent abstracts into a computerised technical information pool available to all group technical departments and including a wide range of other material – abstracts, journals, conference papers, etc. A number of patent managers to whom we talked clearly regard their information retrieval systems as an important part of their activities and take pride in being able to search particular fields better and quicker than the Patent Office and all but the very largest independent firms of patent agents. It appeared that an appreciable portion of the resources of the larger patent departments is devoted to this aspect of their activities. In addition, most departments of any size maintain card-indexed files of their own patents for quick reference; these are essential tools for dealing with renewals, infringements, etc. on any scale.

### Licensing

In some respects, the work of licensing is closely bound up with that of patenting, and personnel in the two areas regularly cooperate and consult each other. However, there are differences in the nature of the work and these are reflected in the skills and training of the people involved and also in the amount of responsibility delegated by senior management.

While the work of the patent specialist is mainly scientific or at least technical in character, that of the licensing specialist has a mainly legal and commercial content. The latter is concerned mainly with the drawing up of licences and licence agreements and the detailed negotiation that often accompanies them, and with the operation of the licences, which entails collecting royalties or other fees, handling renewals or terminations, arranging for exchange of technical information, and otherwise seeing that the terms of the company's licences are being observed. Accordingly a background in the legal or commercial affairs of the company is usually thought desirable for senior licensing personnel.

By contrast with patenting matters, licensing seems to attract active attention from senior management in many companies, and is frequently regarded as a fairly direct responsibility of the commercial or technical director. Arrangements commonly exist for regular approval of new licences by a member of the board, and although the licensing manager's advice is invariably sought on specialist aspects, it is not always taken on commercial ones. Proposals to take or grant new licences may originate at senior as well as middle management levels, and a senior executive will frequently play an active part in the negotiation of an important licence, or in the refusal of one. In short, although the acquisition of patents is generally regarded by top-level management as a matter for specialists, licensing them is felt to involve the economic interests of the enterprise, and licensing policy remains rather more a responsibility for senior management.

More will be said on licensing in the next chapter.

## Litigation

As observed in our opening chapter, patent actions are extremely rare in relation to the total number of patents in existence, and it was not to be expected that our inquiry would collect very much material about them. In fact, three of our 29 companies were involved in U.K. patent litigation in the two years 1967–8, but each said it was an exceptional occurrence. The virtually unanimous view of everyone in industry to whom we talked was that patent litigation is to be avoided 'like the plague', although some firms are driven to it when licensing conflicts cannot be resolved in any other way. The reasons given were very much in line with those mentioned in Chapter 1 (pp. 14–15 and 21–2), *viz.*, the large scope for compromise, the unlikelihood of achieving outright victory, and the time and costs of a court hearing in relation to the other economic stakes involved. One further reason was mentioned – the adverse publicity that tends to attach to a large company involved in a court action, especially where its opponent is an individual or a very small firm.

## Foreign work

A considerable part of the efforts of the typical industrial patent department is devoted to obtaining and enforcing foreign patents. This is partly because the number of foreign patents in the hands of British companies is large in relation to their U.K. patents and partly because foreign patents are relatively expensive in certain respects, e.g., higher renewal fees, difficulties of language and communication, remoteness from headquarters, etc.

An indication of the relative numbers of foreign patents can be gained from Table 6.3, based on information reported by our main sample of firms. These figures suggest that on average a British firm obtains some three to four new foreign patents for every new British patent. However, the ratio varies greatly between companies and between industries; one of the striking features of the table is the relatively high ratio of foreign to U.K. patents in the chemical and allied field, and the rather low ratios in the engineering fields. In general, chemical companies have a greater propensity to patent overseas than engineering companies, for reasons which will be discussed in the next chapter.

Two types of exceptions to the general pattern of foreign *versus* domestic activity may be noted. Firstly, smaller companies in the engineering fields frequently feel that they do not have a sufficiently important stake in overseas markets to warrant obtaining many foreign patents and tend to confine themselves largely to British patents. Secondly, groups of companies that are 'international' in character

TABLE 6.3. *New U.K. and foreign patents, by industry, 1968*

| Industry | (1) New U.K. patents granted (average 1966–8) | (2) Of these, number relating to U.K. inventions | (3) Foreign patents granted on U.K. inventions 1968[b] | (4) (3) ÷ (2) |
|---|---|---|---|---|
| Chemicals and allied[a] | 403 | 385 | 2,038 | 5·3 |
| Textiles and man-made fibres | 185 | 185 | 611 | 3·3 |
| Electrical engineering | 1,102 | 808 | 2,154 | 2·7 |
| Mechanical engineering | 165 | 144 | 366 | 2·5 |
| Total | 1,855 | 1,522 | 5,169 | 3·4 |

NOTES:

Coverage is as in Table 6.1.

[a] Excluding oil companies.

[b] Figures of foreign patents could be obtained for one year only, and in some cases are extremely rough estimates. Comparison with the average of U.K. patents granted in 1966–8 allows for some lag in obtaining foreign patents on U.K. inventions.

frequently have more than one patent department, and some even go so far as to have a department in each of their major market areas. Thus a large American 'multinational' corporation may have, in addition to its principal department at U.S. headquarters, subsidiary departments in, say, the U.K., France or Germany, Argentina, Australia, etc. In such cases, the British department may handle applications for U.K. patents only (possibly even U.K. – originating applications only); alternatively, it may handle some or all Commonwealth or European applications as well, or even all 'Eastern Hemisphere' applications, depending on the particular organisation concerned. Thus, although estimates of all foreign applications that were counterparts to U.K. applications on U.K. inventions reported by departments in our sample are included in Table 6.3, this does not mean that all the foreign patents shown represented work for these departments, although the great majority did.

It would be incorrect to assume that patenting and related costs in the U.K. could be saved in close proportion to the number of foreign patents if foreign patenting were eliminated or much reduced. Certain costs are inescapable if an invention is to be patented at all – such as the drawing-up of the master specification – and others do not vary much with the extent of foreign patenting. We invited participants in our inquiry to estimate the proportion of their patenting and related costs that would be saved if they were not required to obtain and enforce foreign patents and the overall result for our sample came out at approximately 57 per cent, with large variations between companies. Further details will be given in Section C of this chapter, which deals with patenting costs.

*Other aspects*

Apart from its 'professional' activities connected with acquiring and enforcing patents, the industrial patent department typically fulfils the function of a clearing house for technical information within a firm. Where the enterprise is large and complex this role may be an extremely valuable one, although hard to assess in precise terms.

Patent managers and their assistants combine the advantages of familiarity with the work of R & D and technical departments, detailed knowledge of patented developments in the firm's major technical fields and regular contact with the commercial management of the business. Such officials are therefore uniquely placed to act as liaison between the technical and commercial sides of the business, while their background as scientists or engineers helps them to understand the details of technical innovations and communicate them to non-technical managements, and their interest in the commercial aspects of patents helps them to assess technical work from an economic view-point. We were repeatedly impressed with this unusual duality in the skills of company patent officers and it struck us that many firms, particularly in the more technical fields, would find it useful to create an official responsible for coordinating information in this way, had they not already got one in the guise of patent manager.

As was observed earlier, virtually all patent managers keep in close touch with developments in their firms' R & D and technical departments, some taking the task extremely seriously. It is standard practice for the patent manager to receive all research reports and most seem to read them carefully. Apart from that, most patent specialists seem to rely on informal contact with technical managers and assistants to find out what is happening. This is easiest where the patent department and main R & D departments are located together, particularly where both are close to a principal manufacturing establishment, as is usually the case in the smaller companies we visited. The problem is somewhat more difficult in larger groups with several major research establishments and numerous manufacturing centres. However, patent managers seem virtually unanimous in thinking that little if anything of patentable value goes unnoticed by them – although on some occasions the notification is embarrassingly late for obtaining a patent. For this reason, many companies insist as part of routine that all appraisal of serious R & D projects should include an investigation of the patent position affecting them, and the patent department is inevitably involved at this stage, if not earlier.

Furthermore, as has been mentioned, patent departments typically devote a good deal of attention to the filing and retrieval of relevant patent abstracts and other technical information. This activity is naturally more valuable to the firm if an effort is made to summarise and communicate the information to management and technical staff elsewhere in the business. The small patent unit or department will probably content itself with pointing out the occasional new abstract or technical paper to the person concerned, but larger departments often supply a more or less regular technical information service on a group-wide basis – usually in the form of a digest circulated to all senior technical staff. In the largest departments there is likely to be a handful of technical graduates employed fulltime on this type of service, and the companies concerned undoubtedly feel that they obtain considerable benefit of a scientific and technical sort from it.

While a connection with 'professional' patent activity is by no means indispensable to the effective operation of technical information services, as many companies that do not have much in the way of formal patent organisation could doubtless demonstrate, the patent department does appear to provide an extremely convenient focus for such a service. For example, it offers a specialised professional discipline and a career structure, which otherwise tend to be lacking, to the sort of scientist or engineer who finds industrial R & D too specialised or 'backroom' an activity for his taste, but who is not prepared to abandon his technical interests by moving into the wider management field.

It might be expected that the senior patent specialist in a company, equipped as we have seen with the latest technical and commercial information and able to interpret both, would commonly advise senior management on broader business policy involving technical matters. While this undoubtedly happens in the most patent-conscious firms with whom we talked, it does not appear to occur as a regular feature in the majority of the firms investigated, at least to the extent that an observer might expect. Thus, respondents to our inquiry almost always placed a much greater emphasis on their role as advisers to research staff on technical matters than as advisers to management on commercial matters. (The relevant question is No. 2 in Section x of Form B – reproduced on p. 400.) In this respect we are inclined to believe that many companies do not make the fullest possible use of the skills and experience of their patent specialists, although we are clearly not in a position to be dogmatic on the matter.

C.   COSTS

The cost of the patent system is obviously relevant to its economic impact and our inquiry accordingly attempted to assess the costs incurred by industry in connection with the system. Companies were asked to estimate as fully as they could the costs incurred by them in the U.K. on patenting, licensing and associated work in 1968 (see Question 8 in Section II of Form A, reproduced in Appendix B).[1] Amounts were requested under four headings – patent office fees, payments to outside patent agents, etc. (including legal fees and other items of that nature), salaries of employees engaged mainly on patenting and licensing, and 'other'. The latter was intended as a catch-all category for other items, but it was particularly suggested that companies should include in it an appropriate allowance for part-time and occasional work, including time spent by senior management on licensing negotiations, etc. It was stressed that round figures would suffice, and that a comprehensive estimate of relevant costs was being aimed at.

The information sought proved in fact to be not at all straightforward. Our original intention was to concentrate on the costs of the *British* patent system (i.e., patenting and licensing within the U.K.), but we enlarged our approach on learning in pilot discussions with patent specialists that work on foreign patenting accounted for a large share of their activity, and that costs of the British part of the system frequently could not be distinguished at all precisely. On the other hand, several major groups with separate patent activities overseas indicated at an early stage that they could not easily supply information on costs of foreign patenting etc., even for British-originating inventions. Accordingly we tackled the problem by asking firms to report all expenditure on patenting and licensing by their British organisation, including work done on obtaining foreign patents and licensing them, but if possible excluding work on inventions originating overseas. In the great majority of cases this is what was done. Companies were also asked to give the best estimate they could of the proportion of reported expenditure that was attributable to foreign patenting and licensing, so that we could assess the costs of the British part of the system, and virtually all were persuaded to offer an estimate, although some said that it was little more than an informed guess.

Totals of expenditure reported by 26 firms in our main sample (excluding the oil companies and one large electrical group) were as follows:

---

[1] We are talking here of the costs of obtaining and operating patents and licences, i.e., the *administrative* costs of the system that are met by industry. Royalties, licence fees, and other payments for the use of patents are not included, and will be discussed in later chapters.

($£$'000: 1968)

| | |
|---|---|
| (a) Patent Office fees ⎫ | |
| (b) Payments to patent agents, etc. ⎭ | 730[1] |
| (c) Salaries of employees | 860 |
| (d) Other | 250 |
| Total | 1,840 |

As estimates of the full costs to the responding companies of patenting and licensing their British inventions at home and overseas, these figures require adjustment in two respects. Firstly, about half the respondents did not include associated foreign patent office fees and payments to foreign patent agents. On the basis of what other companies reported and of relative numbers of foreign patents, we estimate that about £500,000 should be added for these items to the combined amount for (a) and (b) shown above.

Secondly, several companies could not offer estimates of costs under 'other', but said they might be appreciable. On the basis of what the rest reported, we believe that approximately £100,000 would be a reasonably generous allowance for non-response under this heading.

The amended estimates for expenditure on patenting and licensing at home and overseas by companies in our main sample are then as follows:

($£$'000: 1968)

| | |
|---|---|
| (a) Patent Office fees ⎫ | |
| (b) Payments to patent agents, etc. ⎭ | 1,230 |
| (c) Salaries to employees | 860 |
| (d) Other | 350 |
| Total | 2,440 (say, 2,500) |

This total is no more than an order of magnitude, and it is intended to represent the costs of protecting *British* inventions only.[2] Admittedly, a few companies were unable to deduct costs relating to foreign-originating inventions from their reported totals, and for that reason the estimate may be somewhat on the high side. On the other hand, no expenditures on protecting British inventions by *overseas* patent departments of companies in our sample were included (other than the foreign patent office fees and payments to agents referred to) and this must to some extent counterbalance the previous point, so that our figure may not be too wide of the mark.

It should be noted that the patenting and licensing expenses estimated above are by no means all charged to the British members of a

---

[1] We cannot give a precise split between (a) and (b) because a number of companies that utilise outside patent agents could not easily distinguish official fees from other agents' charges. However, returns from those that could distinguish official fees suggest that they comprise about one third of the combined amount.

[2] The firms concerned reported approximately 1,500 new U.K. patents granted on their British inventions in 1968, and some 10,000 such patents outstanding at the end of the year.

group of companies. A large proportion of expenses for foreign patents, especially official fees and agents' payments, is typically charged to overseas members of a group in markets that benefit from the patents concerned. This is so even where the expenditure is incurred in the first instance by the British department. We shall return to the matter of charging for the patent department's services below.

It is useful for our purposes to calculate the share of the £2½ million of costs referred to above that can be attributed to the British part of the system. This can be done by deducting from each firm's total the estimated percentage that would be saved if foreign patenting and licensing were eliminated, together with foreign patent fees, etc. added by us for non-response. The answer for the British part of the system comes to about £1,050 thousand (say, £1 million), or 43 per cent of their estimated expenditure on British and foreign systems. In other words, firms in our sample spent in round figures some £100 per outstanding patent in 1968 on patenting and licensing their British inventions within the U.K. We would not of course claim that this is a meaningful figure for any particular patent, as there are naturally enormous variations in the amount of patenting and licensing work that different inventions require at different stages of their exploitation. Nevertheless it does provide a very rough indication of the annual cost of protecting and licensing British inventions in the U.K. by means of the patent system in the average case.

A point of some significance that emerges from this part of the exercise is that amounts spent by industry on patenting and licensing are small in relation to those spent on R & D, as might be expected, although they are not entirely negligible if the cost of foreign protection is included. Details from our main sample are given in Table 6.4.

It appears that in 1968 the companies in our sample spent an amount on the worldwide patenting and licensing of their British inventions which was equivalent to approximately 3 per cent of their R & D expenditure in the U.K. in the same year. An amount equivalent to about 1¼ per cent of R & D expenditure was required for obtaining protection and licensing within the U.K. itself.

While these amounts may appear to be pretty small on average, even when foreign patenting is included, it should be pointed out that there was a great deal of variation between companies and that some spent very heavily indeed on patenting etc. in relation to their R & D. As the table suggests, the rate tended to be particularly heavy in the mechanical engineering field, while by contrast in electrical engineering it was well below the sample average. To some extent these differences reflect different degrees of 'patent intensity' in the various industries, which is a subject that we shall return to in later chapters. But the

TABLE 6.4. *Expenditure on patenting and licensing and R & D by industry,*
*1968*

| Industry | (1) Expenditure on patenting and licensing (£'000) | (2) Of which expenditure on British patenting and licensing (£'000) (%) | | (3) Expenditure on R & D in U.K. (£m) | (4) (1) ÷ (3) (%) | (5) (2) ÷ (3) (%) |
|---|---|---|---|---|---|---|
| Mechanical engineering | 430 | 170 | 40 | 4·6 | 9·4 | 3·8 |
| Chemicals and allied | 990 | 370 | 37 | 26·4 | 3·7 | 1·4 |
| Textiles and man-made fibres | 370 | 190 | 52 | 9·8 | 3·8 | 2·0 |
| Electrical engineering | 650 | 320 | 49 | 41·4 | 1·5 | 0·8 |
| Total | 2,440 | 1,050 | 43 | 82·1 | 3·0 | 1·3 |

NOTE:
Coverage is as in Tables 6.1 and 6.3, except that one large electrical group is excluded
(in addition to the oil companies).

picture is not at all consistent even within industries. There is a slight
tendency for rates of patent expenditure to be lower among companies
with large research efforts, but there are notable exceptions. Particular
firms' circumstances in the survey year certainly played some part;
several smaller firms appeared unusually heavily committed to licence
negotiations in that year, while at least one large firm incurred exceptionally heavy legal costs overseas. Some idea of the wide variation
between respondents may be obtained from the fact that only six
companies came within the range of 2–4 per cent, while four showed
less than 1 per cent, and four over 10 per cent.

### Allocation of patent costs within firms

The method generally adopted for allocating patenting and licensing
costs within a firm seems to be as follows. Patent Office fees, payments
to outside agents, and similar items that attach to particular patents,
are charged by the patent department to the operating department or
division of the company most closely concerned. In general, such fees
are charged against the budgets of manufacturing or product divisions
rather than R & D budgets. Other expenses of the patent and licensing
departments (essentially salaries and overheads) are usually allocated
on a more arbitrary basis. Most companies adopt the practice of adding

them to their group or corporate service charge, an all-inclusive over-head that is normally allocated between operating divisions, sub-sidiaries, etc. on the basis of their direct operating costs, or some other rule of thumb. Rather few seem to allocate patenting and licensing overheads on a more rational basis (e.g. in proportion to the amounts of direct work done).

While the use of simple procedures is doubtless warranted by the small size of patenting and related costs in many cases, we did receive the general impression from our inquiry that management on the operating or commercial side of a business, which may exercise a good deal of discretion over the scale of patenting and licensing activities, rarely has a very clear idea of what such activities cost or what the benefits are – except among the more patent-conscious areas of the chemical field. As far as we could tell from conversations with most patent and licensing managers, rather little thought is given at middle-management level to the question of the 'right' amount of patent activity that an enterprise should support, and little discussion of the question appears to take place among senior management. Most patent managers stated that they were fairly content with the level of activity and rate of expansion of their department, and the research and techni-cal directors to whom we talked seemed to be of similar mind. While numerous patent specialists expressed dissatisfaction with particular aspects of the patent system – most notably the failure of the British Patent Office to examine for 'inventive step' – we certainly encountered no feeling among senior management that expenditure on patenting and licensing is not money well spent; nevertheless few senior spokes-men outside pharmaceuticals and certain other special chemical fields appeared to believe that their companies derived more than very moderate benefits from such activities. These considerations lead us well beyond the present account of functions and organisation, and discussion of them will be resumed when we come to consider 'effects' in detail.

# 7. PATENTING AND LICENSING IN PRACTICE: THE ECONOMIC CONTENT OF LICENSING

The practical side of licensing is a complex subject on which a number of specialist books have been written and we do not intend to do more here than examine the aspects that have economic significance. This chapter considers the main provisions found in licences that have economic implications and presents such evidence as our study was able to collect on what is 'typical' in the various industries investigated. (The task of summarising aggregates of patents, licences, royalties, etc. and relating them to magnitudes such as production and research is left for the following chapter.)

Most of the present chapter will be devoted to our principal interest in this part of the study – the licensing of patents and associated know-how between independent companies or groups of companies. However, Section B will offer some evidence on *pure* know-how licensing (i.e., where patents are not involved), while C will deal briefly with intra-group licensing (i.e., licensing between members of the same group of companies).

## A.  INTER-GROUP PATENT LICENSING

It seems useful to enlarge here on what was said in Chapter 1 about the diversity that exists in licensing and, in particular, the wide variation in the know-how content of licences. At its most basic, a patent licence is a short document specifying the parties, the patents licensed, the payments, the duration of the licence, etc. and our practice is to refer to such a licence as a *straight* patent licence. Frequently these are of a standard form and do not leave much scope for negotiation by the parties. At the other extreme, there are 'licences' which are in fact elaborate agreements to provide information, usually of a technical character but occasionally commercial (e.g. marketing know-how) as well. These can be of considerable length with extensive references to engineering specifications, designs, diagrams, blueprints, etc. as well as scores of tightly drafted clauses relating to the conditions of agreement, provisions for enforcement or arbitration and so forth. Such agreements count as patent licences for our purposes if they refer in some definite and explicit way either specifically to existing or future patents held by the parties (in which case they come within our category of 'specific' agreements), or collectively to all patents held by the licensor relating to the product, process, or area of technology designated in the agreement (in which case they are treated by us as 'field' agreements).[1]

Various standard types can be distinguished between these extremes. There are agreements that are essentially patent licences with know-how attached; agreements that give patents and know-how equal emphasis; and agreements that are essentially know-how or technical information agreements but which detail associated patents (and trade marks) either in the main body of the agreement or in the form of separate patent and trade mark licences appended to the main agreement. (The separation of patent licences from the rest of an agreement is increasingly being advised by licensing specialists, essentially so that provisions regarding know-how can survive the expiry of patents – as will be explained in due course.) There are even straight 'field' licences – i.e., licences that simply confer rights to patents in a particular field without specifying them individually, and without providing know-how.[2]

It is important to distinguish as far as possible between these varieties of licences because they represent different types of bargains between firms and their economic significance can be widely different. In particular, it is important so see how much and what kinds of technical information as well as patent rights are exchanged, what conditions attach to their use, the scales of payments involved, and how far the exchange of information depends on patents.

### The parties

One fact which was brought out fairly clearly by the inquiry was that the great majority of licences granted or taken by industrial firms are with other industrial firms. Thus, of a total of some 600 (incoming and outgoing) licences involving only U.K. patents reported by 26 responding firms (the other four in our sample being unable to provide a breakdown), 94 per cent were with other firms.[3] The remainder were

---

[1] It should be noted that we do not include as licences agreements purely for the sale of goods by the patentee, although these may deal briefly with patents. (However, agreements by which the patentee licenses others in particular territories to sell patented products – termed 'selling' agreements – are included.) Neither do we include as licences agreements 'to have manufactured' – i.e., agreements by which the patentee contracts with another to supply him alone (the patentee) with patented products.

[2] Some field agreements, far from being elaborate documents, are no more than brief undertakings to grant patent clearance in a technical field. Such arrangements, although often largely informal, qualify as patent licences in our study if they involve a document referring to patents, however brief.

[3] Answers to this question (Form A, Section III, Q. 16) were limited to licences involving U.K. patents only in order to reduce the load on reporting firms. This narrowing of the picture should if anything exaggerate the degree of non-industrial participation in licensing activity, since virtually all international licensing is done between firms.

with 'non-incorporated organisations' (Government research establishments, the N.R.D.C., universities, private research institutions etc.),
4 per cent, and individuals, 2 per cent.

Moreover, of licences between responding firms and other firms,
over three-quarters were with firms whose main operations were in the
same industrial field (as defined by the groupings that appear in our
tables). Only one or two responding firms tended to have most licences
with firms outside their own industrial fields, and the latter were said
to be less important than those with firms in the same fields.

If this sample can be taken as being roughly representative of the
industries concerned, two conclusions emerge. Firstly, individuals and
non-profit-making research bodies have a comparatively minimal role
as licensors – at least in terms of numbers of licences. (It seems reasonable to assume that these groups *take* very few licences indeed.)
Secondly, companies do not as has sometimes been suggested, have a
strong tendency to grant licences outside their own industrial fields.
The idea that companies prefer to grant licences on inventions whose
application requires technology largely different from their own
appears untrue. The truth is rather that companies tend to license
things which are developed by them or others within their own industrial fields, if not necessarily in their own particular areas of specialisa-
tion or territorial markets.

A third fact which emerged from the inquiry, and one which is of
particular significance, is that the preponderance of licensing by
British firms – and in some fields the great preponderance – is with
foreign firms, or at least relates essentially to their foreign patents.
The detailed figures can be found in the next chapter, but it may be
noted here, for example, that some three-quarters of 'specific' licences
granted by mechanical engineering firms in our sample were on their
foreign patents only, while 90 per cent of their 'field' agreements were
with foreign-based firms. This is clearly an important result, in that it
provides *prima facie* support for the view that U.K. firms tend to deny
others access to patents in their home markets. However, other interpretations are also possible, as will be seen when we come to discuss
selectivity in licensing in Chapter 9.

*Know-how provisions*

The provision of technical information is clearly an important aspect of
licensing, but its economic significance is unfortunately not at all easy
to assess. Many industrialists whom we consulted said quite categori-
cally that the main purpose of licensing is to exchange know-how, etc.,
with patents a minor consideration added in the small print at the end

TABLE 7.1. *Licence agreements with know-how provisions*[a]

|  | 'None' or 'very few' | 'Few' | 'About half' | 'Most' | 'All' or 'virtually all' | Total of com- panies |
|---|---|---|---|---|---|---|
|  | (Number of responding companies) | | | | | |
| Chemicals and allied | 2 | 1 | 1 | 3 | 2 | 9 |
| Electrical engineering | 2 | 1 | 0 | 3 | 2 | 8 |
| Mechanical engineering | 1 | 0 | 0 | 3 | 5 | 9 |
| Textiles and man-made fibres | 0 | 1 | 0 | 2 | 0 | 3 |
| Total | 5 | 3 | 1 | 11 | 9 | 29 |

[a] Companies were asked to state the approximate proportion of all their patent licence agreements that provide for the supply of know-how (whether in the technical field of the patents or in a broader field). The question was restricted to agreements in which the responding company was licensing others to use its patents (including cases where patents were exchanged on a reciprocal basis).

of an agreement to lend an extra element of precision and security to the contract. However, few were prepared to set even rough monetary values on the know-how obtained by their firms under licence.

The strictly factual part of our inquiry was therefore confined mainly to discovering as much as possible about the prevalence of know-how provisions in various fields and the scope of information covered (Form A, Section III, Q. 19 (a) (b) and (c)). While firms were seldom able to give precise answers even to such straightforward questions as the proportion of their licences that contain know-how provisions, most were able to provide reasonable approximations, from which the picture in Table 7.1 was constructed.

If companies are given equal weight, as here, it appears that know-how provisions are most common in mechanical engineering but rather less so in chemicals and electrical engineering, in both of which the position is rather diverse. Within electrical engineering, there is some tendency to confine licensing to patents without know-how, in electronics (particularly in components but also to some degree in finished equipment) and in radio and T.V. Some companies in these fields, however, have a limited number of 'field' agreements (mainly with foreign firms), which provide for the reciprocal exchange of technical information as well as patents and which they clearly regard as important. Explanations for the relative infrequency of know-how provisions in the radio and electronics field are not hard to find. It is a field in wide areas of which manufacturers provide a great deal of technical information on their products through instruction manuals, trade and scientific journals, etc. which are widely available to those interested. Technical advances in this field lie mainly in the design of components and their incorporation into circuits, sets, or systems of equipment; there does not appear on the whole to be a great deal of closely-guarded know-how attaching for example to processes of electronic component manufacture. It seems to be the case here that manufacturers are not in general inclined to be at all secretive about the engineering side.

Know-how provisions are on the whole a much more prominent feature of licensing in the machinery and (non-electronic) equipment branches of the electrical industry, and in telecommunications equipment and systems; although here the picture is fairly diverse.

Our evidence for chemicals suggests that, very broadly speaking, know-how provisions tend to be a regular feature of licensing of processes, but less so where *products* only are being licensed, especially where the novelty lies mainly in particular compounds or formulations (as for example in pharmaceuticals, crop chemicals, toilet preparations, detergents, etc.). However 'field' agreements that provide for the exchange of relatively broadly-based technical information as well as patents are found in branches of the industry that manufacture sophisticated and specialty chemical products (including pharmaceuticals) – the agreements being mainly reciprocal in character and mainly with foreign companies, as in electrical engineering.

It became evident in discussions with licensing specialists that the technical information provided in agreements can be of two broad kinds, which may be termed 'start-up' and 'follow-up' information respectively. Start-up know-how is the information needed to *begin* working a licensed process or product and is usually confined rather closely to the field of the patent or patents licensed. Follow-up know-how is the information that accumulates as experience of working the product or process is gained. Follow-up information may include future patents as well as know-how, and also technical material that, while not being patentable, is hardly know-how in the usual sense. Thus it may relate not so much to ways of doing things as, say, to new data about the performance of the product, new uses for it, etc.

Where know-how provisions are included in an agreement, the licensor almost invariably supplies at least some start-up know-how. The clauses governing this know-how are often extensive and sometimes very elaborate; thus for example they may specify the means of providing know-how, down to methods of personnel instruction, number of factory visits, and even such details as who is to pay the salaries and hotel bills of visiting personnel. In addition, an exchange of follow-up information (and patents) is provided for in the great majority of agreements that include know-how, although several firms (mainly in chemicals) said it was rarely their practice to provide for such exchanges.

The scope and conditions for exchange of follow-up know-how and patents are among the most strongly-contested points in licensing negotiations, since they can involve benefits and obligations for the parties which are often difficult to foresee, but which may turn out to be of appreciable economic importance to them. While the commonest pattern where provisions for follow-up know-how appear is a reciprocal exchange (usually confined fairly closely to the technical area of the licensed products or processes, but not uncommonly extending to a broader field), the transfer is sometimes unilateral, in favour of whichever party has the stronger bargaining position. Where the agreement is essentially for a reciprocal exchange of patents and know-how between the parties (i.e., a 'cross-licence'[1]), the provision for follow-up information on a licensed product or process is normally reciprocal too: however, reciprocal know-how provisions are not uncommon in one-way patent licences as well.

Among the 29 companies that responded to this question, agreements that provide for the supply of know-how 'in the technical field of the patents' appear to outnumber by a substantial margin those that provide for its supply 'on a substantially broader basis'. Thus, 16 companies said either that they did not supply information on a broader basis, or that they did so in only a very few agreements. However six companies (three being in chemicals and three in mechanical engineering) said that most of their agreements supplied information on a substantially broader basis. The remaining seven did so in an appreciable minority of agreements. While the broader exchanges are usually reciprocal, two or three companies said that most of their agreements provide for the supply of such information on an essentially one-way basis.

It appears to be a virtually universal provision that recipients of know-how under licence are bound as licensees not to divulge it to third parties.[2] On the other hand, a licensor is very seldom bound to secrecy with respect to the know-how he transmits as licensor (except in sole or exclusive licences, which will be discussed later), although he sometimes undertakes not to offer the same information elsewhere on more favourable terms. However *both* licensor and licensee appear frequently to

---

[1] A 'cross-licence' provides for the two-way exchange of patents (and often know-how) between the parties. The arrangement is usually bilateral, but multilateral cases – involving perhaps half a dozen different companies – occasionally occur.

[2] Absolute secrecy cannot of course be guaranteed, especially where know-how is of the sort that can be carried in the memory, and is not insisted on. However, licensees are expected to exercise due diligence, for example, in restricting critical documents to personnel directly involved.

agree not to divulge follow-up know-how arising under a licence agreement, including know-how that arises as a return flow to the licensor; this seems to be a fairly common undertaking by the parties to a cross-licence involving know-how. (Clauses providing for an exclusive return-flow of patent rights or know-how from licensee to licensor are commonly termed 'grant-back' provisions.) The admissability of restrictive conditions governing the transfer of know-how in patent licences raises some interesting issues, which will be discussed below (pages 130-4).

Our conclusions regarding know-how provisions on the evidence so far presented may be summed up as follows. The proportion of licence agreements that contain know-how provisions is quite large in most branches of industry examined. (Some 20 out of 29 responding companies said that 'most' or 'all' of their licence agreements contained know-how clauses.) The information supplied is usually in a fairly narrow field (i.e. relating to the particular products or processes licensed), but exchanges of a broader scope are not infrequent, especially in cross-licences. Finally licensees normally undertake not to disclose any know-how obtained under licence, while both licensors and licensees frequently undertake not to disclose follow-up information exchanged under an agreement. Clauses providing for secret return flows of relevant information appear to be a fairly common feature of cross-licensing agreements, and are also found in one-way agreements.

Although the proportion of agreements that contain know-how provisions is fairly large, at least in engineering and 'process-oriented' industries, the number of these in which know-how of outstanding economic importance actually changes hands is probably much smaller. This was suggested both in the answers that were received to our question on licensing benefits (Form A, Section III, Q. 20 and 21), which will be discussed later (Chapter 8, pp. 166-8), and in the discussions which we had with firms. Among the main reasons cited were the tendency of firms to maintain secrecy over critical know-how – if not patentable information – in key technical areas; the comparative rarity of fundamentally new manufacturing techniques in some of the industries covered; and the general difficulties and inertia that have to be overcome if complex technology is to be transmitted rapidly and effectively between independent organisations. Nevertheless quite significant know-how transfers under licence do occur between firms from time to time, as we shall show in later chapters.

### Duration and termination

There appears to be considerable variation in the length of period provided for licence agreements, depending mainly on the nature of what is licensed and the relative bargaining strengths of the parties. (Licensors generally prefer shorter periods and licensees longer, although this is not always the case.) Straight patent licences are usually arranged to terminate at the expiry of the last of the patents to which they relate, although they may terminate earlier. Under Section 58 of the Patents Act (1949), either party has the option of terminating a licence after the patent expires, notwithstanding any provision to the contrary in the agreement, and most straight patent licences are terminated at that stage.

However, this is by no means the standard arrangement in agreements that include know-how as well as patents. Where the essential purpose of an agreement is to supply know-how, with patents a lesser consideration, the parties may agree to continue the exchange well after the expiry of the patents – possibly indefinitely – or they may wish to terminate the exchange well before that date. Several companies, particularly in branches of industry where technology is changing rapidly, said that there is an increasing tendency to provide for the cut-off of know-how flows well before the expiry of the relevant patents, and five years is being increasingly adopted as the preferred maximum period for know-how supply in some fields (e.g., electronics).

Most agreements provide for the right of either party to terminate if the other infringes a substantial condition of the agreement – and it is increasingly becoming the practice to include merger or takeover of either party as grounds for termination by either.

The effect of termination on the subsequent operations of the parties is to some extent a subject for negotiation and is elaborately provided for in some agreements. The major issue relates to the right of the licensee to continue using know-how obtained during an agreement after it has expired. (The right to exercise patent rights freely after the expiry of the patent concerned is not negotiable, since it is explicitly allowed under Section 58.) The issue concerning know-how has not yet been settled decisively by the courts, and we encountered some variation of opinion on it among licensing specialists. It seems universally agreed that know-how provided in association with a patent would be deemed to pass into the public domain along with the patent when it expires, in the absence of any provision to the contrary; but if there is a provision forbidding the use of know-how when the agreement expires, the status of the know-how may nevertheless be uncertain should either party wish not to renew the agreement (as they may be en-

titled to do under Section 58). Some licensing specialists believe that the
courts might uphold the licensee's right to continue using the know-how
in question, notwithstanding an earlier undertaking to the contrary,
on the ground that it is necessary for production of the patented
article – which the licensee must be free to continue. Others maintain
that continued use of know-how where forbidden after expiry of an
agreement would be held to be breach of contract, even where the
know-how is closely associated with the patents licensed in the agreement. Inevitably, the position may be further complicated by the
difficulty of distinguishing between the know-how supplied by the
licensor and that developed subsequently by the licensee, a problem
on which judicial decisions may be hard to predict with confidence.[1]

Licensors who wish to be sure of retaining control of know-how
supplied with patents when the latter expire sometimes attempt to do
so by distinguishing clearly between patents and know-how in their
agreements. In practice this may be achieved by separating patent
licences from the rest of an agreement, and distinguishing between
payments for patent rights and those for use of know-how. Although
this practice is being increasingly adopted in agreements that involve
know-how, it is by no means yet universal. One reason for reluctance
to adopt it is the wish to retain patents as a central part of an agreement
where provisions are included that would otherwise be registrable
under the Restrictive Practices Act (e.g., reciprocal provisions relating
to the markets for output produced under licence). We shall return
to the question of restrictive provisions in due course.

## Payments

The precise form of licence payments depends to some extent on the
industry and type of licence concerned, but two main varieties can be

[1] Among a number of comments on this point made by respondents to our inquiry who were
shown a draft of this chapter, the following should be cited: 'It is agreed that the question
of termination of know-how/patent agreements is not completely clear. A recent case in
*1972 R.P.C.*, pages 229–35, *Regina Glass Fibre Ltd. v. Werner Schuller* adds a little certainty.

Licensing know-how of itself leads to a difficult position in that the buyer is unwilling to
buy until he knows what is for sale and the seller is unwilling to disclose what he has because
secrecy is the only protection he has. The conduct of, and relationship between, the
parties in such a transaction is therefore of great importance.

The buyer or licensee of know-how has always to consider his position in the time after
the contract is signed relative to others who may catch up and be in a better position than
the buyer or licensee because the others do not have to make payment.'

Another licensing specialist commented: 'I should like to draw your attention to the
recent decision reported in *1972 R.P.C.* at page 229 in the case of *Regina Glass Fibre Ltd. v.
Schuller* concerning a patent licence, which appears relevant. As you will see from this case,
the Court held very strongly the view that once an industry has been started on the basis of
confidential know-how and patent rights, the Courts will not lightly close down a company
at the end of an agreement term.'

distinguished – the 'running royalty' and the 'lump sum'. Broadly speaking, the lump sum (or series of lump sums) is favoured where a substantial piece of start-up know-how is supplied, such as designs and engineering expertise for a complete new plant or facility which the licensor guarantees to put into operation effectively. This method of payment is also preferred in cases where there is doubt about the future level of security of licence payments, and is the standard arrangement with licences granted to organisations in Communist countries or in countries where royalty remittances are severely hampered by exchange controls.

The running royalty is regarded more as a payment for use of patent rights or supply of a continuing flow of follow-up know-how, and is generally found when these are prominent features of agreements. It is virtually always related (in the manner of a sales commission) to sales of licensed output and is generally expressed as a percentage of selling value – usually wholesale, net of discounts and sales taxes. However, it is sometimes expressed as a specific rate per unit of licensed output where this seems more appropriate (e.g. where the same patented component is incorporated into a range of products with differing prices).

Combinations of lump sum and running royalty are fairly common and are likely to reflect the joint provision of start-up know-how and patents.

Other types of payments may be encountered, but they are rather rare. One variety that should be mentioned is payment in the form of shares in the licensee's equity capital – in which case dividends are received instead of royalties. This type of arrangement is uncommon, but it has attractions for a licensor in a strong bargaining position who wishes to acquire a stake (and perhaps ultimately a controlling interest) in the management of the licensee; it also offers a potentially long term return in circumstances where the benefits from licensing are of a near-permanent variety, as, for instance, where the licensee acquires 'rights' in the trade reputation or goodwill of the licensor that cannot easily be withdrawn.

Some idea of the relative extent of the various types of payments may be conveyed by the fact that, of the 28 firms that responded on this point, 14 indicated that agreements providing 'running royalties only' accounted for more than two-thirds of their licence income, four stated that a combination of lump-sums and running royalties accounted for the bulk of their licence income and nine said that 'royalties only' and 'combination' agreements each accounted for a substantial proportion (over one-third) of income. Only one firm (a components manufacturer with relatively few licences) said that lump-sums accounted for the bulk of its licence income. Generally speaking, 'royalties only' tends to be the prevalent form of income in radio and electronics and in pharmaceutical and other finished and specialty chemical products, while 'combination' income tends to be found in basic and bulk chemicals where licensed processes are important, and also in the (non-electrical) plant and machinery field.

A frequent concern of licensors in connection with licensing activity is to try to ensure that a prospective licensee will put a reasonable amount of effort into working the licence, and at least make it worth the licensor's while to go to the trouble of licensing.[1] However, while most responding companies said that they needed to be satisfied in an informal way on the ability of a prospective licensee to exploit a licence properly, not a great many (6 out of 28) include explicit guarantees of minimum payments as a normal condition of licensing, and even these generally refer to a rather low guarantee of the sort necessary to reimburse the licensor for his trouble, and seldom to a minimum acceptable return on the patent and know-how licensed. Most licensors insist that regular data on sales and costs of articles licensed should be reported by the licensee, and this in itself helps to keep licensees on their toes.[2]

Minimum payments (lump-sum, royalty, or both) required formally or informally by licensors vary considerably with the nature of the licence, the markets involved and other factors. One large electrical company said that it was contemplating the adoption of a minimum down-payment of £250 to cover the cost of correspondence and servicing on a straight patent licence, with much larger minima where provision of know-how was entailed. An engineering company of medium size said that royalty income of one or two thousand pounds per annum from each licensee would be marginally acceptable on any of its main patents. By contrast, an oil company stated that it would not consider licensing a major petrochemical process for a down payment of less than £50,000; anything less would fail to justify the effort of arranging the licence and providing start-up know-how.

The factors that govern royalty rates are of course complex and it is hard to generalise, except to say that the following principles seem to apply:

(i) The average rate of royalty on a given patent tends to fall, other things being equal, the larger the volume of output produced

[1] It is perhaps significant that licensing managers in general claimed to spend much more effort (both in negotiations and after) on trying to stimulate production on the part of their licensees than on trying to confine it within limits. But see also *Restrictive Provisions* below pp. 125–6.
[2] Licensees sometimes retaliate by seeking a clause providing for the waiving of royalties should the patents concerned be infringed by others, but the parties usually agree merely to consult before taking action should infringement be detected.

under licence. This is explicitly recognised in agreements that relate royalty to output on a diminishing sliding scale, which are fairly common where large volumes of homogeneous output are involved. Accordingly, average royalty rates on products sold in mass markets tend to be very small (sometimes a fraction of one per cent of net selling value), whereas even straight patent royalties on products with limited or specialty markets are likely to be much higher – say 5 per cent or more.

(ii) Elasticity of demand for the patented item also affects the royalty rate. In markets where elasticity of demand for the product sold under licence is exceptionally low (for example, components that vitally affect the safety or performance of aircraft), the royalty rate is likely to be rather high (say 10 per cent or more), especially if the sales volume is also low.

(iii) Inevitably the rate of royalty associated with a particular patent tends, other things being equal, to increase with the amount of know-how supplied. Royalty rates may well increase from 2 per cent on a straight patent licence to, say, 4 per cent on the same licence with supplementary drawings and specifications, and possibly 6 per cent if regular engineers' visits and personal instruction are provided as well.

(iv) In industrial fields where materials or components are produced under licence for incorporation by the licensee in 'finished' products, royalty rates tend to be fixed not in relation to the value of the components etc., but to the value of the finished products. (This is especially likely where sets of numerous components are manufactured under licence from a few patentees for incorporation in larger assemblies, as often happens for example in the radio, T.V. and domestic appliance field.) In these circumstances, the royalty rate will depend a good deal on the ratio of the value of the components etc. to that of the finished product. A royalty of less than a pound may sound small in relation to the price of a T.V. set, but it may be quite high in relation to the value of the components manufactured under licence.

The question of what determines royalty rates and how far they conform to what is 'reasonable' or 'ideal' in a broader economic sense is clearly an important one, and we shall return to it in due course. (It seems, for example, reasonable to argue that royalties should bear some relation to the research cost of a licensed invention, and we shall explore this point further at the end of Chapter 8.)

Although royalty rates proved to be both a difficult and somewhat 'sensitive' subject for detailed investigation, some information on rates was obtained from responding firms (see Form A, Section III, Q. 18) and is summarised in Table 7.2.

TABLE 7.2. *Principal rates of royalty charged in licence agreements*

| Industry | Principal rate of royalty (%)[a] | | | | | |
| --- | --- | --- | --- | --- | --- | --- |
| | Less than 1 per cent | 1–2½ | 2½–5 | 5–10 | Over 10 | Total |
| Chemicals: | (Number of responding companies) | | | | | |
| Finished and specialty | 0 | 1 | 3 | ½ | 0 | 4½ |
| Basic | 0 | 1½ | 2 | 1 | 0 | 4½ |
| Sub-total | 0 | 2½ | 5 | 1½ | 0 | 9 |
| Electrical engineering | ½ | ½ | 5½ | 1½ | 0 | 8 |
| Mechanical engineering: | | | | | | |
| Plant, machinery, equipment | ½ | ½ | 2 | 3 | 0 | 6 |
| Components | 0 | 0 | 1 | 1 | 0 | 2 |
| Sub-total | ½ | ½ | 3 | 4 | 0 | 8 |
| Textiles and man-made fibres | 0 | 1½ | ½ | 0 | 0 | 2 |
| Total | 1 | 5 | 14 | 7 | 0 | 27 |

[a] Companies were asked to state which rates of royalties accounted for a substantial propor-tion (over one-third) of their sales-related royalty income. Companies that reported substantial royalties in one class only count as '1' in the appropriate class in the table. Those that reported substantial royalties in two classes count as '½' in each class. No company reported substantial royalties in more than two classes.

No distinction is made here between types of agreements, know-how content, etc., but it may be safely assumed that companies with predominantly low royalty rates were ones whose licensing activity tended to be either in straight patent licences or in large volume markets, while those with higher rates tended either to provide sub-stantial know-how or to license in 'specialty' markets.

It will be seen that just over half of the 27 respondents were in the class 2½–5 per cent, and that all but one of the remainder were split fairly evenly between the adjacent classes. No company received a substantial portion (more than one-third) of its royalties at rates of over 10 per cent, while only two reported substantial shares at rates of less than one per cent. In both chemicals and electrical engineering the distribution is fairly well concentrated in the median class, while in mechanical engineering it is quite heavily skewed in favour of the higher class (5–10 per cent). Thus, if firms are given equal weight, the mean royalty rate for mechanical engineering comes to 5·3 per cent, compared with a sample mean of 4·2 per cent. It is probably fair to attribute the high mean rate in mechanical engineering to the relative importance of know-how in this field (cf. Table 7.1), as well as to the fact that a good deal of the machinery and equipment licensed by firms in our sample is produced for limited or specialist markets.

The figures in Table 7.2 refer to royalty rates in accordance with their contribution to royalty income. We were not able to collect systematic information on numbers of licences by rate of royalty, but our impression from partial data is that rather over half would come in the '2½–5 per cent' class, with smaller but still appreciable numbers in the '1–2½ per cent' class, rather few in the 'less than 1 per cent' and '5–10 per cent' classes (except in plant, machinery and equipment, where high rates are less infrequent), and that very few indeed would have rates over 10 per cent.

### Restrictive provisions

As explained in Chapter 1, restrictions on patented products and processes are exempt from the Restrictive Practices Act, and patent licensing agreements are not registrable under this Act unless they contain restrictions on things that are not patented. It is part of the legal nature of the patent monopoly that patentees may in general, if they wish and if they have the necessary bargaining power, impose quite onerous restrictions on licensees in such matters as prices and markets for products manufactured or sold under licence. (They may not however, at least in principle, limit the licensee concerning unpatented goods – such as components or materials used in the production of patented items.)[1]

Our inquiry attempted to discover the extent of the main types of restrictive provisions met with in licensing agreements – namely, those relating to (i) quantities, (ii) markets, uses, and methods of distribution, (iii) prices, and (iv) qualities of output produced under licence (Form III, Q. 19).[2] Of the 29 companies that replied to this question, eight stated that agreements in which they were licensors sometimes included restrictions on the quantity of output produced under licence. Five of these were in chemicals and one each in mechanical engineering, electrical engineering and man-made fibres. With one exception (in pharmaceuticals), the companies in question indicated that such provisions were found in only a small proportion of their agreements.

Of the same 29 companies, 25 stated that their agreements either explicitly or in effect limited the markets in which output could be sold under licence. Several made the general point that this is the inevitable consequence of selectivity in licensing particular patents to particular

---

[1] In practice, the position regarding 'tying clauses' relating to unpatented goods is more complicated, and will be dealt with as a special problem in Chapter 9, pp. 192–4.
[2] Restrictions on the disclosure and use of *know-how* under licence were discussed on pages 116–19 above.

licensees. Thus a licensee is effectively confined to manufacturing or selling in the country to which the patent applies, unless the contrary is stated in the agreement. But, apart from this, rather over half the respondents indicated that their agreements commonly included explicit provisions limiting licensees to particular territorial areas.

Limitations on sources, uses and methods of distribution of patented items were said to be fairly common in some fields, but mainly in 'user' or 'selling' agreements (i.e., agreements that license assembly or processing firms to use patented components or materials, or distributors to sell patented products). For example, clauses forcing – or at least strongly inducing – licensees to obtain supplies of bulk materials from the patentee (or his licensees) were said to be common in agreements in the chemical processing field.[1] User and selling agreements in the radio and electronics field and in finished chemicals frequently contain provisions confining the licensee to specified end-uses or applications for patented items. However, such provisions were said to be designed virtually always to protect the patented product against misuse, and not to interfere with the licensee's ability to exploit the licence as actively as possible in the way intended by the manufacturer. The object of most user and selling agreements is after all to maximise sales under licence, not to inhibit them.

While the purpose of provisions limiting the use or distribution of licensed products was generally claimed to be the prevention of damage to the reputation of the patentee, a similar argument could not apply in the case of territorial restrictions. In fact several companies said unhesitatingly that the purpose of territorial restrictions is to prevent or limit competition from the licensee in the licensor's main markets. Thus, it is commonly provided that the licensee will not manufacture or export licensed output to the licensor's home market without his permission and the licensor's main overseas markets are frequently debarred as well.

Such provisions could have important economic implications, and more will be said on them in later chapters. It should however be pointed out that they are frowned upon in some countries, in particular the U.S.A., where they may be found illegal under antitrust legislation unless confined to patented products or processes in one-way patent licences, as also may other restrictive provisions in licensing agreements.[2]

Significantly perhaps, only three of the 29 respondents said that their

---

[1] This is frequently done by the patentee requiring a royalty on supplies obtained from unlicensed sources, whereas licensed supplies are on a royalty-free basis. This type of provision is not always easy to enforce, since it may be difficult for the patentee to detect whether users are obtaining supplies from unlicensed sources.

[2] A. D. Neale, *The Antitrust Laws of the United States of America* (2nd edition, Cambridge University Press, 1970) pp. 300–41, esp. pp. 306, 314.

agreements included restrictions on the (minimum) price of output produced under licence.[1] Only one company (in the components branch of mechanical engineering) said that such provisions were common in its agreements; the other two (both in chemicals) stated that they were included in no more than a few agreements.

Finally, 20 responding companies said that their agreements provided minimum conditions relating to the quality of output produced under licence. Of these, ten indicated that provisions of this kind are fairly normal in their agreements (six being in mechanical engineering, two in electronics, T.V. and radio, one in electrical engineering and one in pharmaceuticals). In several cases minimum safety standards were said to be the main thing enforced and in the rest standards of design or performance were emphasised.

The general picture emerging from our sample regarding restrictive provisions is therefore that a majority of licensors limit the markets available to their licensees as a fairly common feature of their agreements, and in particular attempt to limit competition in their home markets through selective licensing and export restrictions on foreign licensees. Limitations on the quality of output under licence and on uses for which licensed products are sold and for which licensed processes are used are also very common, but these are said to refer almost always to misuse or lowering of standards, and are essentially intended to protect the reputation of the patentee. Limitations on the quantity of output produced under licence are, on the other hand, rather uncommon, except perhaps in chemicals, where they seem to be confined to highly specialised products or sophisticated industrial markets. Restrictions on prices are rare in all the fields investigated, and firms seem for the most part to avoid them with great care. They are undoubtedly influenced in this by the dubious legal status of price restrictions in licences that involve foreign companies, and in particular by the stringent view that is taken of such provisions in the U.S.A. They are nevertheless occasionally found in chemicals and mechanical engineering – in some of the lines of production in which output restrictions are also found.

### Exclusivity

A patentee is permitted under the British and most overseas patent laws to license patents if desired on an 'exclusive' basis (rights confined to licensee alone) or 'sole' basis (rights shared between patentee and licensee). This power is, in theory at least, a feature of the patent system that is much prized by patentees, because it allows the confine-

---

[1] These restrictions related to manufacturers' prices only. Resale price fixing is illegal in the U.K., even where the article in question is patented.

ment of patent rights to one or two manufacturers where the patentee is not in a positive to supply a market on his own. In practice, it appears that exclusivity is more often desired by licensees than by licensors, and that licensors sometimes agree to it rather reluctantly. A licensee frequently has a great deal to gain through securing exclusivity, especially where the market for the product is small, whereas the licensor may favour having more than one licensee in the hope of maximising royalties and possibly playing one off against another if they are dilatory in working the licence.

It was therefore of some interest to discover in our inquiry that exclusive licensing, at least within the U.K., does not seem as widespread or important a practice as has sometimes been supposed. While a number of responding companies had taken or granted sole or exclusive licences on their U.K. patents,[1] usually on a very limited scale, almost no company regarded them as a prominent feature of its domestic licensing activity, although some attached a limited importance to them, more especially in the mechanical engineering field. The picture regarding exclusive licensing overseas by U.K. firms was more variable. In certain fields, the preferred method of licensing key developments is to select one or perhaps two reputable local firms in each major market area and entrust them with exclusive rights, often including rights to sub-licence others in their territory. In other fields, the licensor's approach is less selective, subject almost always to the provision that the licensee will not compete in the licensor's own major market areas.

Responses to the relevant questions (Form A, Section III, Q. 11 and 12) indicated that companies in the electrical field have virtually no interest in exclusive licensing, whether at home or overseas. Only one electrical company in our sample had granted and taken a few 'sole' licences, but these were said to be of negligible importance, involving no royalties and no production of any significance. The picture was almost as blank in man-made fibres, the companies there reporting a handful of exclusive licences involving minimal production and royalties.

Seven out of the 10 companies with substantial chemical activities that responded to this question had granted or taken exclusive licences in the U.K., but in most cases the numbers of patents involved were said to be very small, the royalties negligible and the production affected not economically important. Pharmaceuticals was a notable exception; two of our three companies in this field had taken a total of 15 exclusive licences on British patents, mainly from foreign licensors, the other not having taken or granted any. Royalties paid out on these licences totalled about £20,000 in 1968, and production under them amounted

---

[1] Companies were asked about licences outstanding in 1968.

to about £225,000 in the same year (i.e. about ¾ per cent of the U.K. pharmaceutical production of the companies involved). These amounts are very small in relation to the total pharmaceutical operations of the firms in question, although they could be significant for the particular products concerned. It is when attention is turned to overseas markets that exclusive or sole licensing comes into prominence in this field. A number of important instances were cited to us, outstanding among which was the well-known agreement by which Beecham has granted sole U.S. and Canadian rights on all its synthetic penicillin patents to the American firm, Bristol Myers (also retaining for itself the right to manufacture and sell in these countries). While there are probably few other single licence agreements involving British firms that approach this in commercial importance, the pattern appears a fairly standard one in the international licensing of important new drugs, and will be discussed at greater length in our case study of the industry (see Chapter 10).

Of the 10 companies with substantial mechanical engineering activities that responded on this point, four had granted exclusive licences on their U.K. patents (a total of about 30 patents being involved), and seven had taken exclusive licences (involving 42 U.K. patents, of which most were on machinery and the rest in the components field). One manufacturer of plant and equipment indicated that its usual practice was to award exclusives only, and one components manufacturer had a strong preference for granting exclusives where possible. Incoming royalties on the U.K. licences concerned totalled about £100,000 in 1968 (relating to U.K. output under licence of possibly £2¼ million or so), while outgoing royalties in that year on exclusives totalled about £175,000 (relating to U.K. output of the firms concerned of about £3½ million, i.e. about 4½ per cent of their U.K. sales). One plant and equipment producer reported about one-fifth of its U.K. sales under exclusive licence, while another reported about one-tenth. The rest showed much smaller proportions.

While it would be unwise to draw general conclusions from what are after all fairly small samples of firms, the evidence from this part of the inquiry – and from other companies which we visited but which did not supply information on our main questionnaire – is that exclusive licensing has a perceptibly higher incidence and is more important among plant, machinery and equipment producers than in any other field we examined, apart from pharmaceuticals and certain other chemical specialties. It is the preferred form of licensing at home and overseas for several of the engineering firms to which we talked, although none regarded it as being vital to their operations. (On the other hand, most pharmaceutical firms stressed the critical role played by exclusive, or near-exclusive, licensing in their overseas businesses.) By comparison, exclusivity seems an entirely insignificant feature of licensing in the electrical field, and of relatively little importance in basic chemicals. Whether or not exclusive licensing has any influence on innovation or competition in the fields referred to will be discussed in later chapters.

### *Refusals*

The question of selectivity in licensing is of course vital to our study; if patents are indeed used as a device for suppressing competition in research-based fields, one would expect to find evidence of patentees denying others access to their patents, or at least demanding un-reasonable terms for licences. Moreover, if our figures (mentioned earlier in this chapter and discussed in detail in Chapter 8) concerning the preponderance of international licences in total licensing by U.K. firms really reflect active and widespread discrimination against potential licensees in their home markets, one might expect to find appreciable evidence of unsatisfied demand for licences on U.K. patents among firms operating in the U.K.

Unfortunately, the question of refusal of licence applications is not an easy one to investigate. One problem is that many 'applications' for licences are of a highly informal nature, and refusals may be equally informal. Such instances may not come to the attention of the licensing department, and even when they do they are not likely to be recorded in any systematic way. Secondly, there is the problem that many potential licensees believe that a request for a licence would be turned down, and therefore do not trouble to make one. Thirdly, there is the difficulty of judging whether an application is a serious or reasonable one, and equally whether a 'refusal' is in response to an unreasonable re-quest by the applicant or whether it is a refusal on any reasonable terms.

Consequently, a request for information that merely lists refusals is likely to be misleading. We tried to tackle the problem by inviting respondents to give a rough estimate of the number of clear refusals that came to mind for the period 1966–8, and used this information as a starting point for exploring whether any instances of economic signifi-cance had arisen during the period.

As might be expected, the extent of refusals revealed by this approach was rather small, although not negligible. Of 26 companies that felt able to give a reply, four stated that some of their applications for U.K. licences in 1966–8 had been refused, involving altogether about a dozen patents, including some in all the main fields examined.[1] On no occasion had an applicant been seriously inconvenienced by a refusal.

---

[1] The four companies that would not commit themselves on our questionnaire said in later discussions that the answer would probably be 'nothing of any importance'.

Moreover, only three of the 26 respondents had in turn refused licence applications for their U.K. patents during the period, no more than a handful of applications being involved in total. In one or two cases it was said that the patents were of some consequence to the patentees involved, that they involved appreciable amounts of U.K. production and that they were the sort that would not be licensed to a competitor without some exceptional offer of patents or know-how in return.

We would conclude on the basis of this admittedly slim evidence that outright refusals of 'serious' licence applications are rather uncommon among large firms, although they do occur from time to time where the owner of the patent feels that it gives him a valuable element of protection in one of his principal markets, especially where he is the main established supplier or one of a small number.

It should be added that this evidence on the infrequency of formal refusals does not necessarily imply that licences on important patents are readily available to all serious potential applicants in many or most areas of industry: there are ways by which firms can turn away applicants without giving them an outright refusal. This point will be reviewed and amplified in later chapters.

We should point out that the type of 'considered' refusal discussed above should not be confused with the appreciable number of minor licence approaches and abortive negotiations that customarily take place in some areas of industry. One licensing manager informed us that for every negotiation that bears fruit in his department there are dozens of trivial inquiries, false-starts and intended negotiations that come to nothing. Many approaches are in fact little more than tentative or routine business inquiries from distributors' or suppliers' representatives, which are not carried further. Small, inexperienced applicants are frequently discouraged by the length and complexity of draft agreements presented to them. Many potentially serious applicants change their plans or lose interest before negotiations get very far. Some applications are refused because they come from firms that are manifestly incapable of producing to the licensor's standards or on the scale required to make a licence worthwhile. We were repeatedly assured that the main problem for the licensing department is to interest reputable firms in taking licences rather than dissuading them from doing so, and many licensing specialists to whom we talked were plainly puzzled that their task might be seen in the latter rather than the former light.

### Legality of restrictive provisions

Before leaving this account of patent licensing, we pause to consider an issue that has some bearing on the impact of patents – namely the legality of restrictive provisions in commercial agreements involving patent licences. Although this is a specialist subject on which we venture with some trepidation, the issue seems to us too important to ignore altogether in a study of this kind.

According to our evidence, restrictive provisions are a fairly regular feature of licence agreements in certain fields. Restrictions on territorial markets for output under licence were said to be common by a majority of responding firms, although restrictions on quantities of output under licence were less common and restrictions on prices rare. Furthermore, restrictions on both the *use* of know-how under licence (i.e., its application by the licensee in manufacturing) and the *exchange* of know-how (i.e., its non-divulgence to third parties, as for example in exclusive grant-back provisions for secret return flows of technical information) were said to be common features of licence agreements in certain fields.

The first point is that restrictions relating to prices, outputs, markets etc. for patented products or goods produced using patented processes are expressly permitted under U.K. law. This is justified on the ground that a patent confers a legal monopoly over the product or process concerned (subject to limitations laid down in Sections 37, 41, 46, etc.). This state of affairs is explicitly recognised in U.K. restrictive practices legislation. Thus, Section 8(4) of the *Restrictive Trade Practices Act 1956* exempts patented goods and goods made by patented processes from the application of the Act, with the result that patent licence agreements are not in themselves registrable unless they contain registrable restrictions other than restrictions relating to patented articles covered by the agreement. The patent licence exemption, if validly applied, operates whether there is a one-way patent licence or a cross-licence or patent pool.

As we noted earlier, the exemption for price restrictions in patent licence agreements does not extend to fixing of *resale* prices; the Resale Prices Act 1964 applies to patented goods as to others. Accordingly, a patentee is not permitted to stipulate minimum resale prices in a contract for the sale of patented goods, or to require licensees in their turn to accept or impose restrictions on resale prices. However, Section 1(2) of the 1964 Act declares that the Act is not to interfere with the right of a licensor to fix the price charged by the licensee for *first-hand* sales (including retail sales) of patented goods manufactured by him under the licence.

We are not concerned at this stage to assess the economic case for the principle of exempting genuinely patent-based products or processes from the effect of restrictive practices legislation; exemptions of this type seem inevitable if patent monopolies of the traditional kind are to be allowed. (Whether or not the latter should be allowed, we hope to be able to say in due course.) But we should point out that, quite apart from questions of principle, exemptions of this sort do raise problems of judgment as to whether particular products and processes should be regarded as 'patented' or not, from the point of view of restrictive practices legislation. The impression emerged strongly from our inquiry that in many cases the link between a patent and the product or process to which it applies is a relatively tenuous one – as, for example, when the patent is minor or trivial (or perhaps substantially invalid – or even defunct), or when it attaches merely to one fairly small part, phase or feature of the product or process concerned. Should exemption for restrictive conditions in agreements relating to the markets for such products (imposed, say, by a firm that is a dominant supplier in its field) be obtained on the strength of minimal patent coverage, this would appear to be contrary to the spirit and intention both of restrictive practices legislation and of the Patents Act itself.

We hasten to say that exemption would not necessarily be given for restrictions of a registrable sort in dubious cases of the type referred to, should they come to the attention of the restrictive practices authorities. The important point is that few agreements in which patent arrangements play a part have in fact come to the Registrar's attention, and no decisions defining the extent of exemptions have (so far as we know) yet been made by the Restrictive Practices Court.

The reasons for this are not entirely clear to us as laymen. Undoubtedly the very explicit exemption made in the 1956 Act for restrictions relating to patented goods is an important factor. Firms normally take special care to avoid restrictions in licence agreements that are clearly registrable (e.g., restrictions, accepted by more than one party to the agreement, relating to unpatented goods and processes), and there appears a fairly widespread (and, strictly, incorrect) presumption in industry that all restrictions thought to have any connection with patented goods in licence agreements would be found exempt. While the Registrar, for his part, is required to investigate and take some action on every agreement falling within the Act, he cannot do so in cases that he does not know about, and it is difficult to see, given the Act as it presently stands, how he could effectively proceed to fill this gap.

In this respect, the Patents Act is of very little help. Since there is no sanction in the Act compelling inclusion of a licence on the Register of Patents until litigation is in prospect, and even then only the barest outline of the licence is recorded, the Patent Office's knowledge of the numbers and contents of licence agreements is very incomplete. In the absence of more extensive and precise knowledge, it is hard for anyone concerned with this problem to assess the seriousness of restrictive provisions and the nature and genuineness of the patent coverage involved.

Our second area of concern in this connection is the legality of restrictive know-how provisions in licence agreements. The current legal position in the U.K. is that all restrictions on the *exchange* of manufacturing know-how and similar technical information, including exclusive grant-back provisions, are allowable, whether or not the know-how relates to a patented product or process.[1] On the other hand, restrictions on the *use* of know-how in manufacture, including limitations on the territorial areas in which the know-how can be used or the prices or quantities of output to which know-how is applied, fall within the list of registrable restrictions specified in Section 6(1) of the 1956 Act (provided the other conditions for registration are met) – except that such restrictions are not registrable if they relate to a patented product or process which is licensed. It is also provided in Section 8(5) of the 1956 Act that restrictions on the *descriptions of goods* to be produced by processes which are the subject of know-how agreements are exempt from registration, whether or not the processes are patented.

In other words, where a know-how agreement exists between two U.K. firms (or, as is more likely, between a U.K. firm and a foreign firm with a U.K. manufacturing subsidiary), the grantor of know-how may quite legally insist, not only on non-divulgence of the know-how to third parties, but also on the provision of secret return flows of future know-how. Furthermore, the grantor may quite legitimately restrict the types of goods to which the know-how is applied, whether patents are involved or not, and may stipulate (in a one-way transfer) that the recipient may not use the know-how to compete in his (the grantor's) own territorial markets. Finally, although restrictions on the use of know-how in the U.K., if accepted by more than one party (e.g., in a reciprocal transfer), would normally be registrable under the Restrictive Practices Act, exemption can in effect be obtained if the parties have patents on the product or process to which the know-how applies, and if the restrictions relate to that product or process.

These exemptions for restrictions on the use of know-how relating to patented products raise the same types of problems as those referred to earlier. In many cases, the link between the patent and the product or process in respect of which know-how is supplied appears to be tenuous or minor – as for instance when the patent is on a single stage or feature

[1] The reader should not be misled by the fact that the Restrictive Practices Act was amended in 1968 to give the Board of Trade (now D.T.I.) power to include 'information agreements' by Order. This amendment has been interpreted as not covering agreements for the exchange or use of manufacturing know-how; the only Order so far made applies to agreements for supplying information on prices and terms of trade.

of a multi-stage manufacturing process requiring considerable technical expertise for its implementation – and in these cases it seems questionable whether restrictions on the markets for which the know-how can be used should escape registration. There is indeed no guarantee that complex agreements for the restricted use of processes involving both know-how and patents would be granted exemption if they came before the restrictive practices authorities, but again the problem is that few have been brought to the Registrar's attention, and no decisions defining the exemptions have been made.

As stated earlier, we are not concerned at the moment to assess the arguments in principle for and against exempting genuinely patent-based technology from the provisions of restrictive practices legislation. Our point here is that it is relatively easy to obtain patents of some sort on products or processes in the chemical and engineering fields, with the result that patent licences are almost always incorporated in know-how agreements; consequently, even such know-how restrictions as are registrable under Section 6(1) of the 1956 Act (a type that could, we believe, be of considerable industrial importance) have in effect fallen outside the scope of the legislation. It is probably not an exaggeration to say that, in some branches of these industries, patents are used at least in part as a device for shielding what are essentially restrictive two-way technology-using agreements from the scrutiny of the Restrictive Practices authorities.

It also causes us concern that all restrictions relating to the use of know-how in one-way agreements, and all types of provisions for the non-divulgence of technology covered by licence or know-how agreements (in particular exclusive grant-back provisions), are entirely legal and exempt from official inspection in the U.K. By comparison, know-how restrictions (including restrictions on the divulgence of know-how) appear to be far from immune from official surveillance in the U.S.A., where they may fall foul of antitrust legislation. While the legal status of such restrictions is not wholly clear in the U.S.A., expert opinion suggests that a provision in a licence agreement for a secret return flow of technical know-how, whether accompanied by patents or not, would probably be found illegal.[1] Similarly, restrictions on use of know-how in a cross-licence might well be found illegal, as might restrictions governing prices, markets etc. for patented goods. Because of the highly dubious status of such provisions in the U.S.A. most companies are said to avoid them in licensing agreements with American companies or with subsidiaries of American firms.

---

[1] D. Edmunds Brazell, *Manufacturing Under Licence* (Kenneth Mason, Havant, Hampshire, 1967) pp. 63–4 and 137–8. But see also A. D. Neale, *The Antitrust Laws of the U.S.A.*, pp. 411–12.

*Impact of E.E.C. membership*

It is finally worth noting that the rules of the European Economic Community regarding competition and intra-Community trade forbid certain types of restrictions in agreements involving E.E.C. firms, including patent licence agreements. The relevant parts of the Rome Treaty are Article 36, which provides for the preservation of industrial and commercial property rights, but adds that their exercise shall not be used as a disguised restriction on trade between member states; and the two rules of competition – Article 85, which prohibits all kinds of agreements that restrain competition and may affect trade between member states, and Article 86, which prohibits the improper use of a monopoly position in the Common Market. Article 85 does not apply to purely domestic agreements or those affecting trade between a member state and countries outside the Community, unless such agreements perceptibly affect inter-member trade. Section 3 of Article 85 provides for the exemption of agreements and collective practices which either improve production or distribution or promote economic progress.[1]

The question of what is and is not permissible in patent licensing etc. under the Rome Treaty has been the subject of a number of E.E.C. Commission decisions and judgments by the European Court. Probably the most important recent case was that of *Deutsche Grammophon Gesellschaft v. Metro S.B. Grossmarkt*, the judgment in which seems to be forming the basis of the E.E.C.'s present thinking on this question.[2] The implication of the judgment in this and other cases is that firms operating in the E.E.C. will not normally be permitted to impose or accept restrictions in patent licence agreements that have the effect of restraining trade between member states. Thus, for example, a West German firm will not be permitted to license another firm to supply, say, the French market but not the German one, where this would mean banning exports from France to West Germany. Thus, the E.E.C. must be regarded as a single market for licensing as for other purposes.

It can therefore be seen that membership of the E.E.C. will bring with it quite significant limitations on the freedom of licensing action hitherto enjoyed by U.K. firms.[3] For example, after membership,

---

[1] There are three main regulations concerned with these articles: Regulation 17 of 1962, Regulation 19 of 1965 and Regulation 67 of 1967. See *European Communities; Secondary Legislation* (H.M.S.O., 1972) Part 4.

[2] *1971 Common Market Law Reports 631*. Although this case related to the restrictive use of copyrights, the judgment is regarded as a 'landmark' decision which will probably be applied generally to agreements for the licensing of commercial property rights or know-how.

[3] All agreements, decisions and concerted practices involving U.K. enterprises concluded after 1 January 1973 to which Article 85 of the E.E.C. Treaty or Article 65 of the E.C.S.C. Treaty are applicable will have to be notified to the E.E.C. Commission in conformity

they will not normally be permitted to confine, or accept confinement of, selling rights to particular parts of the E.E.C. in agreements granting manufacturing rights within the E.E.C. Moreover, there is even some question as to whether E.E.C. firms will be permitted to deny others (including non-E.E.C. firms) manufacturing or selling rights for the entire E.E.C. under their patents, where this could lead to a perceptible restraint on intra-Community trade – as, for example, where a prospective licensee might set up a large plant in the E.E.C. to supply more than one member country. Bearing in mind our evidence on the frequency of territorial restrictions and the predominance of international licensing reported earlier in this chapter, it seems clear that these limitations on E.E.C. licensors could impinge on many licence agreements involving U.K. firms after the U.K. joins the E.E.C. Whether these E.E.C. rules, so far as they relate to patent licensing, will greatly increase the competitive pressures felt by U.K. industry is much harder to say; the answer to that must of course depend on the answer to a central question of our study – namely, the importance of patent monopolies in restraining competition (from domestic manufacture or imports) in the U.K.

### B.   PURE KNOW-HOW LICENSING

Since one of the main objects of our study is to assess how far the transfer of technical information between companies depends on patents, it seemed advisable to discover something about know-how licensing that takes place unaccompanied by patents (i.e., 'pure' know-how licensing).

Of the 29 companies that responded to the appropriate section of our questionnaire (Form A, Section V), 19 said that they did have 'pure' know-how agreements with outsiders in 1968, and 10 replied that they did not. All fields of industry were well represented in the positive category but, as will appear below, the more numerous and important agreements tended to be in the mechanical engineering field.

Of those responding with positive answers, only 12 were able to give complete details; the results for these are summarised in Table 7.3, which includes agreements involving no payments as well as those with payments. Several interesting points emerge from this admittedly rather fragmentary evidence. Firstly, it seems that relatively little pure know-how licensing takes place between essentially British firms, and that the amounts of money involved are probably very small – this would be true even if an allowance for under-reporting were made. But on the

with the regulations existing in the Common Market. A six-month transition period before notification will be allowed for agreements in existence on 1 January 1973.

TABLE 7.3. *Pure know-how licensing by twelve responding companies*

| | |
|---|---:|
| 1. Number of outsiders with whom agreements existed in 1968: | |
| (i) companies operating mainly in the U.K. | 18 |
| (ii) companies operating mainly overseas | 102 |
| Total | 120 |
| 2. Industrial field covered: | |
| (i) chemicals[a] | 36 |
| (ii) electrical engineering | 14 |
| (iii) mechanical engineering | 70 |
| Total | 120 |
| 3. Payments to responding companies in 1968 from: | |
| (i) companies operating mainly in the U.K. (£'000) | 60[b] |
| (ii) companies operating mainly overseas (£'000) | 360[b] |
| Total | 420[b] |
| 4. Payments by responding companies in 1968 to: | |
| (i) companies operating mainly in the U.K. (£'000) | 10[b] |
| (ii) companies operating mainly overseas (£'000) | 20[b] |
| Total | 30[b] |

NOTES:

[a] Includes a few agreements in the synthetic fibres field.

[b] These figures are approximate, and incomplete in so far as some firms could not readily distinguish pure know-how payments from other licence payments. In such cases, the normal procedure was to include all payments under patent licences (see Chapter 8, page 162).

other hand it appears that a significant amount of pure know-how transfer takes place between British and foreign firms, and that British firms occasionally obtain appreciable income in this way. (The figures do not, however, reveal the fact that the bulk of pure know-how receipts shown above was reported by one company in the components branch of the mechanical engineering field).

Secondly, more than half the licensing activity shown occurs in mechanical engineering. Since U.K. production by the mechanical engineering firms concerned is only about 8 per cent of total production in this particular sample, it seems safe to conclude that pure know-how licensing is more prominent in relation to productive operations in this field than in the other fields investigated. This impression was confirmed in discussions with firms not in this sample.

Admittedly, numbers of agreements and payments may be misleading indicators of the economic importance of licensing in various fields, especially where intangibles like know-how are involved. In many of the agreements under discussion the purpose is to exchange know-how on a reciprocal basis, payments entering only as a balancing item where required; in a few, the know-how licence is part of an arrangement in which the licensor acquires a financial interest in the licensee which is not reflected in cash payments. It is hardly necessary to point out that these considerations apply equally to patent licensing.

We therefore attempted to supplement these data by asking respondents about the value of pure know-how exchanged under licence, and several companies said that they valued the flows quite highly – although in thousands rather than hundreds of thousands of pounds. There is no doubt that know-how is exchanged quite extensively and quite successfully in some (mainly engineering) fields without the aid of patents. Moreover the exchange is not confined to the industrial giants; it is also found among companies of more modest size that have shown ability to develop new technology in their special areas and have built up technical associations with similar companies (mainly overseas) – albeit sometimes with the help of patents in the initial stages.

Against this evidence we have to set the views of numerous industrialists to whom we talked, who were convinced that patents are normally an essential element in know-how transfers, and that such transfers would be seriously hampered in the absence of patents. This is clearly an issue which is at the heart of our study, and we shall explore it further in due course.

C. INTRA-GROUP LICENSING

One of the striking features of official figures of international technology payments is the large proportion accounted for by payments between subsidiary companies and their parents. According to figures published by the Board of Trade, about one-third of technological and related royalties etc. received by U.K. companies from overseas in 1968 consisted of payments from branches, subsidiaries and associated companies.[1] Intra-group licensing clearly accounts for a substantial portion of all licensing and it can hardly be ignored in the present study. At the same time, we did not wish to devote a great deal of attention to this type of licensing, since it did not promise to raise any new issues of importance.

Several companies in our inquiry pointed out that the use of licensing as a means of transferring technology within a group of companies is primarily a response to the comparative tax situation in Britain and overseas. Where taxes on profits are higher overseas than in the U.K., it is in the interest of a group with overseas investments to minimise the

---

[1] *Board of Trade Journal*, 25 March 1970.

proportion of profit from these investments that arises overseas. One way of doing this is to maximise royalties and similar payments to the parent company, for these are normally tax-free expenses of the paying company, or at least bear relatively low rates of tax. In some tax jurisdictions, royalties are deductible from profits for tax purposes only if they are explicitly provided for in licence agreements; in others, the authorities do not insist on formal licensing, although a reference to patents in a service or management contract may greatly help in per-suading the tax authorities to approve payments. Where the tax authorities are inclined to be strict about royalties, there is therefore an incentive to set up formal intra-group licences, or at least to provide in an explicit general agreement that the overseas subsidiaries have rights under the group's patents.[1]

Replies to the relevant section of our questionnaire (Form A, Section IV) suggest that the policy of the great majority of groups is to make patents and know-how available to subsidiaries wherever they are required.[2] Thus, of the 28 respondents to this section (most of which were large groups or members of groups), only one indicated that a large measure of selectivity was normally exercised in making patents and know-how available to overseas subsidiaries, while three appeared to exercise some minor selectivity in relation to their U.K. subsidiaries.

Of the 28 companies that replied, only five (including those that were 'selective') normally handle intra-group transfers of patents etc. through formal licence agreements. (Three were in chemicals and two in mechanical engineering.) The rest either had no formal arrangements for exchange of technology or normally dealt with it through general group technical service or management contracts. Such contracts can by no stretch of the imagination be termed licence agreements; they typically refer to patents very briefly and in the most general of ways. They provide for technical service or management fees which notionally include patent and know-how royalties but which have no discernible connection with output under licence, being normally calculated on a rather arbitrary basis (a common formula being two or three per cent of subsidiaries' sales).

Inevitably quite large sums can arise in this way and they probably account for a good deal of what appear as international technology payments in the Board of Trade's report. By comparison, royalties and other fees arising from intra-group licensing of the more formal sort

---

[1] In some cases, foreign patents are assigned to principal overseas subsidiaries – especially where the group is distinctly multi-national in character – but this is for administrative rather than tax reasons.

[2] Our questions in this section were confined to licensing between parents and subsidiaries; associates that are not subsidiaries were counted as outsiders. There is no doubt that most parents are more selective in their policy towards the latter than towards subsidiaries.

probably do not add up to very much; thus receipts by the five or so groups in our sample that reported receiving such payments in 1968 were about £600,000 from overseas members and about £100,000 from U.K. members of the group.[1]

We would therefore conclude that while patents are in some cases a useful device for minimising the burden of overseas tax on earnings from foreign subsidiaries, they have no real bearing on the transmission of inventions and associated know-how within groups of companies, either nationally or internationally. If the parent management of a group of companies wishes to limit the spread of technical developments in the group, it does not need the backing of patent monopolies to reinforce its control over subsidiaries, and there seems no inclination whatever in industry to use patents for this purpose.

[1] These amounts do not of course include royalties etc. from outsiders collected by subsidiaries on behalf of their parents.

# 8. PATENTING AND LICENSING IN PRACTICE: RELATIONS TO RESEARCH AND PRODUCTION

When measures of patenting and licensing activity are related to such magnitudes as research and production, large variations are encountered between industries and firms, and generalisation becomes extremely difficult. Much variation is attributable to differences in the research content and supply conditions of different types of output, and our inquiry accordingly sought some information by category of production in the hope that greater consistency might be found within particular categories. The object of the current chapter is to present a summary of these data and to comment on the points arising from them.

Companies were asked to report separately for up to four principal categories of production, with the balance in 'other' if desired. The choice of categories was left to respondents, except that they were referred to the minimum list headings of the Standard Industrial Classification as an indication of the sort of breakdown envisaged. Most managed to provide suitably detailed categories, usually corresponding to their major product groups or subsidiaries for which separate accounting and similar information is normally available. Some preferred for convenience to confine the data to a selection of their major activities, but this did not matter so long as all relevant figures reported by a firm were on the same basis.

A certain amount of grouping of categories was necessary on our part in order to preserve the confidentiality of the data disclosed to us, and for that reason as well as because of the breadth of some reported production, the categories in our tables are more heterogeneous than would be ideal for our purpose. Most of the categories shown are in fact collections of loosely-related products rather than homogeneous outputs and themselves contain quite wide variations in some of the important ratios examined. Nevertheless, they do indicate quite effectively the diversity that exists within broad industrial fields.

With the exception of the oil companies, whose chemical activities could not be included in every table, most companies in our sample of 30 were able to supply all or virtually all the data needed for this part of the exercise and the remainder supplied the great bulk. For the latter, we were obliged to estimate certain items using publicly available information, including annual accounts and other published material, but we made it a rule to consult those concerned in cases where our results were significantly affected. It must be emphasised, however, that our figures are often no more than reasonable orders of magnitude, sometimes reflecting quite heroic approximations by the respondents concerned. Since our conclusions here are seldom sensitive to even quite large margins of error, this is not itself a critical drawback to the exercise.

Further notes on the conduct of the inquiry, the companies concerned, and their importance in national R & D aggregates, etc., can be found in Appendix B.

### A.   PROPENSITY TO PATENT

We examine first the rate at which new patents are generated in relation to R & D expenditure. By introducing the ratio of R & D expenditure to sales of production ('research intensity') we can also obtain a rough idea of the importance of patent activity in relation to output in the various categories.

These considerations are relevant to the impact of the patent system in several ways. For example, the usefulness of the system as a means of protecting industrial research and innovation is likely to be affected to some extent by the frequency with which R & D gives rise to patents; there will probably be little scope for such protection where a mere trickle of patents results from a large R & D effort – unless those patents are of exceptional importance. Furthermore, the impact of patent protection is likely to be affected by the size of R & D expenditure in relation to the total operations of a firm; it seems reasonable to expect that patents will be more capable of encouraging R & D (other things being equal) in a research-based field than in a field where research is, for scientific or technical reasons, a minor activity.

In other words, areas of industry which are highly dependent on invention and innovation are likely to be the strongest candidates for patent protection, while the opportunity for such protection will depend among other things on the rate at which the R & D concerned generates patents.

The relevant information from our inquiry is summarised in Table 8.1, which shows new U.K. patents generated by British R & D in various categories of production, together with R & D expenditure and sales, for the 30 companies comprising our main sample. Industry groups are ranked in accordance with research intensity as measured in the final column, as are categories within each group.

The rate at which R & D effort leads to new patents is shown in column (3). One feature that emerges quite clearly is the large variation in this rate between different categories, even in the same broad industrial field. Thus both the highest and lowest rates shown are found in 'finished and specialty' chemicals, where plastics, dyestuffs, etc., generate nine times as many patents per unit of R & D expenditure as soaps and detergents. The relatively low rates of patent activity in pharmaceuticals and 'cosmetic, food and crop chemicals' (mainly toilet preparations, food flavourings and weedkillers, pesticides, etc.[1]) are particularly noteworthy. They probably reflect among other things the very high proportion of 'unsuccessful' research that goes into the discovery of new drugs, weedkillers and similar products; the high cost of extensive testing for toxic and other undesirable side effects that is prescribed by the food and drug authorities in the U.S.A. and, more recently, the U.K.; and the difficulty of obtaining patents on human treatments, medicines, etc. The latter difficulty may be attributed not only to the non-patentability of human and medical treatments as such, but also to the breadth of coverage of existing patents, and the extent of knowledge held to be already in the public domain in these fields.

Two technical points should be mentioned in connection with these results. Firstly, R & D expenditure is shown before deducting payments from 'outsiders' (primarily the Government). As indicated in the notes to the table, these payments were important in electrical engineering, and quite appreciable in mechanical engineering. However, when patent propensity is under consideration, the gross figures for R & D seem preferable, since propensity to patent is itself not likely to be affected by the source of R & D funds. Secondly, our measure of patent propensity is somewhat depressed overall by the fact that we compare an average of patents granted in 1966–8 (in order to eliminate the large annual fluctuations that sometimes occur in this item within some sections of industry) with R & D expenditure in 1968. Ideally, a lag of several years should be introduced into this comparison to allow for the lapse of time that normally occurs in patent processing, but this was not possible because we felt it necessary to limit our request for R & D figures to the most recent year available. This defect in the data probably has little effect when comparing patent propensities between categories, which is our main purpose here. Had a time lag of about two years been introduced, the rate for each industry would be raised somewhat; for example, that for chemicals would move from 17 to about 21 patents (1968) per £ million of R & D (in 1966).[2]

---

[1] This unusual combination was adopted partly in order to maintain confidentiality of data; but these particular products do have important features in common – they are for the most part relatively specialised, or at least non-bulk chemical formulations manufactured, like drugs, to high non-toxicity and purity standards, and used either directly in human consumption or indirectly through agriculture or food processing.

[2] These figures do not compare closely with those given earlier (for 1958–60) in Table 4.3,

A measure of 'research intensity' in the various production categories appears in column (6). As might be expected, electronic and associated equipment (mainly computers, data processing equipment, automatic control systems, radar systems and other sophisticated equipment in the electronic and radio field), electronic components and pharmaceuticals emerge as the most R & D-intensive lines of activity in our sample. Other categories that register well above the sample average are telecommunications and broadcasting equipment and food and crop chemicals. The ratio is also high in certain lines that could not be shown separately for confidentiality reasons – for example, sophisticated chemicals in the 'plastics and dyestuffs' category, of which silicones and other new plastics materials are special instances reported in our sample. It is also no surprise to find that the ratios for 'other' basic chemicals (mainly fertilisers, industrial gases and other bulk industrial chemicals) and for soap and detergent products are relatively low – as are those for man-made fibres and for the category shown as 'other' at the bottom of the table (a collection of miscellaneous categories that did not fit into the main fields covered).

It must be admitted that the use of sales as denominator of the research ratio for production categories is open to a number of reservations. In particular, the ratio calculated in this way is affected by the relationship between sales and gross output for particular types of production, which may be an appreciable distorting factor where products are largely retained by their manufacturers for further processing or assembly in finished products; and also by the relationship between gross and net output, which will of course vary considerably with the input content of particular categories. While ratios based on net output would doubtless have been preferable, the necessary data were not readily available from responding firms and we had therefore to limit ourselves to the measure as shown. For this and other reasons (see Appendix B, page 375), our figures here probably slightly understate the level of research intensity in finished products and equipment relative to that in components and basic materials.

column (3), for the following main reasons: (i) the figures of patents given earlier include those arising on work done overseas (nowadays about two-thirds of total new U.K. patents) and those attributable to small inventors (now probably about one-third of total new U.K. patents); (ii) growth of U.K. R & D has been much faster than that of U.K.-originating patents. Thus R & D (at current prices) approximately doubled between 1958 and 1966, whereas grants of U.K.-originating patents appear to have risen by only about 15 per cent between 1960 and 1968. (See *Comptroller's Report 1968*, Appendix C.)

TABLE 8.1. *Patents, R & D and sales in selected categories of production, 30 responding companies, 1968*

| Category of production[a] | (1) New U.K. patents[b] | (2) R & D expenditure in U.K.[c] (£m) | (3) New patents per £m of R & D | (4) Sales of U.K. production[d] (£m) | (5) Of which, exports (£m) | (6) Ratio of R & D to sales, (2)÷(4) (%) |
|---|---|---|---|---|---|---|
| **Electrical engineering** | | | | | | |
| Electronic, radio, T.V. and associated equipment | 230 | 24·7 | 9 | 176 | 36 | 13½ |
| Electronic components | 180 | 7·5 | 24 | 101 | 18 | 7½ |
| Telecommunications and broadcasting equipment | 140 | 7·2 | 19 | 132 | 26 | 5½ |
| Other electrical machinery and equipment | 230 | 11·1 | 21 | 251 | 45 | 4½ |
| Total | 780 | 50·5 | 16 | 660 | 125 | 7½ |
| **Chemicals** | | | | | | |
| *Finished and Specialty* | | | | | | |
| Pharmaceuticals | 70 | 7·1 | 10 | 63 | 25 | 11½ |
| Plastics, dyestuffs, paints etc. | 160 | 3·4 | 45 | 162 | 57 | 2 |
| Cosmetic, food and crop chemicals | ⎱ 40 | ⎱ 6·7 | ⎰ 7 | ⎱ 290 | ⎱ 45 | ⎰ 5½ |
| Soap and detergents | ⎰ | ⎰ | ⎱ 5 | ⎰ | ⎰ | ⎱ 1½ |
| Sub-total | 270 | 17·2 | 16 | 524 | 127 | 3½ |
| *Basic chemicals* | | | | | | |
| Petrochemicals[e] | x | 5·2[f] | x | 207[f] | 36 | 2½ |
| Other | x | 3·3 | x | 236 | 42 | 1½ |
| Sub-total | 160 | 8·5 | 19 | 443 | 78 | 2 |
| Total | 430 | 25·7 | 17 | 966 | 204 | 2½ |
| **Mechanical engineering** | | | | | | |
| Plant, machinery and equipment | 110 | 5·1 | 22 | 195 | 35 | 2½ |
| Components and materials | 60 | 2·2 | 28 | 119 | 20 | 2 |
| Total | 170 | 7·3 | 24 | 314 | 56 | 2½ |
| Man-made fibres | 130 | 7·6 | 17 | 362[f] | 90 | 2 |
| Other[g] | 60 | 6·8 | 9 | 745 | 74 | 1 |
| Total | 1,570 | 97·9 | 16 | 3,047 | 550 | 3 |

NOTES:

[a] Categories are as fine as can be given without divulging confidential information. In some cases (e.g., 'cosmetic, food and crop chemicals') groupings were adopted partly to avoid breaching our confidentiality guarantees.

[b] U.K. patents granted on R & D carried out wholly or almost wholly in the U.K.; annual averages, 1966–8; rounded to nearest ten.

(*Notes continued overleaf*)

c Includes R & D financed from external sources (mainly Government). Amounts in 1968 were as follows:

|                        | £m.   |
| ---------------------- | ----- |
| Electrical engineering | 16·4  |
| Mechanical engineering | 1·0   |
| Chemicals              | 0·2   |
| Man-made fibres        | 0     |
| Other                  | 0     |
| Total                  | 17·6  |

d U.K. sales *plus* exports (including sales to overseas subsidiaries etc.), except in the case of petrochemicals and man-made fibres, for which we estimated the selling value of output, including output retained for further processing by the responding company.

e This category comprises the entire U.K. chemical activities of the two oil companies in our main sample, including their agricultural chemicals, plastics and other derivatives; *x* indicates that figures have been omitted on confidentiality grounds.

f Partly authors' estimates.

g A miscellaneous group of products that do not fit into the chemical, engineering and man-made fibres fields.

## *Patent propensity and scale of R & D*

In view of the use that has been made of patents in the empirical literature on innovation and firm size, it seems desirable to review the evidence from the inquiry on the behaviour of patent propensity among firms – or rather R & D programmes – of different size.

As observed earlier, the data collected in the inquiry were not primarily intended for this sort of statistical exercise and are not very well suited to it, since the number of firms in the sample is rather small and they were deliberately chosen to cover a wide range of production categories. There seems to be little to be gained therefore from a simple correlation of patent propensity with R & D expenditure for the 30 firms in the sample without allowing for differences in their industrial activities, diversification, etc.

However, one method of approach that goes some way towards allowing for these factors is to correlate patent propensity with R & D expenditure in each of the main industrial fields covered, counting as separate observations each category of production reported by each firm. In this way patent propensity in broadly related lines of activity is correlated with size of R & D units or 'divisions' within firms. This approach has the advantage that it allows to some extent for diversification of R & D activities within firms, while at the same time following the type of broad industrial classification normally used in empirical studies.

Some results of this exercise are given in Table 8.2, which presents summary figures for the three principal industry groups covered. It should be pointed out that while most of the R & D 'divisions' here represent portions of companies or groups of companies, some represent

TABLE 8.2. *Patent propensity and size of R & D expenditure in divisions of responding companies*[a]

| Size of R & D division (£'000) | No. of divisions | New U.K. patents 1966–8 (average) | R & D expenditure (1968: £m) | R & D expenditure per division (£m) | New patents per £m of R & D |
|---|---|---|---|---|---|
| | | (a) Mechanical engineering | | | |
| Less than 250 | 4 | 7 | 0·18 | 0·1 | 40 |
| 250–500 | 4 | 42 | 1·48 | 0·4 | 28 |
| 500–1,000 | 3 | 67 | 2·25 | 0·8 | 30 |
| Over 1,000 | 3 | 58 | 3·40 | 1·1 | 17 |
| Total | 14 | 174 | 7·31 | 0·5 | 24 |
| | | (b) Chemicals | | | |
| Less than 750 | 4 | 54 | 2·36 | 0·6 | 23 |
| 750–1,500 | 6 | 204 | 6·80 | 1·1 | 30 |
| 1,500–2,250 | 2 | 29 | 3·70 | 1·9 | 8 |
| Over 2,250 | 5 | 140 | 12·80 | 2·6 | 11 |
| Total | 17 | 427 | 25·66 | 1·5 | 17 |
| | | (c) Electrical engineering | | | |
| Less than 1,000 | 3 | 100 | 1·46 | 0·5 | 68 |
| 1,000–2,000 | 3 | 92 | 4·44 | 1·5 | 21 |
| 2,000–3,000 | 3 | 138 | 6·80 | 2·3 | 20 |
| Over 3,000 | 5 | 454 | 37·80 | 7·6 | 12 |
| Total | 14 | 784 | 50·50 | 3·6 | 16 |

NOTE:
[a] A 'division' here corresponds essentially to one category of production reported by one company.

entire companies. The principle behind the table was to combine in one 'division' all categories reported by a firm that have a similar R & D background, and to distinguish as separate divisions those that have different R & D backgrounds.

The main point arising from the table is that there is a pronounced decline in the level of patent activity per unit of R & D expenditure as the size of the R & D division increases. The decline is particularly marked in electrical engineering, but appears quite strongly in the other two groups as well.

Regression analysis is of limited usefulness where the samples are so small and where powerful unmeasured factors affect the behaviour of the dependent variable, but the results of regressing numbers of patents on size of R & D division do suggest that, whereas the decline in patent propensity shown for mechanical engineering might have arisen by chance, reasonable confidence can be placed in the declines in the other two fields. More particularly, the tests suggest that patent propensity diminishes with increasing size of R & D division in the electrical field, while numbers of patents per division are not affected by size of R & D division in our chemical sample. (Inevitably where this is the case the average level of patents per unit of R & D expenditure tends to decrease as size of R & D effort increases.) The regression results for mechanical engineering suggest that patent activity does increase more or less with size of R & D division, but are inconclusive as to the precise nature of the response.[1]

These findings of a decline in patent activity per unit of R & D as R & D increases, for two of the fields examined if not definitely for all three, are capable of interpretation in a number of different ways. One possibility is that large R & D divisions are more secretive about their R & D results (or more neglectful of the patent possibilities) than small, but this seems most improbable; it would conflict, for example, with our earlier finding that very few firms in the inquiry refrain from patenting on grounds of secrecy to any appreciable extent, while in general few patent opportunities were thought to be overlooked.[2]

A second conceivable interpretation is that smaller R & D divisions are more efficient at doing effective R & D than larger ones – i.e., that the former produce more patentable inventions of a given average quality (economic value) per £ of expenditure than larger ones, either because they are better managed or staffed or because there are over-

---

[1] Results for the regression of patent activity ($P$, number of patents granted to an R & D division) on R & D ($R$, £ million spent by the division) are as follows (standard errors being in parentheses):

Electrical engineering:    $P = 21\cdot8 + 9\cdot4R$         $r^2 = 0\cdot33$
                           $(19\cdot8)$ $(3\cdot9)$
Mechanical engineering: $P = 1\cdot9 + 20\cdot2R$         $r^2 = 0\cdot44$
                           $(4\cdot4)$  $(6\cdot6)$
Chemicals: $r^2 = 0\cdot03$

In electrical engineering, the large positive constant (admittedly differing from zero at no more than about the 70 per cent level of probability), together with an $r^2$ of $0\cdot33$, suggest that $P/R$ diminishes as $R$ increases in this field. The constant for mechanical engineering, while positive – and not small when it is recalled that $R$ in this field is typically well under £1 million – is manifestly unreliable when account is taken of its standard error. We cannot therefore rule out that $P/R$ might be fairly constant as between R & D efforts of differing size in this field. In chemicals, there is clearly no association between $P$ and $R$, at least on the basis of this approach, and $P/R$ must therefore tend to diminish as $R$ increases.

[2] One commentator made the point that the number of patents applied for on an invention may vary a good deal depending on the purpose of the patentee and the subject matter of the invention. For example, where the purpose is to bolster up a cross-licence exchange, numerous patents may be applied for on quite minor aspects of an R & D programme, whereas where the purpose is merely to give 'defensive' cover, a handful of applications may suffice.

While this helps to explain the large variations in patent propensity noted between individual R & D divisions, there seems little reason to expect systematic differences between large and small divisions on this account.

whelming diseconomies of scale in the R & D activities covered. Although we do not have enough data to disprove either of these possibilities, it must be said that they both seem very implausible on the basis of impressions obtained in the course of the inquiry. There seemed to be no evidence of widespread scale diseconomies of the strength necessary to explain the differences in efficiency that are implied in this interpretation, while systematic variation in managerial ability, employee ingenuity, etc. with size of R & D unit seems most improbable.

A third possibility and one that seems rather more plausible is that larger R & D divisions tend to undertake more 'development' in proportion to research than smaller ones; if, as seems certainly the case, the development and application of inventions require more resources on average than the research work leading up to them, this would help to explain the apparent tendency for smaller units to patent more in relation to their resource inputs than larger ones.

While this reasoning is attractive, it is not supported by the rather slim information we were able to gather on the relative shares of research and development in R & D expenditure. Only 18 of our 30 sample companies were prepared to offer an estimate on what some regarded as an indefinable distinction, and many stressed that their figures were little more than rough guesses. The results for three size-groups of companies are summarised in Table 8.3, which refers to entire companies since no estimates were obtainable by category of production.

It appears on the basis of this evidence that, if anything, 'research' comprises a slightly higher proportion of R & D expenditure by larger companies in our sample than small, although the underlying figures reveal no clear trend. This is somewhat at odds with what might be expected, but we should again emphasise the arbitrariness of the distinction between 'R' and 'D', together with the lack of a breakdown by production category. (The percentages here are undoubtedly affected by differences in the industry-mix of large and small firms; thus, for example, all the mechanical engineering firms – which tend to do comparatively little 'research' in proportion to 'development' – included here happened to have R & D of less than £1 million in 1968).

If none of the preceding considerations is capable of explaining much of the behaviour of patent propensity depicted in Table 8.2, the variations shown there must be attributable to one or both of two remaining sets of factors. These may be summed up respectively as variations in the average *quality* of patents and variations in the average *patentability* of R & D activities undertaken by large and small R & D divisions.

Taking the latter set of considerations first, it can be argued that

TABLE 8.3. *'Research' as a proportion of R & D expenditure by 18 responding companies*

| Size of company R & D expenditure (£m per annum) | No. of companies | Research expenditure (1968: £m) | R & D (1968: £m) | Share of research in R & D (%) |
|---|---|---|---|---|
| Less than 1 | 7 | 0·59 | 2·42 | 24 |
| 1–3 | 4 | 2·33 | 5·22 | 45 |
| Over 3 | 7 | 15·35 | 55·56 | 28 |
| Total | 18 | 18·27 | 63·20 | 29 |

smaller R & D units engage in work which is on the whole more patent-oriented than that of larger units; there is moreover some evidence from our sample to support this. Thus, R & D in the production categories which appear in Table 8.1 as displaying higher patent propensities – e.g., plastics, dyestuffs and paints, electronic components and industrial plant, machinery and equipment – tends on the whole to be performed in smaller divisions than that in, say, petroleum chemicals, soaps and detergents, electronic computers, data and control systems, man-made fibres and so forth, although the picture is not at all a regular or consistent one. A number of explanations can be suggested. There appears in particular to be some truth in the argument that a good deal of expenditure in the larger R & D divisions is on work that is rather remote from basic technological discovery, being concerned with the organisation, assembly and formulation of sets of equipment, mixtures or combinations of substances such as detergents, motor oils, etc. or with the improvement of large-scale industrial processes, rather than the invention of the materials and components or the basic processes themselves. Such innovatory activities may be both costly and valuable in relation to the more basic work of invention, and they tend in certain of the areas of industry examined to require large organisations to accomplish them effectively. In these cases, they are likely to be counted as formal research activities, whereas in smaller organisations they are inclined to pass as informal management or engineering activities.

Turning finally to the question of the average quality of patents, it is arguable that some part of the decline in patent propensity with size in Table 8.2 reflects a higher average resource input by larger R & D units into the origination (as well as the subsequent development – discussed above) of patented products and processes. Provided that the average return on research activity does not vary greatly between large and small divisions (an assumption which we cannot test because of the non-availability of profit data by category of production, but which seems a reasonable approximation for present purposes), this would imply that the average economic value per patent is higher on the whole for larger than for smaller R & D divisions in the sample. (It does not necessarily imply, of course, that the 'best' patented products and processes of smaller divisions are not as economically valuable as the best of larger divisions – or more.so.) While it is impossible with the information we could collect to test this argument properly, it is at least as plausible as the view that attributes declining patent propensity with size to superior inventive efficiency on the part of smaller R & D units.

Whatever the truth or otherwise of the various interpretations of Table 8.2 discussed above, it seems clear that numbers of patents on their own are a highly defective indicator of total innovative input (or output) for use in a study of innovation and firm size. According to the evidence of our inquiry, this type of analysis is likely to flatter the innovative performance of smaller firms and detract from that of larger firms, and the distortion is likely to be serious, at least in the chemical and electrical fields.

### B. LICENSING ACTIVITY

We turn now to our data on patent licensing, adhering essentially to the sample coverage and categories of production in Table 8.1, although some minor modifications are necessary.

Ideally, we should have preferred to obtain numbers of patents licensed, with some indication of the frequency with which they are licensed, but this was not possible as few firms keep records that would readily yield this information, and moreover it is quite common for agreements not to refer to individual patents, as we saw in the last chapter. The next best course was to invite firms to supply numbers of licence agreements ('licences' for short) in the reported categories (classified by subject matter of the licence), and the resulting data for 1968 are summarised in this section.

It should be emphasised that the figures given are orders of magnitude only. Some firms with large numbers of agreements were understandably reluctant to make precise counts where the necessary information was not readily to hand, and in these cases we had to be content with approximations based on short-cut estimates or expert knowledge of the situation. However, although specific orders of accuracy cannot be guaranteed, we believe that the figures given are reasonably correct and quite adequate for our purposes.[1]

---

[1] As a reminder about orders of accuracy, numbers of agreements shown in the tables are heavily rounded. Although 'field' agreements may cover many patents, each agreement counts as *one* licence here.

Among the various quantitative points which we wanted to explore, we were anxious to preserve the distinction between 'specific' and 'field' agreements, as defined in the previous chapter. The point of this distinction is that it gives some guide to the relative extent of patent licensing which has *patents* rather than know-how as its principal subject. Although 'specific' licence agreements usually contain some know-how provisions, as explained in Chapter 7, it is broadly true that these agreements tend to be ones in which patent rights are the main subject, whereas 'field' agreements tend on the whole to be those in which supply of know-how is the dominant feature. There are of course numerous exceptions to this pattern, but it provides a useful working rule for analysis in perspective.

*Chemicals*

The relevant figures for chemicals are given in Table 8.4. It should be borne in mind in connection with this and subsequent tables that some double-counting of licences may be included, to the extent that companies in our sample licensed each other. However, this is probably a fairly minor component of the totals, and in any case should not greatly affect our conclusions.

The first point to note is that, while specific agreements outnumber field agreements in chemicals as a whole by nearly two to one (column (4)), the position in 'finished and specialty' chemicals is very different from that in 'basic' chemicals, where the frequency of the two types of licensing is about equal. Broadly speaking, this reflects a greater emphasis on straight patent licensing in chemical products than in processes, where agreements tend to centre mainly on know-how rather than patents.

In both the broader categories shown, and in chemicals as a whole, 'licences granted' (i.e., those in which the respondent is essentially licensing others to use its processes or products) predominate over 'licences taken' (where the respondent is essentially the licensee). Although the preponderance is particularly heavy among field agreements in basic chemicals, this is due largely to the activities of a single firm (I.C.I.), as will be explained later; in fact, the numbers here are slightly misleading, in that six of the eleven companies contributing data in this table actually took more licences than they granted, at least in the chemical field.

Figures for cross-licences are given in column (3). Such exchanges appear on this evidence to be more common in pharmaceuticals than in the other fields, representing about one-quarter of agreements in the former and less than 5 per cent in the latter. Although reciprocal

TABLE 8.4. Licence agreements: Chemicals[a]

| | (1) | (2) | (3) | (4) | (5) | (6) | | (7) | (8) |
|---|---|---|---|---|---|---|---|---|---|
| | Number of licences (1968) | | | | Number of licences per £m of R & D in 1968 | Proportion of total licences with payments in 1968 (%) | | Proportion of specific licences granted involving foreign patents only (%) | Proportion of field agreements with firms operating mainly overseas (%) |
| | One-way licences | | Cross- | | | | | | |
| Category of production | Granted | Taken | licences | Total | | In | Out | | |
| **Pharmaceuticals (3 companies):** | | | | | | | | | |
| Specific agreements | 50 | 60 | 30 | 140 | 20 | 40 | 36 | 90 | |
| Field agreements | 20 | 20 | 15 | 50 | 7 | 8 | 6 | — | 72 |
| **Other finished and specialty chemicals (9 companies):** | | | | | | | | | |
| Specific agreements | 170 | 90 | 10 | 270 | 27 | 38 | 19 | 34 | |
| Field agreements | 30 | 10 | 5 | 40 | 4 | 61 | 2 | — | 94 |
| **Basic chemicals (5 companies):**[b] | | | | | | | | | |
| Specific agreements | 160 | 110 | 10 | 270 | 32 | 35 | 21 | 33 | |
| Field agreements | 240 | 10 | 10 | 250 | 29 | 80 | 5 | — | 53 |
| **Total (11 companies):** | | | | | | | | | |
| Specific agreements | 370 | 250 | 50 | 680 | 27 | 37 | 23 | 42 | |
| Field agreements | 280 | 40 | 30 | 350 | 14 | 66 | 5 | — | 61 |

NOTES:

[a] Coverage is as for chemicals in Table 8.1.

[b] Basic chemicals includes figures for chemical licensing by the oil companies that relates to the U.K. part of their operations (i.e., outward licensing attributable to U.K. research and inward licensing attributable to U.K. production). These are partly authors' estimates, although one oil company supplied detailed group figures.

GENERAL:

A field agreement counts as one licence. A licence covering more than one category counts as one in each category. A licence between companies in our sample counts as one for each company. Licensing between members of the same group of companies is not included. Numbers of licences are very approximate, and may not add up precisely, owing to rounding. Numbers of companies in individual categories do not sum to the total because some companies reported licences in more than one category.

exchanges in chemicals take the form of both specific and field agreements, it is fair to assume in general that the broader exchanges are on average the ones of more significance, although this is by no means true in all cases.

Contrary to what might be expected, cross-licensing is apparently not much practised by the oil companies, in either their chemical or other activities. Furthermore, they tend to avoid field agreements and to confine know-how exchange rather narrowly to the field of the patents, unlike some other companies in the basic chemicals category.

Column (5) of the table gives a rough indication of the extent of licensing activity in relation to R & D expenditure in the U.K. in the various production groupings. While this evidence is admittedly far from comprehensive and owes much to the activities of I.C.I. in the basic chemicals field, it does suggest that chemical companies are more ready to license their patents in the production of basic chemicals than in finished and specialty chemicals (especially the more novel and sophisticated kinds) – bearing in mind that average patent propensity in these broad groupings is roughly similar. This conclusion applies in particular to the licensing of know-how and patents through the medium of field agreements.

As with patents, the economic importance of individual licence agreements is likely to vary considerably, and it may be seriously misleading to compare numbers without taking this into account. One step in this direction is to look at the proportions of licences that actually involved financial payments in the survey year, since these at any rate are of some tangible value to the licensor. (Those that involve returns in the form of patents or know-how were also of value, but they are harder to identify and assess.)

The proportions of licence agreements in chemicals that involved royalty payments, know-how fees, etc. in 1968 are shown in column (6). The main point that emerges is that, allowing for the (fairly small) number of licences that involved payments in both directions, quite a high proportion – roughly two thirds – of both specific and field agreements involved payments in one or other direction.[1] The main exception occurs in field agreements in pharmaceuticals, few of which entailed payments in 1968.

A second point is that in all three categories a greater proportion of (total) agreements involved receipts by the respondents than payments by them; in basic chemicals the proportion was much greater. Thus, roughly one-half of specific licences involved receipts, and one-quarter expenditures. A much higher proportion of field agreements involved receipts than payments, except in pharmaceuticals, and in all three

[1] However, payments were small in the great majority of cases, as will be seen in due course.

groupings few field agreements involved expenditures. If paying licences only are taken into account, the balance of outward to inward licensing in chemicals is substantially improved, both overall and in terms of individual companies. The preponderance of 'valuable' licensing activity in basic chemicals as compared with the other fields is, moreover, increased.

The question of selectivity in licensing is of course one that is of outstanding interest to us, and some of the figures obtained shed interesting light on an important aspect of this question – namely, the extent to which British licensors confine their licensees to non-U.K. markets. Many firms in the chemical and other fields with whom we had discussions told us that they are in general much less reluctant to licence other firms to produce or sell overseas than in the U.K., and indeed this is borne out by the evidence on territorial and market restrictions discussed in the preceding chapter. The point is further illustrated in columns (7) and (8) of Table 8.4. Column (7) shows the percentages of one-way specific licences granted by responding firms (column (1)) in which the licensor restricted the licensee to producing or selling under his foreign patents. (The others granted rights to both foreign *and* U.K. patents, or U.K. patents only.) It will be seen that 90 per cent of such agreements in pharmaceuticals involved foreign patents only, while about one-third of those in the other two groupings were so restricted. The figure for pharmaceuticals is particularly noteworthy, suggesting as it does that pharmaceutical firms do not as a rule license competitors in their domestic markets. Although the rate in the other groupings is not so high, it is still high enough to support the view that licences on important patents are not on the whole granted to domestic competitors.

While corresponding details are not available for field agreements, which are harder to pin down in this way, our impression is that they are in general even more solidly confined to overseas licensing. Some confirmation of this is offered in column (8), which shows the proportions of all types of field agreements that were with firms operating mainly overseas. The percentages are high in both pharmaceuticals and other finished and specialty chemicals, although less so in basic chemicals.[1]

Although field agreements between companies based in different

---

[1] The pattern of licensing in basic chemicals is influenced by the extensive licensing activity of I.C.I.'s Agricultural Division, which obtained basic patents in 1964 on the important Steam Naphtha Reforming Process used for the manufacture of hydrogen and thence synthetic ammonia. This process proved to be suitable for the production of town gas, and has been widely licensed for that purpose in the U.K. It has not however been licensed for the production of ammonia in this country, although quite extensively for that purpose overseas. (A fuller discussion of the Steam Reforming Process can be found in Chapter 11).

countries rarely confine the licensee to his domestic territory, especially where international groups are involved, we were widely informed that the licensee in such agreements seldom obtains rights under the licensor's domestic patents, and frequently the latter's main export markets are also ruled out. If this information is correct we may conclude that the bulk of field licensing by the chemical firms in our sample related either to overseas markets or to licensees in the U.K. who do not compete with their licensors.

*Mechanical engineering*

Details for the two principal production categories covered are given in Table 8.5. In contrast to chemicals, specific agreements outnumber field agreements by an overwhelming margin, owing to the figure for 'components and materials', where field licences are virtually non-existent, at least in our sample. While these figures admittedly represent the experience of a fairly small number of companies, the contrast between the position in components etc. and that in basic chemicals is very marked, and illustrates quite effectively the difference in licensing patterns between these industries. In basic chemicals, licensing typically relates to plant design, use of catalysts, process know-how, etc., with patent clearance added as a necessary but subsidiary condition of the exchange; in engineering components, the licence typically centres on the provision of patent rights covering a particular article, probably with a certain amount of manufacturing expertise attached.

For related reasons, cross-licences are on the whole a less common feature of licensing in the mechanical engineering field than in chemicals. They do, however, occur in certain branches of the industry, notably among manufacturers of heavy industrial plant and equipment, where they take the form of continuing exchanges of know-how etc., with patents a lesser consideration – usually with companies based outside the U.K.

While the components and materials manufacturers in the table are heavy net licensors (in terms of a preponderance of 'licences granted' over those taken), this is not on the whole the position in plant, machinery and equipment. Taking mechanical engineering as a whole, seven of the 13 companies contributing data took more licences than they granted (in this field).

The percentages in column (5) suggest that licences are more numerous in relation to R & D in components and materials than in any other category so far examined. Licensing seems a somewhat more common activity in mechanical engineering than in chemicals as a whole, at least on the basis of this evidence.

TABLE 8.5. *Licence agreements: Mechanical engineering*[a]

| | (1) | (2) | (3) | (4) | (5) | (6) | | (7) | (8) |
|---|---|---|---|---|---|---|---|---|---|
| | One-way licences | | Cross-licences | Total | Number of licences per £m of R & D in 1968 | Proportion of total licences with payments in 1968 (%) | | Proportion of specific licences granted involving foreign patents only (%) | Proportion of field agreements with firms operating mainly overseas (%) |
| Category of production | Granted | Taken | | | | In | Out | | |
| Plant, machinery and equipment (9 companies): | | | | | | | | | |
| Specific agreements | 40 | 70 | 5 | 110 | 21 | 27 | 39 | 46 | — |
| Field agreements | 40 | 30 | 10 | 80 | 15 | 38 | 45 | — | 90 |
| Components and materials (5 companies): | | | | | | | | | |
| Specific agreements | 180 | 50 | 2 | 230 | 104 | 73 | 14 | 78 | — |
| Field agreements | 0 | 2 | 1 | 3 | 1 | 0 | 100 | — | 100 |
| Total (13 companies): | | | | | | | | | |
| Specific agreements | 210 | 110 | 10 | 330 | 46 | 58 | 22 | 73 | — |
| Field agreements | 40 | 30 | 10 | 80 | 11 | 37 | 47 | — | 90 |

NOTES:
[a] Coverage is as for mechanical engineering in Table 8.1.

For other notes and explanations, see the *General Note* to Table 8.4 and the text.

If account is taken of the share of licences that involved financial payments (column (6)), the components and materials producers emerge even more strongly as net licensors, at least in numerical terms, owing especially (but not entirely) to the prolific licensing activity of one components manufacturer, while plant, machinery and equipment firms appear on balance to be net takers of 'paying' licences. If the percentages involving payments in one or other direction are combined, mechanical engineering shows an even higher rate of paying licences to all licences than does chemicals (i.e., about 80 compared with about 65 per cent).

Owing mainly to the influence of components firms, the proportion of specific licences granted in which the licensee is confined to manufacturing or selling under the licensor's foreign patents appears high (about three-quarters in the mechanical engineering industries combined). Furthermore, some 90 per cent of field agreements in mechanical engineering were with companies operating mainly overseas. These figures clearly suggest that a great deal of the licensing undertaken by British mechanical engineering firms is limited to foreign markets or to obtaining patents and know-how from essentially foreign manufacturers.

### Electrical engineering

Licensing data for the four categories of production distinguished in this field are summarised in Table 8.6. Our figures for licensing in the first three categories – electronics, radio, telecommunications and related fields – are more than usually approximate because of reporting difficulties affecting two of the six responding companies, essentially in connection with field licensing (see the notes to the table). However, we believe that these rough estimates give a reasonably correct impression of the frequency and type of licensing in the categories concerned.

The overall division between specific and field agreements in the electrical engineering industries resembles that in chemicals, field agreements being particularly prevalent in 'other electrical machinery and equipment' (a category which consists in our sample mainly of cables, smaller electric motors and generators, batteries, and a wide range of electrical equipment for the automotive and aviation industries, mainly of a non-electronic character).

Cross-licences appear to be somewhat more numerous than in the other two main industrial fields so far examined, the proportion here being about 13 per cent of total licensing, compared with 8 per cent in chemicals and 5 per cent in mechanical engineering. They are relatively frequent in electronics, radio and related categories, where they

TABLE 8.8. *Licence agreements: Electrical engineering*[a]

| | (1) | (2) | (3) | (4) | (5) | (6) | | (7) | (8) |
|---|---|---|---|---|---|---|---|---|---|
| | Number of licences (1968) | | | | Number of licences per £m of R & D in 1968 | Proportion of total licences with payments in 1968 (%) | | Proportion of specific licences granted involving foreign patents only (%) | Proportion of field agreements with firms operating mainly overseas (%) |
| | One-way licences | | Cross-licences | Total | | In | Out | | |
| Category of production | Granted | Taken | | | | | | | |
| **Electronic components (3 companies):** | | | | | | | | | |
| Specific agreements | 15 | 30 | 5 | 50 | 6 | 21 | 26 | 0 | — |
| Field agreements[b] | 0 | 0 | 10 | 10 | 1 | (very few) | 90 | — | 80 |
| **Electronic, radio, T.V. and associated equipment (5 companies):** | | | | | | | | | |
| Specific agreements | 80 | 100 | 10 | 190 | 8 | 29 | 25 | 35 | — |
| Field agreements[b] | 30 | 15 | 30 | 80 | 3 | 43 | 19 | — | 73 |
| **Telecommunications and broadcasting equipment (3 companies):** | | | | | | | | | |
| Specific agreements | 0 | 15 | 0 | 15 | 2 | 0 | 67 | — | — |
| Field agreements[b] | 0 | 0 | 15 | 15 | 2 | (very few) | 73 | — | 80 |
| **Other electrical machinery and equipment (3 companies):** | | | | | | | | | |
| Specific agreements | 80 | 70 | 5 | 150 | 14 | 25 | 33 | 59 | — |
| Field agreements | 70 | 110 | 15 | 190 | 17 | 49 | 35 | — | 86 |
| **Total (8 companies):** | | | | | | | | | |
| Specific agreements | 180 | 210 | 20 | 410 | 8 | 25 | 30 | 43 | — |
| Field agreements | 100 | 120 | 70 | 290 | 6 | 44 | 35 | — | 83 |

NOTES:

[a] Coverage is as for electrical engineering in Table 8.1.

[b] Two of our six companies in the electronics, radio and telecommunications fields were unable to supply full data on licensing, owing to membership of an international group in which some licensing (mainly field agreements) is handled on a group basis by the overseas parent. Figures for these companies, which between them supplied one return in each of the first three categories, are therefore estimated partly on the basis of more general information.
See also the *General Note* to Table 8.4.

account for about 20 per cent of all agreements and form an important type of licensing.

Numerically, licences granted exceed those taken in all four categories, while for the sum of categories the proportions involving expenditure and receipts were about equal.

The licensing picture in telecommunications and broadcasting equipment requires special comment. The virtual absence of one-way licences granted by responding firms in this field is attributable to the fact that most U.K. sales of telecommunications and broadcasting equipment are to Government purchasers, and subject therefore to contract provisions such as those in the Bulk Supply Agreements between the U.K. Post Office and leading suppliers, which dominated the communications equipment industry until the last of them (on telephones) expired in 1969. For reasons that will be explained later (see Chapter 12), these supply agreements made formal licensing between U.K. manufacturers largely unnecessary – although they did not affect their overseas licensing.

Even allowing for this factor, it appears quite clearly from column (5) that the rate of licensing activity is extremely low in relation to R & D expenditure in all three categories in the electronics, radio and telecommunications fields. The point is especially noteworthy in electronic components, where the propensity to patent is well above average. The generally low rate of formal licensing activity in the electronics field was said by the companies to reflect a widespread preference in the industry for informality in patent licensing and for dealing with patents in large blocks – in response to the enormous volume of patents that has been generated in this field and the impossibility of handling them through individual licences. The principal electronics firms have tended to license patents in large collections, either in formal patent clearance or 'patent and know-how' agreements with other large (and mainly foreign) firms, or less formally at home through patent-pooling or bilateral clearance arrangements of a relatively informal kind. By contrast, the rate of formal licensing activity in the non-electronic branches of electrical engineering is markedly higher.

It can be seen from column (6) that the electronic components and telecommunications equipment producers were heavy net takers of paying licences, while the balance was the other way in the other two categories. It appears that just over one-half of all specific agreements involved payments in one or other direction (somewhat fewer than in the other fields so far examined), while over three-quarters of field agreements involved payments (about the same as in the other fields). As in other fields, the great majority of payments were relatively small.

Finally, the proportion of specific licences granted that were confined to the licensor's foreign patents (column (7)) is similar to that in chemicals, while the proportion of field agreements that were with companies operating mainly overseas (column (8)) approaches the very high percentage reached in mechanical engineering. These results again confirm the emphasis on overseas licensing activity discovered elsewhere in the study. Indeed several electrical companies with whom we had discussions stated that most if not all important cross-licences in this field are with international groups based overseas and that British electrical manufacturers do not have extensive cross-licensing arrangements with each other.

### Man-made fibres

The three companies in our sample that contributed data on man-made fibres together reported a total of some 150 licence agreements in this industry, of which about 30 were field agreements and the remainder specific. Licences granted heavily outnumbered those taken, especially in the case of field agreements. Some dozen or so agreements were cross-licences.

On average, licensing activity was undertaken at the rate of about 16 specific agreements and 4 field agreements per £ million of R & D expenditure, which suggests that manufacturers in this industry, as in the electronics and related areas of electrical engineering, are much less active in licensing than are the chemicals and mechanical engineering firms in our sample.

A very high proportion (over 90 per cent) of both specific and field agreements in man-made fibres involved financial payments in 1968. Of these about two-thirds involved receipts for the responding companies, while about one-fifth involved expenditures, indicating that the firms concerned were substantial net licensors of technology in this category of production.

All but one of the field agreements reported were with firms operating mainly overseas, while about one-half of outgoing specific agreements were confined to foreign patents. This suggests that most of the important licensing in man-made fibres is with essentially foreign firms or is confined to foreign markets, which is much in line with the findings for the other industry groups examined.

### Other

While the miscellaneous production included as 'other' in Table 8.1 is too mixed to be of much interest, the figures are of some use in that they illustrate licensing activity in a collection of industries which are

6

for the most part neither very research-intensive nor patent-conscious. The amount of sales involved is in fact quite large – roughly £750 million in total – and the main products covered are processed foods, animal feeding stuffs, gramophone records, paper, printing and packaging and natural textiles.

Some 60 specific and a half-dozen or so field agreements were reported in these categories, most being found in textiles and printing and packaging. (Figures were in some cases said to be incomplete, or very approximate.) This represents an average of about 10 agreements per £ million R & D expenditure. Approximately two-thirds of these agreements involved payments, and about 60 per cent of specific licences granted were confined to foreign patents. The numbers of agreements are, of course, extremely small when related to production and so are the payments involved, as will be seen in the next section.

C.   ROYALTIES AND LICENCE FEES

Although financial payments are by no means the only type of benefit that may accrue from licensing – and indeed a number of companies in the inquiry pointed out that money is often not the major consideration – they are the easiest to measure and they do provide a minimum indication of the scale of returns involved. Our questionnaire accordingly invited firms to report amounts paid and received for licences in the relevant categories of production in 1968 (Form A, Section III, Q.9 and 10), and the resulting information is summarised in Table 8.7.

While it was explained to respondents that we wished if possible to include only payments which relate to genuine patent or 'patent and know-how' licensing, some companies could not readily distinguish these from related payments, such as those for use of trade marks, designs and copyrights, technical service fees, 'pure' know-how payments, etc. (This difficulty was noted in connection with pure know-how licensing in the previous chapter.) The figures in Table 8.7 may therefore rather overstate the true amounts of payments associated with patent licences, although the degree of exaggeration is probably nowhere very large. Since we are anxious not to understate the amounts of money involved in patent licensing, this defect is not serious, but we again stress that the figures here, like those on numbers of licences, are rough orders of magnitude only.

Two other technical points should be mentioned. Although firms were requested where possible to exclude income attributable to patents or know-how stemming from the operations of their overseas affiliates, a few international groups were unable to comply fully, with the result that some (fairly small) part of the income shown in Table 8.7 is in payment for R & D etc. done outside the U.K. On the other hand, these figures fail in some cases to include income attributable to U.K. R & D but received by foreign affiliates of responding firms. (This particularly applies where responding firms are subsidiaries of foreign parents, and assign their foreign patents and know-how to the latter either cheaply or free of charge.) This tends to counterbalance the previous point, but in any case the amounts involved in this particular sample are probably relatively minor.

The 28 companies in our sample that contributed details of licence fees etc. received total patent royalties and licence fees (columns (1) and (2)) of some £10·5 million from outsiders in 1968, in turn paying some £3·1 million. These amounted to about 12 and about 3½ per cent respectively of their R & D expenditure on the relevant categories of production in the same year.

While there are no official figures of domestic licence payments to use as a yardstick, comparison with international royalty and related transactions published by the Board of Trade is possible and suggests that our sample accounts for roughly one-third of licence receipts by U.K. firms in the industries we covered, and for rather under one-quarter of expenditures.[1] In other words, our coverage of total licensing activity by U.K. companies seems to be rather higher for outward than inward licensing – at least as far as payments are concerned.

The main point arising from the table is that the firms in question received very much more from licensing their patents and associated know-how overseas than in the U.K. As can be seen from columns (1) and (2), receipts from overseas licensing amounted to more than 80 per cent of total licence receipts of the responding firms. This agrees closely with the split reported publicly by certain major companies (e.g., I.C.I., which has stated publicly that 80 per cent of its group licence income arises overseas). It is moreover very much in line with our findings noted earlier on the restriction of important licensing to overseas markets and on the predominance of agreements with overseas firms.

The share of licence income arising overseas is particularly large in mechanical engineering, and somewhat lower than average in the electrical field, but the general division seems to be about the same in all the industries covered.

A corresponding distinction for licence expenditures (not shown in the table) shows a fairly even split between payments on British and foreign patents etc., but this has little meaning as an indicator of the

[1] For official figures see *Board of Trade Journal*, 25 March 1970. For the purpose of this comparison, our figures for pure know-how payments (Table 7.3) are included.

TABLE 8.7. *Royalties and licence fees, 1968*

| | (1) | (2) | (3) | (4) | (5) |
| | Receipts | | | As proportion of R & D expenditure in 1968 (%) | |
| | From U.K. patents | From foreign patents | Expendi- ture | | Expendi- |
| Category of production | (1968: £m) | | | Receipts | tures |
|---|---|---|---|---|---|
| Chemicals (9 companies):[a] | | | | | |
|   Pharmaceuticals | 0·1 | 3·6 | 0·4 | 52 | 5 |
|   Other finished and specialty | 0 | 0·2 | 0·2 | 2 | $1\frac{1}{2}$ |
|   Basic[a] | 1·2 | 1·2 | 0·1 | 74 | $2\frac{1}{2}$ |
|   Total | 1·3 | 5·0 | 0·6 | 25 | $2\frac{1}{2}$ |
| Mechanical engineering (13 companies): | | | | | |
|   Plant, machinery, equipment | 0 | 0·9 | 0·7 | 19 | 13 |
|   Components and materials | 0·1 | 0·4 | 0·1 | 21 | 6 |
|   Total | 0·1 | 1·3 | 0·8 | 19 | 11 |
| Electrical engineering (8 companies): | | | | | |
|   Electronic components | 0 | 0 | 0·1 | $\frac{1}{2}$ | $1\frac{1}{2}$ |
|   Electronic, radio, T.V. and associated equipment | 0·2 | 0·5 | 0·5 | 3 | 2 |
|   Telecommunications and broadcasting equipment | 0 | 0 | 0·1 | 0 | 1 |
|   Other electrical machinery and equipment | 0·1 | 1·1 | 0·6 | 11 | $5\frac{1}{2}$ |
|   Total | 0·4 | 1·7 | 1·2 | 4 | $2\frac{1}{2}$ |
| Man-made fibres (3 companies) | 0·2[b] | 0·5[b] | 0·3[b] | 9 | 4 |
| Other (5 companies) | 0 | 0·1 | 0·2 | $1\frac{1}{2}$ | 3 |
|   Total (28 companies) | 1·9 | 8·6 | 3·1 | 12 | $3\frac{1}{2}$ |

NOTES:
[a] Excluding the oil companies. Otherwise coverage in this table is as in Table 8.1.
[b] Includes authors' estimates for one producer.
   In this table, 'o' means less than £50,000. Numbers of companies in individual industries do not sum to the total because some companies reported for more than one industry.

importance of overseas licensors. The meaningful distinction here is that between payments on foreign-owned and those on British-owned patents. Although we cannot give details on this, we can safely say from what companies told us that the bulk (probably over three-quarters) of payments are to foreign licensors. That is to say, the pre-dominance of international as compared with domestic licensing applies whether we examine licences granted or licences taken by the respond-ing firms.

Columns (4) and (5) in Table 8.7 give an indication of the importance of licence payments in relation to R & D expenditure in the U.K. by the firms in question. In basic chemicals, pharmaceuticals and both categories of mechanical engineering, licensing receipts are quite substantial (i.e., over one-fifth) in comparison with R & D expenditure, and in some categories and firms very substantial. Licence expenditures by firms in the sample are much less substantial in most fields, an exception being machinery and equipment in both the electrical and non-electrical fields, where they amount to $5\frac{1}{2}$ per cent and 13 per cent of R & D respectively. Apart from 'other', the only categories where expenditures exceed receipts are electronic components and telecommunications and broadcasting equipment, in both of which the amounts involved are small. The low level of licence payments in the electronics and related fields reflects the relatively low incidence of formal licensing in these categories, noted in the preceding section.

It should be pointed out that the bulk of licence payments shown in the table was heavily concentrated among a relatively small number of companies. Thus, only 12 of the 28 companies concerned reported licence income in 1968 of more than £100,000 and of these six had income exceeding £500,000. The three largest recipients (two in chemicals and one in electrical engineering) accounted for 68 per cent of total reported licence income.

Licence expenditures were also quite heavily concentrated. Ten of the 28 companies had expenditures in excess of £100,000 in 1968, and of these one had expenditure exceeding £500,000. The three largest spenders (two in electrical and one in mechanical engineering) accounted for 39 per cent of total reported licence expenditure.

Some idea of the frequency of 'major' licence incomes among firms is given by the fact that licence receipts amounted to a third or more of R & D expenditure in 1968 in eight of the 28 firms (two in chemicals, two in electrical engineering, and four in mechanical engineering), while they exceeded R & D expenditures in two of these. By comparison, licence expenditures were equal to a third of more of R & D expenditures in three firms (all in mechanical engineering), and in no firm did they exceed R & D expenditures.

In only a few returns for categories of production by individual firms were licence payments appreciable in relation to sales. Thus, licence receipts exceeded one per cent of sales (including exports) in only five instances (two in chemicals, one in electrical engineering and two in mechanical engineering), while licence expenditures exceeded one per cent of sales in only 2 instances (one in chemicals and one in mechanical engineering). For the 28 firms, licence receipts averaged about 0·4 per cent of sales (including exports), while expenditures averaged about 0·1 per cent of sales. Chemicals showed the highest rate of receipts at 0·8 per cent, and mechanical engineering the highest rate of expenditures at 0·3 per cent.

A corresponding calculation for profits revealed that licence receipts averaged about 4 per cent of gross profits (1968) for the sample as a whole, with chemicals showing 7 per cent, mechanical engineering 6 per cent and electrical engineering 2 per cent. Licence receipts exceeded one-tenth of gross profits in five companies – two in pharmaceuticals and three in mechanical engineering.

Although we were unable to obtain figures of licence payments from the oil companies in our sample, we would guess on the basis of what the companies told us that licence expenditures on their chemical production in the U.K. were probably equivalent to about 1 per cent of sales – i.e., about £2 million in 1968, or about two-fifths of their estimated R & D expenditure on chemicals in the U.K. in that year. (These are our own best estimates, based on discussions with the companies and material supplied by them, but not confirmed by them.) Licence income arising from their R & D in the U.K. is harder to estimate, since they both undertake a good deal of R & D outside the U.K. The most we can say is that, taking both groups as a whole, there is a tendency for licence expenditures to exceed receipts quite substantially in the petrochemical field – in contrast to the oil processing side of their activities, where they are both substantially net licensors. It is also safe to say that the great bulk (probably well over 80 per cent) of licence income of these companies in both the chemical and the oil processing fields arises outside the U.K.

### D.   MAJOR LICENSING RETURNS

Although a high proportion of licence agreements involve payments or other benefits which are extremely modest in comparison with such magnitudes as sales or profits in the category of production concerned, we were frequently assured in discussions with companies that licensing returns can be important in some cases – and indeed the figures for royalties and licence fees given in the previous section go some way towards substantiating this. We attempted to pursue the matter further by inviting respondents to refer specifically to as many of their patented inventions as they could which they considered to have yielded outstanding licensing benefits in recent years – in terms either of payments or a return flow of patent rights, know-how, etc. (The relevant questions are 20 and 21 on Form A, Section III.) We could not be very exact as to

TABLE 8.8. *Inventions yielding major licensing returns in 1968*

| Industry | Companies citing inventions | Number of inventions cited | Number yielding a major financial return | Number yielding a major return of know-how, patents, etc. |
|---|---|---|---|---|
| Chemicals[a] | 3 | 6 | 5 | 2 |
| Electrical engineering | 5 | 5 | 3 | 2 |
| Mechanical engineering | 5 | 7 | 6 | 2 |
| Man-made fibres | 2 | 2 | 2 | 0 |
| Total | 15 | 20 | 16 | 6 |

[a] Including petrochemicals.

what was meant by a 'major' return, but in cases of doubt it was suggested that inventions yielding an annual licence income of about £100,000 or more – or the equivalent saving of payments for know-how or patent rights – should be included. In fact, several inventions yielding lesser benefits were cited by the smaller companies in our sample, and these were also included.

The information obtained is not easy to summarise, but the principal figures are shown in Table 8.8. It can be seen that half the companies in our main sample felt able to cite patented inventions that were considered to have yielded a major licensing return in recent years. Some twenty inventions (or groups of inventions) were specifically referred to, and most of these involved a major financial return in 1968, while about a third involved (alternatively or in addition) a major return in the form of free or cheap technical information or access to others' patents. Principal among the products and process mentioned were the following: penicillin products and processes; manufacture of hydrogen by the Steam Reforming Process; manufacture of methanol by the low-pressure process; dyes for synthetic fibres; manufacture of ethylene oxide; electronic semi-conductors; developments in television; small-core coaxial cables; variable speed electric motors; diesel fuel injection systems; printing, packaging and laundry machinery; hydraulic gear pumps; fasteners; automotive suspension components; zoom lenses, and developments in polyester fibres. Total royalties etc. involved in 1968 were of the order of about £8½ million, the bulk of which was in chemicals and electrical engineering, and about 85 per cent of which was received from overseas.

While we would not claim that this list is exhaustive, it does include the major instances referred to us and it does effectively illustrate two important points. Firstly, the bulk of licence income in the fields covered is accounted for by a relatively small number of patented products and processes, licensed predominantly overseas. Secondly, instances of major returns in the form of technical information or patent rights appear, on this evidence at least, to be rarer than those of major financial returns. However, it should be admitted that technical information is sometimes very hard to evaluate; our figures on this point should therefore be treated with a good deal of caution.

## E.   PRODUCTION UNDER LICENCE

Although we did not invite firms to supply information on the extent of production under licence, an estimate of these amounts can be attempted with the aid of the data obtained on royalty rates and licence income.

Since the bulk of licence payments are in the form of running royalties, and since in the majority of cases the royalty is specified as a percentage of the net selling value of output produced under licence, a reasonable estimate of the latter can usually be obtained by dividing income from a particular licence by the appropriate rate of royalty. Adapting this approach to the information in the inquiry, we can estimate the annual net selling value of output produced under licence in a particular category of production by dividing the annual licence receipts reported in that category by the relevant rate of royalty.

There are admittedly several practical sources of inaccuracy in this approach. It takes no account of output under licence on which no financial payment is charged: that is to say, the answer is limited to output under 'paying' licence, and for that reason may well understate the value of total output produced under licence, especially in the case of cross-licences, where payments, if made, are likely to be on a net basis.

Furthermore, some licence payments are in the nature of lump sums, the treatment of which as running royalties in this exercise will clearly exaggerate the particular output concerned – although figures derived in this way for a whole industry may not be unduly inflated (since they may be considered to allow for output under licence on which 'lump sums only' were paid before 1968).

A further problem is that our data on royalty rates do not always distinguish between categories of production, although supplementary detail was supplied by some firms. Some estimation of appropriate rates for individual categories was therefore necessary on our part, based on the sort of consideration discussed in the previous chapter. Where firms indicated wide variations between different categories and we had no supplementary information to draw on, we chose rates towards the lower end of the scale, because we were anxious not to understate the value of output under licence. While a high degree of precision is not claimed for our estimates of rates, the resulting figures are sufficiently accurate for our purposes; if anything, the estimates of output under 'paying' licence are probably on the generous side.

The results of this exercise for the three main groups of industries in our sample are given in Table 8.9. Column (1) shows the averages of royalty rates charged by 28 responding firms in the various categories: the figure for 'total' here differs from that in the previous chapter – 4·2 per cent – (page 123) mainly because the system of weights used to produce the average is different. The bias in our estimates for some categories here in favour of rates at the lower ends of indicated ranges was probably also a factor.

The estimated net selling value of output under 'paying' licence from responding firms in 1968 is shown in columns (2) and (3), which relate to output produced at home and overseas respectively. It can be seen that the bulk occurs in chemicals (mainly pharmaceuticals and basic), while quite large amounts are also found in plant, machinery and equipment (virtually all overseas), electronic, radio and associated equipment, and other electrical machinery and equipment.

Owing to the tendency of licensing in the U.K. to occur in fields with low royalty rates, the overall share of overseas licensees in total production under licence – about 72 per cent – comes out rather lower than the share of overseas in total licence income shown for these industries in Table 8.7 (82 per cent). Thus, the domination of the overseas component in total licensing by respondents in our inquiry noted earlier is reduced somewhat if production under licence rather than licence income is used as the criterion.

An indicator of the relative importance of production under licence in the various categories is presented in column (6), where it is expressed as a percentage of 'total sales' in the appropriate category (i.e., sales of production by the licensor at home and overseas *plus* sales under licence from him).[1] Pharmaceuticals and basic chemicals emerge as the categories where output under paying licence is relatively most prominent, while the percentages are negligible or very low in telecommunications equipment, electronic components and other finished and specialty chemicals. In all categories where production under licence is substantial in relation to total production, percentages for overseas are higher than for home – and except in basic chemicals much higher.

---

[1] Overseas sales here include estimated sales by overseas branches and subsidiaries of responding firms as well as U.K. exports and overseas output under licence (column (3)). Exports are as reported on the questionnaire forms.

TABLE 8.9. *Production under 'paying' licence, 1968 (£m)*

| | (1) Rate of royalty charged (%)[b] | (2) Production under licence[c] U.K. | (3) Overseas | (4) Total | (5) Total sales[d] U.K. | Overseas | Total | (6) Production under licence as percentage of total sales U.K. (%) | Overseas (%) | Total (%) |
|---|---|---|---|---|---|---|---|---|---|---|
| **Chemicals[a]** | | | | | | | | | | |
| Pharmaceuticals | 6·7 | 0·8 | 54·1 | 54·8 | 39·5 | 119·7 | 159·2 | 2 | 45 | 34½ |
| Other finished and specialty | 2·7 | 0 | 8·0 | 8·0 | 359·1 | 154·0 | 513·1 | 0 | 5 | 1½ |
| Basic[a] | 2·0 | 60·3 | 57·2 | 117·5 | 253·9 | 196·6 | 450·5 | 23½ | 29 | 26 |
| Total | 3·5 | 61·1 | 119·3 | 180·4 | 652·5 | 470·3 | 1,122·8 | 9½ | 25½ | 16 |
| **Mechanical engineering** | | | | | | | | | | |
| Plant, machinery and equipment | 4·3 | 0·3 | 22·2 | 22·5 | 160·6 | 120·9 | 281·5 | ¼ | 18½ | 8 |
| Components and materials | 4·3 | 1·9 | 8·6 | 10·5 | 100·2 | 60·2 | 160·4 | 2 | 14½ | 6½ |
| Total | 4·2 | 2·2 | 30·8 | 33·0 | 260·8 | 181·1 | 441·9 | 1 | 17 | 7½ |
| **Electrical engineering** | | | | | | | | | | |
| Electronic components | 4·7 | 0·6 | 0·5 | 1·1 | 83·2 | 30·2 | 113·4 | ½ | 1½ | 1 |
| Electronic, radio, T.V. and associated equipment | 2·4 | 7·9 | 21·9 | 29·7 | 148·0 | 101·0 | 249·0 | 5½ | 21½ | 12 |
| Telecommunication and broadcasting equipment | — | 0 | very small | very small | 105·8 | 59·8 | 165·6 | 0 | very small | very small |
| Other electrical machinery and equipment | 5·1 | 2·7 | 21·7 | 24·4 | 209·3 | 99·9 | 309·2 | 1½ | 21½ | 8 |
| Total | 3·7 | 11·1 | 44·1 | 55·2 | 546·3 | 290·9 | 837·2 | 2 | 15 | 6½ |
| Total of above | 3·9 | 74·4 | 194·2 | 268·6 | 1,459·6 | 942·3 | 2,401·9 | 5 | 20½ | 11 |

NOTES:

[a] Excluding the oil companies; otherwise the coverage of the industries shown is as in Table 8.1.

[b] Averages of royalty rates reported by individual companies, weighted by production under licence from them.

[c] Estimated net selling value of production by 'paying' licensees of responding firms. o means 'less than £50,000'.

[d] Equals total sales of production by responding firms in the appropriate category *plus* production under licence from them. 'Overseas' includes sales by overseas branches and subsidiaries of responding firms as well as their U.K. exports (to outsiders) and overseas sales under licence from them. In some cases, figures of sales by overseas subsidiaries are extremely rough estimates based on information in annual

### F.   COMPARISON OF ACTUAL AND 'CORRECT' RATES OF ROYALTY

The information presented in this chapter can, with the help of one or two fairly bold assumptions, be used to illustrate an approach to the assessment of licensing activity drawn from the theoretical discussion of Chapter 2. Central to this approach is the concept of a 'correct' rate of royalty chargeable in licence agreements.

Briefly, the suggestion is that, in any licensing situation, the economically desirable or 'correct' rate of royalty is such that the licensee contributes to the cost of discovery and development of the licensed product or process at the same rate per unit of output as the licensor. If R & D expenditure (*plus* an allowance for normal or 'necessary' profit) by the licensor on the product or process is taken to represent the relevant costs, and sales of the product or process as the relevant measure of output, the correct rate of royalty occurs when:

$$\frac{\text{Royalties}}{\text{Sales of production under licence}} = \frac{\text{R \& D costs less royalties}}{\text{Sales of production by licensor}}$$

It can easily be shown that this occurs when the royalty rate is equal to R & D costs/total sales for the licensed product or process.[1] It follows that the licensor's net research ratio (on the right in the above equation) will exceed the rate of royalty charged if the latter rate is less than the 'correct' rate; and will be less than the rate charged if that rate exceeds the correct rate.[2]

This rate of royalty is correct in the following sense. If anything less is charged, the licensee will have a competitive advantage over the

---

[1] We have said that the 'correct' rate of royalty is charged when:

$$\frac{L}{P_L} = \frac{R-L}{P_P}$$

where $L$ = royalties, $P_L$ = sales of production under licence, $P_P$ = sales of production by the licensor ($P_L + P_P = P$, the total production of the licensed item) and $R$ = R & D costs of this item. Then $\dfrac{L}{P_L}$ is 'correct' when:

$$\frac{L}{P_L} = \frac{R-L}{P-P_L}$$

i.e., when $LP - LP_L = RP_L - LP_L$

i.e., when $\dfrac{L}{P_L} = \dfrac{R}{P}$.

[2] Denoting the licensor's 'net research ratio' by $n\left(=\dfrac{R-L}{P_P}, \text{i.e.,} \dfrac{R-L}{P-P_L}\right)$, it follows that:

if $\dfrac{L}{P_L} = \dfrac{R}{P}$, $n = \dfrac{L}{P_L}$; if $\dfrac{L}{P_L} < \dfrac{R}{P}$, $n > \dfrac{L}{P_L}$; and if $\dfrac{L}{P_L} > \dfrac{R}{P}$, $n < \dfrac{L}{P_L}$.

licensor, and innovative activity will tend to become unprofitable – unless the licensor has offsetting advantages on the manufacturing side[1] (or unless he in turn gains in a similar way as a licensee in an industry where innovative activity is spread fairly evenly among a number of firms). Conversely, if anything more than the 'correct' rate is charged, the licensor will have a competitive advantage over the licensee and inventive activity will tend to become abnormally profitable, with consequent loss to the consumer, as explained in Chapter 2. Given the existence of roughly 'correct' royalties, and reasonably competitive conditions in the markets concerned, price differences between products of licensors and licensees will tend to reflect differences in quality, differences in rates of profit will tend to reflect differences in manufacturing efficiency and the objectives of a market economy will be approximately achieved, at least so far as licensing is concerned.

Needless to say, any attempt to apply the concept of a 'correct' royalty in practice is fraught with difficulties, of which three are likely to be serious. Firstly, there is the difficulty of deciding what is a 'normal' or 'necessary' rate of return on R & D. Secondly, there are problems of timing to consider. Should one use annual rates of R & D, royalties, sales, etc. or should these be converted to capital values using rates of discount, and if so, what should the discount rate be? Thirdly, and most difficult of all, there is the practical question of which R & D costs and which sales are to be counted in any particular case of licensing. The latter problem is likely to be especially difficult where large multi-product firms are involved, where R & D is highly diversified and where its results can be applied in a variety of uses.

As regards the latter type of problem, we can do no better here than count as relevant the R & D expenditures, sales and licence receipts reported by firms for particular categories of production. This is admittedly a rough and ready procedure, and might be objected to on a number of grounds. For instance, it could be argued by licensees that a good deal of what appears as R & D by licensors in the various categories is not connected with licensed products and processes, but is related mainly to other things; if so, a 'correct' rate of royalty based on the entire R & D shown would, in the absence of other compensating factors, tend to be too high and licencees would find themselves subsidising the non-licensed activities of licensors. On the other hand, licensors might well argue that much of their own sales in the reported categories owe little or nothing to the R & D shown; if so, a 'correct' rate of royalty based on the total sales reported would be too low.

We have no way of testing the relative importance of these opposing

---

[1] One such advantage might be the 'head start' that an innovating firm often expects to gain by being first to apply a new invention on an industrial scale.

arguments. We simply assume that the 'research intensity' of licensed products, etc. in the categories reported is not very different from that of the unlicensed products (so that $\dfrac{R}{P}$ can be taken as the appropriate research ratio for licensed products). We further assume that, when data for a range of products and a number of firms are combined, the amounts for R & D, sales and licence receipts in a single year, 1968, are reasonably representative for the purpose of calculating average research ratios, royalty rates, etc. (Thus, for instance, we hope that totals for particular categories will contain a roughly representative cross-section of 'mature' ventures, in which R & D is diminishing or petering out, and 'immature' ones, in which sales have not yet obtained their full operational level and R & D is at its height.)

Finally, it is assumed for simplicity in the present exercise that the 'normal' rate of profit on R & D for the sample as a whole is in the region of 20 per cent before tax, and that it does not vary much between categories.[1] Accordingly, a margin of 20 per cent is added to R & D expenditure shown in Table 8.1. (Certain other minor adjustments were made to these R & D figures before arriving at the 'gross R & D costs' shown in Table 8.10[2]). 'Correct' rates of royalty are then arrived at by dividing R & D costs in each category by 'total sales' (Table 8.9, column (5)).

The results for the three principal industrial fields covered in our main sample are shown in Table 8.10, along with actual (predominant) rates of royalty charged (as in Table 8.9), and the implied 'net research ratio' borne by licensors (i.e., R & D costs including normal profits *less* licence receipts, expressed as a percentage of licensor's sales, all amounts being for 1968).[3]

---

[1] Readers who find this assumption too sweeping can easily substitute alternative rates in the various categories.

[2] In the case of responding groups of companies which do substantial R & D overseas, an allowance was made for the cost of overseas work that is of substantial relevance to their central technical efforts in the U.K. The adjustment was based on information collected in an earlier study by the Department of Applied Economics. (See W. B. Reddaway *et al.*, *Effects of U.K. Direct Investment Overseas: Final Report* (D.A.E. Occasional Paper No. 15, Cambridge University Press, 1968), especially Chs. xxiv and xxv.)

An allowance was also made for expenditure on market research by responding firms, based similarly on data collected in this earlier study. Market research accounts on average for less than three per cent of total R & D in the engineering field, but is more important in chemicals – especially pharmaceuticals and other finished specialty lines – and is arguably a legitimate cost for the purpose of fixing licence fees.

[3] The licensor's net research ratio, it should be noted, depends not simply on the difference between the 'correct' royalty rate and that actually charged, but also on the size of production under licence in relation to total production. Thus, given the 'correct' rate and the rate actually charged, the licensor's net research ratio increases as the share of output under licence increases if the 'correct' rate exceeds the actual rate; and decreases as the share of output under licence increases if the actual rate exceeds the 'correct' rate.

TABLE 8.10. *'Correct' and actual rates of royalty, 1968*[a]

| | (1) | (2) | (3) | (4) |
|---|---|---|---|---|
| | | | | Licensor's |
| | Licensor's | 'Correct' | Rate of | net |
| | gross R & D | rate of | royalty | research |
| | costs | royalty | charged | ratio |
| Category of production | (£m)[b] | (%)[c] | (%) | (%)[d] |
| **Chemicals** | | | | |
| Pharmaceuticals | 12·0 | 7·6 | 6·7 | 8·0 |
| Other finished and specialty | 17·0 | 3·3 | 2·7 | 3·3 |
| Basic | 4·8 | 1·1 | 2·0 | 0·7 |
| Total | 33·9 | 3·0 | 3·5 | 2·9 |
| **Mechanical engineering** | | | | |
| Plant, machinery and equipment | 6·9 | 2·5 | 4·2 | 2·5 |
| Components and materials | 2·8 | 1·8 | 4·3 | 1·3 |
| Total | 9·8 | 2·2 | 4·2 | 2·0 |
| **Electrical engineering** | | | | |
| Electronic components | 9·9 | 8·7 | 4·7 | 8·8 |
| Electronic, radio, TV and associated equipment | 33·1 | 13·3 | 2·4 | 14·8 |
| Telecommunication and broadcasting equipment | 9·7 | 5·8 | — | 5·8 |
| Other electrical machinery and equipment | 4·5 | 1·5 | 5·1 | 1·1 |
| Total | 57·1 | 6·8 | 3·7 | 7·0 |
| Total of above | 100·7 | 4·2 | 3·9 | 4·2 |

NOTES:
[a] Coverage is as in Table 8.9.
[b] R & D expenditure in U.K. (Table 8.1, Column (2)), *plus* allowances for R & D by overseas subsidiaries of responding companies, for market research, and for 'normal' returns to R & D.
[c] Equals column (1) divided by column (5) of Table 8.9.
[d] Equals column (1), *minus* licence receipts (see Table 8.7), divided by sales of licensor's production (including overseas production).
For other explanations, see the text.

Comparison of columns (2) and (3) in this table gives an indication of the relative levels of 'correct' and actual royalty rates charged by responding firms in the various categories of production. It can be seen that for the total of industries shown, actual rates were on average very close to 'correct' rates: indeed they may be considered on this evidence to be about the same, bearing in mind the wide margins of error present in the figures. However, the similarity disappears when individual categories of production are examined. Only the pharmaceuticals and other finished and specialty chemicals firms in our sample appear on average to charge roughly 'correct' rates of royalty. The 'correct' rate is exceeded in basic chemicals, in both branches of mechanical engineering and in other electrical machinery and equipment, while rates in electronic components and electronic, radio, T.V. and associated equipment are on average much below the 'correct' levels.

Comparison of columns (3) and (4) enables one to see the extent of competitive advantage obtained by licensors (or licensees) in the course of licensing – supposing output under licence is potentially competitive with that of the licensee. It appears on this approach that licensors have a competitive margin in their favour (i.e., that the rate of royalty charged exceeds the licensor's net research ratio) in basic chemicals, both branches of mechanical engineering and electrical machinery and equipment, while licensees seem on the whole to have the advantage in electronic, radio and related branches of the electrical industry; in pharmaceuticals and other finished specialty chemicals the balance seems about even.

We are well aware that the analysis described here is exceedingly rough and ready, being based in part on crude data and sweeping assumptions, and we are therefore reluctant to read very much into the results. The differences in the three variables examined are nevertheless quite large for some categories, and can hardly be explained away completely by defects in the analysis. In particular, they lend some tentative support to the idea that licensing charges tend to be on the high side in the engineering industries, both in the mechanical and electrical (non-electronic) fields, and possibly also in basic chemicals. They also support the view that paying licences are fairly cheap in the electronic, radio and associated fields, although it should be borne in mind here that the volume of output under licence is fairly small (especially in components); that most, as in engineering, is overseas; and that telecommunications and broadcasting equipment is a special case where formal licensing is relatively rare. Finally, it should be said that, while the competitive position between licensors and licensees in pharmaceuticals and other finished and specialty chemicals appears fairly evenly balanced on the surface, there are large differences in the results for individual pharmaceutical companies, while the volume of output under licence in dyestuffs, plastics, paints and detergents etc. in our sample is very small. Moreover, in these branches of the chemical field, unlike basic chemicals, virtually the whole of output under paying licence from responding firms is produced overseas.

# 9. IMPACT OF PATENTING AND LICENSING

## A. PRELIMINARY CONSIDERATIONS

Having reviewed the predominantly factual part of the investigation, we now turn to the difficult task of assessing the economic consequences of patenting and licensing activity. In doing so, we shall rely mainly on the responses of firms to the second half of our questionnaire (Form B, reproduced in Annex 2 of Appendix B, pp. 396–400), but we shall also draw on material and opinions arising from discussions with the fourteen or so 'supplementary' firms which could not reply to the questionnaire in a formal way.

Our main problem in describing this phase of the study is that the impact of the patent system depends very much on the circumstances of particular cases. Any attempt to deal with it fully must consider special cases and industries in detail if real light is to be shed on the problems. It therefore seemed best to treat the present chapter as an account of the overall picture with regard to effects, and to supplement it with a series of detailed studies seeking to corroborate and pursue the findings summarised here. These studies will be found in Part III below.

An unavoidable feature of our results here is that they contain a large element of judgment, both by participants in companies and by us. The key questions in this phase of the inquiry sought impressions rather than facts, and although some answers were expressed in precise quantitative terms for the purposes of 'adding up', it would be wrong to imply that they are at all exact. This chapter is the outcome of an exercise in rough estimation of effects for a large number of particular cases, responsibility for which lies jointly with us and those participating on the industrial side. Any claim to reliability for these results must rest on the care with which the exercise was undertaken and the knowledge and frankness of those responding.

On the latter it is important to point out that the results were obtained in the course of an extensive programme of meetings and discussions between the spokesmen of the firms concerned and the authors. It was essential to the effectiveness of the exercise that those responding should be absolutely clear on what was being asked, that they should be encouraged to consider the issues with great care and that we should be able to discuss replies with them in as much detail as we could reasonably wish. In every case where replies are incorporated in our results we were able to subject respondents to something approaching a cross-examination, and in some cases this led to a modification of their original estimates. The interview programme entailed some eighty visits and meetings with firms conducted over a period of more than 18 months, the extent of sessions depending on the importance and complexity of the various firms. It was usually found necessary to have at least two separate sessions with the larger firms in the sample, and a point was made of consulting managing or research directors as well as patenting and licensing specialists in the important cases. (One major group was visited on seven separate occasions, and managers from three operating divisions were consulted as well as patent and licensing specialists.)[1]

A second essential feature of the investigation was the construction of a clear and simple analytical framework within which the impact of the patent system could be judged. This was achieved by proposing to respondents that they should compare their actual patenting and licensing activity (as reported in Form A of our questionnaire) with what would have happened had the patent system during that time been different in certain basic respects. The alternative situation suggested as a 'yardstick' was the compulsory licensing system outlined in Chapter 5, i.e., a system in which patent licences would be granted more or less on request, much as happens with *licences of right*, except that licence fees at 'commercially reasonable' rates, would be payable.

It was emphasised to respondents that the suggestion of a compulsory licensing system was intended by us purely as an analytical device for the purposes of assessing effects. We did not wish them to consider the 'transitional' implications of *changing* to a system of the sort described, and in no sense were we urging the adoption of compulsory licensing in place of the existing system. We sought to make our approach as objective as possible – and indeed we had very little idea at the outset what conclusions would be likely to emerge.

Two further points should be stressed in connection with our compulsory licensing alternative. Firstly, successful applicants under the type of scheme we had in mind could, if they wished, work the licence through import rather than local manufacture. There would be no question of refusing a licence to sell in the U.K. on the ground that the applicant was expected to supply via import. Secondly, the compulsory element in the system would apply to *patent* rights only. Thus a successful applicant would obtain clearance (i.e., freedom from infringement proceedings) under the patents in question, but he would *not* be entitled to demand access to unpatented information. In other words, compulsory licensing as imagined here would not extend beyond the

[1] Further details of the inquiry can be found in Appendix B.

matter of published patent specifications: a patentee would not be required to go further in supplying know-how etc., than he would do in 'voluntary' agreements. This latter point is important in principle and in practice. It concentrates attention on the impact of patents as opposed to secret know-how, as protective devices, and it recognises that any attempt to extend compulsory licensing to know-how would probably prove to be impractical in the real world.

### The effects in more detail

Having selected an alternative for the analysis, we set out to consider the impact of the patent system under four main headings, as follows:

(a) *Impact on competition.* The essential characteristic of patents is that they may enable patentees to monopolise their patented inventions; thus, once an invention has been made and patented, the owner may restrict its use to one or a very few producers and this may lead to high prices and limitations on supply, as explained in Chapter 2. We clearly needed to assess the degree of restraint on competition attributable to patent monopolies. In practice, this meant identifying products or processes that are confined to one firm or to a few licensees under existing arrangements, and that would not be so confined under a compulsory licensing system (assuming for this purpose that the rate and direction of inventive activity would not be affected).

(b) *Impact on research and development.* The traditional justification for granting patent monopolies is that they induce enterprises concerned mainly with the profit motive to devote more resources to invention as an outgoing activity than would otherwise be the case. We needed to assess how much more industrial inventive activity (measured by R & D expenditure) is done in the U.K. than would be done under a compulsory licensing system, and which types of production are affected.

Furthermore, it seemed desirable to inquire into possible alternative uses for the resources in question. A related issue is the question of the extent to which patent monopolies encourage wasteful R & D – such as that done solely to circumvent others' patents. We therefore investigated how far the existing patent system encourages *duplication* of inventive activity.

(c) *Impact on innovation.* In modern industrial circumstances, the traditional defence of the patent system has been extended to cover the activity of innovation – the first introduction of new products and processes on a commercial scale. Large sums are nowadays spent on 'innovatory investment' and on the creation of new markets, and these are thought to be dependent to some extent on patent protection; it therefore seemed desirable to try to assess the extent of this impact. Since few firms identify expenditures on innovation in the way that most identify R & D, we approached this problem by attempting to distinguish 'patent-based' production and to assess how far technologically novel items in this area depend on patent protection. We also investigated what alternative types of production would emerge under a compulsory licensing system.

(d) *Impact on the spread of technical knowledge.* The prospect of patent protection seems likely to induce firms to *publish* more information of a technological kind than they otherwise would, either as patent specifications or as technical literature of other kinds. We tried to make an assessment of the loss of such information that could come about under a compulsory licensing system.

Moreover, the greater facility for the *control* of information supplied under patent licence may well encourage firms to *exchange* more (unpublished) technical information, principally engineering know-how, under private contract than they otherwise would. On the other hand, the exercise of patent monopolies could conceivably result in *less* information of this sort being exchanged, since innovating firms may tend under the present system to confine such licensing rigidly to non-competitors. We needed if possible to assess the net effect of these influences on the exchange of technical knowledge.

While these headings may not be exhaustive, they probably embrace the principal *direct* economic effects attributable to patent monopolies (i.e. effects which are likely to be evident to individuals concerned with patenting and licensing policy in industry, since they stem largely from deliberate responses to the patent system). Admittedly, the patent system may affect R & D and innovation, etc. in ways which are not obvious to those 'on the ground'; for example, research and patent-oriented firms may grow faster than others in their industry through the exercise of patent monopolies, and this may result in an increase in the industry's R & D without any conscious response to patent protection on the part of research management in the firms concerned. We tried to bear in mind the possibility of such *indirect* effects, and raised them in general discussions, but we can say less with confidence about them than about the direct effects. They are by their nature extremely difficult to assess and it is doubtful whether any approach could do so satisfactorily.

It should be noted that the effects listed above are related in some senses to one another. Thus, it seems a necessary condition for patents to encourage R & D and innovation that they should have (or appear to have) a restrictive effect on competition, although the latter is by no means a sufficient condition for the former. Similarly, it seems necessary for patents to have (or appear to have) a restrictive effect on competition if they are to encourage the publication and exchange of knowledge, although again this is by no means a necessary result. It seems evident that if patents are thought to have no effect on competition they are likely to have little effect under the other headings, although the reverse does not apply (i.e., patents might well affect competition, but not inventive activity or publication of knowledge).

Finally it should be said that, while we shall be essentially concerned with effects on U.K. research, innovation, etc., it is not possible or desirable to confine the discussion wholly to domestic considerations. Accordingly, such matters as overseas licensing policy will be brought into the picture, and a special section will be devoted at the end of the chapter to impacts on the U.K.'s overseas trade.

### B.    IMPACT ON COMPETITION

Our investigation under this heading required a thorough examination of the licensing policies of firms in our sample, with some consideration of the implications for prices of patented products. The answers are not easy to summarise, and they sometimes involve confidential matters. While we were on the whole impressed with the frank and scrupulous response to our questions, we are unfortunately unable to reveal as much detail of the replies as we should like.

It seems advisable to start by recapitulating briefly what was discovered on licensing in Chapters 7 and 8. Licensing was found to be most active in relation to R & D in the two branches of mechanical engineering examined and in electrical machinery and equipment outside the electronic and radio field; it was found to be moderate in both basic and finished chemicals, and relatively light in the electronic, radio and associated field (both in components and finished equipment). Approximately one-third to one-half of 'specific' licences granted by chemical and electrical engineering firms were confined to their foreign patents, while the bulk of such licences in mechanical engineering (especially components) and pharmaceuticals were similarly confined. The great majority of 'field' agreements in all industries (with the exception of basic chemicals, for the special reasons explained) were with foreign firms. Similarly, over 80 per cent of reported licence income originated overseas. Territorial restrictions on the sale of output under licence were said to be common by a majority of firms, and this was said to mean usually the exclusion of licensees from the licensor's domestic market and frequently from his main overseas markets. Exclusive licensing was found to be of negligible overall importance within the U.K., but a strongly preferred practice for licensing overseas in some fields (especially pharmaceuticals and certain other finished chemicals). The refusal of formal licence applications was said to be uncommon, although a few cases were found in all fields investigated. In no industry were 'high' royalty rates (i.e., rates in excess of 10 per cent) found to account for a substantial proportion of licence income. An exercise comparing actual and 'correct' royalty rates found that actual rates were higher than seemed to be warranted by R & D expenditures in mechanical engineering and 'other' electrical machinery and equipment, about right on average in chemicals, and very low in the electronic and radio field, but it was emphasised that these results are based on rather crude methods and assumptions.

### *Selectivity in licensing*

The picture that emerges is quite compatible with the view that there is considerable selectivity of licensing of major patents by British licensors in their home and principal export markets, especially in mechanical engineering, pharmaceuticals and other branches of chemicals. However, it could also reflect other circumstances, such as the lack of suitable licensees in the home market or, in some areas of electrical engineering, a relatively informal attitude to licensing among the major firms. It is of particular interest that there seem to be very few refusals of formal licence applications among major companies, although this fact is capable of a number of different interpretations.

Turning to the responses to Form B of our questionnaire, firms gave a wide variety of answers when invited to describe their licensing policies (Section VII, Q. 1), from which the following general points emerge. All firms have some patents which they are glad to license to any genuine applicant on 'reasonable commercial terms' with no important restrictive conditions – other perhaps than that the output under licence should satisfy quality specifications laid down by the licensor, in order to protect his reputation. A few firms (two in the electronic and radio field and one in each branch of mechanical engineering) were willing to license *all* their patents in this way, but most had reservations about licensing their more important patents.

Of the great majority which had such reservations, all had some patents which they would not license to a competitor without territorial restrictions. In most cases this meant that manufacture and sales would not normally be permitted in the U.K. and, less frequently, in major overseas markets, depending on the licensor's own interest in these markets. Exceptions *might* be made in such cases where access to patents or technical information of equal importance were offered in exchange, but financial payments would rarely provide an adequate inducement.

Of the 30 companies in the main sample, 16 said they had some important patents (usually a fairly small number) which they would license only in return for exceptionally valuable patents or know-how. Of these, eight said it was their normal policy not to license anything of key importance to their own operations, except where the applicant was very clearly not a prospective competitor. The categories of production mainly concerned were pharmaceuticals, crop protection chemicals, moulded plastics, industrial machinery and synthetic fibres. In addition, a further five said that although they might consider licensing some things of key importance overseas, there were certain patents for which they would probably refuse *all* conceivable U.K. licence applications.[1] The main types of production affected, in addition to those already mentioned, were industrial chemicals (phosphoric acid derivatives), detergents, fuel injection systems for aero engines, electrical instruments, telephone equipment and synthetic fibre processes. All related to products in which the responding firm claimed to be meeting the U.K. market satisfactorily through its own production, and most were sold in markets of a rather limited and specialised character.

The general impression from these replies was that, outside the chemical and synthetic fibre field, almost all patents for which U.K. licence applications will normally be refused cover fairly narrow ranges of output, although there are very occasional exceptions in the mechanical engineering and 'other' electrical equipment fields. In finished and specialty chemicals, however, particularly pharmaceuticals, weed killers and pesticides, plastic products and materials, and certain industrial chemicals of a specialised kind, the ranges of output affected appear to be rather wider, and in pharmaceuticals and crop chemicals extend to the bulk of the research-intensive part of output.

In view of the importance of the question, an attempt was made in Form B to pursue the subject of licence refusals as seen from the viewpoint of the applicant. This subject was investigated on Form A, but the question in the second phase of the inquiry (Form B, Section IX, Q. 3) was restricted to 'important' patents, at the same time being broadened to include informal as well as formal licence approaches.

Of the 30 companies in the sample, spokesmen for seven could think of important cases in which their applications (informal as well as

---

[1] The relevant question is VII.2 of Form B. This differs from the similar question in Form A, which referred to instances in which formal licence refusals could actually be recalled (see Chapter 7, page 130).

formal) for others' patents had been refused in recent years; of the remainder, 21 could recall no such instances, while two were unable to give an answer. Of the seven companies that had been unsuccessful in some instances, one was a chemical company, two were mainly in the electronic and radio field, two were in the components branch of mechanical engineering and one was in man-made fibres. It is perhaps significant that in the case of the chemical company no refusals were for chemical patents. Some twenty or so instances were cited, of which the main ones were in electronic welding equipment, numerical control of machine tools, telephone receivers, automotive components, plastic moulding, textile machinery and synthetic fibre processing. In virtually all cases the applicant was essentially seeking British manufacturing (and selling) rights, with foreign rights needed only as a secondary requirement. In about half the instances the patentees making the refusals were British firms, and in the other half foreign. In most instances a licence was not available on any terms, while disagreement over royalties or 'other factors' was mentioned in a few.

Although the patents in question were all of importance to the responding firms, no refusal was sufficiently important to cause a radical change in their research or production programmes. In almost all cases the respondent was seeking to introduce a product or process improvement of a relatively minor sort or to augment an existing product range and was able to overcome the setback without very much difficulty, either by developing a substitute on the basis of its own R & D, by switching to something slightly different or, as in the case of the telephone receiver, by purchasing the patented component from the patentee. In one case an application for a compulsory licence was made and this proved to be unsuccessful. In another instance, not among those under discussion, a *threat* of application for a compulsory licence was made, which proved effective. Only three companies said that they had had to undertake R & D work they would not have needed to do if licences had been available, and the amounts involved were said to be minor. (More will be said on the latter point in Section C below.)

It therefore seems that while licence refusals are not perhaps quite so rare as appeared when formal approaches alone were considered, they rarely add up to much more than a minor inconvenience for the minority of firms in our sample that experienced them. This seems to be as true in the chemical field as in electrical and mechanical engineering, at least on the basis of the evidence available to us.

On the surface, this comparative rarity of, and unconcern about, licence refusals among major industrial firms may seem to contrast oddly with the appreciable selectivity that was found in licensing policy generally, and particularly in the chemical field. However, explanations are not far to seek. Among the variety of reasons that were suggested to us, the following should be mentioned. Firstly, spokesmen in a number of firms said that in recent years there have been no technical developments of real importance in their fields from which patents have barred them. Several ventured the view that the era of the 'master' or 'basic' patent has largely gone and, although others (particularly in chemicals) would not agree entirely with this, it seemed commonly accepted among engineering and electronics firms that basic patents of great commercial significance (comparable to Western Electric's transistor patents in the 1950s or, on a lesser scale, the pre-war patents on xerography) are nowadays extremely rare. However, they still occur from time to time, one notable recent example being the patents on the P.A.L. colour television system (see Chapter 12).

A second and not unrelated answer was encountered typically among manufacturers of plant and machinery: this was that in lines of activity where the basic technology is well established and has passed into the public domain, firms attempt to secure recognition for their products through variations in design and minor improvements which are either not patentable or, if patented, can be easily circumvented. Indeed, where this happens, it commonly proves difficult to find licensees, for each manufacturer is keen to develop his own individual designs and modifications and is reluctant to be found relying on the patented items of others if this can be avoided. This is particularly the case in industrial plant and machinery and other specialised capital equipment, where orders tend to go to the firm with the best technical 'name' in the field, and where manufacturers are consequently reluctant to have 'made under licence from...' stamped on their products.

A third type of explanation was found, more particularly among manufacturers of specialty chemicals, where patents are capable of protecting valuable, if usually limited, markets. The argument, which might be termed 'keeping off the grass', was put to us somewhat as follows: 'The instinct in this industry is to keep off other people's grass and this applies to patents as to other things. Patents are needed to map out the technical territory belonging to each firm, and when it is marked out we stick to it, and there is very little poaching.' The firm in question was working on the development of a polyvinyl chloride stabiliser for use in the manufacture of rigid plastic containers. It had no patents in the field, which is process-dominated, and if patents were obtained by another firm it would abandon the field. It would not apply for a licence on something for which it planned to supply a specialised ingredient, for the market for the stabiliser would be too small to allow more than one profitable producer; neither would it want a licence to use the stabiliser in manufacture, since it had no interest in manufacturing containers, although the market for these is large.

Similar to the above was the type of explanation which said that licences were seldom actively sought on major patents because it was well known among leading manufacturers that requests for these would be refused. This line of argument, like the previous one, seemed particularly common in finished and specialty chemicals and non-bulk industrial chemicals. Firms in this field, more than any other, tend to take patents seriously and to respect the protection offered by them, for most have valuable patents and are therefore reluctant to challenge what are thought to be valid or well-entrenched patent holdings without an exceptionally good reason; many, after all, would be liable to retaliation in like manner by others. Of course, not all respondents to our inquiry would subscribe to this 'live and let live' policy, but a number did appear to be saying this or something similar, and they were by no means confined to industries which can be classified as economically or technically stable; in fact, some of the most competitive and technically most progressive firms in the inquiry seemed to adopt this attitude.

By contrast, firms in the engineering fields seemed much less impressed with the protective value of patents as such. They frequently made the point that patent clearance on its own is seldom worth much compared with unpatented expertise, which can be very critical to developments in sophisticated machinery and equipment, mass-produced components and bulk chemical processes. We gained the impression that many U.K. engineering firms (both non-electrical and electrical) have little interest in straight patent licences from other U.K. firms, because the associated know-how etc. would be too costly for them to develop themselves (bearing in mind the size of the U.K. market and the entrenched positions of established manufacturers), and because it would not be made available under licence to them as potential competitors. Moreover, in most specific cases of selectivity in these fields that we investigated from the licensor's point of view, secret know-how or highly specific technical skills emerged as the effective barriers to imitation, and patents were rarely if ever a crtical factor.

A final point which should be made here is that the question of selectivity in licensing is academic where the patentee is for some reason already a monopolist of the product or process concerned – possibly as a result of the exercise of patent monopolies in the past. One can point to many British markets for both basic and specialty chemicals in which there is essentially only one major domestic supplier, owing primarily to the operation of economies of scale in production and in the use of R & D results; in these circumstances no demand for U.K. manufacturing licences is to be expected, at least from established firms in the U.K. Foreign firms may seek licences on U.K. patents, but they are only likely to be granted for manufacturing in their own home markets or for export markets that do not conflict with those of the licensor.

*Impact of compulsory licensing*

It is clear from the foregoing that the impact of the patent system on competition cannot be judged properly without some consideration of particular cases, and we shall attempt to do this for selected industries in Part III. We cannot do much more here than state our general impression that there seems on the whole relatively little unsatisfied demand for licences among major established firms operating in the U.K. This does not of course imply that licensing activity would be totally unaffected by a system of compulsory licensing. As far as we can tell, such a system would lead to increased licensing of certain types of new chemical products within the U.K., especially in more sophisticated areas such as pharmaceuticals, crop chemicals, plastics and complex industrial chemicals – assuming that the rate and direction of inventive activity were unaffected. There would probably be a similar effect on a smaller scale in specialised machinery, equipment and components in mechanical and electrical engineering, but very little in the electronic and radio field, except perhaps in colour television.

However, the evidence of our inquiry suggests that there would not be any general tendency among *established* firms in British industry to take advantage of the system, although a number of cases could be cited in which compulsory licences would be utilised by major research-based firms on a minor scale. The types of output concerned would be narrow and specialised, and would probably be mainly in machinery and components in the mechanical engineering field, although some special types of electrical machinery and apparatus might also be slightly affected. We can point to almost no area of the basic chemical industry where licensing among the established producers would be very much affected.

The principal reasons for this lack of widespread impact among major producers will be pursued further in Part III. At the risk of undue generalisation, we would say that the existence of unpatented manufacturing know-how seems an overwhelming factor in the engineering fields and in the areas of chemicals dominated by bulk process technology; unless a compulsory licensing system could encompass know-how etc. in addition to patent clearance – which we assume not to be the case – it is unlikely that licensing would occur much more readily under such a system than at present. Furthermore, even in the chemical areas mentioned where patents do provide a significant element of protection, it is hard to believe that established firms with patent holdings of their own would make much resort to compulsory licensing, were it possible for them to do so. As argued earlier, such firms are in the main highly conscious of their stake in patents and of their own vulnerability under the present system to vociferous or insistent re-quests for licences (especially if accompanied by prospects of legal battles over patent claims, or other retaliatory steps): they would be doubly so under a 'thoroughgoing' compulsory licensing system.[1] Moreover, when established firms seek licences on drugs, etc. they have a strong preference for exclusivity, and this would of course be unobtain-able under a compulsory licensing system.

For these reasons it seems unlikely that established U.K. or major international chemical firms would make much use of a compulsory licensing system. They would probably still compete, as now, essentially through individual R & D and innovative efforts and, in the cases of consumer goods industries, through advertising and market promotion.

If, as we believe, additional demand for U.K. licences in the specialty chemical field would be forthcoming under a compulsory licensing system (assuming no change in R & D programmes), it would therefore have to come from firms which are not established U.K. producers, and it can be argued fairly convincingly that these would mainly be smaller firms with little previous claim to any serious or sustained inventive or innovative activity. If we extend our alternative of compul-sory licensing to cover all major industrial countries, which seems necessary in view of the international nature of the patent system, the arguments that have been applied above to established, research-intensive firms in British industry also apply to established firms over-seas, since they would be as vulnerable to retaliation through com-pulsory licensing as would their British counterparts. This leaves the class of firm that seeks to rely essentially on manufacturing and market-ing of products developed by others as the main type of contender for compulsory licences.

The opinion of the majority of company spokesmen to whom we talked was that such firms would not present a serious competitive threat under a compulsory licensing system. This was particularly the view of larger firms in electrical engineering, and in basic chemicals the answer was similar. In both these fields the minimum size of output necessary to produce economically is so large that it is most unlikely

---

[1] Experience in the U.K. pharmaceutical industry under Section 41 tends to bear this out, as will be seen in Chapter 10.

that any producer could remain in the field without a large technical effort. Opinions in mechanical engineering were more varied, but most machinery and components firms were of the view that new suppliers must specialise in some technical way if they are to make much of an impression on the market, and for that reason would be as vulnerable to compulsory licensing (and therefore as unlikely to rely much on it) as their larger rivals.

On the other hand, spokesmen in finished and specialty chemicals were on the whole much more impressed with the competitive threat that could be posed by new or non-research-based firms in a compulsory licensing regime of the sort described. It was said that while it is hard for smaller firms that concentrate solely on manufacturing, formulating and packaging to make reasonable profits under existing patent arrangements, they might well flourish under a compulsory licensing system, particularly if compulsory licensing were given more official encouragement than was currently the case in pharmaceuticals under Section 41. The view in a number of companies, particularly in pharmaceuticals, fine chemicals, crop chemicals, and other fields where formulation and packaging are major activities and economies of scale in production are not very significant, was that competition might well expand appreciably in these activities under a compulsory licensing system. It was emphasised moreover that such competition would be unlikely to stem from the research-based firms, who would be the ones to suffer under such a system. (These arguments will be taken up in Chapter 10, using pharmaceuticals as an illustration.)

### *Royalties and pricing policy*

Respondents were invited in this phase of the inquiry to comment on their policies with regard to the fixing of royalty rates; in particular we were interested in how far the costs of producing information licensed to others are normally taken into account in fixing rates.

Many firms stressed the general point that royalty rates are normally determined in the course of licence negotiations and that it is misleading to think of them as being 'fixed' in the same way that a seller sets a price. However, it was admitted that in many cases of routine licensing the licensor in effect sets the rate, while even where considerable bargaining is involved the licensor usually has a clear idea of the range within which he will be prepared to settle.

Virtually all companies said that they mainly took account of the 'normal' charges in their industry for the type of licence and the type of product or process concerned, and most seemed to have a fairly definite idea of what can be regarded as typical charges for particular licences in their field. Most took some account of the maximum that potential licensees could be expected to pay, and this was often said to be very similar to the 'standard' rate for a licence, although it was admitted that it might be higher for an invention of exceptional importance.

Rather less than a third of the companies in our sample made a serious attempt to assess the R & D costs of the technical information provided under licence and took these into consideration when arriving at royalty rates.[1] While the rest usually had a rough idea of the overall ratio of their R & D expenditure to their sales, this was seldom taken into account in licence negotiations and the idea that R & D costs of specific types of output might provide an explicit basis for licence charges seemed strange to many. On the other hand, a few firms (mainly in chemicals and man-made fibres) had detailed knowledge of their R & D costs in various product fields and did take explicit account of them in licence negotiations.

This general neglect of R & D costs as a factor in determining royalty rates may to some extent explain the wide disparities between R & D ratios and royalty rates observed for individual firms and categories of production (as indicated for instance in Table 8.10). One conclusion at least emerges: most firms do not have a very clear notion of licence income as a return to their R & D, and are inclined to view this income very much as 'gravy'. In most cases where 'high' royalty rates are charged, this is done in the expectation that the licensee will pay rather than in the knowledge that the costs of the invention or know-how covered in the licence are high.

There can be no general presumption, using R & D costs as a criterion, that royalties paid on existing licences under a compulsory licensing system would be very much lower on the whole than they are under the present system. If Table 8.10 is roughly correct, a system in which royalties were related to the R & D and associated costs of production under licence would tend to raise charges in electronics and radio, lower them in mechanical engineering and 'other' electrical machinery and equipment, and leave them little changed on average in chemicals – although rates on some key drugs and other chemical products might be somewhat reduced.

Turning now to our questions on pricing policy (Section IX, Q. 1 and 2), we found very little direct evidence that firms deliberately exert patent monopolies to charge higher prices for their patented products than they otherwise would. The main point that emerged from this

---

[1] These comments do not apply to R & D done under Government contract or otherwise financed by the Government (mainly in the electronics field), since special accounting procedures are normally adopted by firms in relation to this type of work.

line of questioning is that few companies differentiate between patented and non-patented products when fixing prices. The usual procedure for pricing of patented as well as unpatented products is to price on the basis of 'full cost' (including an allowance for R & D and marketing expenses along with other current overheads – generally in the form of a percentage added to direct costs that might vary somewhat between divisions or members of a group of companies), plus an allowance for 'reasonable' profit. However, it was sometimes said that this procedure is not suitable for 'new' products of a technically advanced character, for these would be likely to have exceptionally high R & D and pre-market outlays associated with them. In these cases the main consideration seems to be 'what the market will reasonably bear', and the prices of such products in their early years tend to be high in relation to their longer-run levels. It was emphasised however that this applies equally to non-patented and patented products.

It might of course be argued that the denial of patent rights to competitors could affect what the market will bear, and that patents may have an influence on pricing in this way. As far as we could tell from the inquiry, this does not seem to be true in general, although there are important exceptions in the chemical field and lesser ones in mechanical engineering. When asked whether the prices of patented products tend to fall as the expiry of the patent approaches (which is to be expected if the argument is to hold), the great majority of firms replied either that this was not the case, or that, where it does happen, the fall in price has no connection with patents but is a feature of all technically novel products. Many firms made the point that the price of such products tends to fall some years after their introduction, partly because the initial outlays on R & D and market promotion have then been 'paid off' and partly because other firms introduce superior or at least similar products in due course. We were widely assured that vigorous competition via new products is typical of research-intensive fields and that there are very few lines of activity in which patents are capable of preventing the emergence of competing products once the market and the main lines of technical approach have been established.

By far the most important exception to this general response came in the pharmaceutical field. Spokesmen for the pharmaceutical firms in our inquiry referred to a number of important cases in which the expiry of a patent had been followed by appreciable (and sometimes, very substantial) cuts in the prices of affected drugs, and said that the emergence of competition permitted by cessation of patent cover was a prime factor in such cases. We were told that such cases were not uncommon in the drug field, and were especially notable where new 'wonder' drugs were involved.[1] Similar (but less frequent) instances of an association between price cuts and expiry of patent protection were said to occur in other 'fine' chemicals and chemical specialties (e.g., crop chemicals). Apart from these, only one of all the companies to whom we talked could cite instances in which the expiry of a patent had been responsible for a fall in the price of a patented article; the company in question was a chemical company and the cases referred to were additives used in the manufacture of plastic materials. Otherwise, the general consensus of companies outside the finished and specialty chemical field was that patents in themselves have little perceptible impact on the prices of patented items, except in a few cases.

We are well aware that it would be unwise to accept this evidence on its own, and if the picture is examined more closely one or two qualifications can be added. Firstly, some firms (outside as well as within the chemical field) stated that patents can sometimes help to delay the stage at which the price of a research-based product falls to what can be called its long-run level. However they said that in most cases the delay attributable to patents (among other factors) is very short, i.e., probably not more than 'a very few years'.

Secondly, while it may indeed be true that it is only in the area of sophisticated or specialty chemicals that patents are likely to be effective in resisting potential competitive pressures for price reductions, the products involved may nevertheless be economically very important. Major drugs are the obvious example, and there is considerable evidence (from our inquiry and from other sources) to suggest that patents have in the past played a critical part in maintaining high prices for drugs – although they probably now have a diminished effect in the U.K. following action by the Government in the 1960s, as we shall see in Chapter 10. Synthetic fibres are another area in which patents probably had an important impact on U.K. prices some years ago; we discuss the evidence for this with reference to nylon and Terylene in Chapter 14. Other examples from the past can be cited, almost entirely from the finished chemical and related fields; it is much more difficult to identify present-day instances.

Despite these important cases, we believe it to be broadly true, even for a good deal of the finished and specialty chemical field, that patents nowadays seldom have much impact on prices – at least compared with what would happen under a compulsory licensing system.[2] This is suggested both by our direct evidence on pricing policy and by

[1] The impact of patents on drug prices is discussed more fully in Chapter 10.
[2] There are of course quite significant exceptions, particularly in mechanical engineering, and even in electronics. (See, for instance, our discussion of the recent conflict in Europe over licensing the P.A.L. colour television system (pages 298–9)). But they only occasionally add up to much in terms of sales, etc.

our earlier conclusions on licensing and royalty rates. If licensing and royalties would on the whole be little affected in a world of compulsory licensing, except in the special chemical areas mentioned, it is fair to conclude that competition would not increase very much in such a world and that pressure for price reductions of patented items would be little changed. It is even possible to argue that prices in some fields might ultimately be higher than otherwise if compulsory licensing were introduced, should the switch have the effect of discouraging inventive activity. We shall examine the impact of patents on invention and innovation in Section C of this chapter.

*Patents and 'tied' leasing*

It seems appropriate to add something here about a particular kind of monopolistic practice involving patents that has at times attracted strong criticism – namely, 'tied' leasing. The inclusion of British United Shoe Machinery in our sample enabled us to consider this practice in the context of shoe-making machinery, a branch of industry in which tied leasing has in the past been specially prevalent (it was abandoned in 1951).

Towards the end of the nineteenth century, machinery producers in certain fields developed the practice of 'tied' leasing, under which machines were leased to users on condition that the latter should obtain all their auxiliary equipment and materials (including unpatented items), as well as new machines, from the lessor. Where the machinery manufacturer was able to acquire strong patents on one or two important machines, this practice offered him a powerful means of extending his monopoly throughout an entire range of machinery and equipment, especially where his customers were numerous and ill-organised. The best known example is probably the virtual monopoly over shoe machinery and materials built up in America by the United Shoe Machinery Corporation before 1918, partly through tied leasing of patented machines.[1] A comparable monopoly was established by

[1] This practice was the subject of an action in the U.S. Supreme Court under the Clayton Act, in which the tying clauses were found (in 1920) to be illegal and to have a substantial effect on competition. (See Neale, *The Anti-trust Laws of the U.S.A.*, p. 326.) The U.S.M. monopoly had earlier been attacked (unsuccessfully) under the Sherman Act in 1918 and was again the subject of a celebrated anti-trust action in 1953. (See Neale, pp. 101–3, 114–18, 407–8.) In the latter, the Government's case was upheld, and it was ordered *inter alia* that U.S.M.'s patents on shoe machinery applied for before 1955 should be subject to compulsory licences with 'a reasonable royalty' – to be determined, in default of agreement, by the Court. At the same time, U.S.M. was ordered to divest itself of part of its shoe machinery business, and to assign or give royalty-free licences under its patents relating to the divested business. (The final Consent Decree is dated February 1969.) A detailed account can be found in C. Kaysen, *United States v. United Shoe Machinery Corporation*, Harvard Economic Studies 99 (Cambridge, Mass.; Harvard University Press, 1956).

U.S.M.'s British subsidiary in the U.K., and this was the subject of considerable friction between the company and rival shoe machinery manufacturers after the 1914 war.

The U.K. Patents Act has since 1907 explicitly disallowed tying clauses relating to unpatented goods in contracts involving patented goods, on the ground that the patent monopoly should relate solely to the patented invention, and should not be extended to cover other goods supplied by a patentee. (A licensee may be confined to obtaining supplies of the patented item from the licensor and, as was mentioned in Chapter 7, such provisions are not uncommon in 'user' agreements, but he may not be confined, say, to specified sources for other items, except spare or replacement parts for the patented item.) However, the Act has from the same time also included an 'escape' provision which enabled B.U.S.M. and others to continue to operate tied leases, and this provision has survived to the present day.[1]

The practice of tied leasing persisted until the Second World War, by which time B.U.S.M. supplied 80–90 per cent of the U.K. market for general shoe-making machinery. In 1946, a Board of Trade report on the shoe industry found that, although B.U.S.M.'s leasing arrangements had operated to the benefit of its customers over the years, there were important potential dangers in the tied lease system, and its abolition was recommended.[2] As a result, the Company agreed with the Federation of Boot and Shoe Manufacturers in 1951 no longer to include compulsory lease or purchase clauses in its contracts and to release both parties to existing tied leases from the ties binding them under those leases, although in fact very few tied leases had been entered into after the outbreak of the war.

There seems little doubt that patents were a significant contributory factor in the creation of U.S.M.'s monopolies over the manufacture of general shoe-making machinery in the U.S.A. and the U.K. in the early years of this century, for without patents on key new machines it would probably have been more difficult to persuade large numbers of customers to agree to tying clauses in the years when U.S.M. had serious rivals – in spite of the alleged benefits for shoe manufacturers

---

[1] Under Section 38 of the Patents and Designs Act 1907 and Section 57 of the Patents Act 1949, tying clauses were and are allowable in a contract for the sale or lease of patented goods, or for the use of a patented process, provided that the purchaser or lessee has the option of obtaining the patented goods or using the process without such conditions on 'reasonable terms', and provided that he can terminate the contract on payment of compensation to the lessor or seller. The majority of shoe manufacturers opted for the tied system (which among other benefits enabled them to obtain further machines at the same rentals notwithstanding any inflation) and had no objection to it, while those who preferred freedom to obtain other machines usually found the alternative higher terms for 'free' leases to be acceptable.

[2] Board of Trade, *Working Party Reports: Boots and Shoes* (H.M.S.O., 1946) pp. 15–18.

from the tied system. However, it cannot be said that patents are nowadays a factor sustaining this particular monopoly, both because tied leasing of shoe machinery was abandoned in the U.K. twenty years ago, and also because patents in this field can nowadays be more readily designed round than they could be before the war.[1]

So far as we could discover in the inquiry, tying clauses relating to unpatented items nowadays play very little part in licence agreements in mechanical engineering or any other industry, although we were informed that they are still to be found in some fields. The 'loophole' in the Patents Act still remains, but industrialists seem of the opinion that the Court's interpretation of 'reasonable terms' for a restriction-free option of the type referred to in Section 57 would probably be so unfavourable to the licensor as to rule out any prospect of building up powerful new monopolies by means of tying clauses. This general conclusion seems to be *a fortiori* applicable in licence agreements involving American companies or their subsidiaries, as the latter are said studiously to avoid anything resembling unfair restrictive conditions in licence agreements for fear of invoking anti-trust investigation. The whole matter seems, therefore, to have become a dead issue, whatever its historical interest.

## C.   IMPACT ON RESEARCH AND DEVELOPMENT

In assessing the impact of patents on inventive activity in industry, the main object was to arrive at a joint estimate with those participating on the industrial side of how far their R & D would be affected under a compulsory licensing system. We also investigated a number of subsidiary questions which were designed to shed light on this central question.

A start was made by exploring the extent to which patent considerations enter into the planning of research at a fairly early stage (Form B, Section VI, Q. 3). It appears that virtually all firms with a substantial R & D effort take some trouble to inform their research and engineering staff about patent possibilities and procedures. This is usually done through literature presented when they join the staff, which may include a special section on patents, or even a separate pamphlet. Patent-conscious firms (especially larger chemical firms) are likely to go further, for example, by holding introductory seminars at which patents are discussed and follow-up sessions in which the need for vigilance

[1] Kaysen similarly finds that patents have not been an important factor in sustaining the market position of the American parent company post-war. See Kaysen, *United States versus United Shoe Machinery Corporation*, pp. 78–91.

on patent matters is pointed out. We even encountered two firms in which opportunities are regularly offered to research staff to work for a short period in the patent department. However, outside pharmaceuticals and one or two other highly patent-conscious fields, the task of considering whether new research is patentable and of watching for possible patent infringements is left very much to patent specialists, as explained in Chapter 6.

Except in pharmaceuticals and other sophisticated branches of finished chemicals, the patent manager is seldom a permanent member of the committee for research or technical planning found in most enterprises that undertake substantial R & D. While he may be consulted from time to time by such a committee he rarely expects to have much influence in the planning of research programmes – although it is his job to be familiar with these plans and to deal with the patent matters arising from them. In most cases where such matters are raised, the difficulty is likely to be infringement of an existing patent, and the patent specialist's main role is to give advice on whether to risk being sued for infringement or seek a licence and if so what the chances of success will be; or on what to do if the company's patents seem to be infringed by another firm.

As a forerunner to the central question, respondents were asked to estimate the proportion of research projects in recent years in which patentability was a decisive criterion for deciding whether or not to go ahead with the project (Section vi, Q. 4). Of 34 returns received from 29 companies,[1] the answers were as follows:

|  | Number of returns | (%) |
|---|---|---|
| Never | 7 | 21 |
| In very few cases | 18 | 53 |
| In a significant proportion (up to 10%) of cases | 5 | 15 |
| In over 10% of cases | 4 | 12 |
| Total | 34 | 100 |

Of the 9 returns in which patents were said to be decisive in a significant proportion of projects, six were in finished and specialty chemicals (with pharmaceuticals and crop protection chemicals prominent), one in basic chemicals, one in industrial plant and one in automative components.

It should be noted that stress was laid on 'decisive' in this question. A number of companies observed that, although patents were seldom if ever decisive, they were often one of many factors affecting research

[1] In general, returns on Form B referred to the 'main activity' of the responding firm. Some respondents made returns for more than one main activity.

decisions. But it was also said that the relevant consideration was usually the danger of infringing others' patents rather than the possible protective value of the researcher's own patents.

In an attempt to quantify responses on this subject more precisely, respondents were invited to give their best estimate of the proportion of R & D undertaken in recent years that would not have been carried out had effective patent protection not been available (Section vi, Q. 6). In discussions on this question, which tended to require a good deal of debate, it was explained that we were trying to assess the strength of the inducement offered by the patentee's right to monopolise the resulting product or process, or license it selectively (say, overseas only).[1]

Not surprisingly, some participants in the inquiry, although sympathetic to our general aim, hesitated to venture judgments on what they felt to be a somewhat 'hypothetical' question. On the other hand, a larger number than we expected had few doubts about the answer. Most however wished to consider the reasoning behind their replies in detail, both with colleagues and in the sessions with us. They were encouraged to give separate consideration to their various main categories of R & D where this seemed appropriate, and to illustrate their answers with examples where possible. In cases where a large area of uncertainty remained, it was usually possible to agree on a reasonable maximum figure, and since our object in this as in the other key questions on Form B was to avoid understating the impact of patents, the benefit of the doubt in such cases was given to those who seemed to us to be erring on the high side in their assessments. For that reason, our findings are likely if anything to exaggerate rather than minimise effects.

Ultimately, usable returns were obtained for 32 major activities or categories of production in 27 companies from our main sample and these are summarised in Table 9.1. It can be seen that in 24 out of the 32 returns it was estimated that R & D was either not, or very little, affected by prospective patent protection, while in the other

---

[1] We did not ignore the possibility that some firms might actually spend more on R & D in the absence of patent protection, because they would not then be inhibited by the patents of others. However, all those replying felt that this type of impact would be of very minor importance, for patents seldom if ever interfere directly with R & D programmes, and can virtually always be circumvented at the manufacturing stage of a genuinely research-based project. There are of course exceptions – e.g., in electronic equipment, where it is often difficult to avoid using basic patented inventions such as the transistor – but these tend nowadays to be in areas where patent clearance is generally made readily available to all firms that make a genuine contribution in the relevant research fields. Where patents do have a significant inhibiting effect, it is almost invarably on the skilled imitator – usually a firm on the fringes of the industry that would wish to avoid extensive involvement in R & D regardless of patent circumstances.

TABLE 9.1. *Estimated proportions of R & D expenditure dependent on patent protection: 27 responding companies*

| | Proportion of R & D affected[a] | | | | |
| --- | --- | --- | --- | --- | --- |
| Industry | None or negligible | Very little (less than 5%) | Some (5–20%) | Substantial (over 20%) | Total of returns |
| | (Number of returns) | | | | |
| Chemicals: | | | | | |
| Finished and specialty | 1 | 2 | 1 | 4 | 8 |
| Basic | 1 | 2 | 1 | 0 | 4 |
| Sub-total | 2 | 4 | 2 | 4 | 12 |
| Mechanical engineering | 7 | 1 | 0 | 2 | 10 |
| Man-made fibres | 1 | 1 | 0 | 0 | 2 |
| Electrical engineering | 7 | 1 | 0 | 0 | 8 |
| Total | 17 | 7 | 2 | 6 | 32[b] |
| *Percentage of returns* | *53* | *22* | *6* | *19* | *100* |

NOTES:
[a] Percentages refer to the estimated reduction in annual R & D in recent years that would have been experienced, had patent monopolies not been available.
[b] Some companies made returns for more than one activity.

eight there was thought to be at least some appreciable effect. The six returns in which R & D was thought to be *substantially* affected were in the fields of pharmaceuticals (2), crop chemicals, special industrial chemicals, heavy industrial plant and automotive components. The majority of mechanical engineering firms felt that their R & D was probably very little affected, while all but one of the electrical firms replying were firmly of the belief that their R & D was not at all sensitive to patent protection, certainly so far as its overall size was concerned. The two man-made fibres firms which felt able to give an answer believed that their R & D was probably very little affected.

Of those replying that the size of their R & D would be little affected by the absence of patent monopolies, a number pointed out that the type of project undertaken might be slightly different under a compulsory licensing system, although none believed that any radical redirection of their programme would be required. The most that was claimed for patent protection in these cases was that its absence might make management slightly more reluctant to undertake the more speculative type of scheme than they are under the present system. However, it was also observed that the expectation of a pay-off in such schemes is normally so remote at the start that patents are often an academic consideration at that stage, while by the time patents emerge it may be too late to withdraw.

The estimates given above can be expressed in terms of amounts of R & D expenditure dependent on patent protection, and this is done for our three principal industry groups in Table 9.2. Since several of the replies to this question were deliberately imprecise, it was sometimes necessary to use our own judgment to convert them to the percentages on which the table is based. In the one or two cases where considerable latitude existed, the maximum figures that seemed reasonably justifiable were chosen.

The returns included here account for about two-thirds of the R & D expenditure reported in our sample proper. (The gap is due both to the inability of some firms to supply answers, and to the fact that many of those replying restricted themselves to one major activity.)

It emerges on the basis of these figures that roughly 8 per cent of R & D expenditure in the three fields combined was judged to be essentially dependent on patent protection. The areas substantially affected were pharmaceuticals, in which it was judged that approximately two-thirds of R & D was so dependent, and other finished and specialty chemicals, in which about a quarter of R & D was dependent on patents. By contrast, basic chemicals, plant, machinery and equipment and components and materials were thought to be only marginally affected and electrical engineering hardly at all.

Apart from the man-made fibres producers, the main absentees from Tables 9.1 and 2, compared with our sample proper, are in pharmaceuticals (one company) and basic chemicals (an oil company), estimates for which could not be obtained. Our own judgment, based on discussions with the companies concerned, is that the orders of magnitude shown in the table would not be greatly affected, had they been included. The man-made fibres industry is rather more difficult to assess, but estimates supplied by two of our three companies in this field suggest that the effects of patents on R & D in man-made fibres are nowadays probably very small. However, this conclusion may not properly reflect past experience in the basic development of synthetic fibres and it will be reviewed in greater detail in Chapter 14.

While it would be unwise to base solid conclusions on these assessments alone, they are very much in line with evidence produced elsewhere in the study, and particularly that in the previous section. It is reassuring, for example, to find that the industries in which patents are thought to have by far the largest impact on R & D of those examined – namely, finished and specialty chemicals – are also those which felt themselves to be most vulnerable to competition under a

TABLE 9.2. *Estimated impact of patent protection on R & D expenditure in 1968: 25 responding companies*[a]

| Industry | (1)<br>R & D<br>expenditure<br>in the U.K.<br>(£m) | (2)<br>R & D<br>dependent<br>on patent<br>protection<br>(£m) | (3)<br>(1) as<br>proportion<br>of (2)<br>(%) |
|---|---|---|---|
| Chemicals: | | | |
| Pharmaceuticals | 4·9 | 3·1 | 64 |
| Other finished and specialty | 7·1 | 1·8 | 25 |
| Basic | 5·5 | 0·2 | 5 |
| Sub-total | 17·5 | 5·2 | 17 |
| Mechanical engineering: | | | |
| Plant, machinery and equipment | 3·6 | 0·3 | 7 |
| Components and materials | 2·1 | 0·1 | 2 |
| Sub-total | 5·7 | 0·3 | 5 |
| Electrical engineering | 42·7 | negligible | negligible |
| Total of above | 65·9 | 5·5 | 8 |

NOTE:
[a] Coverage is as in Table 9.1, except that man-made fibres are excluded.

compulsory licensing system. Thus, pharmaceutical firms stressed their conviction that the royalties likely to be received under a compulsory licensing system would do little to compensate for the market losses they would experience. It is also reassuring that those who were least concerned about the competitive implications of compulsory licensing – namely, major firms in the electronics and radio field – believe that their R & D effort is not at all sensitive to patent protection. (Those who were most definite in this view were among firms that receive substantial support for R & D from the Government.)

A more extended discussion of findings for selected industries will be postponed until Part III. We review next a parallel set of quantitative results for 'innovation', but before that we consider briefly a subsidiary question relating to the nature of R & D that is encouraged by the patent system.

### Duplication of R & D

It might be argued that some significant part of the impact on R & D referred to above may constitute the sort of work that is needed essentially to circumvent another's patents, for such efforts would presumably become unnecessary if patent monopolies were eliminated. While this argument seems inherently somewhat implausible – on the ground that R & D which is typically dependent on patent protection is of a different kind from that which 'designs around' a minor obstruction or can easily be 'designed around' – it cannot be ignored altogether.

Accordingly, respondents were invited to judge how much R & D would have been saved by their companies in recent years if they had had access (on reasonable commercial terms) to all the patents they wished. The question (Section IX, Q. 7) follows the one relating to the accessability of licences which was discussed in the previous section of this chapter (page 183). As stated there, almost all companies replied on this point, and of these only three felt they had been caused to undertake R & D which they would otherwise not have done, and in all three cases the amounts were said to be very small. If these judgments are correct, the view that patent monopolies cause a considerable amount of wasteful R & D seems largely unfounded.

In fact, the latter view was heavily discounted by the patent and research managers to whom we talked. Most agreed that a certain amount of essentially immitative R & D activity takes place, but the universal opinion was that this is attributable largely to a desire for product differentiation rather than to obstructiveness on the part of patentees. Several made the point that companies in some fields customarily undertake a substantial amount of research which is directed to solving the same core of basic technical problems, but this was defended on the ground that competitive research of this more fundamental nature has frequently led to important and unforeseen discoveries.

Whatever the truth of the latter contention, the relevant point for us is that most immitative work of a more trivial nature would proceed regardless of the patent system. A resolute and competent manufacturer with some patents of his own to offer can usually gain access to patents attaching to the subsidiary features of a product or process, if he wishes to do so. He may well meet more obstruction if he pursues licences on patents of a more crucial nature, but if so his usual reaction is to adopt a different line of approach which involves a more original contribution than the mere duplication of another's research.

For this reason, we are inclined to conclude that little of the R & D judged above to be dependent on patent protection can be dismissed as wasteful in an obvious sense, and therefore that there would probably be little genuine economy of R & D from this source under a system of compulsory licensing. The question of alternative uses for the resources in question nevertheless remains a relevant one, and this will be touched on in the following section.

While the sensitivity of R & D to patent protection is an important part of the picture, it seemed desirable to broaden the investigation to consider the larger question of the impact on innovation – the first introduction of new products and processes on a commercial scale. This is a difficult subject to tackle, since firms do not in general identify expenditures on innovation in the way that most identify R & D expenditures. The approach adopted was to assess the impact on the annual selling value of technologically novel production by finding out what proportion of total production in various categories is 'patent-based', and how much of that would not have been produced had patent protection not been available. The R & D costs associated with the patent-based production were also obtained and this enabled a check to be made on the results of the previous section.

*Patent-based production*

As a first step in this part of the exercise, respondents were asked to estimate the proportions of their sales of U.K. production in the various categories in the survey year that were 'patent-based', in the sense that patents attached to them in a significant way, either directly or via components or processes used in their manufacture. It was suggested in the notes to the questionnaire (see especially pages 401–2) and subsequent discussions that a product should be considered to be 'patent-based' if the patentee could use his patents – should he wish to do so – to deter others from producing or selling a *closely* similar product, through having a patent either on the product or on a process or material needed for its manufacture. In some cases the answer proved to be relatively straightforward – as where sales consisted of patented articles, substances, components, machines, etc. – but in others the position was inevitably a matter of judgment – as for instance where sales consisted of machines on which some part, component or special design feature was patented. The resulting figures were in most cases rough estimates based on the knowledge and opinions of patent specialists and, in some cases, of management on the production or commercial sides. Proportions vary considerably between companies in the same general industrial field, depending on the research content and technical nature of their major production categories.

The relevant figures are summarised by category of production for our three main industrial fields in Table 9.3. It can be seen from column (1) of this table that sales of U.K. production (including exports) of the 22 companies in these industries that were able to supply answers

TABLE 9.3. *Estimated impact of patent protection on U.K. production in 1968: 22 responding firms*

| Industry | (1) Sales of U.K. production (£m) | (2) Of these, sales of 'patent-based' production (£m) | (% of (1)) | (3) R & D expenditure on patent-based production as proportion of (2) (%) | (4) Production dependent on patent protection (£m) | (5) (4) as proportion of (1) (%) |
|---|---|---|---|---|---|---|
| Chemicals:[a] | | | | | | |
| Pharmaceuticals | 63·2 | 42·7 | 68 | 13½ | 42·7 | 68 |
| Other finished and specialty | 332·0 | 116·8 | 35 | 3 | 16·3 | 5 |
| Basic[a] | 170·1 | 105·8 | 62 | 1½ | negligible | negligible |
| Sub-total | 565·3 | 265·3 | 47 | 4 | 59·0 | 10 |
| Mechanical engineering: | | | | | | |
| Plant, machinery, equipment | 194·2 | 33·1 | 17 | 4½ | 3·7 | 2 |
| Components and materials | 91·0 | 19·1 | 21 | 1½ | 1·1 | 1 |
| Sub-total | 285·2 | 52·2 | 18 | 3½ | 4·8 | 1½ |
| Electrical engineering: | | | | | | |
| Electronic, radio, T.V. and associated components and equipment | 364·7 | 100·9 | 28 | 8 | negligible | negligible |
| Other electrical machinery and equipment | 251·2 | 69·4 | 28 | 2 | 8·6 | 3½ |
| Sub-total | 615·9 | 170·3 | 28 | 5½ | 8·6 | 1½ |
| Total of above | 1,466·4 | 487·8 | 33 | 4½ | 72·4 | 5 |

NOTES:

[a] Excluding the oil companies.

Column (2) 'Patent-based production' is production that has patents attaching to it in a 'significant way,' – see page 201.

Column (4) 'Production dependent on patent protection' is patent-based production that would be abandoned or replaced under a thoroughgoing compulsory licensing system. See page 205.

amounted to about £1,470 million, or just over 75 per cent of total sample sales in these categories. (There was a high response among mechanical and electrical engineering firms and in pharmaceuticals, but several chemical firms were unable to supply answers, including the two oil companies.)

Column (2) shows that on the whole about one-third of this production was patent-based, the highest proportions being found in chemicals and the lowest in mechanical engineering. As might be expected, the highest proportion in a single category occurs in pharmaceuticals, although basic chemicals (as far as they were covered) are not on average far behind. In general, bulk industrial chemicals tend to be patent-based on account of the reliance of many of them on patented processes, although there are notable exceptions (e.g., certain bulk industrial gases). Finished chemical products with a high research content, such as weedkillers and pesticides, dyes, industrial adhesives and the newer kinds of plastics, are highly patent-based, whereas others (e.g., toilet preparations, food chemicals, paints, detergents, fertilisers) are only moderately so, at least on the evidence of our sample.

The picture in mechanical engineering is very mixed. Some types of industrial plant and machinery are fairly heavily patent-based (e.g., printing, baking and shoe machinery) but others have patents only minimally attaching to them. Similarly, some types of components and materials are strongly patent-based (e.g., certain automotive suspension and engine components), while those of a less specific or more conventional character are not. On the whole, about one-fifth of sales by mechanical engineering firms in our sample turned out to be patent-based.

In the electronic, radio and associated areas of the electrical engineering industry, the situation appears to be more straightforward. As a rule respondents in this field tended to regard components (e.g., semiconductors, valves, capacitors, switches, microcircuits, etc.) as mainly patent-based, while assemblies and sets of equipment (e.g., transmission and telephone equipment and systems, computers and other data processing equipment instrumentation and control systems, radio and television equipment for both broadcasting and domestic use) were on the whole regarded as non-patent-based, although they would be likely to incorporate large numbers of different patented components. (There were some exceptions, of which colour television equipment was the most notable.) In 'other' electrical machinery and equipment, however, the position is as mixed as in mechanical engineering. Thus, certain types of electric motors are patent-based by virtue of some patentable feature in their construction, while others are not;

some types of insulated cable (e.g., small-core co-axial cable) are patent-based, while more conventional cable is not. Novel types of electric storage batteries are patent-based, but conventional varieties are not, etc. The overall answer for this category – 28 per cent – is very much the outcome of 'educated guesswork' on the part of the patent specialists concerned.

The essential point about these estimates of patent-based production is that, although rough in many cases, they supplied an upper limit to the maximum proportion of a firm's output in various categories that could reasonably be considered to be dependent on patent protection. Such a narrowing of the field for possible answers helped to bring the question of effects into proper focus and helped to prevent respondents from generalising about the whole of their business on the basis of its patent-oriented sectors. This was a tendency which we tried hard to guard against, while at the same time erring as far as seemed reasonable on the high side in selecting figures where a range of possibilities was put to use.

Most participants in this part of the exercise were able to give some indication of the ratios of R & D expenditure to selling value of output in their patent-based lines, and the results are summarised in column (3) of Table 9.3. It is worth noting that, although the average R & D ratio in all patent-based lines, $4\frac{1}{2}$ per cent, is almost exactly the same as that for non-patent-based lines, the position in individual industries is very different (as can be seen by comparing these percentages with those in Table 8.1, column (6)). Thus, R & D ratios in patent-based lines exceed those in other lines in all three chemical categories and in plant, machinery and equipment (including 'other' electrical), while the reverse is true in the electronics, radio, and associated field. Broadly speaking, patent-based lines tend to be the research-intensive ones in chemicals and mechanical engineering, while the opposite seems true in electrical engineering.

Replies to our question concerning the profitability of patent-based production were for the most part too vague to be incorporated in the results. However, such answers as were received suggested that the profitability of patent-based lines (reckoned as a percentage of their selling value after charging R & D and other current overheads) was usually higher than on other lines in the same category, although rarely a great deal higher. More general responses to this question also indicated that profitability of patent-based production would in most cases be slightly higher, but seldom very much higher, than that of other production in the same category.

*Effect of patent protection*

Amounts of patent-based production judged to be dependent on patent protection are summarised in column (4).[1] As in the assessment of effects on R & D described earlier, the replies on which these figures are based were for the most part rough estimates by those closely concerned, reached after discussing the issues and the method of approach with us. In some instances – usually where production was thought to be unaffected (or very little affected) by patent protection – participants made it clear that their answers were quite definite; in others – more particularly where patents were thought to have an appreciable impact – replies were more tentative, and in the latter we gave the benefit of the doubt to those claiming large effects, as in the exercise on R & D.

At the risk of wearisome repetition, we again draw attention to the limitations of these estimates – viz., that they arise from a fairly small selection of firms and even for these firms are quite rough. Thus, the figure of five per cent in column (5) for 'other' finished and specialty chemicals really means no more than that we think the true result is unlikely to be greater than about seven or less than about two per cent, while one per cent for components and materials means merely that the true share is probably not negligible but probably not more than about two or three per cent.

These limitations do not matter much where the impact for an industry is clearly seen to be small or relatively modest, but they do make difficulties for interpreting the results in pharmaceuticals, which is the one field of those distinguished where the reported impact is large. It can be seen from column (4) that the bulk of production judged to be dependent on patent protection in the table occurred in pharmacticceuals and in other finished and specialty chemicals, with much smaller amounts in components and materials and in 'other' electrical machinery and equipment. The production thus affected accounted for over two-thirds of total production in pharmaceuticals (i.e., essentially all 'patent-based' production of the responding firms), a proportion approached by no other category of those shown, although certain branches of finished chemicals, such as crop protection chemicals, were judged to be heavily affected.

The estimates for pharmaceuticals stand out so sharply from the rest that some comment seems necessary here, although the industry is

---

[1] The relevant question is Section VIII, Q. 4 of Form B, reproduced on page 398. In the notes to this section and in subsequent discussions it was suggested, as earlier in connection with R & D, that respondents should approach the problem by comparing their actual production in 1968 with what it would have been under a compulsory licensing system of the sort outlined.

dealt with as a special study in Chapter 10. Briefly, all three pharmaceutical firms were able to argue convincingly and with great conviction that essentially none of their patent-based lines (corresponding roughly to their newer prescription medicines) would have been embarked upon in the environment of 'thoroughgoing' compulsory licensing we put to them. Two out of the three respondents went so far as to say that they would probably not have ventured into the drug industry on a substantial scale, had patent protection not been available. Admittedly, these estimates may well overstate the true impact on the entire research-based wing of the pharmaceutical industry in the U.K., for two principal reasons. Firstly, the industry as a whole contains a number of longer-established firms, likely to be rather less sensitive to patent protection, and 'effects' for these might well be lower. Secondly, the estimates in the table make no allowance for the possibility that if the rate of introduction of basically new drugs fell away very drastically in a compulsory licensing world, the pressure of unsatisfied demand for new drugs might be so strong as to attract other firms to expand their pharmaceutical R & D, in the hope of making high gains on the strength of secrecy, lead times, large production volumes, etc.

For a variety of reasons we think it would be a mistake to allow this latter possibility to detract radically from the figures in Table 9.3. Thus it is of the very essence of the case in pharmaceuticals that secret technology, lead times and large-scale manufacturing seldom provide much protection from the sort of 'instant competition' that can arise quite rapidly after the introduction of important new drugs that do not have patent protection. Moreover, the operation of official price regulation in the U.K. nowadays[1] has greatly weakened firms' prospects of earning really spectacular profits on prescription medicines sold to the National Health Service, however scarce new ones might become. Finally, it seems improbable that governments in the U.K. or other advanced countries could tolerate a serious cut-back in R & D expenditure on drugs by private industry for very long without being impelled to assume major responsibility for the task themselves in some way or other. For these reasons it seems best to retain these estimates for the firms concerned, while pointing out that the figures should not be taken too literally and that the true impact for the U.K. industry as a whole would probably be somewhat lower. We shall return to these matters when we come to discuss pharmaceuticals in Chapter 10.

Apart from pharmaceuticals, the main specific types of production found to be sensitive to patent protection were automotive suspension units, advanced types of nuclear and industrial boilers, small core

---

[1] Reinforced in 'intractable' cases by the investigative powers of the Monopolies Commission, as shown by the latter's recent report (11 April 1973) on the supply of tranquillisers.

co-axial cables and certain types of electrical and mechanical equipment for the automotive and aircraft industries. Almost without exception, respondents in basic chemicals and in the electronic, radio and associated field (including components) were fairly sure that their production was not dependent on patent monopolies to any perceptible extent, while this was also the general answer among plant and machinery manufacturers – although several exceptions were pointed out in this field. Overall, the proportion of total U.K. production by the 22 companies that was judged to be dependent on patent protection came out at about five per cent.

The difference between this percentage and the percentage for impact on R & D in Table 9.2 (applying to a slightly different sample of firms) can probably be attributed largely to differences in the R & D content of affected lines as compared with other lines of production. Consideration of the results for 'other' finished and specialty chemicals, for example, (five per cent in Table 9.3 as compared with 25 per cent in 9.2) suggests that the R & D content of patent-based lines was much higher than in other lines in this field, and also possibly that the R & D content of patent-based production 'lost' or 'replaced' was higher than in other patent-based lines. (However, it could also be the case that some R & D would be abandoned without withdrawing or measurably altering the production associated with it. This could be imagined to happen, for example, where the research affected is of a particularly basic or long-term sort, whose loss would not affect immediate production plans in any discernible way.)

It should finally be mentioned that, of the 22 companies included in Table 9.3, only seven stated that patent protection had had a perceptible effect on their production, and of these only four claimed that one or more major portions of their business were substantially dependent on patents (i.e. more than 10 per cent of their production affected).

As far as we can judge from the information provided and from subsequent discussions with those concerned, it seems unlikely that the results of Table 9.3 would have been very different, had it been possible to include all our thirty sample companies. The main quantitative gaps are in basic chemicals, where the oil companies are notable absentees, and man-made fibres. As will be explained in Chapter 11, which discusses bulk petrochemicals and other basic chemicals, our impression with regard to the bulk chemical side of their activities is that patent monopolies have in recent years had very little impact on the rate at which they have introduced new products and processes, and their inclusion here would if anything probably reduce slightly the estimates given for chemicals as a whole in column (5). It is harder to generalise with confidence about man-made fibres, but our tentative conclusion is that compulsory licensing would not have affected the pace of innovation there in the last decade, although it may well have affected the development of nylon and Terylene in their early years. This conclusion will be reviewed more fully in Chapter 14.

### *Alternative production under compulsory licensing*

Firms were invited to say what alternative action would have been followed in cases where their patent-based production would have been reduced under a compulsory licensing system. (The relevant question was Section VIII, Q. 5, reproduced on page 398.) Broadly speaking two types of answers were given, depending mainly on the extent of the 'loss' of patent-based production that was anticipated in these circumstances.

In the three cases of major activities in which more than half of production was thought to be essentially dependent on patents, it was said that the divisions of the firms concerned would probably not have existed under a compulsory licensing system. This was the view, for example, of the two pharmaceutical producers who were able to supply answers to this question. The implication was either that these companies would have expanded their operations in essentially unrelated types of output, or that they would have released the relevant resources, at the same time distributing more profits or raising smaller amounts of capital from outside, for use elsewhere in the economy. It was not possible to establish by our interview approach how far the 'surplus' resources would have been redeployed within the corporate groups concerned as opposed to being utilised elsewhere, but in either eventuality it seems reasonable to think that the alternative use would largely be in lines which would not be patent-based, and which would on the whole be much less research-intensive than the output displaced.

The likelihood of this outcome is reinforced by the replies that were received in the four or five cases where production was found to be more moderately dependent on patent protection, although still appreciably so. The view of these respondents was that the affected production would be replaced by other lines that would not be patent-based. It was thought that some part of the alternative production might be of the kind that is based on secret (i.e., non-patented) R & D, but that it would mostly comprise an expansion in lines with a low research content.

One point that seems fairly clear is that, as stated earlier, established research-based firms would not be among the ranks of compulsory licence applicants – at least in the early years following a switch from the existing system to a (thoroughgoing) compulsory licensing system. Consequently, little of whatever 'alternative production' they would develop would consist of the patent-based products of others. On the other hand, it is of course more than likely that some 'alternative production' would be production by non-research-based firms under compulsory licences obtained as a result of the switch, and in so far as this would happen there would be no immediate loss of research-based production in the economy. (Indeed consumers might be temporarily better off, since prices of some goods subjected to compulsory licensing might fall quite sharply after the switch.) These benefits, however, would probably be short-lived, for it is an important part of our argument that if research-based firms had because of compulsory licensing to abandon a substantial part of their production in a particular line, the R & D associated with that line would sooner or later also be abandoned and not be taken up by any other firm. Should that stage be reached, compulsory licensing would largely disappear, except as a marginal activity in some fields.

It therefore seems fair to conclude that, from the point of view of the industrial fields concerned, if not of the specific firms affected, the marginal increase in resources devoted to patent-based production attributable to the exploitation of patent monopolies has as its counterpart a roughly corresponding decrease in resources devoted to non-research-intensive lines. In other words, had the industries covered in our inquiry operated for many years under a system of compulsory licensing, rather than under the existing system, recent levels of output in research-intensive lines would have been marginally lower, overall, and output in other lines would have been marginally higher. If the effects estimated above are roughly correct, the substitution would be negligible in the electronic, radio and associated branches of electrical engineering, and in basic chemicals; very small in plant, machinery and equipment (including 'other' electrical); and marginal on the whole in finished and specialty chemicals. However, some important research-intensive branches of the latter, of which the outstanding one is undoubtedly pharmaceuticals, would probably be very seriously depressed and several leading British producers might not have entered the field, at least in the opinion of those closely concerned.

Consideration of the implications of the results in Table 9.3 for R & D expenditure lends support both to the foregoing and to the estimates given in Section C of this chapter. Assuming that the research-ratios for lines of production judged to be dependent on patent protection are similar to those for other patent-based lines in the same category, it can be calculated that the R & D expenditure associated with production that would be displaced in the absence of patent protection was roughly £7 million in 1968 for firms included in Table 9.3, or some 10 per cent of all R & D done by them. This compares quite closely with the estimate of 8 per cent for the impact on R & D given in Table 9.2 for a slightly larger collection of firms. The implication is clearly that patent protection has a larger proportional impact on R & D than on sales of production by the firms in question, reflecting the fact, suggested above, that the R & D content of lines responsive to patent-protection is higher on average than that in other lines.

E.   IMPACT ON THE SPREAD OF TECHNICAL KNOWLEDGE

In the course of discussions on the impact of patents on research and innovation, industrialists frequently made the point that although the size and direction of their R & D programmes would probably not be much different in a world of compulsory licensing, their policy with regard both to patenting and to publication of their R & D results in other ways would probably be more selective. A few firms (mainly in the chemical field) even went so far as to suggest that they would probably not patent anything. Most were less categorical, but, although few were willing to venture quantitative estimates, a common theme was that certain types of inventions or improvements which are at present patented would not be patented or otherwise published under a compulsory licensing system.

The general characteristic of inventions that might be kept secret under these conditions (apart from their being of the type that firms wish to monopolise or license selectively) is that some essential step or feature should remain undetectable to outsiders after their implementation in manufacture. (Clearly, there would be little point in refraining from patenting inventions all of whose essential technical features are revealed once they are put into practice, for such inventions if unpatented could be freely copied by outsiders, whereas they might command royalties if patented under a compulsory licensing system.) Broadly speaking, the former inventions include many of those that apply to manufacturing *processes* (the essentials of which are not revealed by examination of the product), and those that have substantial secret know-how attaching to them, which may well include some process inventions. While it is not possible to be precise about the proportion of patents that would fall into these categories, it is perhaps relevant to recall that the majority of patents in basic chemicals (and a fair proportion in finished and specialty chemicals) attach to processes, and that, as was shown in Chapter 7, the bulk of patent licences in all fields contain know-how provisions of some sort.

On further consideration, however, it is not clear that all or virtually all inventions involving essential know-how would necessarily be candidates for secrecy under a compulsory licensing system. Several arguments are possible in this connection. It might for instance be suggested that, where know-how is essential to the successful implementation of an invention, the rational inventor would choose to patent the invention (even under a compulsory licence system) rather than keep it secret, for he would thereby gain something in security for the invention while at the same time retaining an element of control – which would remain with him by virtue of the secret know-how, without which a straight licence on the invention would not be of great help to outsiders. But this assumes that secret know-how alone is an adequate protection for the invention, whereas the opinion of most industrialists to whom we talked was that most types of know-how can be kept secret for no more than a limited period of time, the main problem being that key personnel cannot be prevented from changing their employer and taking the secrets with them. (By comparison, industrial espionage was rated a minor problem.) In their view, the most that could be hoped for was usually that know-how might be kept secret for a small number of years, perhaps sufficient to establish a lead which would put a firm with a rapidly developing technology ahead of its rivals in the medium term. It might nevertheless be argued that even if the know-how cannot be kept secret for very long, the inventor would still do better to patent the invention under a compulsory licence system and take what royalties he could, relying on temporary know-how secrecy to control access to the technology. However, some firms pointed out that the period of control through secret know-how would probably be shortened if attention were drawn to the invention by patenting it, and these thought they would do better to refrain from patenting this type of invention under a compulsory licence system.

While it was not possible to arrive at orders of magnitude on this point, it seems fair to conclude that a considerable number of process inventions and improvements that have been patented under the existing system would not have been patented in a world of compulsory licensing, although perhaps not quite as many as some companies were prepared to claim. What does seem fairly clear is that important process improvements whose essential features are revealed *in the patent* would almost certainly be kept secret, for a large element of control over them would be lost by the patentee under a compulsory licensing system, whereas it might be retained for a useful period if they were kept secret. An example of such an invention would be the introduction of a new catalyst for use in the production of some basic chemical by a method which otherwise departed little from standard processes used in the field. There have been a number of inventions that might fall into this category in recent years, as will be seen in Part III.

It is extremely hard even to begin to assess the economic importance of the reduction in the quantity of technical information generally available to industry that this decline in patenting would represent. We did scratch the surface of the question by inviting firms to comment on published patent specifications as a source of information on general technical developments in their fields and on the research work of competitors – not including knowledge gained through taking licences (Form B, Section x, Q. 1 and 2). Most firms in our sample said that specifications were of 'some' value to research staff on technical details and to management on general research trends and the work of competitors, but less than a third of these were prepared to term these benefits 'substantial'. Those that did so were in chemicals, machinery and man-made fibres, while respondents in electrical engineering were on the whole very sceptical.

This line of approach was pursued further by inviting respondents to put a money value on the general information that they obtain through patent specifications. The question (Section x, Q. 3) sought to discover the *maximum* fee that firms would have paid the Patent Office in 1968 for access to patent specifications published in that year, had they been confronted with an 'all or nothing' choice, and had there been no other way of obtaining specifications (e.g., through an Abstract service or from overseas). In the event, virtually all those replying, usually after discussion of the issues with us, placed rather low values on this benefit. Thus, the overall answer for 22 responding firms averaged about three-quarters of one per cent of their combined R & D expenditure in the same year, industry figures ranging from about $1\frac{1}{2}$ per cent in chemicals and man-made fibres to less than $\frac{1}{5}$ per cent in electrical engineering.

These figures are admittedly based on no more than 'educated guesses' by the patent and research managers concerned on a question which by its nature is hard to answer with any confidence. Furthermore, they make no allowance for the value of information which is published under the protective umbrella of patents. A number of firms said that their research results frequently appear in scientific and technical journals, conference papers and other kinds of technical literature, and this was especially emphasised by firms in the electronic, radio and associated field, where such literature is a major source of information for customers, as well as for other manufacturers in the field.[1] Several firms (although none in the latter field) made the point that they would probably be more selective about publishing their results in this way

[1] Publication of this sort is generally delayed until patents have been granted.

under a compulsory licensing system, particularly if it were decided not to patent them.

It is not easy to gauge the order of magnitude of the economic loss that this decline in the broader type of technical publication would represent. In general, chemical firms tended to rate patent specifications and the related technical literature as of about equal value to them, while respondents in mechanical engineering were inclined on the whole to value patent specifications more highly than the literature. By contrast, electrical engineering firms clearly valued the technical literature much more highly than patent specifications, especially in electronics and radio. Altogether, and bearing in mind that technical publication in the latter field would proceed for the most part regardless of the patent position, it seems reasonable to conclude that firms in our sample valued the technical literature associated with patented inventions and improvements somewhat, but not a great deal, more highly than the patent specifications themselves.

If these assessments are roughly correct, and we again emphasise that they reflect the best guesses of those concerned and relate to a question which does not lend itself easily to this sort of approach, the value of the general information derived by responding firms from patent specifications and associated technical literature is equivalent to no more than a few per cent of their R & D expenditure. This valuation might perhaps be thought to be on the low side, but even if it were greatly increased and the view were taken that an extremely high proportion (say, a third) of patented inventions would not be patented under a compulsory system, the impact of patent monopolies in this connection cannot be put at very much more than 5 per cent of the R & D expenditure of the firms involved. That is to say, the loss of general technical information that would be experienced by responding firms if patenting were curtailed under a compulsory licensing system would, on this reckoning, be of very small value in relation to their R & D expenditure.[1]

While we would hesitate to place great reliance on this finding alone, it agrees very much with more general impressions received in the inquiry. For instance, all research managers with whom we discussed the point were clear that, if presented with the choice of spending a modest addition to their budgets either on greater access to (and retrieval of) patent specifications and other technical literature or on their own research activity, they would unhesitatingly choose the latter; or perhaps more significantly that, if obliged to make an equi-proportional cut in graduate staff employed either on retrieval of technical

[1] We are not including here any loss to the economy that would come about through a reduction in licensing attributable to increased secrecy. This is discussed later (pp. 214–16).

information or on research, they would unhesitatingly choose the former.

For these reasons, we are inclined to think that the additional technical information in the form of patent specifications and related literature which is attributable to the influence of patent monopolies is a benefit of rather marginal value for industry as a whole, although it may be important in particular cases. We did not collect any information on the benefits derived from such publication elsewhere in the economy, but our judgment is that these benefits are probably very small: it is hard to believe that the sort of information concerned – namely that relating to the vital details of improvements in large scale industrial techniques, product engineering, etc., – is of any great economic value outside the industrial sector of the economy.

### Exchange through licensing

Quite apart from the question, discussed in Section B of this chapter, of whether the licensing of patented inventions would tend to expand under a compulsory licensing system, we have here to consider the possibility that some types of licensing might diminish if the rate at which inventions are patented fell under such a system.

Although it has been argued above that many inventions, especially in the process field, would probably not be patented in a world of compulsory licensing, this does not necessarily mean that they would not be licensed in such a world. As was pointed out in Chapter 7, some 'pure' know-how licensing takes place on an arms'-length basis quite successfully without the assistance of patents, mainly in mechanical engineering, and there is reason to think that this kind of transaction could be expanded if firms desired to utilise it more. However, it seems doubtful whether the development of pure know-how licensing could fully replace whatever patent licensing would be 'lost' under a compulsory licensing system, for the following reaons. Firstly, to the extent that inventions at present patented became wholly confidential, firms in general would be less informed about technical developments in their field, and would accordingly seek fewer licences. Secondly, there is a widespread conviction among industrialists that the existence of patents greatly facilitates licensing. That is to say, other things being equal (the rate and direction of inventive activity, the state of general awareness about technical developments, etc.) technical information is thought to be transferred much more readily between firms if there are patents attaching to it than it otherwise would, for reasons that are mainly legal in nature.

The essential point here, as we are given to understand it, is that a patent comprises a specific item of property which is specially recognised in law. There is little room for doubt in a patent licence agreement as to what the subject matter of the agreement is and what rights are being granted. This is not equally true of know-how or other information that is not patented – because it is usually less easy to define and identify, and its status in law is less straightforward. For example, it appears to be the case that if know-how (without patents) obtained under licence is passed to a third party in contravention of an agreement, that party can seldom be restrained by legal action from using the know-how or passing it to others. The licensor may of course sue the licensee for breach of contract (although difficulties may be encountered if the licensee claims that the information passed was the outcome of his own research, using the licensor's results), but by then the damage is done and it can rarely be undone.[1] A major source of uncertainty lies in the difficulty of distinguishing between know-how etc. supplied under licence – particularly where extensive personal contacts are involved – and that developed independently by the licensee; such uncertainty can be greatly reduced where the heart of the information transferred is contained in a patent, especially as it will then have been subjected to the intensive scrutiny of patent examiners.

While not all those with whom we discussed this point had similar qualms about controlling pure know-how, it was evident that in some sections of industry, particularly basic and bulk chemicals, man-made fibres and other fields where processes are important, there are strong misgivings about licensing unpatented information. It seems reasonable to believe that the amount of information on processes transferred under contract in these fields would be somewhat diminished under a compulsory licensing system in which a reduction would take place in the patenting of process improvements of the sort described.

More will be said about the impact on information transfers in particular cases in Part III, but it can be observed in summary here that licensing in some fields, especially basic chemicals, might be quite seriously hampered. However, the impact should not be exaggerated. Not only would many inventions (probably the majority) continue to be patented under a compulsory licence system; it must also be

---

[1] The unease about licensing know-how without patents felt by many respondents to our inquiry is summed up by the following comment by one patent manager: 'The main difficulty in relation to a know-how licence is that neither party has any security. As you point out it is very difficult to define the boundary of the know-how being transmitted, so that the licensor has little redress if the licensee builds upon it, and the licensee has no redress if a third party obtains by independent effort or otherwise, an equivalent know-how. Thus there is very little legal basis for a know-how agreement.' See also the comments noted in Chapter 7 (p. 119 n.).

remembered that the industries likely to be affected – namely, those which operate large-scale manufacturing processes in which patents protect some critical step or ingredient – tend to be composed of small numbers of large companies in circumstances of near monopoly, or oligopoly if considered from the viewpoint of international markets. The established firms in these industries, many of which are multinational corporations, are accustomed to exchanging patent rights (and, to a lesser extent, associated know-how or other technical information) either in formal 'field' cross-licensing agreements with minimal balancing payments, or sometimes, where patents alone are involved, informally through tacit agreement on mutual non-enforcement of patent rights. They would in general, we believe, be no more likely to pirate each others' confidential know-how etc. under a compulsory licensing system than they would to exercise compulsory licenses against each others' patents. (Furthermore, leakages of secrets through bidding away of key staff seem a fainter possibility where the senior managements of the firms involved are in fairly frequent contact.) In these circumstances, uncontrolled leakage of know-how would probably occur mainly via small, unestablished and non-research-based firms on the fringes of these industries: as was explained earlier, the major established producers in basic chemicals, man-made fibres, and similar fields do not believe that such peripheral firms would constitute a serious competitive threat in a world of compulsory licensing, owing to the existence of barriers to competition which have little to do with the current patent position in those fields.

### F.    IMPACT ON OVERSEAS TRADE

In view of the large volume of foreign patenting undertaken by British firms and the stress laid by them on the international character of the patent system, it seems desirable to attempt some assessment of the impact of patents on overseas trade, however tentative. Although information was collected on exports and international royalty payments in the course of the inquiry, and the topic was discussed with company spokesmen, it was not possible to obtain a great deal of detailed material on this question, and a fuller investigation would have added considerably to the already onerous task confronting participants. Accordingly, the best estimate we can make here is necessarily extremely rough, although we believe that its order of magnitude is probably correct. It unfortunately cannot include a detailed treatment of the impact on flows of overseas investment and profits, since our information on them is extremely sketchy, but these cannot be left entirely out of account and some general comments are offered on them as well.

There are two principal reasons for thinking that the patent system may encourage both international trade and overseas manufacturing investment. Firstly, the shares exported of the kinds of technology-oriented production that are sensitive to patent protection are likely to be higher than those of more conventional, non-patent-sensitive lines. It is widely recognised that the technological content of internationally-traded manufactures is higher than that of manufactures in general – for new technology is a major source of the cost and quality differences that make international trade and international investment profitable. Thus, if the patent system is effective in bringing about a shift of production in favour of patent-based goods, as suggested for certain industries in the previous sections, it should also bring about a shift of resources into exports by those industries.

The second point is that, even where patents have no significant impact on decisions at home regarding invention and innovation, they may affect exports if overseas sales are, as might be expected, more subject to competition and therefore more sensitive to patent protection than are a firm's sales in its own home market. This is likely to be so since research-based firms are frequently near-monopolists or at least capable of avoiding head-on price competition in their domestic markets, whereas overseas they are likely to be in keen competition with numbers of other research-based enterprises, especially in markets which none regard as their home territories – i.e., those outside the major industrial research centres of North America and Western Europe.

It is possible, using data collected in the inquiry, to arrive at a rough evaluation of the earlier point, at least in so far as exports and royalty earnings by participants themselves are concerned, and this will be our main concern in the remainder of this section. The second point, which can be called the 'foreign market shares' argument, is both more debatable and more difficult to assess, but we shall return to it briefly at the end of the section.

*Exports*

For the purpose of estimating the impact on exports, we make the working assumption that, for any category of production reported by a participating firm, the ratio of exports to U.K. sales of production dependent on patent protection is equal to the export ratio for all the firm's production in the relevant category.[1] This assumption is adopted in the absence of better information, and it may underestimate the

[1] Data on exports by broad category for the main sample were given in Table 8.1, p. 145.

TABLE 9.4. *Estimated impact of patent protection on U.K. exports of patent-based production in 1968: 22 responding companies*[a]

| Industry | (1)<br>U.K.<br>exports<br>(£m) | (2)<br>Exports<br>dependent<br>on patent<br>protection[b]<br>(£m) | (3)<br>(2) as<br>proportion<br>of (1)<br>(%) | (4)<br>(2) as<br>proportion<br>of 'patent-<br>based<br>production'<br>(%) |
|---|---|---|---|---|
| Chemicals: | | | | |
| Pharmaceuticals | 24·5 | 17·1 | 70 | 40 |
| Other finished and specialty | 48·9 | 6·0 | 12¼ | 5 |
| Basic[a] | 21·4 | negligible | negligible | negligible |
| Sub-total | 94·8 | 23·1 | 24¼ | 8¾ |
| Mechanical engineering: | | | | |
| Plant, machinery, equipment | 35·1 | 0·8 | 2¼ | 2½ |
| Components and materials | 18·6 | 0·2 | 1 | 1 |
| Sub-total | 53·7 | 0·9 | 1¾ | 1¾ |
| Electrical engineering: | | | | |
| Electronic, radio, T.V., and associated components and equipment | 77·1 | negligible | negligible | negligible |
| Other electrical machinery and equipment | 44·6 | 1·8 | 4 | 2½ |
| Sub-total | 121·7 | 1·8 | 1½ | 1 |
| Total of above | 270·2 | 25·8 | 9½ | 5¼ |

NOTES:
[a] Coverage as in Table 9.3.
[b] Obtained by multiplying exports in categories of production reported by individual firms by their estimates of shares of U.K. production dependent on patent protection.

export content of patent-dependent production. However, the under-estimation is probably not serious, since in the few industries where the impact of patents is thought to be relatively large (such as pharmaceuticals), the patent-dependent lines comprise either essentially the whole or at least the bulk of categories for which separate information on exports was given.

The results for the twenty-two firms included in Table 9.3 are given in Table 9.4. It is apparent from column (3) that, in correspondence with the effects on patent-based production discussed earlier, the industries significantly affected are pharmaceuticals and, to a much smaller degree, other finished and specialty chemicals. In none of the other groups does the impact reach 5 per cent of exports, and in most it is

very small indeed.[1] A similar conclusion holds if patent-based production is used as the basis for comparison, as is shown in column (4).

It should be pointed out that the effects in Table 9.4 are 'gross',
in the sense that they do not allow for exports of whatever 'alternative'
production would be forthcoming under a compulsory licensing system;
they relate solely to exports of production dependent on patent protection, whereas it seems reasonable to think that these would be partly
replaced under a compulsory licensing system by other kinds of exports.
It is not easy to allow for the latter factor since we can make no precise
guess as to what alternative production would arise under a compulsory
licensing system, except that it would consist for the most part of non-
patent-based lines – and some would presumably comprise output produced under compulsory licence. However, a tentative impression of
the net impact of patent protection can be gained if we make the further
assumption that, in the industrial fields affected, the share of exports in
'alternative' production would be similar on average to that of production in categories with a 'low' patent-based content (say, those with
patent-based production less than one quarter of the total). For chemicals, the only group of industries shown as being significantly affected
in Table 9.4, the share of exports in all categories of production with
a 'low' patent-based content averaged 10½ per cent (considerably
lower than the average share of exports in more heavily patent-based
lines). If this is taken as the average share of exports in 'alternative'
production, the net impact of patent protection on chemical exports
in our sample comes to £17 million (i.e., £23·1 million less 10½ per
cent of £59 million, the latter being 'alternative' production equal in
size to chemical production dependent on patent protection, as shown
in Table 9.3). The net figure amounts to some 18 per cent of chemical
exports reported by this particular sample.

While it would be stretching our conclusions rather far to translate
these figures into an estimate of the overall impact on U.K. exports,
it is of interest to see how far our results in this context are affected by
the particular mix of industries covered. Using as weights the values of
U.K. manufacturing exports by major industry group in the official
trade accounts for 1968,[2] and counting as 1¾ per cent the impact on

---

[1] Readers are reminded that these effects take account only of exports of U.K. production
that would be abandoned in a compulsory licensing world. In addition, it is reasonable to
think that exports of some lines which would still be produced in the U.K. in the alternative
situation would be lost if overseas patent protection were not available, while exports of
other lines might increase if compulsory licences could be obtained on all overseas patents.
These effects are not included here because we have no basis for estimating their size,
or even whether they would on balance be positive or negative. They are discussed at
greater length in the section on 'foreign market shares' (pp. 225–7).

[2] So far as these can be separately distinguished in the summary figures published, for
example, in the U.K. *Annual Abstract of Statistics*, 1970. Exports in chemical classes 51, 52

exports of industries not included in our sample (i.e., the same percentage as in mechanical engineering), the average impact on U.K. manufactured exports comes to $3\frac{1}{2}$ per cent, or about £200 million. (This is the 'gross' impact of patent protection, before allowing for offsetting exports of alternative production.) Clearly, the relatively heavy concentration of chemicals in our sample produces an average result for the collection of industries covered which is markedly higher than the corresponding figure for U.K. manufacturing as a whole.

### Royalties and licence fees

In so far as the patent system encourages R & D, it encourages the flow of royalty earnings and licence fees associated with that R & D. Some assessment of the impact of the patent system on the U.K.'s international royalty earnings therefore seems desirable, to put alongside the results for exports.

A rough estimate for royalty earnings (net of payments) can be made on the basis of two further heroic assumptions. The first is that the effect on overseas royalties received by a responding firm is proportional to the impact on its U.K. patent-based production, on the ground that the impact on foreign patent-based production under licence from participating firms is likely to be roughly proportional to the impact on the licensor's own patent-based production in the U.K. (royalties on a licence being approximately proportional to production under the licence). Alternatively, it could be assumed that the impact on royalty income is roughly proportional to that on R & D expenditure by the licensor, but this would not make a great deal of difference to the answer.[1] Secondly, it is assumed for purposes of our standard compari-

and 59 were arbitrarily divided two-thirds to 'finished and specialty' and one-third to 'basic' chemicals.

[1] It might be argued that this approach overlooks an important item, namely the international royalties that U.K. patentees would receive on licences which they would be compelled to grant overseas under a worldwide compulsory licensing system. However, such receipts would, we believe, be for the most part merely a short-run consequence of a switch from the present system to the compulsory licensing alternative. In time, R & D associated with patented items that would be abandoned in a compulsory licensing world would likewise largely be abandoned, and receipts from the compulsory licensing of such research would largely disappear. In the case of pharmaceuticals, for example, this would mean the disappearance of virtually all the U.K.'s overseas royalty earnings, assuming that essentially all patent-based production and associated R & D would be abandoned. Pharmaceuticals is admittedly a special case; other industries would in general abandon rather little patent-based production in a world of compulsory licensing, if our findings are correct, and they might well find themselves compelled to grant compulsory licences (including some on their overseas patents) on things which at present they licence only selectively. Even so, the resulting flow of international royalties would probably be fairly small in the long run, for R & D results of the sort likely to attract compulsory licensing applications would probably not be patented on the same scale as at present. If so, international royalty receipts in these industries would not be a great deal higher than they are under the present system. (Similar arguments hold in relation to payments in the reverse direction.)

son that, in any category of production for the sample in question, the impact on the U.K.'s royalty receipts from overseas is offset by an equi-proportional impact on its payments in the opposite direction, reflecting the impact of foreign patent protection on invention and innovation overseas. This is admittedly a rather shaky procedure, but the figures for royalty payments in our sample are so small that the precise assumptions made here do not materially affect the overall conclusions.

Briefly, the main result of this approach (under which percentages obtained by dividing column (4) by column (2) in Table 9.3 were applied, by broad category of production, to royalty receipts in Table 8.7) is that some 46 per cent of the £8.6 million or so of U.K. overseas royalty receipts shown in Table 8.7 is associated with invention and innovation that would have been 'lost' under a compulsory licensing system. Almost all the impact on royalties occurs in pharmaceuticals, partly because the major impact on R & D and patent-based production is found there, and partly because a substantial share of reported royalty receipts arises there.

If the percentages mentioned above are applied, by industry, to official figures of U.K. overseas royalty receipts in 1968 (including receipts from overseas branches and subsidiaries and other 'related' operations of British firms), the overall impact on receipts comes to about 28 per cent (or £20 million).[1] Furthermore, if the same percentages are applied by industry to U.K. royalty payments in the same year, the impact on them comes to about 18 per cent (or £12 million). By this reckoning, the impact of the patent system (as compared with a worldwide system of compulsory licensing) on net U.K. overseas royalty earnings appears to be of the order of £8 million or so in the survey year – a very much smaller figure than that for exports, even after effects on imports are allowed for, as described below.

### Imports and the balance of trade

So far, nothing has been said about imports, but it is reasonable to think that these may be affected if the patent system influences domestic output of technologically-novel kinds of production, and some allowance for this factor should clearly be made if an acceptable estimate of the net impact on trade is to be arrived at.

By way of illustration of the type of point to be considered, it was suggested by spokesmen for pharmaceutical firms consulted that, if the level of U.K. R & D in pharmaceuticals in recent years had been very

[1] For this calculation, the percentage applicable to 'other manufacturing' was taken to be 5 per cent, while that for 'distribution' was put at zero.

TABLE 9.5. *Impact on U.K. trade in pharmaceuticals – two alternative cases*
All amounts are £ per £100 of U.K. pharmaceutical production by reporting firms in 1968[a]

| | (1) Existing patent system | (2) Worldwide compulsory licensing system | (3) Compulsory licensing in U.K. only |
|---|---|---|---|
| Exports | 40 | 12 | 12 |
| *Less* | | | |
| Imports | −10 | −3 | −10 |
| Additional imports to replace 50% of reduction in home sales of U.K. production | — | — | −20½ |
| Net exports | 30 | 9 | −18½ |
| International royalty receipts | 5½ | —[c] | — |
| *Less* royalty payments | −½ | —[c] | −2 |
| Exports of 'alternative' production[b] | — | 7 | 10 |
| Balance of above | 35 | 16 | −10½ |

NOTES:
[a] Coverage as in Tables 9.3 and 4.
[b] Assumed to be chemical production not based on patents.
[c] See the footnote to page 220.

much lower than it actually was, U.K. demand for the newer kinds of drugs would have shifted heavily towards imports – or at least towards production by U.K. subsidiaries of foreign firms whose main research efforts are located overseas. However, this argument ignores the overseas side of the picture, for it is logical to assume that under a worldwide compulsory licensing system the rate of invention and innovation in overseas drug industries would be affected to a degree similar to that in the U.K., if not more so, with the result that production and exports of technologically-novel lines by foreign firms would be similarly reduced.

It is not at all clear what would happen to U.K. pharmaceutical imports in those circumstances, but the most neutral assumption we can make is that they would be lower by the same percentage as that applying to U.K. exports – roughly 70 per cent. Since U.K. pharmaceutical imports have recently been about one-quarter of exports, the loss of net exports of pharmaceuticals on the basis of our sample would be about £21 per £100 of U.K. production in 1968; i.e., the difference between columns (1) and (2) in Table 9.5.

If net overseas royalty earnings are included, the figure for the impact on U.K. pharmaceutical trade (in comparison with a worldwide compulsory licensing system) becomes £26 (i.e. £35 less £9), while if exports of 'alternative' production are also allowed for it is reduced to about £19 (i.e., £35 less £16).

In the case of other finished and specialty chemicals, where exports are roughly 20 per cent of U.K. production, and imports roughly 13 per cent, and where exports might fall by slightly over 12 per cent in the absence of patent protection (Table 9.4), the impact on net U.K. exports of patent-based lines would on similar reckoning be about £1 (i.e., $20 - 13 \times 12\frac{1}{4}$ per cent) per £100 of U.K. production in 1968, and this figure would be about £$\frac{1}{2}$ if effects on royalties and 'alternative' production were included.

If these round figures are applied to total U.K. production in 1968 for the industries concerned (including that of firms not in our inquiry), the impact on U.K. trade and royalty earnings in patent-based chemicals comes to some £90 million which can be credited to patent protection in the sense described, but against this must be offset some £28 million of exports of 'alternative' chemical production that would arise under a (worldwide) compulsory licensing system. The combined impact on net U.K. overseas trade and royalty earnings in the chemical field can thus be put at rather over £60 million in 1968, of which the great bulk would be attributable to pharmaceuticals.

Official figures of earnings (interest and profits) from direct investment overseas do not give very much detail by industry, but such data as are available suggest that U.K. post-tax earnings in chemicals amounted to about £45 million in 1968, compared with some £40 million of profits etc. paid on 'inward' chemical investments in the same year. While we have no direct evidence on the extent to which these flows are affected by the patent system, it seems reasonable to argue that in our standard case the (relative) impact on U.K. receipts is not likely to be very different from that on U.K. payments, on the ground that the technological efforts of both British and foreign companies concerned would on average be equally affected under a worldwide compulsory licensing system. If so, the impact of patent protection on *net* U.K. earnings from direct investment overseas is likely to be fairly small – although of course the flows of payments in each direction would probably be quite appreciably affected, at least in the field of finished and specialty chemicals.

### Modification of the standard case

The importance of being explicit about the choice of alternative situation for assessing the patent system is highlighted if we consider briefly the implications for U.K. trade of an alternative in which Britain *alone* had a compulsory licensing system, arrangements elsewhere being unchanged. The argument can be confined to chemicals as the group of industries principally affected, but on this occasion it is assumed that no reduction takes place in overseas R & D or patent-based production as a counterpart to the reduction in these activities in the U.K.: indeed it might well increase. In these circumstances, it can fairly be expected that the bulk of unsatisfied U.K. demand for new types of drugs, etc. under a compulsory licensing system would be transferred to substitutes based on foreign R & D. For the sake of illustration, it is assumed here that about one-half of the reduction in U.K. patent-based production sold domestically would be offset by higher imports, and the remainder by increased production either by U.K. subsidiaries of major foreign-based firms, based on their overseas R & D, or by compulsory licence applicants or copyists with U.K. manufacturing operations.[1] The result in the case of pharmaceuticals would almost certainly be a large deterioration in net U.K. trade, as shown by comparing columns (1) and (3) in Table 9.5.

Column (3) of this table presents a tentative estimate of exports, etc. of pharmaceuticals by our sample of firms in 1968, had a (thoroughgoing) compulsory licensing system been in existence in the U.K. only, systems elsewhere being unchanged. Pharmaceutical exports of the reporting firms are shown as being lower by 70 per cent, as in column (2), but imports are increased from £10 per £100 of U.K. production to over £30, the additional £20½ corresponding to roughly one-half of the drop in home sales of drugs based on British R & D. The resulting adverse trade balance is worsened if reductions in U.K. net royalty earnings are also allowed for, as U.K. receipts would fall essentially to zero in reflection of the impact on U.K. R & D., while it is assumed that additional royalties would be payable to foreign parents at the rate of roughly 7 per cent of the increased production by their U.K. subsidiaries. On the other hand, the adverse balance is partly alleviated by additional exports of 'alternative' production (shown higher than in column (2) to allow for the comparative expansion of U.K.

[1] Although quite substantial compulsory licensing activity in pharmaceuticals might emerge initially after unilateral adoption of (thoroughgoing) compulsory licensing in the U.K., it seems unlikely that such activity would be more than marginal in the long run. According to the inquiry, U.K. research-based firms would greatly reduce their R & D in lines likely to attract compulsory licences, while foreign-owned firms would be less likely to patent their important discoveries and would be much more secretive on technical matters. Their new drugs would doubtless be the target for considerable 'piracy' by some locally-based imitators (although others might take compulsory licences – and pay associated royalties – where possible, as for example has happened in Italy in the absence of pharmaceutical patents. While copyists might ultimately account for a significant share of the U.K. market, their competition could hardly be serious enough to affect the central R & D efforts of foreign-based firms; moreover it is doubtful whether the U.K. consumer would gain very much net advantage through lower drug prices, as will be explained in Chapter 10.

pharmaceutical production by foreign-owned firms), but the deterioration is still over £45 as compared with column (1).

The corresponding figure for other finished and specialty chemicals is a deterioration of some £4 per £100 of U.K. production by reporting firms.

If these estimates are applied to total U.K. production by British-owned firms in the industries concerned (including that of firms not in our sample), the deterioration in net trade and royalties is approximately £54 million in the case of pharmaceuticals and £56 million in the case of other finished and specialty chemicals.[1] On this basis the impact of the patent system on net exports and international royalties can be put at roughly £110 million in the chemical field – appreciably more than the earlier estimate of £60 million or so based on the alternative of a worldwide compulsory licensing system. The impact would moreover be even larger if earnings on direct investment overseas were also included, for it is to be expected that U.K. earnings by foreign-owned chemical concerns would increase in the circumstances envisaged here, whereas earnings of British chemical firms overseas would diminish appreciably if our earlier conclusions are broadly correct.

### The 'foreign market shares' argument

The impacts on trade so far discussed arise from the idea that patent protection directly affects the rate and direction of invention and innovation in certain industries; quite apart from this, however, it was also suggested earlier that patents may affect exports and overseas production through their influence on firms' shares of sales in foreign markets, which are thought to be more sensitive than home market shares to the sort of competitive advantages that patents can sometimes give. The latter point is difficult to assess in any precise way but it could conceivably be important and we therefore consider it here.

On the one hand, it seems pretty clear that the possession of key foreign patents by British firms has in some cases helped both U.K. exports (either direct sales in overseas markets or sales of intermediate products to affiliated companies overseas for further manufacture) and production by overseas affiliates of U.K. firms quite considerably. An outstanding example is probably the stimulus given in recent years by Terylene patents both to U.K. exports of polyester fibre and to overseas production of Terylene fabrics by or under licence from British

---

[1] It is estimated that pharmaceutical production by British-owned firms amounted to some £120 million (or 40 per cent of the industry's sales) in 1968, while production of other finished and specialty chemicals by British-owned firms is put at very roughly £1,400 millions (or about 85 per cent of the industry's sales).

firms. (This is an important case and more will be said about it in Chapter 14, when the question of effects in the man-made fibres field is discussed.) Other leading examples can be found in the field of electronic capital equipment, and lesser instances in a number of chemical or engineering lines came to our attention in the course of the inquiry.

Other firms, especially in the pharmaceutical and fine chemical industries, pointed out that the principal immediate effect of a thoroughgoing compulsory licensing system (whether worldwide or in the U.K. alone) would in their view be that foreign firms would apply for U.K. licences to import or manufacture locally, and that this would tend to reduce the British companies' share of U.K. markets, quite apart from the consequences of a reduction in R & D by those companies.

The trouble with both these arguments is that they are in danger of seeing only part of the overall picture. The essential counterargument from a national standpoint is that, under a worldwide compulsory licensing system, British firms would be much freer in their turn to apply for compulsory licences on both foreign and U.K. patents in the hands of overseas concerns. It seems perfectly possible that such exports and overseas profits as are obtained by British firms on the strength of their patent protection in overseas markets may be at least equalled in value, if not surpassed, by market 'losses' attributable to the patent holdings of foreign firms. It may well be, as was frequently suggested to us, that established, research-based enterprises in the U.K. would be reluctant to make much use of even a thoroughgoing compulsory licensing system in their home territories, for fear of retaliation, but it is by no means so clear that they would be unwilling to do so in overseas markets, especially those outside the major research centres. It was impossible to collect quantitative evidence on this, but most firms consulted seemed to be in general agreement with the point, and it is perhaps significant that, in cases where responding firms had actively sought licences (although without success), about half related to patents in the hands of foreign firms.

Moreover, in a similar vein, it seems perfectly possible that in some industries increases in domestic market shares obtainable by British firms at the expense of foreign-owned firms under a compulsory licensing system would go some way towards counterbalancing losses suffered by British firms in other industries, so that the net impact on imports and overseas profit payments from the national viewpoint might not be very large.

It is not easy to gauge the relative strength of these arguments, but we are inclined to think that such evidence as is available does not add up to a large credit in favour of the patent system. There are, after all, many more patents in foreign than in U.K. hands and, apart from adverse consequences operating against research-intensive firms, which have been dealt with earlier, there is little to indicate that British firms would not gain on balance from the greater accessibility of patented inventions, providing this existed on a worldwide basis.

As in the earlier discussion, this verdict depends very much on the particular alternative chosen for purposes of assessment. There is little question but that our view on this point would be distinctly more favourable to the patent system if the alternative were the unilateral adoption of a compulsory licensing system in the U.K. For then foreign firms would be able to apply for compulsory licences in the U.K. without fear of like retaliation from British firms in foreign markets, and the outcome would probably be an appreciable net decrease in both U.K. and export market shares obtained by British-based firms in research-intensive fields.

# PART III

---

## SPECIAL STUDIES

# 10.  PHARMACEUTICALS

We now turn to a series of more detailed studies of particular industrial fields. Limitations on space and time make it necessary to concentrate on four fields of special interest – pharmaceuticals, basic chemicals, electronics (defined very broadly) and the 'small inventor'. In the industry studies, we start by describing the main economic features of the industry, especially market structure, scale, R & D and technical innovation, as well as patent and licensing activity. We then discuss the role and importance of the latter activity in an attempt to amplify the conclusions outlined in Chapter 9. Finally in each case consideration is given to a major patented innovation as an illustration of the preceding points.

Material for these studies was obtained from a wide range of sources, including of course our industrial inquiry itself. Respondents to the inquiry who gave particular help with the case studies were shown drafts of the relevant study and their comments were taken into account – although of course we retain final responsibility for matters of economic interpretation. Where no other reference is indicated for key statements of fact, it should be understood that we are drawing on information arising from our industrial inquiry.

The pharmaceutical industry stands alone in the extent of its involvement with the patent system. No other major industry approaches pharmaceuticals in its degree of attachment to patent protection; in no other field have critics of patent monopolies been so severe. One side in the argument appears convinced that the entire survival of the research-based industry depends on the unassailability of its patent rights, especially since the emergence of a 'penny-pinching' National Health Service as a monopsonistic buyer of drugs. The other is equally convinced that patents are merely a means of obtaining excessive profits on products which are vital to the consumer.

The truth as far as it can be discerned from the present study appears, as might be expected, to lie somewhere in between.

### A. OUTLINE OF THE INDUSTRY

Although the preparation of vitamins and hormones from natural materials on an industrial scale was commenced soon after the first world war, while insulin was developed in the 1920s and sulphonamides in the 1930s, the rapid growth of the international pharmaceutical industry dates from the discovery and development of large-scale production methods for the major antibiotics. The first of these was penicillin, which although discovered by Fleming in 1928 did not reach the stage of a stable substance reproducible on a useful scale until 1941. As is well known, the industrial development of penicillin was then transferred (without patent protection[1]) to the U.S.A., which alone had the resources during wartime – and, at that time, the applied skills – to tackle an enormous cooperative development task involving universities, hospitals, government departments and industrial firms.

When, in due course, it became apparent that the earliest penicillin (penicillin *G*), although outstandingly successful as the first mass-produced antibiotic, had limitations and that the search for new antibiotics was at a beginning rather than an end, a number of interested American firms spent large sums on research into alternatives, and were successful in the early 1950s in developing the tetracycline group of 'broad spectrum' antibiotics, which until recently were the most widely used of the various antibiotic drugs available.

Unlike penicillin and its early derivatives, the tetracyclines *were* patented, and their worldwide exploitation has been closely controlled by the innovating firms through overseas production, export and selective licensing. Through their monopoly position in these drugs the firms involved (principally Pfizer, Cyanamid and in chloramphenicol, Parke, Davis) were able to dominate the important antibiotic market in the U.K. and elsewhere until the expiry of the patents in the mid-1960s, and this is one factor explaining the large share of the British industry owned by American firms. More recently, research developments have taken place in the U.K. which have given British firms a larger share in the antibiotic market, and these have likewise been extensively patented, as will be described later.

Since the war, pharmaceuticals has been one of the most rapidly growing sections of the chemical industry in the U.K., as it has overseas (although exceeded by heavy organic chemicals, plastics materials and crop chemicals). Real output of the industry in the U.K. rose by about

---

[1] Patents were not applied for on the early penicillins, as the work was carried out by academic researchers who were not involved in the commercial exploitation of their discoveries. Fleming is said to have been 'very disappointed' at the lack of early commercial development of his work on penicillin.

120 per cent between 1958 and 1968. Sales of U.K. output amounted to some £300 million in 1968, the bulk being accounted for by about 80 firms each employing over 100 persons. One feature of note is that in the U.K., as elsewhere, the industry has grown mainly as a subsidiary activity of major chemical, food or 'popular medicine' firms, which have found in it a suitable and fast-growing avenue for diversification from their traditional lines. Very few of the larger U.K.-owned groups of companies involved are centred primarily in the industry, although there are some exceptions.

Approximately 75 per cent of U.K. pharmaceutical output consists of prescription medicines (i.e., those by law or in normal circumstances obtainable only through a doctor's prescription), and these comprise the research-intensive area of the industry's operations. The remainder consists of household (i.e. popular, or 'over-the-counter') medicines, the research content of which is comparatively low, and veterinary medicines, research on which is moderate. Approximately 36 per cent of the industry's total output (mainly prescription medicines) is exported.

An outstanding feature of the U.K. industry is the extent of participation in it by foreign-owned firms. It is estimated that about 60 per cent of the assets and a similar proportion of the sales of the U.K. industry are in the hands of subsidiaries of foreign companies, among which American firms are dominant, while Swiss and to a lesser extent French and other European firms also have appreciable shares. These shares seem to have stabilised in recent years, and there are now altogether about 40 foreign-owned concerns manufacturing prescription medicines in the U.K., accounting for rather over two-thirds of sales to the N.H.S. and a slightly smaller proportion of U.K. exports of these items.[1] The foreign stake in the research-based wing of the industry is thus seen to be very large indeed (although the foreign-owned firms do most of their R & D overseas). In turn, it should be noted, the leading British-owned firms have substantial markets overseas, as can be seen from Tables 8.1 and 8.9.

Apart from the patent-based ascendancy of American firms in the 'broad-spectrum' antibiotics, mentioned earlier, there are a number of more general economic influences tending to promote the 'international' character of the industry. Most major diseases are world-wide, so that there is frequently a world market for given chemotherapeutic products. Moreover, the minimum R & D programmes thought necessary to obtain a satisfactory rate of improvement in a

[1] In 1965, U.K.-owned firms exported 41 per cent of their total sales of prescription medicines and foreign-owned firms 24 per cent. See *Report of the Committee of Enquiry into the Relationship of the Pharmaceutical Industry with the National Health Service 1965–67* (Sainsbury Report) (H.M.S.O., 1967) p. 101.

particular field of prescription medicines are typically large in relation to the size of the market in any one country (with the exception perhaps of the U.S.A.). According to an authoritative spokesman for the industry in 1963, annual expenditure of between £150,000 and £200,000 was needed at that time to build up a valuable R & D capacity in a particular type of drug, while at least £1 million annually was needed to maintain a substantial stake in a broad field.[1] (Inflation had probably increased these amounts by about 40 per cent by 1968.) By comparison, very few therapeutic groups of drugs command sales of more than £10 million per annum in the U.K., and it would have to be a very successful effort indeed to obtain, say, a quarter of the U.K. market in one of these major fields (antibiotics, hormones, cardio-vascular drugs and one or two more).

There are consequently strong pressures for pharmaceutical firms to look overseas for their markets. At the same time, optimal *manufacturing* facilities are, for most drugs, typically not large in relation to the principal national markets, while manufacturing costs are in any case normally relatively small in relation to other expenses. Accordingly, the major firms tend to manufacture in a number of countries, while their R & D efforts are usually concentrated in one, or perhaps two, locations – almost invariably in the U.S.A. or Western Europe, although Japan is now becoming an important centre for research.

Finally, both official medical authorities and patent systems tend to encourage local manufacture where possible, as will be seen later.

An indication of the importance of R & D in the cost structures of British drug firms was given in Table 8.1, where it was shown that R & D expenditures approach 12 per cent of sales of the companies concerned. Their average research ratio for prescription medicines alone is probably about 15 per cent.[2]

The U.K. research costs of foreign-owned drug firms in the U.K. are probably proportionately much lower, since they do by far the greater part of their R & D in their home locations and only about one-half of the leading companies have research establishments in this country.[3] However, if allowances for overseas R & D expenditures and other overheads are included, the cost structure of prescription medicines in the U.K. industry is as in Table 10.1.

It can thus be seen that the ratio of manufacturing costs to the selling

---

[1] H. W. Palmer (now Deputy Chairman of the Glaxo Group), 'The Pharmaceutical Industry' in *Proceedings of the Royal Society of Medicine* (July 1963, Vol. 56, No. 7).

[2] These percentages would be reduced by about a quarter if the sales and research of overseas subsidiaries were included, since most British-owned firms do the bulk of their R & D
in the U.K.

[3] W. G. Jensen, 'Pharmaceuticals', a case study in J. H. Dunning, *The Role of American
Investment in the British Economy* (P.E.P. Broadsheet 507, Feb. 1969) p. 185.

TABLE 10.1. *Cost structure of National Health Service products: 50 leading U.K. manufacturers, 1965*

|  | (%) |
|---|---|
| Manufacturing cost of sales | 40·5 |
| Distribution and sales promotion | 17·0 |
| Royalties, patent and trademark expenses | 2·2 |
| General administration and service charges | 9·9 |
| Research and development | 9·7 |
| Profits before interest and taxation | 20·7 |
| Total | 100·0 |

SOURCE:
Sainsbury Report, p. 119.

value of drugs in 1965 was relatively low compared with that of most other industries. Not surprisingly, this feature has attracted a good deal of attention in a field where the public interest is closely involved and where, since the advent of the National Health Service, there is an almost complete separation between those ordering the products (the doctors) and those paying for them (the taxpayers). Stimulated perhaps by the Report of the Kefauver Committee in the U.S.A. (1961), which was strongly critical of the pricing practices of major American drug companies, the feeling gained ground in the early 1960s in the U.K. that pharmaceutical firms were making excessive profits from prescription medicines on the strength of patent monopolies, assisted by a lack of economic motivation on the part of those prescribing drugs. This belief was further fed by the knowledge that a substantial part of the research-based wing of the industry was in foreign hands.

This wave of criticism precipitated an upheaval in the affairs of the industry which shook the established companies and from which they have only recently begun to emerge – much chastened and doubtless much more on the defensive as regards pricing and profit policies than they were ten years ago. No study of the industry would be complete without some account of this phase.[1]

[1] Our account cannot unfortunately be fully up-to-date: this work was in the press before the full emergence of the dispute between the Department of Health and Roche Products following the report of the Monopolies Commission on *Chlordiazepoxide and Diazepam* (H.M.S.O., 11 April 1973). However the basic issues seem to us to remain unaffected, as are our views on them.

B. PRICES, PROFITS AND PUBLIC INTERVENTION

There is not space here to narrate in full detail the background to the dramatic events of the early 1960s in the pharmaceutical industry, or cover all the issues raised.[1] We must be content here with an outline stressing the aspects that relate to patents.

*Use of section 46*

At the end of the 1950s a number of British hospitals found they could obtain supplies of major patented antibiotics – principally the tetracyclines, and also chloramphenicol and the chlorothiazides, from unlicensed importers at about one-third of the price charged by the U.S. patentees and their licensees. The main ultimate source of the imports was Italy, which still (1972) does not grant patents on pharmaceuticals, and for that reason has been a source of potential weakness in the pattern of international licensing built up by the innovating companies. This weakness became actual when a number of Italian producers obtained essential production information on the tetracyclines from employees of the U.S. firms, and began offering cheap supplies in the hope that patent infringements might not be detected or prosecuted.

The U.K. Ministry (now Department) of Health banned the import by hospitals of unlicensed drugs, but in 1961 bowed to the pressure for price cuts by introducing new plans for central buying of hospital drug supplies by tender, stating that, where necessary, Section 46 of the Patents Act would be invoked to obtain supplies from the cheapest source. (As explained in Chapter 1, this section provides that patents on products purchased for the services of the Crown can be set aside at the latter's discretion, with compensation payable to the patentee in due course.) This was the first resort to Section 46 on behalf of the National Health Service, and a fundamental departure from the use that had been made of the Section in the defence and other public service fields.

Tenders for hospital contracts were accepted from importers at a fraction (approximately one-tenth in some cases) of the patentees' prices. Although the latter were reduced several times in subsequent years, they did not approach the importers' tenders until 1965, when the tetracycline patents were almost due to expire. From that time, all centrally-negotiated N.H.S. contracts were awarded to licensed U.K. manufacturers, but the Minister warned that Section 46 would be kept in reserve for use on any future occasion when patentees' prices seemed unduly high.

[1] A forceful case against the 'majors' can be found in B. Inglis, *Drugs, Doctors and Disease* (André Deutsch, 1965) and a more objective study of the industry in M. H. Cooper, *Prices and Profits in the Pharmaceutical Industry* (Pergamon Press, Oxford, 1966).

Pfizer sued the Ministry of Health for infringement of its U.K. patents and took an appeal to the House of Lords. In a famous judgment in 1965 it was held that the hospital services of the N.H.S. were services of the Crown and the appeal was dismissed by a majority of three to two, a small royalty (about 5 per cent) being awarded to Pfizer in compensation.[1] In the course of the judgment it was also held that the application of Section 46 to purchases for the much larger General Practitioner services of the N.H.S. would not be legitimate – a state of affairs strongly criticised by the Sainsbury Committee, as will be seen in due course.

A number of consequences followed from this unprecedented resort to Section 46 and its confirmation by the Courts. The established pharmaceutical companies were aghast at what they felt to be abrogation by the State of the fundamental principle of patent rights. Prophesies were made that the British industry would wind up its drug research and become totally dependent on foreign developments. In a number of the developing Commonwealth countries, the health authorities copied the U.K. Ministry's action in awarding contracts to the cheapest source, usually without compensation, and in several such countries where the patentees took action for infringement the local patent legislation was amended to permit such a policy.

*Use of section 41*

For their part, the unlicensed importers, encouraged by their success under Section 46 and wishing to expand their market into the larger and more remunerative area of the General Practitioner and Pharmaceutical Services, switched their attention to Section 41. Several applied for compulsory licences on tetracycline and the other drugs and, without waiting for a decision, proceeded to supply retail chemists at about half the patentee's price. (As explained in Chapter 1, Section 41 provides that anyone may apply to the Patent Office for a licence on any pharmaceutical patent at any time after grant, and must receive one on terms fixed by the Comptroller, unless in his judgment there are 'good reasons' for refusal.) In due course, a small number of compulsory licences were granted.[2]

Prior to 1963, when the wave of applications from unlicensed importers started, Section 41 had been very little used. Except in one or

---

[1] *Pfizer Corporation v. Minister of Health* [*1965*] *R.P.C. 261.*
[2] Numbers of applications under Section 41 have been as follows: 1960, 7; 1961, 3; 1962, 4; 1963, 8; 1964, 15; 1965, 0; 1966, 3; 1967, 0; 1968, 1; 1969, 9; 1970, 13; 1971, 1.

There were no applications before 1960. Four applications were allowed in the 1960s, seven were refused, and the rest withdrawn. However, in 1970–1, of those decided only one was refused, while ten were allowed and four were withdrawn. (See Comptroller's Reports, 1966 and 1971.)

two instances under its predecessor (Section 38A), established research-based pharmaceutical companies have not resorted to compulsory licence applications and are hardly likely to do so, since they have an interest in maintaining a strong patent system and would be vulnerable to retaliation in a compulsory licence 'war'. Only smaller companies, mostly of the sort that concentrate on import, formulation and packaging – deprecatingly termed 'middlemen' by the research-based wing of the industry – have been prone to invoke Section 41, and virtually without exception they have attacked foreign-owned patents, as indeed was the case in the episode referred to.

Apart from the reluctance of the 'majors' to resort to compulsory licensing, it is not hard to understand the general low level of activity under Section 41. One explanation is that the Comptroller and the Courts have been obliged by the wording of the Section to consider reasons for not awarding licences. Thus, applications may be refused if the applicant is judged not to have suitable staff or equipment for working the licence, although smallness is not in itself necessarily a disqualification. Furthermore, despite the awards in 1963, there is still a strong doubt as to whether applications for licences to import will be allowed, decisions on this and other points turning on whether substantial advantages are likely to accrue to the public.[1] Moreover, the wording requires that the patentee should derive a 'reasonable advantage' from his patent rights. Thus, despite the apparent intention of Section 41, a successful applicant has to show that the patentee will not be unreasonably deprived in the event of a licence, and this may be difficult to demonstrate convincingly.

A related explanation is found in the length and complexity of Section 41 hearings, which normally take well over a year to complete, and much longer if taken to appeal.[2] It is of course to be expected that patentees will contest applications tenaciously if given the opportunity to do so, and this is likely to be a strong deterrent to prospective applicants, especially small firms.

In the view of some patent experts, the basic jurisprudence under

---

[1] However, recent decisions in the courts have added a degree of certainty on this point. Thus, in refusing Roche's request for 'certiorari' against the Comptroller in 1972, the Queen's Bench Division upheld the Comptroller's power to grant a compulsory licence including the right to import the affected drug in bulk form, where the patentee himself relies on imports of the drug in that form. However, it was not ruled that a licence for bulk imports should be awarded if the patentee manufactures the drug in bulk in the U.K. See *1972 Fleet Street Law Reports* (7), p. 385.

[2] In the application by Biorex for a licence under Geigy's Patent in 1961, three and a half years elapsed before the Comptroller's final Order was issued (granting the licence) and nearly a year more before this Order was confirmed on appeal. (*Geigy's Patent, 1964 R.P.C. 391; 1966 R.P.C. 251.*) While this was an unusual and precedent-setting case, a tenacious patentee can normally expect to delay an award under Section 41 for at least three years after application.

Section 41 has now been established and future cases are likely to be dealt with somewhat more rapidly. Moreover, there are signs that interest in the Section is again reviving, for a further burst of activity took place in 1969–70, after the quiet period following 1964.[1] Significantly, perhaps, the recent round of applications seems to have been relatively successful, for only one of those recently decided has been refused by the Comptroller or the Court and, although a number have been withdrawn, these are thought to be instances in which the two sides have come to a compromise arrangement.

Despite these recent indications that Section 41 is at last beginning to bite, it would not, we believe, be fair to argue that experience under Section 41 has so far proved a major sustained attack on patent monopolies in the drug field. The industry has not so far experienced sustained and widespread pressure from compulsory licence applicants, such as we believe would happen in due course under the sort of thoroughgoing compulsory licensing system envisaged in our industrial inquiry. On the other hand, it is possible that, given further increases in the speed and success of applications under this Section, the level of activity under it (were it retained in more or less its present form) might quite rapidly mount up and assume much greater importance than in the past. If so, the research-based wing of the industry would find itself moving into the sort of compulsory licensing environment described in our inquiry.

While this does not appear to have happened yet, the major companies are clearly concerned about Section 41, and are becoming increasingly so. Most were perturbed at the success achieved by the unlicensed importers of tetracycline and other drugs, and many believe that the Section is an important potential source of weakness that could in the future be widely exploited by copyist firms, and indeed is being used by a few at present, albeit on a relatively narrow front. (It was admitted that overt threats to use Section 41 are extremely rare, but these were said to be superfluous, given the existence of the Section, which has led to a certain amount of 'reluctant' licensing that otherwise would not take place.) Many also feel that Section 41 creates an unfortunate precedent for foreign legislation modelled on the British system, as is the case in most Commonwealth countries. Accordingly, the repeal of the section, as recommended by the Banks Committee,[2] would doubtless be heartily welcomed by the industry.

[1] This activity reflected in part the applications by Berk Pharmaceuticals and DDSA Pharmaceuticals for licences under Hoffman–La Roche's tranquillizer patents. See Monopolies Commission, *Chlordiazepoxide and Diazepam*, Ch. 3.

[2] Banks Report, Sections 408–10. The Committee thought that Section 46, together with its extension in 1968 to cover the general medical and pharmaceutical services, provides a sufficient safeguard against unfair patent exploitation in the drug field.

*Prices and profits*

The attack on patented drugs via Sections 46 and 41 was followed by some notable reductions in patentees' prices for the drugs concerned. Between 1961 and 1968 Pfizer reduced its price for tetracycline on six separate occasions, the total reduction being about 60 per cent from the level in 1961, which had been unchanged for the preceding ten years. Doubtless some reductions would have happened anyway, as for instance when the relevant patents expired. Thus, in 1966 when Pfizer's patent on oxytetracycline, another important antibiotic, expired, I.C.I. launched its own brand (Imperacin) at one-third of Pfizer's price. Pfizer responded, after negotiations with the Ministry of Health, by cutting the price of its own brand (Terramycin), to a level close to that of I.C.I.

The controversy stimulated by the resort to sections 46 and 41, and the price reductions which followed, led to the setting up in 1965 of the Sainsbury Committee to investigate the relationship between the industry and the National Health Service. The Committee produced a report (1967) that was critical of the industry in a number of respects; in particular, it considered that the risk element in pharmaceutical research had been exaggerated by the industry and that in some cases profits were excessive for this reason.[1] It was found that, while the average rate of profits (at book values, after charging R & D but before depreciation and tax) on gross assets was not unduly high at 19 per cent in the period 1963–5, compared with $14\frac{1}{2}$ per cent for all manufacturing industry, some firms made extremely high returns. Thus, eight out of 27 major firms showed rates in excess of 30 per cent, three of them coming within the range of 50–5 per cent. (Not all firms were able to confine their figures to N.H.S. business, but most did.)[2]

A great deal of discussion has been devoted to the adequacy or otherwise of these rates as realistic indicators of profitability in drugs. Major issues are the separation of drug operations from other sorts of business, the inclusion of returns from overseas operations, and the treatment of R & D expenditures as items of current rather than capital expenditure. The Department of Health has calculated in some instances of negotiations with suppliers that true profit rates may be as high as twice those claimed by firms, and the Department's estimates have in turn been strongly contested by the suppliers. One explanation advanced for the rates shown by foreign-owned firms, which are on average appreciably higher than those for British-owned firms, is that

---

[1] Sainsbury Report, para. 178.    [2] *Ibid.*, para. 122.

the former contain a higher proportion of businesses specialising in formulation, packaging and distribution, in which fixed assets are small and profit rates likely to be misleadingly high. Moreover, foreign-owned firms tend to have a high ratio of current liabilities to capital and reserves; it has been argued that a large slice of these liabilities is in the nature of debt to the parent company, and should be included as capital for purposes of calculating rates of return.[1]

One of the principal recommendations of the Sainsbury Report was that Section 46 of the Patents Act should be made applicable to the General Medical and Pharmaceutical Services as well as the Hospital Services of the N.H.S. – thus overcoming the judgment of the House of Lords in the Pfizer case. This was enacted in the *Health Services and Public Health Act 1968*, Section 59, and has become a powerful sanction in drug price negotiations between the industry and the Department of Health, as the Banks Committee has pointed out.[2]

A further recommendation of the Sainsbury Committee was that the Department's hand should be strengthened in price negotiations with the suppliers by requiring the latter to provide detailed cost data and estimates of overall financial returns on N.H.S. products. This suggestion was adopted by the Department as part of its 'voluntary' arrangements with the industry.

### Price regulation

Schemes for voluntary drug price regulation have operated in the U.K. since 1957, but the Sainsbury Committee found them deficient in that they relied mainly on prices in export markets as criteria of 'reasonableness'. As the Committee observed, 'most of the factors that cast doubt on the competitiveness of prices in this country exist in equal measure in most export markets' (para. 285). Under the latest scheme (in operation since November 1969), the bulk of sales of major drugs to the N.H.S., whether for hospital or general service use, are subject to price negotiations between the Department of Health and the companies. The latter provide annual information on costs and rates of return in divisions of their business concerned with prescription medicines, and prices are agreed that are thought to provide a reasonable return to the supplier.

While strong disagreements arise from time to time between the industry and the Department's experts as to what are acceptable rates of return, and management dislikes the official surveillance, the industry

[1] M. Cooper and J. Parker, 'Are Drug Profits Excessive?' in *The Times Review of Industry*, August 1965.
[2] Banks Report, pp. 116–19. It should be noted that, unlike Section 46, the new Section included the right to 'vend' and covered drugs and medicines, but not surgical devices etc.

seems now to have accepted the general principles of price regulation, albeit with great reluctance.[1] There is no doubt that, for the major U.K. research-based companies, 'voluntary price regulation', backed by the monopsonistic buying power of the Department of Health and the threat of Section 46, has so far been a more onerous limitation on their ability to exploit patents than Section 41. Sales of prescription medicines to the N.H.S. comprise some 40 per cent of the industry's total sales, and include products for which demand is least price-elastic – and therefore most likely to yield profits if exploited in a monopolistic fashion.

There seems little doubt that prices and profits in the U.K. pharmaceutical industry have fallen appreciably in response to the pressures described above. The heavy reductions in tetracycline prices throughout the 1960s have already been noted, and these, according to the Association of the British Pharmaceutical Industry, are indicative of price trends in other important established drugs. An O.E.C.D. committee has estimated that British prices of the leading branded prescription medicines have recently been falling at about 4 per cent per year.[2] (The same report concludes that price indices, which tend to show moderate upward trends in most countries, are not a satisfactory indicator because they are affected by the mix of 'new' to 'established' products on the market, and do not allow for improvements in the general quality of drugs.[3]) There is moreover some direct evidence that drug profit rates in the U.K. are now lower than they were in 1965. Thus, according to the Department of Health, there were in 1969 probably only six firms (three British-owned, two American-owned and one European-owned) showing rates of profit of 25 per cent or more. Leading companies were typically found in the 10–20 per cent range, while small and medium-sized firms on the whole made very small profits or even losses.[4] Admittedly, the general rate of profit in manufacturing has declined since 1965, but our belief that drug profits in particular are being squeezed and that the large companies are having to look more critically at their research programmes was

[1] The scheme was reviewed in 1972 and a number of modifications, mainly to relax the reporting burden on small firms, were announced. (See the statement by the Secretary of State for Social Services, *Hansard*, 26 July 1972, pp. 328–9.)

[2] O.E.C.D., *Pharmaceuticals*, a report in the *Gaps in Technology* series by the Committee for Science Policy (Paris, 1969) p. 60.

[3] In fact, the official index of wholesale prices of pharmaceutical preparations sold in the U.K. moved as follows (1963 = 100): 1965, 98·1; 1967, 94·8; 1969, 94·8; 1971 (prelim), 101·4. (See *Trade and Industry*, 9 March 1972, p. 394.) If, as we calculate, unit costs of labour and materials combined rose by some 15 per cent in the drug industry between 1965 and 1971, manufacturers' profit margins on home sales must have fallen very sharply on average in that time.

[4] Evidence of the Department of Health on 10 March, in the *First, Second and Third Reports from the Committee on Public Accounts, 1968–69* (H.M.S.O.) p. 284.

on the whole confirmed in our discussions with firms in the industrial inquiry.

To some extent, the fact that a large proportion of the U.K. industry's markets are overseas has mitigated the impact on the industry of pressures within the U.K. However, these pressures have had repercussions overseas, and indeed are seen by some as part of a worldwide trend to weaken patent monopolies in the pharmaceutical field. Thus, although nothing precisely comparable to Section 46 is found in actual or proposed patent legislation overseas (with the exception of certain developing Commonwealth countries, mentioned earlier) some form of official or semi-official price regulation is practised in about half the industry's main foreign markets. Moreover, prices in drug contracts with a number of foreign medical authorities are influenced by those paid by the U.K. National Health Service, and are thought by the industry to reflect the reductions which have been brought about in the U.K. in recent years. There is probably some truth in this: the price of tetracycline to retailers in the U.K., for example, has been some 20–30 per cent below the mean world price (excluding the U.K.) since 1961 and, although the percentage gap has progressively widened, the world price has fallen steadily more or less in step with the British price. According to the industry's association, this pattern has been followed by other major drugs, although in general the percentage falls have not been so large. On the other hand, the international industry has benefited from growth of the market provided by expanding medical care schemes, particularly in developing countries. There is in fact no clear evidence that the profitability of the drug industry in other countries has been falling, and indeed rates in the U.S.A. and Japan seem to have been rising in recent years.[1]

Perturbed at the lead given by the U.K. authorities on price regulation and the overruling of patent rights, the industry's association has warned that drug research in the U.K. would become depressed and that the country's large net trading balance in pharmaceuticals would suffer.[2] So far as can be seen from the latest published data, there is no clear evidence that these changes are taking place. The ratio of R & D to sales in the industry has been remarkably constant over the last decade and currently shows no sign of diminishing, although several companies have stated that they are tending to spend more on 'imitative' and 'second line' products (on which the risk of loss is minimised) than hitherto. The U.K.'s share of world exports of pharmaceuticals

[1] O.E.C.D., *Pharmaceuticals*, p. 63.
[2] See, for example, Association of the British Pharmaceutical Industry, *Annual Report, 1967/8*. A fuller public statement of the Association's case can be found in its pamphlet *Medicines and the Patent System* (1972), (obtainable from Manager, Information Services, ABPI).

has remained relatively constant, although perhaps declining slightly.[1] On the other hand, the ratio of U.K. import to export values, having fallen suddenly from about 20 to about 10 per cent at the end of the 1950s, has since grown steadily and is currently running at above its pre-1959 level. It remains to be seen whether this is merely the result of fairly short-term movements in the pattern of drug utilisation and other temporary factors, or whether it represents the start of a long-term deterioration in the U.K.'s balance of trade in pharmaceuticals, as the industry fears.

## C.  IMPACT OF THE PATENT SYSTEM

### Competition

In a field where the 'customers' (primarily, medical doctors) are more than usually anxious to obtain superior products, with price a secondary consideration, and where it has repeatedly proved possible with the expenditure of large sums (probably upwards of two million pounds at 1968 prices) to discover and develop new drugs which will supersede others in important medical treatments, it seems inevitable that competition between the principal research-based firms should occur through innovation rather than through price, and that innovating firms should attempt to monopolise new products with exceptional tenacity. The industry itself makes no bones about its view that the exercise of whatever monopoly is possible within the limitations imposed by the short life cycle of most drugs is both legitimate and economically necessary if technical progress is to be maintained at a rate that satisfies the authorities and the public.[2]

There seems little question that keen competition to discover and introduce new drugs indeed takes place among the established firms of the industry. This is illustrated by the comparative instability of rankings of major drugs and major firms over quite short periods of time. Thus, only two of the world top ten drugs (by value of sales) in 1967 were in the top ten in 1962, and four were not marketed then.[3] Of the world top ten firms in 1962, four had been replaced by others in 1969.[4] Seven of the top ten in 1962 had lower rankings in 1969, their average drop in the listings being seven places.

[1] We calculate using United Nations trade statistics that the U.K.'s share of pharmaceutical exports (S.I.T.C. 541) by 15 leading exporters, all expressed in U.S. dollar values at prevailing rates of exchange, moved as follows: 1962, 15·6%; 1966, 14·3%; 1969, 13·6%. The U.K.'s share in 1971 is estimated at about 14½ per cent.

[2] H. W. Palmer, *Proceedings of the Royal Society of Medicine* (July 1963), p. 550.

[3] A 'drug' here means a 'branded product'.

[4] *The Times*, 9 November 1970, Special Report, p. vii. In the U.K., the company with the largest N.H.S. sales in 1969 stood fifth in 1962. The leader in 1962 had dropped to thirteenth by 1969.

There equally seems little question that new drugs, once introduced, are typically monopolised or at least closely controlled by the innovating firm for periods of five, ten or fifteen years, according to circumstances, and that patents are usually the main protective factor in this control – although brand names, too, play a part, and survive far longer. The pattern of behaviour among innovating firms is somewhat as follows. The research-based firms, of which there are probably some fifty or so independent ones of various sizes in the U.K., about half of which are foreign-owned, tend to specialise in one or a very small number of generic or therapeutic fields (of which the former might be penicillins, tetracylines, steroids, etc., while the latter might be antibiotics, hormones, vitamins, etc.) and at any time there are likely to be several working independently on an important new drug or improvement in each of these fields. Provisional applications will be filed as soon as there is anything to patent – i.e., at the stage when new compounds are synthesised – but their value will not be known until a year or two later when potential products have been selected and given preliminary tests (e.g., for possible therapeutic activity in animals).[1] If eventually a promising substance emerges it will be subjected to extensive toxicity tests and clinical trials,[2] and if it survives these the innovating firm will, after an intensive promotion campaign aimed at doctors, proceed to supply the drug as a monopolist during the life of the patent – except that a limited number of reputable licensees will probably be granted exclusive licences to supply overseas markets not accessible to the patentee.

If, on the other hand, the basic breakthrough is achieved more or less simultaneously by two or more firms, patent priorities may be disputed, both privately or through opposition before the Patent Office. In such cases, compromise solutions are invariably reached whereby one firm obtains the patent and licenses the other contenders to share its monopoly.

Since it frequently happens when major new drugs are introduced that an innovating firm cannot supply the entire world market on its own, international licensing agreements conferring straight patent rights on major drugs are not uncommon, and indeed form the dominant kind of licensing in the industry, as was seen in Table 8.4 (p. 153). That this is true of American no less than British experience is confirmed by the (Majority) Report of the Kefauver Committee, which investigated the U.S. pharmaceutical industry, 1956–61. The Report's description of international licensing by U.S. firms is worth noting:

Patents are also of vital importance in the formation of cartels

---

[1] Some firms are more selective, and therefore take longer, in identifying potential products before they file provisionals.
[2] More will be said on this phase in *Research and Development*, especially pp. 251–2.

for the international control of drug prices. In each of the major
drug fields examined by the subcommittee, the use of patents to
restrict competition in international trade was spelled out in great
detail in patent agreements among the world's major drug companies. Even in the domestic licensing agreements, restrictive provisions of highly doubtful validity were found. A typical limitation,
for example, is that the licensee can market in final packaged form
only; this, of course, is designed to prevent the smaller companies
from securing access to the product in bulk form.

This, as well as more far-reaching restrictions, has been written
into the patent-licensing agreements with foreign firms. In cortical
steroids, tranquillizers, antidiabetic drugs, and the broad spectrum
antibiotics, the licensing contracts contain such provisions. Typical
license agreements may be found in the appendixes of the hearings.
In general the pattern is the same. The patentee – or sometimes
merely the applicant for a patent which has not as yet been issued –
grants to a single company in each of a related group of countries
the exclusive right to sell in that market. Where the foreign companies are large and economically powerful, the license usually
covers the right to make and sell; if the licensee lacks the requisite
bargaining power, it may secure the right to sell, and the contract
specifically provides that the product in bulk form is to be purchased
from the licensor. A geographical limitation upon the marketing
area of the licensee is usually imposed, which is often buttressed by a
specific provision that he will not engage in export of the product.
The geographical confines of his marketing territory are rigidly
imposed for companies in the highly industrialized countries such as
the United States and the individual countries of Europe. Usually
the British Commonwealth is regarded as a single unit for exploitation by the British licensee. In less industrialized countries, the various areas may be parceled out in a variety of ways; often because of
the limited markets, they are open to those licensees who can meet
the local regulations of these countries.[1]

The account is illustrated with the example of chloramphenicol, one
of the 'broad-spectrum' antibiotics in relation to which Section 46 was
exercised in the U.K. in 1961, and the Report concludes:

Effective worldwide control of chloramphenicol by Parke, Davis
has resulted from this structure of patent licensing agreements.
To be sure, it lacks the perfection of a one-company monopoly of
production and sale throughout the world – the goal toward which
Parke, Davis first directed its efforts. But as a device for subduing

[1] Antitrust Subcommittee of the U.S. Senate Committee on the Judiciary (Kefauver Committee), *Administered Prices, Drugs* (Washington, 1961) pp. 147–8 (footnotes omitted).

splinter groups – particularly the activities of the Italian companies – and avoiding price competition in European markets and elsewhere, it has been strikingly successful. As the price information obtained by the State Department reveals, there is nothing like the widespread variations in the prices of chloramphenicol as among different countries which are to be found in other drug products where the scheme of control over European producers has been less effective.[1]

The main conclusion reached by the Kefauver Committee was that patent monopolies result in considerably higher drug prices than would exist in their absence. The Committee was, however, unable to decide whether patents had any effect of the rate of inventive activity in the industry.

Although firms working in the same research field may contest the award of basic patents, the resulting monopolies, or oligopolies if the award is effectively shared between several, are rarely if ever challenged by other established firms in the industry. This finding emerged clearly from our industrial inquiry, in which drug companies were frank about their unwillingness to licence important patents to competitors without a 'very substantial' *quid pro quo* in terms of patent rights or know-how. Their attitude however is seldom put to the test because of the reluctance of the 'majors' to poach on each others' patented territory. (Imitation of a remunerative product *after* the patents on it expire is quite another matter, as is shown for instance by I.C.I.'s introduction of Imperacin in competition with Terramycin, referred to earlier.) When a profitable new (patented) drug appears on the scene, the usual reaction of competitors is to intensify their own efforts to discover something that will supersede it, or at least a substitute that will have similar effects without infringing. If success is not forthcoming, they will wait until the patent expires and then break into the market, although the patentee may sometimes forestall them by adding patented improvements in the meantime.

In the process, the price of the drug tends to fall rapidly as competing products are introduced, although it may be relatively stable for a number of years after introduction. The price reductions may be quite substantial as the expiry of the patent approaches and the patentee moves to forestall competition from unpatented analogues. U.K. price reductions of the order of a quarter to a half or more have been noted at this stage of the life-cycle of important patented drugs. Yet larger reductions in the American prices of many important patented drugs came to light in the evidence to the Kefauver Committee.[2]

[1] *Ibid.*, p. 150.
[2] A summary and discussion of the more dramatic examples can be found in H. Steele, 'Patent Restriction and Price Competition in the Ethical Drugs Industry', *Journal of Industrial Economics* (July 1964).

This picture of the role of patents in restricting price competition in pharmaceuticals is supported by the conclusions of most other economists who have studied the industry. Of many American economists who have written on the subject, W. S. Comanor may perhaps be cited:

> The impact of the patent system has not been to create monopoly positions which remain active throughout the seventeen-year life of the patent, but rather it has been to foreclose to a great extent rivalry between identical chemical entities or standardized commodities about which price competition might develop. It has strengthened and encouraged the high degree of chemical product differentiation which is the primary form taken by technical change within the pharmaceutical industry.[1]

It should be noted that Comanor sees a strong link between the impact of patents in encouraging competition through product differentiation and the growth of industrial research in the drug field.

*Prices*

The argument so far points to the conclusion that patent protection has been a significant factor in sustaining drug prices and profits in the U.K., at least before the episode of Section 46 and the subsequent tightening of price regulation. This conclusion is in agreement with that of the Kefauver Committee for the U.S. industry. (Implicit in it is the assumption that the drugs in question would have been introduced in the absence of patent protection. This assumption is very debatable, as we shall see in due course.)

It is not possible to gauge from the available information how much higher U.K. prices and profits were in the pre-Section 46 era than they might otherwise have been, except to say that on the evidence of the price reductions which occurred after the exercise of Section 46 and the wave of compulsory licensing that followed it, the impact was probably appreciable for a number of important drugs, of which the tetracyclines and other broad spectrum antibiotics are leading examples.

Several points are relevant to this conclusion. Firstly, it must be emphasised that the ability of a patentee to charge in excess of 'competitive' price levels is not unlimited. A pharmaceutical patent on its own seldom confers a complete monopoly over more than a particular drug: a patentee is rarely if ever in a position to control the sole effective method of treating an injury or disease, for a number of alternatives are usually possible. Moreover, the National Health Service nowadays urges upon doctors the need to exercise economic as well as

---

[1] W. S. Comanor, 'Research and Competitive Product Differentiation in the Pharmaceutical Industry in the United States', *Economica* (November 1964).

medical discrimination in prescribing branded remedies for given medical problems. The price of any drug is therefore governed to some extent by those of substitutes, and the more exceptional a new drug appears to be as an answer to a particular illness, the more likely are substitutes to be stimulated to compete with it.

A fairly recent example of such competition can perhaps be seen in the antibiotic field with the development of the new antibiotics known as cephalosporins, which have been rated as important as penicillin and capable of destroying penicillin-resistant bacteria.[1] Cephalosporin, developed initially at Oxford before 1964 and then by Glaxo laboratories under licence from the National Research Development Corporation, has proved to be a strong competitor with some of the important and highly remunerative 'semi-synthetic' penicillins, developed by Beechams as patented successors to the early biological penicillins. More will be said about the semi-synthetic penicillins in due course, but it is perhaps not without significance that 20 per cent reductions occurred in prices of ampicillin and methicillin in 1968, at a time when the cephalosporins were rapidly increasing their sales in British and American markets.

For these reasons, it can be seen that the prices of even the most successful of patented drugs are far from immune from competition from new products well before the end of their patent terms. In such cases, and they are probably the rule rather than the exception, the effect of patents is to delay price competition by forcing others to search for patentable alternatives, rather than to suspend it for the term of the patent. Moreover, as will be seen later, the effective life of a 16-year patent will in many cases not be more than twelve years, because of the normal lapse of time between the date of a patent and the first introduction of the product based on it.

The second point is that, owing to the events described in the previous section, the U.K. industry now operates in an environment of price control, reinforced by the ultimate sanction of Section 46 should the voluntary regulation scheme break down. Most of the evidence suggests that the prices of important prescription medicines sold to the N.H.S., while being somewhat higher than they would probably be under a compulsory licensing system,[2] are no longer *in general* unreasonably high – for 'fair' pricing is after all the purpose of the scheme and the suppliers' accounts are now periodically open to

[1] Cephalosporins are a class of compounds akin to penicillins. We were informed that there are currently about six different makes of cephalosporin on sale in various countries.
[2] Whereas prices agreed under the V.P.R.S. include a full allowance for the R & D costs of innovating firms, this would probably not be so under a compulsory licensing system, for reasons which will be discussed later (pp. 253–4).

scrutiny by the Department's experts.[1] Provided some effective form of official price regulation exists, there is probably little to be feared from patent monopolies as far as prices and profits of U.K.-owned drug companies are concerned. Whether there is anything to be gained will be seen in the next section.

### Research and development

This brings us to the crucial question of the impact of patent protection on the rate of inventive and innovative activity in pharmaceuticals. The question cannot be dismissed on the ground that the exercise of Section 46 has 'drawn the teeth' of pharmaceutical patents, because the section is still kept very much in reserve and the Government has indicated that it will not set aside drug patents so long as their owners charge reasonable prices on their supplies to the N.H.S. So long as drug prices can be amicably agreed between the industry and the Department of Health, as occurs in most (but not all) cases, the former are perfectly entitled to exercise their patents in the accepted way (i.e., restrict others' access to the market, provided they themselves can meet the demand).

Neither can it be argued that thoroughgoing compulsory licensing already operates in this field through Section 41, since licensing under this section has not so far been the near-automatic procedure envisaged in our alternative, although a movement may now be taking place in this direction.

The conclusion of our industrial inquiry was that the situation in the research-based wing of the industry would be very different under a regime of compulsory licensing of the sort we put to companies. The estimates in Chapter 9 were that some two-thirds of the R & D expenditure of responding firms and a similar proportion of their U.K. pharmaceutical production (corresponding to essentially all their 'patent-based' lines) would be 'lost' in a world of thoroughgoing compulsory licensing. The two companies in our main sample whose major pharmaceutical divisions have been built up from a modest scale since the 1950s were firmly of the opinion that these operations would not have been created had effective patent protection not been available, and their arguments appear on the whole convincing. The third, although much longer established and more heavily committed to the ethical chemical field relative to its other group operations, would probably

---

[1] However, there are indications that the Department of Health sometimes has difficulty in establishing what is a fair rate of profit where an overseas supplier is involved or where a U.K. supplier is part of a foreign-owned group which does its basic research overseas, imports the active ingredient, etc. This was clearly so in its dispute with Hoffman–La Roche. See *Chlordiazepoxide and Diazepam, op. cit.*, Ch. 7.

have cut back its activity in new patent-based pharmaceuticals very heavily, rather than embark on its expansion programme in this field begun several years ago.

(a) *Vulnerability to imitation.* The essential point is that most new drugs, once discovered, developed and marketed, are capable of being copied at minimal research and marketing expense by any firm with experience in the relevant field of manufacture. This is to some extent a feature of all innovation in the chemical field where the inventive step consists in the synthesis of new compounds and the discovery of their properties, but it is particularly so in pharmaceuticals, for reasons which will appear.

A great deal of time and expense in discovering new drugs is devoted to synthesising new products (or isolating them from natural substances) and putting them through elaborate laboratory tests in order to identify their active properties.[1] This is a laborious 'hit and miss' procedure in which several thousand new compounds per year are screened, of which with luck a handful will have useful activities and perhaps one or two will be short-listed as possible products. It may take anything from one to four years to establish the properties of a promising compound, and a further year to perform preliminary tests before selection for probable manufacture. Then comes the development phase proper, in which the selected compound is transformed into a marketable product and production processes mastered. The main expenditures here are on (i) toxicity tests, which are necessary to satisfy the requirements of such regulatory bodies as the U.S. Food and Drug Administration and the U.K. Medicines Commission (the successor to the Dunlop Committee on the Safety of Drugs); (ii) the development of a bulk manufacturing process; (iii) the development of formulation methods to present the drug in dosage form; (iv) clinical trials at specialty hospitals and in general practice, both in the U.K. and overseas; and (v) market promotion. The development phase may take from two to four years, making the total period for the introduction of a new drug from four to nine years (although only highly novel ones would take more than six or seven). A further period of one to two years after introduction will probably be needed before a successful drug receives full acceptance by doctors.

Total amounts spent on the R & D in these phases vary considerably, but are not likely to be less than £1½–2 million on a major drug. (Glaxo Laboratories are said to have spent £1½ million on the development of cephalosporin, and this did not include the initial discovery.)

---

[1] Pharmaceutical firms perform rather little 'pure' research on basic principles of medical treatment; this is left to universities and research institutions.

The point about these R & D expenditures is that they can almost all be avoided by a skilled copyist. The compounds concerned are in most (but not all) cases fairly simple in chemical terms and synthesis, bulk manufacture and formulation methods can be readily copied once the right compound and the right processes are established. The results of many of the tests, clinical trials, etc. are likely to be made publicly available by the innovator with a view to increasing the acceptability of the product.[1] Admittedly, manufacturing know-how is important in some types of drugs, while certain essential details such as the precise strain of an organism used in a critical reaction are sometimes not divulged in patent specifications or in any other way. These may deter or hold up the work of a copyist, and in some areas his manufacturing efficiency may not be as good as that of the innovator. This is true for instance in the production of penicillin, where deep culture fermentation methods involve a highly specialised technology which cannot easily be copied by the inexpert. However, it does not apply to the bulk of other drugs, which are based mainly on synthetic compounds, the large scale production of which is relatively well understood. Moreover, production secrets cannot always be kept secure, as was found when Italian firms were able to produce tetracycline quite effectively.

*(b) Unpredictability.* A second point is that the outcome of much pharmaceutical research is highly uncertain. The special problem here is the extreme unpredictability of the behaviour of new chemical compounds, and even modifications of familiar ones, in the human body. It seems generally accepted by scientists that this unpredictability is of a much higher order than that found in non-biological areas of chemical research – and very much higher than that in engineering fields. By contrast with the latter, where the basic technological effectiveness of a development project can usually be established in the early stages, the decisive stages in drug research come near the end of a project, in the crucial toxicity tests and clinical trials. Even a suspicion of a harmful side effect can in these post-thalidomide days invalidate hundreds of thousands of pounds of R & D effort, and most major

---

[1] The question of the *efficacy* of a new drug, as opposed to its safety, purity and conformity to chemical specifications, admittedly remains almost entirely a (joint) matter for the developing firm and medical doctors. Although independent trials are sometimes undertaken with the agreement (and sometimes the encouragement) of the developer, the majority of clinical trials are, so far as we understand it, controlled by the developer, who may choose what results he communicates to doctors. While critics have argued that there is a need for compulsory independent trials, the relevant point here is that the developing firms must provide doctors with a great deal of accurate and detailed information about the composition, central properties and known side-effects of new drugs if they are to create a market for them, and virtually all research-based firms do so.

companies can cite instances of important late setbacks in promising research programmes.

The main implication of the uncertainty of pharmaceutical research is that rates of return on successful products have to be high enough to cover losses on unsuccessful research. Profit margins (before charging R & D) on successful drugs have therefore to be relatively high; hence their attractiveness to compulsory licence applicants.

There may of course be less defensible factors making for high margins on such products. Marketing expenditure is one such factor, and equally provides an incentive for the copyist seeking to exploit a market created by the patentee. It is not necessary here to debate the desirability of promotional expenditures from a social viewpoint. The research-based firms themselves have misgivings about some types of promotion that are practised, but they remain entirely convinced that large expenditure on 'proper' kinds of promotion (such as an accurate communication service and reminder advertising to doctors) are necessary if markets are to be created for new drugs.

What does seem unlikely is that the scale of drug promotion is increased by patent monopolies. Indeed, it can be argued that such expenditures would be larger in the absence of patent protection, for the pressure to build up brand loyalties would then be greater. Italy, the only European country without drug patents, is often cited as the market where promotion expenditures are highest, and published data seem to bear this out. Thus 'marketing' expenditures of Italian firms appear to be well over 20 per cent of total sales on average, whereas 'distribution and sales promotion' of U.K. firms are about 17 per cent.[1]

(c) *Royalty rates.* An important element in the objections of pharmaceutical companies to an automatic compulsory licensing system is the view that royalties awarded under such a system would fail to compensate them properly for all R & D and marketing expenditures incurred in the course of their pharmaceutical operations. In other words, royalties awarded under such a system would be at less than the 'correct' rate (i.e., the rate at which all relevant R & D and other necessary pre-market costs are shared between licensee and licensor equally per unit of sales of the licensed item). It should perhaps be added that this is not their only objection. They have, in addition, an entirely rational preference for manufacturing rather than licensing, as will be explained in due course.

Objections to the level of royalties likely to emerge under compulsory licensing arise from the belief that any system of the sort described in

[1] O.E.C.D., *Gaps in Technology–Pharmaceuticals*, pp. 56, 57.

our inquiry would fail to cope adequately with all the subtleties met with in individual cases and would have a built-in tendency to set rates too low, so as to be on the safe side in seeking to protect the public interest. More specifically, it is feared that an official arbitrator would tend to underestimate the proper level of research charges against successful drugs, for example, by failing to allow sufficiently for the need to subsidise unsuccessful research from the proceeds of successful products, and for the uncertainty associated with research in the drug field. He would also disallow substantial portions of marketing expenses, which the companies see as quite legitimate charges against successful drugs.

Experience under Section 41 suggests that these fears are not groundless. Thus, in fixing royalty rates for compulsory licences the Comptroller has in the main ruled that the relevant research ratio is that arising from the *whole* of the patentee's business, not the much higher rate on medical specialties which the companies advocate and which has been accepted under the Government's price regulation scheme.[1] Furthermore, the Comptroller has disallowed substantial portions of market research and promotion expenditures on the grounds that they are not legitimate changes against the drugs in question, or that they are excessive.

(*d*) *Other objections.* But apart from the issue of the levels of royalty rates, the companies are critical of compulsory licensing for several other reasons. Firstly, there is the point that, while manufacturing economies are typically not an important feature of the industry and the minimum efficient size of plant is usually not large in relation to the major national markets, this is not true for all types of drugs. If the U.K. market for more specialised, low-volume drugs were shared by, say, a dozen manufacturers each with his own bulk production facilities, the result for these drugs would be excess capacity and higher rather than lower costs to the N.H.S. Even where this would not be the case, it is argued that decisions by innovating firms concerning size of plant usually have to be made well before the establishment of the product as an effective drug – and therefore well before the stage at which compulsory licences would be sought. (An innovator might well anticipate that some compulsory licence applications would be forthcoming, but would find it very difficult to estimate how many, and how far sales would be affected.) Under a compulsory licensing system, innovating firms would be extremely uncertain as to the share of the U.K. market they should plan to obtain, and they might well guess wrongly, whereas under the present system they can

[1] Smith, Kline and French's Patent, *1967 Fleet Street Patent Law Reports 2*, p. 97.

usually foresee their own and any intended licensee's shares well in advance.

Admittedly, if compulsory licensing were confined to the U.K., the problem of excess capacity might be avoided by exporting output surplus to domestic requirements. However, this escape route would not be possible under a worldwide system of compulsory licensing, which is the alternative that should be borne in mind as a true yardstick for the patent system as an international institution. Moreover, as argued in Chapter 9, British research-based firms would be at a strong competitive disadvantage under a *unilateral* compulsory licensing system, for they would not obtain compulsory licences overseas, whereas their competitors could obtain compulsory licences in the British market.

Secondly, the companies point out that licensees under a compulsory system are for obvious reasons likely to wish to greatly undercut the patentee's selling price, and their ability to do so will reflect not simply that the rate of royalty awarded may be too low (especially if calculated using a selling price equal to or only slightly below that of the licensor), but also that a licensee in such circumstances would probably be content with a return on his capital much lower than that required by an innovating firm. Two points are implicit in this argument. The first is that the target rate of return on an investment involving substantial basic R & D expenditures in the pharmaceutical field will on average be higher – and probably much higher – than that on a 'routine' manufacturing investment, because of the much higher risks involved in the former. Companies emphasised the high degree of uncertainty attaching to fundamental drug research, reflecting the speculative nature of work on the discovery of 'first line' drugs.

The second point is that, when companies contemplate risky research ventures, it is the size of expected total profits in relation to outlays *at high risk* that specially concerns them. Since profits from manufacture under the present system are thought to be typically much larger than returns expected through licensing, compulsory or otherwise (even though royalties may be on a 'reasonably commercial' basis), it is argued that a switch to a compulsory licensing system would sooner or later greatly reduce incentives to continue with basic R & D programmes in the drug field.

These points can be illustrated with the aid of a hypothetical example based on the cost structure of the 'average' N.H.S. supplier (see page 235). Thus, a typical pharmaceutical firm with annual sales of prescription drugs of, say, £10 million, an R & D programme of £1 million and marketing expenditures (not including distribution) of roughly the same amount, currently makes total profits (after charging R & D and marketing, but before interest, depreciation and tax) of

TABLE 10.2. *Annual sales and expenditures, etc. of 'average' research-based pharmaceutical firm (£m)*

| | (i) Under present system | | | (ii) Under thoroughgoing compulsory licensing | | |
|---|---|---|---|---|---|---|
| | Patent-based products | Other | Total | Patent-based products | Other | Total |
| Sales | 5 | 5 | 10 | 2·13 | 5 | 7·13 |
| *Less* Costs of manufacture, distribution, administration etc. | −2 | −4 | −6 | −1 | −4 | −5 |
| R & D and marketing | −2 | 0 | −2 | −2 | 0 | −2 |
| *Plus* Royalty receipts | 0 | 0 | 0 | 1·2 | 0 | 1·2 |
| *Equals* Profits | 1 | 1 | 2 | 0·33 | 1 | 1·33 |
| Total net assets (say) | 2 | 4 | 6 | 1 | 4 | 5 |
| Gross profit on net assets (%) | — | — | 33·3 | — | — | 26·6 |
| 'Risk-free' return (20% of net assets) | — | — | 1·2 | — | — | 1·0 |
| Profit on outlays 'at high risk' (after deducting return to net assets) | — | — | 0·8 | — | — | 0·33 |

about £2 million – see case (i) in Table 10.2. (Royalties are assumed for simplicity here to be zero and sales etc. are assumed to be divided between patent-based and other products as shown.)

Assuming that net assets are valued at about £6 million, the firm's gross rate of profit comes in this case to 33·3 per cent. Assuming further that a rate of some 20 per cent (or £1·2 million) is regarded as an acceptable 'risk-free' return (before depreciation and tax) on net assets, this leaves £0·8 million as profits on outlays 'at high risk' (i.e., the annual outlay of £2 million on R & D and marketing.)

Now suppose this firm were compelled to license others (non-research-based firms) to supply half its market for patent-based products, royalties being fixed on a 'correct' basis, as defined in Chapter 8 (i.e., total R & D and marketing costs – unchanged – plus an allowance of 20 per cent – equal to the gross profit margin on sales of the average N.H.S. supplier – would be shared at an equal rate per unit of patent-based output between the licensor and firms manufacturing under compulsory licence). Suppose also that entry of new (non-research-based) suppliers taking advantage of compulsory licences would result in an average fall of about 15 per cent in the prices of the licensor's patent-based products – which is probably roughly what could be expected on average in these circumstances for a range of patented drugs – while total sales volumes would be unchanged (reflecting low price-elasticity of demand for generic types of drugs). Suppose finally that the licensor could in due course reduce his manufacturing and other 'routine' expenses on patent-based products in proportion to the cut in his production of them (i.e., 50 per cent), and similarly his net assets. (For his 'other' products, these would be unchanged.) If so, the outcome would be as in case (ii) in the table. The licensor's annual royalty income would be £1·2 million (half of £2·4 million), and his gross profits would be £1·33 million.

It is evident, firstly, even under these very moderate assumptions, that the licensor's total return on his (reduced) net assets would be quite substantially reduced – although not disastrously so. But secondly it appears that the profitability of the patent-based part of his business would be much reduced; for example, his profit after deducting the 'risk-free' return on capital is more than halved, while his outlays 'at high risk' (R & D and marketing) are unchanged.

Needless to say, the prospect for the licensor would be yet worse if inroads into his patent-based business were larger or if less generous royalty rates were allowed, should large portions of R & D or marketing expenditure be disallowed for compulsory licensing purposes. The latter would have the effect both of diminishing the licensor's royalties, and reducing the minimum price at which compulsory licence applicants would find it profitable to supply the market, hence reducing the licensor's own profits on sales.

The preceding arguments assume, of course, that home markets are relatively small in relation to the R & D and marketing outlays needed to sustain them, and that licensees cannot be relied upon to open up new markets. This is very much the case in pharmaceuticals, where the U.K. market for most drugs is incapable of supporting more than a few major research programmes, and where markets, once created, are not highly sensitive to additional selling efforts or price reductions.

For these reasons, established U.K. pharmaceutical companies are convinced that they would suffer heavily under a thoroughgoing compulsory licensing system and that such a system would not be compatible with the continuation of industrial R & D into new drugs on anything like the scale that has been witnessed under the present patent system. The introduction of automatic compulsory licensing and the encouragement of non-research-based firms to use it would in their view go beyond price regulation, backed by Section 46 (and far beyond the present Section 41), in deterring major drug research programmes.

### D.   THE NEW PENICILLINS

As an example of the sort of pharmaceutical venture that might well be in jeopardy in a world of compulsory licensing, we consider the important new antibiotics developed by the Beecham Group as successors to the first or 'biological' penicillins (Penicillins *G* and *V*).

The history of the discovery and development of the early penicillins is well known, but that of their semi-synthetic successors is less familiar.[1] Briefly, a significant breakthrough was achieved in 1957 in Beecham's laboratories, which were set up as a new venture after the war to pursue basic pharmaceutical research. The breakthrough consisted in the isolation of the penicillin nucleus (6-amino penicillanic acid, or '6-APA') and the discovery that, by adding 'side chains' using synthetic chemical methods, the molecule could be variously modified to produce new 'semi-synthetic' penicillins, which were found to be effective in destroying staphylococci resistant to the biological penicillins, as well as having a broader spectrum.

Patents were applied for on the isolation of 6-APA and work began on its extraction in pure form and on the synthesis and screening of new compounds derived from it. A series of new penicillins resulted and were patented, of which the most important became ampicillin ('Penbritin') in 1961, a highly effective broad-spectrum antibiotic. In the process, the size of the Group's R & D effort in drugs was increased more than tenfold and cumulative R & D expenditure of about £10 million was incurred between 1957 and 1966.[2]

Beecham's complete lack of manufacturing experience in antibiotics had to be overcome rapidly, and this was done by means of an exchange agreement with Bristol Myers, an American firm experienced in deep fermentation techniques. Under this agreement, Beecham granted Bristol Myers sole rights under its U.S. and Canadian penicillin patents, including rights to sublicense, together with rights in other non-Commonwealth countries, all royalty-bearing. (Beecham retained the right to manufacture and sell in these markets, and exercises it in many, including the U.S.A.) In return Beecham obtained know-how and assistance in the building and operation of a large-scale deep fermentation and extraction plant in the U.K. Bristol Myers entered into a research agreement on penicillin with Beecham, and subsequently a considerable amount of information in this field was exchanged. Beecham granted a number of patent and know-how licences on its new penicillins to other overseas companies, all of which have been royalty-earning. In addition, Beecham entered into agree-

---

[1] See Jewkes *et al.*, *The Sources of Invention*, p. 351.
[2] *Ibid.*, p. 353.

ments in many countries for the local compounding and packaging of penicillins, bulk material being supplied by Beecham itself.

By 1968–9, world sales of all brands of ampicillin alone amounted to some £70 million annually, and this has now become the leading broad spectrum antibiotic sold on world markets.[1] Sales of all new penicillins produced by or under licence from Beecham then amounted to approximately 20 per cent of all world antibiotic sales. Total royalties received by the Group in 1968–9 were £3·7 million, mostly from the new penicillins.[2]

Beecham has one existing licensee in the U.K. for one of its penicillins (propicillin, not ampicillin). Otherwise licensing is confined to selected companies overseas in return for royalty payments.

Prices of the new penicillins to the N.H.S. are negotiated with the Department of Health and these are said to have an important influence on prices charged in overseas markets.

When asked what part patent protection has played in the development of the new penicillins, spokesmen for the Group felt that, under a regime of 'thoroughgoing' compulsory licensing, the original decision to expand drug research would probably not have been taken, and basic work such as that which led to the discovery and development of the new penicillins would not have been launched. Beecham would have continued to rely essentially on its traditional product lines, proprietary medicines, toiletries and beverages, and would probably have been hard pressed to find alternative research-based ventures within its field of interest. Had effective patent protection been generally available, but not on penicillins, the research would have proceeded in other pharmaceutical directions. Had active requests for compulsory licences materialised after the launching of the penicillin programme, the main ultimate effect would probably have been to cut the programme hard back, as royalty receipts would have been much lower in these circumstances and they have been very much the mainstay of new research. Moreover, had effective sole patent protection been lacking in the U.S.A., it would have been extremely difficult to persuade Bristol Myers to divulge its manufacturing know-how. A pure know-how agreement might conceivably have been obtained had Beecham kept essential information secret and offered it in exchange, but such an arrangement, far from yielding royalties, would probably have necessitated payments in the reverse direction. Had manufacturing expertise of this sort not been obtained, Beecham would not have entered the field as a manufacturer, for delay would have invalidated its research lead and lack of patent protection would have put it entirely at the mercy of competitors.

[1] Beecham Group, *Annual Accounts, 1968/69*.    [2] *Ibid.*

Finally, we examine published data on the pharmaceutical industries of the leading research countries in the hope that this may shed some light on the question. Such relevant data as are available stem principally from the O.E.C.D. report in the *Gaps in Technology* Series, and this, with minor additions and modifications, is summarised in Table 10.3.

The data here refer to the R & D programmes of pharmaceutical firms on drugs and related products *within* the various countries, and cover the great majority of all such expenditure outside the Communist countries. Some of the figures are fairly rough, but the orders of magnitude are probably right.

Column (1) shows expenditures in 1965, converted to U.S. dollars at the prevailing rate of exchange. One drawback of these figures is that they fail to allow for differences in national salary levels and on that count over-estimate the real resources content of expenditure in high-wage countries. Accordingly, numbers of scientists and engineers employed on R & D are given as an alternative measure in column (2); it can be seen, for instance, that the predominance of the U.S.A. is much reduced by the latter measure. However, this measure too has serious limitations, since it fails to reflect differences in capital employed and in the quality or productivity of both technical and supporting staff. (Moreover, national definitions of 'scientists and engineers' do not always match closely. The figure for Japan in column (2) is almost certainly an overestimate on this account.)[1]

Despite these limitations, it is clear that the bulk of world pharmaceutical research outside the Communist sphere is done in seven countries, of which the U.S.A. is by far the most important.

Information on the growth of R & D is unfortunately sparse, but the indications are that expenditure in the U.K. grew roughly in step with that in Western Europe as a whole between 1960 and 1965, but not so rapidly as in the U.S.A. No country matched the phenomenal increase shown by Japan.

Columns (4) and (5) give alternative measures of 'intensity' of research in the various countries. Even allowing for differences in salary rates, per capita expenditure in the U.S.A. is well ahead of most other countries, with the exception of Switzerland, where pharmaceuticals are an unusually important sector of industrial activity. The level in the U.K. seems approximately in line with that of its two largest European competitors.

---

[1] To the extent that differences in international salary levels reflect genuine differences in productivity between countries (due perhaps to higher training standards, a more stimulating atmosphere, the need to justify higher costs by extra effort, etc.), column (1) is preferable as a measure of 'effective work done', which seems the relevant consideration.

A more revealing figure for present purposes is found in column (5), which gives approximate ratios of R & D to drug sales of production in the various countries. A fair degree of consistency is shown, ratios for all the major research countries being between 6 and $8\frac{1}{2}$ per cent.

Two points of special interest can be made on the basis of the figures mentioned so far. Firstly, there is no indication here of a 'depression' in the U.K. research effort, as prophesied in some quarters after the exercise of Sections 46 and 41 in the early nineteen sixties. The U.K. ratio of R & D to sales in 1965 was the highest for any of the major research countries (with the possible exception of Switzerland), and according to figures in the same O.E.C.D. report, the U.K. ratio increased to just over 10 per cent in 1967 – having risen steadily from under 6 per cent in 1958.[1] There is accordingly no sign as yet in published data that drug price control is having the effect that was feared.

Secondly, the figures for Italy, the only country of those shown which did not grant pharmaceutical patents, do not give a clear indication that the level of drug research is depressed there. Admittedly, expenditure per capita of total population was only half that in France and the U.K., but it must be remembered that per capita expenditure on *all* R & D in Italy was only about one-sixth of that in France and the U.K. at the time.[2]

In fact, Italy employs a much higher proportion of her R & D scientists and engineers in pharmaceuticals than does the U.S.A. Moreover, the ratio of R & D to sales of Italian drug companies, while slightly on the low side, is not far from that in France and West Germany, as can be seen in column (5).

On the other hand, it is quite possible to argue that drug research would have been higher in Italy, had patent protection been available. It is well known that most of the large Italian drug firms were in financial straits in 1965, owing at least in part to fierce competition from non-research-based firms.[3] Pharmaceuticals is a major industry in Italy, and for that reason it might be expected that per capita drug research levels would be nearer to those in France and W. Germany – although still lower, because of lower income per head in Italy.

The picture is very much less favourable to Italian research when we consider the figures in column (6). These represent essentially the whole of the O.E.C.D.'s compilation of the world's most important

[1] O.E.C.D., *Pharmaceuticals*, Table 19.
[2] O.E.C.D., *The Overall Level and Structure of R & D Efforts in O.E.C.D. Member Countries*, Report 1 in the Series for the International Statistical Year on Research and Development (Paris 1967) Table 2.
[3] *Sunday Times*, 28 March 1965, p. 47.

TABLE 10.3. *R & D effort, 1965, and major drug inventions, 1950–67, by pharmaceutical firms: ten countries*

| Country | (1) R & D expenditure | | (2) Scientists and engineers | (3) Growth of expenditure, 1960–5 | (4) R & D per capita | (5) R & D as per cent of drug sales | (6) Major drug inventions 1950–67 | |
|---|---|---|---|---|---|---|---|---|
| | ($ U.S. m) | (%) | | (%) | ($ U.S. m) | (%) | Number | (%) |
| U.S.A. | 365 | 63½ | 8,900 | 72 | 1·87 | (7½) | 67 | 50 |
| W. Germany | (44) | 7½ | n.a. | n.a. | (0·70) | 7 | 15 | 11 |
| Japan | (42) | 7½ | (5,100) | (310) | (0·40) | (6) | 1 | ½ |
| U.K. | 33 | 5½ | 1,600 | 55 | 0·59 | 8½ | 10 | 7 |
| France | 28 | 5 | 900 | n.a. | 0·58 | 6½ | 11 | 8 |
| Switzerland | (About 20) | 3½ | n.a. | n.a. | (about 5) | n.a. | 20 | 15 |
| Italy | 15 | 2½ | 875 | 44 | 0·29 | 6 | 1 | ½ |
| Sweden | 11 | 2 | n.a. | 184 | 1·30 | 14 | 0 | 0 |
| Netherlands | 10 | 1½ | n.a. | n.a. | 0·80 | 8½ | 5 | 4 |
| Belgium | 5 | 1 | 100 | n.a. | 0·55 | n.a. | 4 | 3 |
| Total of above | (573) | 100 | (about 20,500) | n.a. | (about 1·5) | (about 7½) | 134 | 100 |

SOURCE: O.E.C.D., *Pharmaceuticals*, Tables 17, 18, 19, 20 and page 131. Figures in brackets have been adjusted to 1965 levels, or are authors' estimates. n.a. = not available.

drug innovations since 1950, by country of origin.[1] It can be seen that while the distribution of inventions coincides very broadly with the pattern of expenditure by country in 1965, certain countries performed extremely well in terms of inventions relative to R & D (particularly Switzerland) and others (Italy, Japan and Sweden) performed badly. In the cases of Japan and Sweden, this can probably be attributed principally to the fact that drug research has grown very rapidly in both countries during the relevant period, and that in Sweden at least the absolute size of the R & D effort was fairly small until quite recently. This is not the case in Italy, however, where drug research has been established on a large scale for much longer.

The poor record of major drug invention in Italy does appear to suggest that, although drug research may not have been depressed in that country, the research effort there has been directed mainly at imitative products, whose proliferation on the Italian market was

[1] For the method of compilation and the list of drugs, see O.E.C.D., *Pharmaceuticals*, pp. 130–1, and 141–5. The list is accepted as reasonably correct by British patent experts, in contrast to an earlier list produced by the Kefauver Committee, which has been much criticised.

The O.E.C.D. list includes 138 drugs, only four of which originated in countries not shown here.

acknowledged to be particularly notorious by the Italian Parliamentary Commission on Monopolies which investigated the industry in 1965.[1] This history can hardly be attributed to lack of competence on the part of Italian researchers; the Italian record of invention in other chemical fields (e.g. petrochemicals), where patenting has been permitted, has been one of notable successes. It rather suggests that lack of patent protection of new drugs has led the Italian companies to concentrate on variants and derivatives of established drugs, stimulated no doubt by the knowledge that these could be sold in their home markets without infringing patents.

F.   CONCLUSIONS

It is hard to escape the conclusion that R & D activity by British companies on basically new drugs would be substantially reduced under a system of 'thoroughgoing' compulsory licensing on a world-wide basis. The evidence of our industrial inquiry seems convincing on this point and such other evidence as is available tends to lead to the same conclusion.[2] It is hazardous to venture precise figures for the possible impact, but our estimate for the firms in our main sample would be that about two-thirds of their pharmaceutical R & D, including the bulk of that on fundamentally new drugs, would be 'lost' (see Table 9.2). Corresponding to this, there would be a heavy reduction in their production of patent-based pharmaceuticals, perhaps equivalent in value to about two-thirds of their total U.K. pharmaceutical output (see Table 9.3), this reduction being counterbalanced by an equivalent expansion (by these firms or others) of alternative lines – mainly non-research-based pharmaceuticals or other products

[1] *Financial Times*, 18 August 1965.
[2] In an interesting study which was received too late for full consideration here, an American economist has reached conclusions concerning the impact of patent protection on the U.S. pharmaceutical industry which in some important respects resemble ours for the British case quite closely. (See H. D. Walker, *Market Power and Price Levels in the Ethical Drug Industry*, Indiana University Press, Bloomington, London, 1971.) Using an entirely different approach, Walker estimates that the short-term impact of abolishing patent protection on U.S. drugs would be that large firms would be obliged to cut their pharmaceutical production by about one-half as a result of intensified competition from small (non-research-based) firms (page 148). He argues (pp. 150–1) that in the long run the American 'majors' would be compelled to abandon virtually all their pharmaceutical research in affected lines in order to maintain reasonable profits on their manufacturing operations, and that competition would henceforth take place mainly through selling effort, expenditure on which would not be reduced. While we have reservations about some of the estimating procedures that Walker uses, and although circumstances in the U.S. pharmaceutical field differ quite strongly from those in the U.K. (with respect, for example, to Section 46 and price control, for which there are no exact U.S. counterparts), it seems significant that an entirely independent study should conclude that the removal of patent protection would have a crippling effect on the research-based wing of the American industry.

(e.g., over-the-counter medicines, beverages, health foods, toiletries, etc.). Bearing in mind that these particular results are heavily influenced by the experience of firms whose expansion in this field has been relatively recent and rapid, and which might therefore be expected to be more sensitive to patent protection than others, we would guess that the answer for the entire pharmaceutical industry in the U.K. (including foreign firms, who would also be subject to compulsory licensing, overseas as in the U.K.)[1] would probably be somewhat lower – but hardly lower than, say, one-half of R & D, etc. on pharmaceuticals (because of the importance of the responding firms in the national total). The bulk of the cut would be in R & D on new generic types of drugs, and on the more fundamental variations of existing types. Correspondingly, there would be a substantial fall in total U.K. production of such drugs – although its size is difficult to assess because it is extremely hard to judge how foreign-owned firms would behave in such a situation – and this would be replaced by additional production of low-research lines.

To avoid any misunderstanding, it should be pointed out that this is an estimate of a *long run* effect; it does not purport to say what would happen in the years immediately following the introduction of a (thoroughgoing, worldwide) compulsory licensing system. Supposing that this step were to take place in present circumstances, we would imagine that the immediate impact would be a wave of compulsory licensing applications on important patented drugs from non-research-based firms, leading to a rapid increase in market shares of such firms at the expense of their research-based rivals. Prices of affected drugs would fall appreciably and profit margins of research-based firms (before charging R & D and marketing expenditure) would be considerably reduced. Established research-based firms would sooner or later react by reducing basic R & D on new drugs of the sort that are currently patent-based to relatively low levels, and would confine their pharmaceutical activities much more than they have done to the manufacture of established products and the search for minor product differentiation based on brand-names and superficial variations in existing products (development of 'second-line' products, diversification through packaging, dosage forms, etc.), much as has been done in Italy. As a result, the number of significant advances and entirely new drugs developed by industrial firms would in due course (perhaps five to ten years, the time taken to perfect a new family of drugs) begin to diminish, eventually reaching a fraction of levels experienced in the post-war era, and at that stage compulsory licensing activity would 'wither away' for want of new material to feed on.

[1] We are dealing here with the alternative of *worldwide* compulsory licensing.

In pharmaceuticals, unlike other high research fields, it does not seem relevant to argue that firms are obliged to spend large amounts on R & D in order to stay in business. Most of the larger British Groups involved have diversified rapidly into the field, attracted by potentially high returns in a fairly risky extension of their main activities. Had patent protection not offered a reasonable prospect of exploiting successful drugs, several of the largest ones would have preferred to remain with their traditional if less profitable mainstays, or to seek alternative (and probably less research-intensive) fields for expansion.

A certain amount of pharmaceutical research of a non-patent-based kind would of course survive in a compulsory licensing world, and some development of basically new drugs would probably be undertaken on the strength of 'lead-time' and secret technology. Very little of the latter would be patented, and this would inevitably reduce the exchange of know-how through licensing, although some would probably continue through secret deals and 'pure' information agreements. In the atmosphere of greater market insecurity, research on 'second line' products and minor variations of existing lines would, if anything, increase, as probably would expenditure on advertising and other forms of market promotion.

Total pharmaceutical output in physical terms would probably be somewhat smaller than at present, for there would be fewer 'wonder' drugs available, and those that were (on the basis of secret R & D) would probably be more expensive (because of their greater rarity) than they would be under the present system. (However, this might not be too important if prices were subject to effective Government supervision.) A much greater proportion of the industry's output would doubtless be composed of established products or minor variations of them, but it does not seem likely that these would be available on average much more cheaply in the long run, because profit margins on most of these items are not exorbitant (owing to V.P.R.S.),[1] because expenditure on promotion of them would probably increase, and because there would be few economies obtainable from increasing their scale of manufacture, either overall or by individual firms.

It is not easy to speculate on the ultimate structure of the industry in a compulsory licensing world. Firms in our inquiry maintained that the principal threat of compulsory licensing applications under Section 41 came from importers and 'middlemen', and that the same would

---

[1] Some drugs presently sold to the N.H.S. are doubtless overpriced in spite of V.P.R.S but serious cases are probably few. The Monopolies Commission itself termed Roche's tranquillizer monopoly an 'exceptional case' (*op. cit.*, para. 232). In our view, these can best be dealt with by more effective (perhaps *compulsory*) price regulation, not by a further weakening of patient protection in the drug field.

probably be true (but on a greater scale) in a thoroughgoing compulsory licensing system. However they felt that very few major established firms would resort to compulsory licensing even in the latter conditions. It is hard to judge whether they are right on this point, or whether in such a different situation the 'majors' would be obliged in self-defence to poach more on each others' territories. Whichever would be the case, it seems clear that the older-established drug firms would survive, albeit with a much more restricted research base, but that the non-research-based wing of the industry (firms concentrating on manufacture, packaging and distribution) would be relatively more important and more numerous than under the present system.

It seems likely in these circumstances that the 'majors' would be driven to react through mergers and takeovers of their smaller competitors. Since, in such a sensitive 'public interest' field, it is doubtful that they would be allowed to exploit or even build up permanent monopoly positions in particular drugs comparable in size with those of existing patentees (limited, as the latter are, by the length of the patent term as well as Sections 37, 41 and 46), and since the manufacturing advantages of large size in this field are generally not very great, a movement of this kind would probably be centred on achievement of market domination through massive advertising and marketing outlays, spread over a wide range of products. In particular, even greater efforts than at present would be made to promote brand names and the minor product differentiation that goes with them. Such a development would hardly be calculated to encourage the re-emergence of genuinely basic R & D in the industry on anything approaching the present scale.

It is possible to conceive of a strange polarisation ultimately occurring in the structure of the industry, for the largest firms would become yet larger and fewer in number, while at the same time the industry would attract a much greater proliferation of small firms specialising in the non-research phases of the industry. In other words, the industry would become both more concentrated, and yet comprise in total a larger number of (on average) smaller firms. If so, this would pose problems for public policy, in controlling major structural monopolies at one end of the industry spectrum, and in ensuring high standards of drug purity and efficacy at the other. The prospect is intriguing, but not attractive.

# 11.  BASIC CHEMICALS

### A.  THE INDUSTRIAL BACKGROUND

Basic chemicals have been termed the 'building blocks' of the chemical industry. They comprise a limited number of items manufactured in bulk and used almost exclusively as materials for a vast range of 'secondary' chemicals and finished chemical products. They can be divided into *inorganics*, which have traditionally been obtained mainly from non-carboniferous minerals, and *organics*, which have a basic structure of carbon atoms combined with hydrogen and other elements, and which have traditionally been obtained from coal. The principal bulk inorganic chemicals are sulphuric acid, ammonia, chlorine and caustic soda, while the principal bulk organics consist of the olefins (ethylene, propylene, etc.), the aromatics (benzene, toluene, etc.), the paraffin methane, methanol (methyl alcohol) and acetylene (used for P.V.C., vinyl acetate, neoprene rubber and acrylonitrile, but now tending to be overtaken by more economic alternatives).

The growth of bulk organic chemicals has greatly exceeded that of inorganics in the post-war era. For example, between 1958 and 1968, U.K. production of organics rose by just over 160 per cent, compared with 60 per cent for inorganics. A major supply factor in this growth has been the rapid increase in the availability of cheap petroleum feedstocks as the main raw material for organic chemicals and as an increasing source of ammonia and sulphur. Whereas before 1950 the organic chemical industry of Europe had been based almost entirely on coal, growth since then has depended very largely on petroleum feedstocks, a development reflecting the rapid expansion in refinery capacity in Europe after 1950 and the consequent abundance of light naphtha feedstock at a cost much less than coal.[1] It is estimated that petroleum now provides the basis of some 85 per cent of the tonnage of organics, about 80 per cent of ammonia, and about a quarter of sulphur produced in the non-Communist world.

For obvious reasons, manufacture of most basic chemicals is exclusively carried out in large production complexes owned by the major oil and chemical companies. Minimum efficient capacity for the latest type of ethylene plant is now approximately 300,000 tons per year[2]

---

[1] F. A. Fidler (Research Manager of B.P. Ltd), *The European Petroleum Chemical Industry*, (unpublished lecture, February 1969), p. 2.
[2] Even larger plants are being planned. See C. F. Pratten, *Economies of Scale in Manufacturing*

(compared with total U.K. production of approximately 1,200,000 tons), and for such a plant to be fully utilised it must be accompanied by a series of derivative plants which can absorb the olefins. The proposal by Shell Chemicals in 1969 for a new olefins cracker and accompanying plants at Carrington and Stanlow amounted to a total investment of £150 million, and only the largest companies can invest on this scale. According to Shell, one-third of all U.K. capital expenditure on basic chemicals is currently provided by the oil companies (Shell, Esso and B.P.), and one-third by I.C.I. British Oxygen, Albright and Wilson and British Celanese (a subsidiary of Courtaulds) probably account for the bulk of the rest.

Although large sums are spent by companies on R & D in the basic chemical field, R & D costs are not on the whole a major item in relation to the total selling value of output. Our estimate in Table 8.1 was a ratio of U.K. research to selling value of some 2 per cent for the companies in our sample, which is probably about half the overall ratio in finished and specialty chemicals, and much lower than that in specialised areas, especially pharmaceuticals and crop protection chemicals. The expenditures on basic chemicals are nevertheless high in absolute terms, and it is probably correct to think of them as being 'research-based' industries in which reliance on R & D is mitigated by the large size of markets and the operation of economies of scale in the use of R & D as well as on the production side.

The recent history of technical progress in basic chemicals has been very much that of the introduction and improvement of large scale production processes, especially those utilising petroleum as a feed-stock. The range of products has not widened very much over half a century, although naturally their relative importance has greatly changed. Most research efforts are directed towards the reduction of unit costs and improvements in the purity and consistency of standard products. There is relatively little work on new products, although increasingly the industry has been obliged to investigate new uses both for its principal outputs and for the by-products which are a common feature of large-scale chemical processes. 'Applications technology' is coming to be an important sub-area of research, although up to now results are mainly in the nature of sidelines to the main activity. There are however exceptions, of which probably the most significant in recent years has been B.P.'s discovery of protein from oil, a new product development which has now reached the commercial stage and which could be of great importance in the long run.

A further sub-area of research which is much stressed nowadays is

*Industry*, Department of Applied Economics, Occasional Paper 28 (Cambridge University Press, 1971) pp. 46–7 and 59.

. work on environment problems created either by the industry's own
operations (e.g. waste disposal) or utilisation of its products. For
example, processes for the desulphurisation of heavy oil feedstocks
have been available for a considerable time and will probably be further
developed and extensively used in the near future.[1]

A good deal of R & D activity in the basic chemical field is of the sort
that gives rise to patents. As was shown in Table 8.1, rather more
patents are granted per unit of R & D expenditure in basic than in
finished and specialty chemicals, and basic chemical patents are more
numerous than in the other chemical fields in our sample. Furthermore,
as can be seen from Table 9.2, nearly two-thirds of basic chemicals
output in our sample was 'patent-based' (in the sense that it was
produced using patented processes that could be denied to others if the
patentee wished). Licence agreements are considerably more numerous
in relation to R & D in this field than in other chemical fields, as was
shown in Table 8.4. On this evidence, companies in the basic chemical
industry are at least as active in patenting, and about twice as active in
licensing, as are those in finished and specialty chemicals.

### B. IMPACT OF THE PATENT SYSTEM

Despite the fairly high rates of patenting and licensing activity noted
above, and the large proportion of output based on patented processes,
companies in our sample were uniformly of the view that patent protection has a rather marginal effect on their basic chemical operations.
(They were careful to distinguish between basic chemicals and their
'down-the-line' derivatives on this point.) The estimates for basic
chemicals given in Chapter 9 were that some 5 per cent of R & D
and a negligible proportion of output would be 'lost' under a thoroughgoing compulsory licensing system. This is clearly in contrast with the
appreciable impacts estimated for finished and specialty chemicals,
as well as belying the appearance of a high stake in patents given by
figures of patenting and licensing activity, and merits some explanation.

### Economies of scale

The first point that can be made is that, because of the limited range of
products involved (which assists the exploitation of economies of
scale) and the large size of markets available for them, there is not the
same pressure to protect research results here as in finished and specialty

---

[1] Dr H. Hoog, *Conserving Our Environment*, Presidential Address to the Institution of Chemical
Engineers, London, 1970.

chemicals – and the same is true of promotional and selling expenditures, which are small in comparison with those in, say, pharmaceuticals or detergents. Although innovations in important production processes can certainly lead to large reductions in unit costs for firms with access to them, the competitive advantage obtained by copyists is quite slight, since ongoing R & D programmes typically comprise a relatively small fraction of the total costs of innovating firms. By comparison, economies obtainable from large scale production are virtually always overwhelming.

The existence of powerful economies of scale in manufacturing, and the cost advantages that arise from vertical integration of processes and bulk supply contracts, mean that there is little place in the industry for the medium-sized firm, let alone the small one. Even in basic chemicals, for which there are relatively small or fragmented markets, the giant manufacturer is usually at a considerable cost advantage because of the fact that such products are frequently joint products or by-products of the bulk outputs. In the U.K., very few basic chemicals are produced by more than a small handful of companies, and in a number of important cases there are essentially only one or perhaps two manufacturers.[1] Leading examples are ammonia (I.C.I. and Shellstar), chlorine, caustic soda and soda ash (I.C.I.), oxygen (British Oxygen and Air Reduction), phosphorus and compounds (Albright and Wilson), hydrogen peroxide (Laporte Industries), methanol (I.C.I., B.P.), acetylene (British Oxygen), borates (Borax Holdings), and there are many more.

Owing to the existence of powerful 'physical' barriers to entry, patents are seldom if ever required to provide protection against competition from the small or medium-sized firm. The only sort of competition that can take place in the basic chemical industry is that between large manufacturers, and these are few in number in most markets – even in the U.S.A.

Because of ultimate limitations on production economies of scale (at present, it is doubtful whether there are any significant cost advantages in building an ethylene plant in excess of 500,000 tons annual capacity),[2] competition between a small number of large firms is at least a possibility in major industrial markets such as the U.K. Moreover, international competition is possible through exports and through overseas investment. In normal circumstances, the latter is the prevalent form, since bulk chemicals are costly to transport in proportion to their value, except perhaps by pipeline in very large volumes.

---

[1] There are exceptions, notably in the manufacture of sulphuric acid and hydrochloric acid, on which several dozen firms are engaged, including some of fairly moderate size.
[2] Correspondence with Dr F. A. Fidler.

In these circumstances, which approximate in many respects to the economist's stereotype of 'oligopoly without product differentiation', it is very much in the interest of producers to refrain from outright competition in any of its various forms, and behaviour to this end might be expected to be a feature of the industry. Although a proper investigation of this subject was beyond the scope of our inquiry, our general impression from talking to management of the firms concerned is that collusion of even the most tacit kind on prices and supply is nowadays strictly avoided, for fear of attracting the attention of anti-trust and restrictive practices authorities in the major industrial countries. The most that appears to happen in some industries where there is a dominant supplier is that price leadership of a rather informal kind may tend to emerge, but even this is relatively rare. It is in fact possible to point to a number of important product areas closely linked with basic chemical production where keen price competition has manifestly taken place in recent years. Fertilisers and plastics materials are outstanding examples of industries in which international competition through exports and international investment has squeezed prices and profits.

It might be thought that basic chemical patents would provide a welcome and quite legitimate device for forestalling such competition, but they do not in practice appear to be much used for this purpose. The main reasons, so far as we can tell, are as follows. Where firms are unable to rely on natural monopoly or dominant supplier positions based on economies of scale or other manufacturing advantages (in which cases patent monopolies are anyway redundant), they have found it in their mutual interest to share basic innovations through licensing rather than attempt to monopolise them – hence the considerable volume of patent and know-how licensing mentioned in Chapter 8. The fact that such licensing is mainly with foreign companies is due largely to the relatively small number of U.K.-owned companies in the basic chemical field. The tendency to confine licensees to a few foreign markets appears rather less pronounced here than in finished and specialty chemicals, and exclusive licensing is definitely rare.

The incentive for technology exchange in the basic chemical field comes partly from the fact that firms in this industry are in many cases producing the same range of (identical) products from an essentially similar series of processes, while no single firm has a monopoly of patents on more than a few of those processes. It is therefore doubtful whether any company could hold the others to ransom on an important process without fear of retaliation on some other process. In this situation, patents are bargaining counters in licensing deals rather than monopoly-giving devices.

This situation is reinforced by the fact that there are very few patented processes of unique technical importance in the basic chemical field. There are often alternative methods for producing the principal items, and if this is not so it is usually possible to introduce variations into the patented features of a 'standard' process in order to avoid infringements. Patents are likely to cover a particular catalyst or a modification of a well-known chemical reaction to suit a particular reactant and variants can usually be substituted without incurring prohibitive extra costs, although some loss of efficiency or quality may be experienced in comparison with the best patented solution. The number of patented 'winners' in the basic chemical field is relatively rare. Developments of considerable importance do occur from time to time – for example, I.C.I.'s Steam Naphtha Reforming Process, which will be discussed below – but even these are capable of being varied or in some circumstances by-passed altogether, as will be seen.

In short, patents rarely if ever offer the prospect of a complete monopoly over the only commercially feasible method of producing a basic chemical, and even if they did it is doubtful that patentees would attempt to exercise exclusive rights over the process, although they might be tempted to do so in their own domestic markets in the unlikely event of competition there from newcomers to the industry. Even in the latter case, the patentee might license a domestic competitor who could offer some reasonably important piece of technology in exchange, which is often possible in an industry where research concentrates on a fairly narrow range of technical problems.

### Importance of know-how

Even were firms as prone to selectivity in licensing of basic chemical patents as they are in finished and specialty chemicals, it seems doubtful whether they would be much affected under a compulsory licensing system which merely provided (automatic) access to patents and nothing more. We were assured that in many cases know-how is a vital ingredient in licence agreements in this field, and this would be no more readily obtainable under a compulsory licensing system than it is under the present arrangements. (To envisage, as an alternative to the existing patent system, a system that required the compulsory licensing of know-how as well as patents would take us far beyond an assessment of the patent system.)

Some idea of the sort of supporting information that is normally provided in standard licensing agreements in this field is given by the following excerpt from the licensing prospectus offered by Shell Chemicals on its ethylene oxide process, which has been licensed for use by a number of firms in the U.K., Europe, U.S.A. and Canada:

The final design 'package' furnished by Shell for an Ethylene Oxide unit includes: a set of process flow diagrams showing all process equipment, process conditions and duties, material balance and recommended instrumentation; process specification sheets for auxiliary equipment showing duties, process-side fouling factors, process conditions, flow rates, and physical properties of process fluids; column specification sheets showing process conditions and flow rates, column diameters, number and type of trays, feed tray locations, and recommended general tray configuration. This 'package' contains all process information required by the client and/or his contractor to prepare the mechanical design of the unit.

Although Shell does not perform the mechanical design of the unit, a review is made of the mechanical drawings and specification sheets for all major process equipment from the standpoint of process adequacy and operability.

After completion and review of the final mechanical design, Shell issues the following material:

1. A report containing the process design summary and reference material for an operating manual, including general considerations of operation, start-up and shutdown. The preparation of detailed operating orders is, of course, handled by the customer consistent with his operating practices, nomenclature, etc.

2. An analytical manual for the unit, containing the analytical information needed for plant control and analysis of process streams including detailed descriptions of the analytical methods, and recommended sampling schedules.

3. A basic data report, containing a sufficient range of physical and equilibrium data to permit the operating staff to evaluate operation of the unit for the achievement of maximum efficiency.[1]

A licensee here is clearly obtaining access to far more information than that contained in the patent specification, and without it he would probably be ill-equipped to work the process in competition with a fully-licensed firm, or Shell itself. Moreover, the nature and scope of the information offered here is typical of that in most processes of no more than moderate novelty and complexity licensed in the field. Support of a considerably more expensive sort is likely to be offered on the more advanced or complex processes, as will be seen in the case of the Steam Naphtha Reforming Process.

It therefore seems fair to argue that, in chemical process technology at least, the ability of a firm to monopolise its inventions depends at least as much on secret know-how as on its patents, and that the former

[1] Shell Chemicals Ltd., *Shell Ethylene Oxide Process*, p. 3.

would continue to offer a comparatively effective means of controlling the spread of technology in a world of compulsory licensing. Naturally, the effectiveness of the deterrent to would-be copyists would depend on preserving the secrecy of know-how, and it is widely recognised that production secrets cannot be kept indefinitely. However, the type of technical expertise needed to construct and operate the more advanced processes goes far beyond 'production secrets'. Without such expertise, even a licensee with considerable experience would need to spend several years solving the design, materials and operating problems associated with a major new process. For this reason, it seems highly unlikely that the compulsory licensing of mere patent rights would in itself have much impact on the spread of new process technology in this field.

### Pressures to innovate

Finally, even if patents were a unique or more powerful means of exercising monopolies in basic chemicals and firms were more inclined to use them for that purpose, it seems highly doubtful in present circumstances that their removal would affect the industry's R & D effort to any marked extent. The pressures on firms to sustain their research programmes in basic chemicals are strong, once they are committed to producing in this field. Basic chemical manufacture requires a high ratio of fixed capital to labour (in the region of £25,000 per employee compared with about £2,500 for all manufacturing in 1969), and large losses would be unavoidable if plant became idle. Substantial unit cost reductions and quality improvements are steadily achieved by many of those who do research, and no firms could afford to stand aside from this activity even if (as seems unlikely) research results in this field became more difficult to protect as a consequence of compulsory licensing. Moreover, programmes that are directed at finding major new applications for by-products and solving environmental problems are hardly likely to be sensitive to patent protection. The latter are not primarily influenced by immediate profit-and-loss considerations, while the compulsion to push ahead with the former is not likely to be affected by considerations of monopoly profit, at least where large potential markets are concerned.[1]

The types of R & D in this field that might be affected would be work on highly specialised applications, returns on which can be highly sensitive to competition from imitators. Some small-volume industrial

---

[1] There is, for example, no question in the mind of B.P.'s management that the pioneering work on protein from oil would have gone ahead had patent protection not been available – although B.P. is naturally extremely pleased that it has been able to secure basic patents on this work, and is not keen to license them in territories where it plans to manufacture itself.

chemicals come within this category, as well as product sidelines in such areas as novel building materials, some of which have provided profitable minor outlets for basic chemicals. The amounts of R & D involved in these areas are however relatively small.

For similar reasons, prices and profits in the basic chemicals field are not thought to be much affected by patent protection. The degree of competition between large producers would not be significantly altered in a world of compulsory licensing, for there is no indication that key technology would become more widely available under such a system. The pricing and licensing policies of firms would probably operate much as under the existing patent system.

### Greater secrecy

The principal impact of patent protection in this field, so far as we can tell from the evidence available to us, is that a good deal of public disclosure of technical information takes place which would otherwise tend to be kept secret. This occurs through both patent specifications and technical literature of various other sorts, but the patent specifications probably contain the essential pieces of information at issue. All firms stressed the point that they would tend to be more secretive about process technology in a compulsory licensing environment. The sort of information affected would above all be the precise specifications of catalysts, construction materials, etc. together with operating details (pressures, temperatures, rates of flow, etc.) which are often of crucial importance in chemical processes, and which are normally revealed in, or on the strength of, patent specifications under the existing system.

The main impact of greater secrecy would be to retard the general progress of process research in the industry, and it also seems likely that licensing would suffer to some extent. Apart from the reduction in general awareness of process improvements among potential licensees, it is doubtful that pure know-how licensing could fully compensate for a fall-off in patent licensing in this field, because of the additional legal difficulties and uncertainties involved. Furthermore, the greater pressure for secrecy would interfere with the normal licensor's practice of commissioning engineering contractors to construct plants for licensees and providing them with full supporting information. The leakage of secret know-how through contractors and fabricators is a problem that all licensors have to deal with in normal circumstances and there is no doubt that patents are a useful means of checking this leakage. Under a compulsory licensing system, much greater supervision of contractors would be required.

For these reasons, it is arguable that the exchange of technology in basic chemicals might well be reduced, rather than increased, in a world of compulsory licensing.

Lest our conclusions regarding the marginal impact of patent protection in basic chemicals appear to contrast somewhat oddly with the high level of patent activity observed, it should be said that firms in this industry do, of course, derive benefits from the patent system which are in some cases of appreciable value. In simple terms, the most obvious of these is royalty income, which amounts to several million pounds a year for each of the largest companies, but such advantages as 'recognition' for technical achievements, and the usefulness of patents as bargaining counters in licence negotiations, are also valuable. If this were not so, firms would not go to the trouble they do to obtain patents and suppress infringements. However our point here is that, apart from the tendency to promote public disclosure and the associated increase in process licensing mentioned in the previous paragraph, these benefits are not significantly dependent on the monopoly element in the patent system. (Thus, royalties received on basic chemicals would probably not be very different under a compulsory licensing system, other than for the reasons mentioned above.) Here, as elsewhere, it is the comparison with a compulsory licensing world in which we are essentially interested.

## C.  THE STEAM NAPHTHA REFORMING PROCESS

The preceding arguments can be illustrated by reference to a major patented innovation in basic chemicals – I.C.I.'s Steam Naphtha Reforming Process. This process represents an important advance in the 'reforming' of hydrocarbon feedstocks (principally liquid naphtha, a light petroleum distillate) to produce hydrogen, ammonia synthesis gas or town gas.

It was evident as early as the 1950s that the traditional 'water gas' method of producing ammonia (in which steam and air were successively passed over hot coke) was becoming uneconomic and that the future probably lay with the steam reforming of hydrocarbons. Well before the war I.C.I. had introduced the steam reforming of by-product methane on a limited scale and was examining methods of reforming petroleum feedstocks. However, the impetus of the search was much increased in the mid-1950s, when cheap natural gas became available in a number of European countries and the prospect of competition from ammonia derived from methane in natural gas threatened I.C.I.'s major production centres. Unable to foresee the discovery of North Sea gas, I.C.I. believed that its only course was to develop an efficient method of reforming cheap naphtha from oil refineries which were being built all over Europe, and its Agricultural Division (the chief producer and user of ammonia for fertilizers) turned its research efforts heavily in that direction.

The result was a new reforming process which totally eclipsed the traditional 'water gas' and 'producer gas' methods, and is by far the most economic process for manufacturing bulk ammonia and hydrogen in any location where cheap natural gas is not available. It uses much cheaper raw materials and is capable of being used on a much larger scale than traditional methods, and it has the useful advantage that it can be operated at high pressures, thereby permitting economies in subsequent gas compression for ammonia synthesis, or in gas distribution. The process can, with modifications in plant design, be adapted for producing pure hydrogen or town gas, and has great superiorities in both over traditional methods. Although the process was developed over a number of years, the main breakthrough was made in 1959 and basic patents were applied for in 1960 and granted in 1964.

Among the various patented features, the one of most importance is the use of a novel nickel reforming catalyst in place of standard catalysts used to reform natural and refinery gases. This overcame the problem of carbon formation which blocked the reaction tubes and which could otherwise be dealt with only by using uneconomic quantities of steam. Although I.C.I. had used nickel catalysts for hydrocarbon reforming before the war, it was many years before the 'alkalised supported' nickel catalyst was invented. However, once invented, it was quickly proved to be very effective.

A second novel feature is the use of a hydro-desulphurisation process to prevent deactivation of the nickel catalyst by the sulphur contained in all petroleum feedstocks. This process, which was patented, was a considerable advance on processes commercially available at the time.

Research on steam reforming of hydrocarbons has been carried on at Billingham for a long period, and two pilot plants as well as several laboratory scale units continue to operate. I.C.I. estimates that £1–2 million had been spent (up to 1968) on inventing, developing and improving this particular process, but this of course excludes the substantial investment in large scale units on which the process was commercially proven, prior to licensing. It has been licensed throughout the world, contracts having been signed for the construction of some 300 plants in 30 countries. Annual royalties received by I.C.I. are stated to have been in the region of '£1 million plus'.

The method of licensing is of some interest. I.C.I. have appointed six internationally-known contractors (two British, three American and one German) as main licensees, and have provided them with full supporting know-how. (Major chemical and oil companies do not as a rule enter the construction field themselves.) Customers normally obtain no more than a straight patent licence via the contractor in which I.C.I. does not directly participate, although undertaking to give expert technical advice and to train operating staff if necessary. (Moreover, I.C.I. is a main supplier of the catalysts.) The contractors naturally operate within licensing policy guidelines laid down by I.C.I.

The advantage of this type of arrangement is that I.C.I. is relieved of the construction problems involved in 'package' licensing agreements, and does not have immediate responsibility for commissioning plant and ensuring its successful operation. These activities can make for enormous demands on engineering staff when major new processes are licensed, and although this pattern is not by any means the commonest form of arrangement, it is increasingly being adopted by the industry for licensing major process innovations.

I.C.I.'s policy on licensing the process depends on the purpose for which it is intended. Any serious applicant may have a licence to produce town gas, and every Gas Board in the U.K. has been licensed for this purpose. The policy with regard to chemical industry uses (e.g. manufacture of hydrogen, ammonia, carbon monoxide or methanol) is more selective. Any manufacturer who is not a competitor in one of I.C.I.'s main markets may have a licence on standard terms. This means in practice that chemical licences are readily available except in countries where a member of the I.C.I. Group produces the chemicals concerned, and in fact nearly 100 chemical contracts have been signed. Very few licences for chemical purposes have however been granted to outsiders in I.C.I.'s main territories (e.g. U.K., Australia, Canada, South Africa), and none for ammonia in the U.K.

In commenting on the role played by patents in the development of the process, spokesmen for the Agricultural Division were of the opinion that the prospect of patent protection was not an important factor in decisions to undertake the work; the R & D would have gone ahead without such protection, given the absence of major patent impediments, owing to the need to meet competition from gas-based ammonia. Patents were essentially a bonus, in that they facilitated the licensing of the process somewhat – although there was no doubt that I.C.I. would have been able to license it on almost as large a scale without them, at least in the early years of its exploitation, because of its technical superiority and the high level of demand for petroleum-based gas. More recently, patents have assisted royalty earnings to a larger degree, for the know-how has inevitably become dispersed and competitors have been developing their own variations and alternatives. There would probably have been a tendency to keep more of the critical details secret in conditions of compulsory licensing, but the basic patents would still have been applied for and secret know-how relied on for security to the extent possible.

It therefore seems safe to conclude that this particular innovation was not dependent on patent protection, and that I.C.I.'s R & D effort on the process would not have been significantly reduced in a world of compulsory licensing. Whether utilisation of the process for chemical purposes would have been any more widespread in the latter conditions is also highly doubtful. The element of know-how is clearly most essential to the successful operation of the scheme, and straight patent licences would not in themselves be of great assistance to an outsider. Moreover, although the process has (in I.C.I.'s terms) revolutionised the economics of ammonia production, this is only true in comparison with methods not utilising natural gas. While readily adaptable to the latter, it offers only marginal advantages over alternative processes – its main advantage being suitability for operation under high pressure, whereas other natural gas processes are low pressure methods. As has been observed, the serious threat of competition in I.C.I.'s main markets comes from gas-based ammonia.[1] It thus seems probable that I.C.I.'s reluctance to license the process for ammonia synthesis in the U.K. and its other principal production centres has had very little impact on supply conditions for ammonia and the fertilisers that are its main derivative product.

[1] The only other major supplier of ammonia in the U.K., Shellstar, is basing its large planned expansion in capacity on North Sea Gas. Some 50 per cent of output in the non-Communist countries is based on natural gas, and this proportion is expected to increase.

# 12. ELECTRONICS

## A. THE INDUSTRIAL BACKGROUND

### Outline of the industry

The electronics industry is customarily divided into three broad product fields – components, capital goods and consumer goods. Although exact measures are impossible because of quality changes, it is estimated that total real U.K. output has in recent years risen at roughly 8 per cent annually. Growth in components and capital goods has for some time considerably exceeded that in consumer goods, which has been relatively sluggish in most advanced industrial economies since the boom of the nineteen-fifties.

In 1968 deliveries of components by U.K. firms totalled £205 million, while those of capital goods (not including telecommunications equipment) were £454 million, those of telecommunications equipment were £199 million and those of consumer goods were £181 million (the value of components in each case being included in that of finished equipment).[1] Proportions exported are about one-fifth of components, one-third of capital goods and telecommunications equipment and one-twentieth of consumer goods. Imports are roughly equal in value to exports in 'active' components (valves, tubes and semi-conductor devices, including transistors and integrated circuits) and in consumer products and are about half the level of exports in 'passive' components (a wide range of items from capacitors, resistors, transformers and relays to aerials, loudspeakers and microphones) and capital goods; imports of telecommunications equipment are very small.[2]

In some areas of the industry a substantial proportion of U.K. production is accounted for by subsidiaries of foreign companies. This is particularly true in components, where several of the largest manufacturers are foreign-owned (e.g. Mullard and S.T.C., which are wholly-owned subsidiaries of Philips N.V. and International Telephone and Telegraph respectively) and probably control over half of U.K. output of active components. Foreign-owned firms are also important in computers, where they account for about 20 per cent of U.K. production,[3] in telecommunications equipment (where S.T.C. and Pye, now a wholly-owned subsidiary of Philips, are two of the four

[1] Gross value added in these industries totalled £622 million in 1968. See Appendix A.
[2] N.E.D.O., *Statistics of the Electronics Industry* (Electronics E.D.C., June 1967) Tables 22, 24.
[3] O.E.C.D., *Electronic Computers*, a report in the *Gaps in Technology* series (Paris, 1969) p. 79.

established U.K. suppliers), and in measuring and test equipment, where the American firms Hewlett Packard, Tektronix and Beckman Instruments have U.K. manufacturing operations which are dominant in their special fields. In electronic equipment for chemical and medical laboratories Pye Unicam is the leading U.K. manufacturer and its major competitor is the British subsidiary of the American firm Perkin Elmer.

The share of overseas firms in key U.K. electronics markets is moreover much increased if imports are included. In computers and other data processing equipment, for example, imports amount to about 30 per cent of the domestic market,[1] so that the total foreign share in the U.K. computer market is probably nearly 50 per cent. This is in line with the fact that, in 1967, some 55 per cent of all computer installations in Britain were of foreign (essentially American) design, a percentage that had grown from 21 per cent in 1962.[2] The U.S. share was probably of the same order of magnitude in measuring, test and other instrumentation, but much lower in radar, radio and tele-communications equipment and process control systems.

### *Invention and innovation*

There is not space here to give a full account of the phenomenal technical changes that have taken place in the electronics field since the first demonstration of radio communication at the end of the nineteenth century.[3] Briefly, the history of the industry until the second world war was essentially that of radio, and later television. Most of the basic inventions in radio had been made (and patented) by British, German and American inventors before 1920, and by then regular marine and international radio telegraph services had been established, mainly in the hands of the two pioneering radio companies, Marconi and Telefunken. During the next 20 years a series of advances in radio receivers and components was introduced, mainly by R.C.A. and Philips, but the chief developments in radio were the growth of public broadcasting, the development of worldwide short-wave communication networks and the introduction of frequency modulation (FM) in Germany and America in the 1930s. The basic work on television transmission tubes was done in America by Zworykin in the 1920s, and Zworykin's work was later taken up by R.C.A. in the

---

[1] C. Freeman, 'Research and Development in Electronic Capital Goods', *National Institute Economic Review* (Nov. 1965) p. 50. The share seems to have changed little since 1964.

[2] O.E.C.D., *Electronic Computers*, p. 128.

[3] A useful account can be found in Freeman, *op. cit.*; detailed accounts of recent developments are available in O.E.C.D., *Electronic Components* and *Electronic Computers*, reports in the *Gaps in Technology* series.

U.S.A. and E.M.I. in the U.K., as will be described later.[1] The world's first regular high definition public television service was introduced in the U.K. in 1936. It was not until 1940 that a similar service was inaugurated in the U.S.A.

Industrial research on radar began in the early 1930s, but the work was greatly accelerated in the U.K. and Germany by the approach of war, when large Government and university research teams in both countries were brought into the field. The U.K. obtained and held a narrow wartime lead over the Germans and Americans, but by the end of the war all three countries had developed advanced radar-based navigational and guidance systems. The main post-war developments have been in airborne and marine navigation equipment, in which British firms (most notably Cossor,[2] Marconi and Decca) have been among world leaders, and in air traffic control and weapons guidance systems, in which American firms are now slightly ahead of their European competitors. Radar is of interest in that it was the first field in which large-scale R & D efforts were launched by governments, leading to technical advances of extraordinary rapidity by pre-war standards.

It is not easy to summarise the rapid technical progress that has been made in the electronics field since the war, but the following features are outstanding: the development of the electronic computer and successive improvements to it; the application of the computer in data processing, industrial process control and special military and scientific applications; the miniaturisation of components based on semiconductors, beginning with the transistor, and the development of solid-state electronics based on the transistor; and the development of colour television.

A common feature of all these basic post-war innovations, with the exception perhaps of industrial process control and other special computer applications, where British and to a lesser extent other European firms have made important contributions, is that their principal industrial development, if not always the discovery and applied research, has been undertaken almost entirely by large American firms. In computers, for example, the first commercially available models were produced by Remington Rand (UNIVAC, 1951) and I.B.M. ('650', 1954), although the basic theoretical work had been done before the war in Europe, and the first 'breadboard' model was built by Zuse in Germany in 1942. Such has been the size and effectiveness of development work in computers by American firms that in

[1] Pioneering work on mechanical systems of television was done by the Scottish inventor J. L. Baird, but these systems proved far inferior to those based on the cathode ray tube.
[2] Cossor was taken over by the U.S. Raytheon Corporation in 1962.

recent years some three-quarters of all computers installed in Western Europe, as well as all those in America itself, have been installed either by American manufacturers or under licence from them.[1]

In the component field, both the basic research and the important industrial applications have been undertaken essentially by large American firms. The transistor was invented in the Bell Telephone Laboratories (the R & D organisation of American Telephone and Telegraph) in 1949, and its subsequent industrial development was carried out at very considerable expense by Western Electric (the manufacturing and supply organisation of the same Group).[2] Most other pioneering advances in semiconductor technology have been made by American firms, prominent among which have been the basic work of Fairchild in planar technology and the development of integrated circuits by Texas Instruments. Microcircuitry, although still a relatively high-cost technology and therefore not yet generally adopted for consumer products, offers great advantages in terms of lightness, efficiency and reliability in more demanding uses and probably now accounts for a third to a half of 'active element groups' (circuitry) in the U.S. industrial component market.

The basic development of colour television has been undertaken almost entirely by American firms, principally R.C.A., although many others cooperated on the American system (N.T.S.C.), including important contributions by Hazeltine and General Electric. R.C.A. produced the first colour tube in 1950 and subsequently pursued the development at enormous cost[3] and in the face of strong official discouragement and slow market growth.[4] More recently refinements and additions have been made independently in Europe by Telefunken (now A.E.G.–Telefunken) – the P.A.L. system – and the French firm Campagnie Française de Télévision (C.F.T.) – the S.E.C.A.M. system – both based essentially on the American technology.

The P.A.L. system has been officially adopted as the standard system in the U.K. and a number of other European countries, but France has opted for S.E.C.A.M. and has persuaded the Soviet Union to do

---

[1] O.E.C.D., *Electronic Computers*, Table 4.

[2] It is estimated that R & D expenditure on the transistor up to the patenting stage (1946–50) was $140,000, while development expenditure in the next ten years was some $28 million. See Jewkes *et al.*, *The Sources of Invention*, p. 215. For a general account of the formidable basic contributions of Bell Telephone Laboratories in the electronic field since 1925, see H. W. Bode, *Synergy: Technical Integration and Technological Innovation in the Bell System* (Bell Laboratories, Murray Hill, New Jersey; 1971) Chs. 7 and 8.

[3] Freeman, *Research and Development in Electronic Capital Goods*, pp. 54–5. R.C.A. are estimated to have spent $130 million on launching colour television between 1946 and 1960, including large sums on setting up a broadcasting system, programmes, etc.

[4] Slow growth was attributable mainly to the relatively poor picture quality offered by the earlier American colour T.V. receivers.

likewise, while others (e.g. Italy) have yet to choose between the two.

A great deal of debate has taken place concerning the reasons for post-war American technical leadership in the electronics field. It is generally agreed that although wartime disruption in Europe was in some cases an important contributory factor, the main considerations are firstly the large scale of U.S. Government support, especially in the early development of computers, which initially were thought to have their main applications in the military field, and more recently in miniature components, where the U.S. military-space programmes have financed large amounts of R & D and have provided large orders for products; and secondly, the large size of the U.S. civil as well as military market for electronic products, which even in recent years has dwarfed that of Europe.[1] This means that although the largest American electronics firms typically spend on R & D roughly ten times the amounts spent by their largest European counterparts, their R & D/ sales ratios tend to be no higher than those of European firms.[2] In other words, where the rate of technological advance in a particular field depends, within limits, on the absolute size of firms' individual R & D programmes, the size of the American domestic market has been a crucial factor in this advance.

### Research and development

While electronics is sometimes cited as the field *par excellence* in which an R & D programme has to be large in order to be effective, this is by no means true of all types of electronic products. Freeman, in the article cited above, estimates that the 'threshold development cost' (i.e., the absolute volume of R & D expenditure necessary to develop a product sufficiently novel to supersede established products) ranges from £80–150 thousand (at 1965 prices) for something as straight-forward as a new radio receiver to £8–16 million for a complete range of E.D.P. computers, software and peripherals.[3] If the appropriate 'maximum lead times' (i.e., the estimated maximum time that can elapse between the commencement of work on a particular new product and its introduction on the market, if a firm's share of that market is to

---

[1] The selling value of U.S. computer production (including exports) was estimated at $3,200 million in 1966, whereas production in all other O.E.C.D. countries combined was probably less than $1,000 million. See O.E.C.D., *Electronic Computers*, Table 1.

[2] *Ibid.*, Table 9. The Bell Telephone Laboratories, probably the world's largest private research organisation, employed 17,000 persons at the end of 1969; nevertheless, its R & D undertaken for the A.T. & T. Group amounted to no more than 6·4 per cent of Group sales. (See Bode, *Synergy*, pp. 18, 51.)

[3] It was suggested by I.C.L. in our inquiry that these computer costs seem very low even for 1965, and might be four times as high for the present day (1972).

be kept above what is held to be a minimum viable economic level) are two and four years for radio receivers and E.D.P. computers respectively, the minimum annual R & D expenditures (at 1965 prices) necessary for a 'defensive' strategy are £40–75,000 in the case of the former and £2–4 million for the latter.[1] The R & D threshold is thought by Freeman to be quite low for radios and smaller electronic instruments, moderate for machine tool controls, research satellites and small computers, and high for general purpose computers, fully-electronic telephone exchanges and communications satellites. Although these figures are very rough orders of magnitude it is clear that only the largest firms, with annual sales of at least £50 million, can hope to survive in one of the latter fields, and that much larger turnover is required to support a diversified R & D programme with a reasonable margin of security against unsuccessful projects.

All firms in our inquiry specialising in the electronics field have £ multi-million R & D programmes. (Six companies between them reported R & D of nearly £40 million.) Some, but not all, produce components as well as finished products, and one (Mullard) is essentially a components manufacturer. The average R & D ratio in 'equipment' (nearly 14 per cent), was much higher than that in components (nearly 8 per cent – see Table 8.1), mainly because 'development' is much heavier in the former than the latter, in relation both to 're-search' and to sales.[2] On this evidence, electronics is best thought of as a highly 'development-intensive' field, in the U.K. at least. While we do not have information for smaller firms specialising in measuring and test instruments, etc., we doubt whether their R & D ratios would be very much different, for although R & D programmes in such areas can be quite small, the markets in these areas tend on the whole to be small as well.

*Role of the government*

An outstanding feature of R & D in the electronics industry is the extent of Government support, which is far in excess of that in any other field covered in our inquiry. Although we do not have enough data to give a precise breakdown between electronics and other categories, we estimate that the great bulk of the £16·4 million of Government finance to electrical engineering shown in Table 8.1 was in the electronics and telecommunications fields. If so, it appears that roughly 40 per cent of

[1] Freeman, *Research and Development in Electronic Capital Goods*, p. 69.
[2] The division between 'development' and routine technical activity is extremely difficult to draw in the electronic equipment field; it is particularly hard to distinguish between 'development software' and 'routine software', and the former accounts for about a quarter of all development in computer-related areas. The figures in Table 8.1 should therefore be treated only as broad orders of magnitude.

R & D expenditure by large companies in the electronics field is financed by the Government. This is naturally somewhat higher than the 32 per cent implied for the whole of electrical engineering in Table 4.2, although it does not approach the extremely high level of Government support in the aircraft industries. It should perhaps be pointed out that although the bulk of the finance in question is in the nature of payments for R & D done under contract for a Government department or research establishment, or the N.R.D.C., or as a joint project with them, it also includes general financial support for company R & D, such as that granted by the Ministry of Technology to I.C.L. for basic work on computers.[1]

The Government's interest in the electronics industry is not of course confined to its sponsorship and subsidisation of R & D. It is an important purchaser of electronic capital goods and other equipment, most notably in the spheres of defence and telecommunications, and there are frequently links between the R & D it supports and the equipment it buys. The Ministry of Defence (now including Aviation procurement) is by far the largest domestic customer for radar and navigational aids, aircraft and weapons guidance systems and other 'avionics' equipment, while the Post Office has until fairly recently been virtually the only U.K. buyer of telephone equipment and equipment for long distance telecommunication systems.[2] The public sector is also a major customer in other areas, e.g. public broadcasting equipment (B.B.C.), medical and scientific apparatus (hospitals, universities and government research establishments) and computers (for the largest types of which the Atomic Energy Authority and the Post Office have been major customers).

Where the U.K. Government commissions R & D or is a major purchaser of research-based products, and where defence secrets are not involved, it normally encourages firms with which it has contracts to make the resulting technology available to other British manufacturers on reasonable commercial terms. A standard arrangement in a Government research contract would be that any patents arising from the work belong to the firm that does it, while the Government reserves free clearance for use of the patents by all firms working on Government supply contracts. The Government does not normally require that free rights be granted for other (i.e., commercial) uses, and indeed as a rule insists on the payment of royalties in such cases (including a share payable to itself), but it would be unlikely to approve refusal by the

[1] Ministry of Technology, *Industrial Investment: The Computers Merger Project 1968* (Cmnd. 3660). See also International Computers (Holdings) Ltd., *Annual Report and Accounts, 1968.*
[2] In the last few years a number of major installations have been supplied to large British firms wishing to set up private microwave communications systems.

patentee to license others on reasonable commercial terms. According to firms in our inquiry, it is usually provided that the Government will receive a standard royalty if the patents are licensed for commercial uses or if the patentee utilises the technology in his own commercial operations; a levy of $7\frac{1}{2}$ per cent of the selling value of output under licence is normally payable to the Government for use of manufacturing know-how and patent rights arising from Government contract work in the electronics field.

Whether or not it finances the R & D, the Government normally invokes its statutory patent licence under Section 46 of the Patents Act in contracts for the purchase of electronic and similar equipment by the Crown – i.e., primarily for the defence services and the Post Office (in the days before this became a public corporation) – and this is reflected in the terms of major departmental supply agreements.[1] For example, under the terms of the G.P.O. Bulk Supply Agreements, through which the Post Office for many years obtained nearly all its electrical equipment requirements, contracts were allocated at common prices between the main established U.K. manufacturers. The latter worked to a common set of specifications laid down by the Post Office and were held to have free clearance under each others' patents in the relevant field for supplies to the Post Office.[2] (This explains the absence of straight patent licensing between U.K. telecommunications manufacturers noted in Chapter 8.) However, the Bulk Supply Agreements were terminated when the Post Office became a public corporation in 1969, and Section 46 is no longer applicable in the field they covered. It remains to be seen what domestic licensing policy telecommunications firms will choose to adopt in the new 'competitive' era. If, as seems likely, they wish to follow the industry's generally liberal policy on straight patent clearance (which we discuss below), some extension of formal licensing arrangements in this field will presumably be necessary.

### Structure of the industry

Although the electronics industry has the appearance of being dominated by a small number of very large firms which manufacture a

---

[1] See Ministry of Aviation (now Ministry of Defence), *Standard Conditions of Government Contracts for Stores Purchases* (H.M.S.O., October 1970), especially Section 32A. The use of Section 46 of the Patents Act in the electronics field is essentially to protect Government suppliers against infringement proceedings by patentees (whether or not the patents arise from Government-financed research). There is rarely if ever, any call in the defence field for this section to be invoked against a patentee in respect of his own supplies, unlike the experience in the pharmaceutical industry (discussed in Chapter 10).

[2] This point was made by several respondents to our inquiry, and confirmed by the industry's association (TEMA).

wide range of components and equipment, this picture needs qualification in certain respects. Firstly, even the largest corporate groups tend to specialise in one, or perhaps two, broad areas; thus I.B.M. concentrates mainly on data processing equipment, International Telephone and Telegraph on telecommunications equipment, Philips mainly on consumer goods, etc. Secondly, there are certain areas, notably passive components, measuring and test instruments and audio equipment, where, although the bulk of output is produced by a relatively small number of larger firms, there are relatively numerous 'tails' of medium-sized and small firms. There is not space here to explore reasons for this state of affairs in full; the essential points are that R & D 'threshold' expenditures are quite small in some areas, as was noted earlier, while manufacturing economies of scale, which are especially important in component production, cannot operate where demand is relatively limited, as is the case in high performance audio equipment, scientific instruments and some specialised types of passive components for industrial uses. In these areas, a relatively small manufacturer who concentrates on a narrow range of products may build up an expertise in his field which is at least equal to that of the giant corporation. Moreover, he may be assisted by the generally permissive attitude to patent licensing, as we shall see in due course.

It is nevertheless the case that in the more complex equipment and the 'mass market' components the large firm is at an advantage, owing not only to large development 'thresholds' and economies in the use of R & D results, but also to other types of scale economy. The operation of economies of scale in these fields is attributable not to bulky capital equipment, which is not a feature of the electronics industry, but rather to the superiority of large organisations in the planning and manufacture of extremely complex products, and in maintaining the highly trained staffs necessary for effective selling and servicing on a broad front.

It is therefore no surprise that the principal world markets for the more complex electronic capital goods are dominated by a small number of large firms. For example, while there are fifty or so companies capable of supplying computers in the non-Communist world, the majority of these either manufacture under licence or confine themselves to small computers for special industrial or scientific purposes. Approximately half are American and of these four (I.B.M., Honeywell, Sperry Rand and National Cash Register) account for over three-quarters of American domestic installations, as well as perhaps two-thirds of those in Western Europe, either directly or through licensing of local manufacturers.[1] Virtually all non-American firms

[1] O.E.C.D., *Electronic Computers*, Annex I.

rely heavily on versions of American-designed computers. In 1967, only two firms (I.C.T. in the U.K. – now I.C.L. – and Fujitsu in Japan) were capable of supplying a broad range of general purpose computers without an American manufacturing licence.[1]

In the U.K., only I.C.L. and I.B.M. (and, on a smaller scale, Honeywell) now (1972) manufacture a wide range of computers, although several U.K. firms continue to produce special purpose machines, mainly designed for industrial process control or for weapons control systems. Principal among these are Elliott–Automation, (now part of G.E.C.–E.E.), under licence at one time from N.C.R., Marconi (also part of G.E.C.–E.E.) and Ferranti, whose main E.D.P. computer range ('Atlas') was taken over by I.C.T. in 1962 (and has now been superseded), but which still produces special purpose machines (the 'Argus' range). The latter account together for the bulk of industrial control installations in the U.K., while Ferranti and increasingly Plessey are dominant in military and aviation control systems. Since its acquisition of the numerical control interests of Ferranti and Airmec in 1970, Plessey has become the leading U.K. manufacturer of electronic controls for machine tools.

The picture in other complex electronic equipment fields is broadly similar, except that technical superiority is less concentrated in American hands. In radar and navigational system, British firms continue to be among the technical leaders, and several (notably Marconi, now a part of G.E.C.–E.E., and Decca) have built up large export sales and have licensed a number of European manufacturers. In telephone equipment, there are four U.K. manufacturers (Plessey, G.E.C., S.T.C. and latterly Pye) capable of supplying a complete Post Office telephone exchange, and all rely essentially on their U.K. development efforts, although S.T.C. has access to I.T.T.'s basic research in the U.S.A.

In components, the situation is rather more diverse. There were in 1967 only three U.K. manufacturers of valves and tubes for the mass consumer good markets, but a further nine or so produced valves and tubes for industrial uses.[2] In the rapidly growing field of semiconductors, there were some twenty U.K. manufacturers, including some small specialised firms as well as giants such as Plessey, which was the first to introduce silicon integrated circuits in Britain.[3] The numbers were much larger in passive components, although again the more research-intensive or mass-market items are dominated by large firms. Plessey, for instance, is the largest producer of ferrite core computer memories

[1] *Ibid.*, p. 49.
[2] N.E.D.O., *Statistics of the Electronics Industry*, p. 25.
[3] The Plessey Company Ltd., *Report and Accounts for 1969/70*.

in Europe, and is making a bid to become the largest supplier in the American market.

Although minimum development expenditures are not large in the field of radio and T.V. receivers, or in the audio reproduction field, the electronic consumer goods industry has in recent years become highly concentrated, especially in Western Europe. A number of factors have brought this about, principal among them being the need to reduce capacity following general overestimation of demand in the early 1960s, the transistor revolution, which has made valve-based radios largely obsolete, fierce Japanese competition and the advent of colour T.V. There are now for example only six independent manufacturers of domestic T.V. receivers in the U.K. (G.E.C., Thorn, Pye/Philips, Rank Bush Murphy, Decca and S.T.C.). On the other hand, there are numbers of relatively small firms in the high quality audio-reproduction field, making a variety of high performance equipment and components for the 'hi-fi' enthusiast. (However some of these are members of larger groups; e.g. Leak is now a subsidiary of the Rank Organisation.) This is typically a smaller-scale industry where flexibility, limited production-runs and specialist expertise in a narrow field can give the smaller firm a competitive advantage over the large corporation.

### *Patenting and licensing*

The overall rate of patenting activity in relation to R & D expenditure in electronics is roughly similar to that in chemicals, but it is significant that the rate in components is much higher than that in finished equipment (with telecommunications something of an exception – see Table 8.1). While it is usually fairly easy to obtain a patent of some sort on a component (on the manufacturing process if not on the product itself) or on some aspect of circuit technique, it is usually hard to patent a complete assembly of equipment or a system involving several sets of equipment, and even harder to patent the software or other operating expertise that goes with it.[1] Yet a very high proportion of R & D in the equipment field is on the design of sets of equipment and the development of applications for them.

The difference between the patentability of components and that of finished sets of equipment is reflected in the proportions of these items which are judged to be 'patent based' (see Table 9.3). Although there are exceptions in each of these broad categories, respondents to our inquiry were of the view that virtually all components are covered by

---

[1] As observed in Chapter 1, computer software is not *per se* patentable in most countries; it can only be protected by patent in so far as it is specific to a patentable piece of hardware, or to a patentable process or control system.

patents in some substantial way, whereas equipment seldom has more than very marginal patent coverage.

Such is the proliferation of patents in the components field that the situation is nowadays referred to in quite serious terms by patent practitioners as a 'jungle'. The manufacture of complex electronic equipment requires the right to use extremely large numbers of patented components, circuit configurations, etc.; a television receiver, for example, normally contains several dozen different patented items (involving perhaps 600 separate patents), while a large computer contains thousands of different patented components. It would be quite beyond the resources of licensing departments of equipment manufacturers to take licences and check for possible infringements on each component patent separately,[1] and for that reason it is common practice in electronics, more than in any other field, to licence patents in large clusters, or to grant blanket patent clearance in a defined field without specifying patents individually. This practice inevitably tends to reduce the number of licence agreements concluded, and does much to explain the low rate of licensing per unit of R & D expenditure in electronics noted in Chapter 8 (page 160). The apparent infrequency of licence agreements in electronics should not in general therefore be interpreted to indicate a highly selective approach to patent licensing, and indeed the approach in this field is normally quite liberal, as will be seen shortly.

### Patent pools

The difficulty of licensing large numbers of patented components and design improvements for assembly in sets of equipment has in the past led to the creation of formal 'patent pools' in the electronics field. These pools, all of which are now defunct in the U.K. (according to participants in our inquiry), were essentially arrangements by which the major patentees in a particular field pooled their patents for licensing *en bloc* to any firm on payment of a standard royalty, the receipts being divided among the patentees in proportion to their contributions to the pool. At various times, there have been pools in radio, television, radar and computers. The first, in radio, was started by Marconi's in 1923 and survived several transformations until its expiry in 1964. The last, in marine radar, was wound up in 1968. The radar pool was sponsored by the Government, which owned most of the basic patents from wartime work. A principal member of the computer pool was the

---

[1] Under most standard conditions of sale, a supplier of components is responsible for indemnifying the buyer (e.g. the equipment manufacturer) against patent infringement, but it is normally in the interests of the buyer to check that the supplier is in a position to grant indemnity – through being the patentee, or having a licence to manufacture and sell the component.

National Research Development Corporation, which held basic patents on the Manchester tube storage system (now superseded), and for a number of years was a leading financier of industrial projects for the development of digital computers. The computer pool was wound up in 1967.

So far as we have been able to discover, patent pools (at least, those involving formal arrangements) have not existed outside the radio and electronics fields, and have not been an important feature in other countries, although their existence in Canada and Australia was pointed out to us. The pools have at times attracted criticism – mainly from smaller equipment manufacturers obliged to take licences – and even now they tend to be viewed in retrospect with a certain amount of suspicion, unjustifiably in our view. The most important one was the radio and television pool, and this will be discussed more fully in due course (see page 301).

A variety of reasons for the disappearance of formal patent pools were suggested to us. Principal among them were the expiry of basic patents held by U.K. firms, the considerable reduction in the number of equipment manufacturers that has taken place in most branches of the industry, and the passing of the lead in basic research to the U.S.A. It is said for example that it was the reluctance of R.C.A. to pool its television patents that led to the winding up of the Broadcast Receiver Licensing Pool (i.e. the radio and T.V. pool). In their place are now found a series of bilateral field licensing agreements between the major firms, supplemented by a larger number of plain patent licences in narrower areas of interest.

Patent pools as described above should not be confused with informal (sometimes purely tacit) agreements between companies to permit mutual infringement of each other's patents. Such situations – described to us as positions of 'armed neutrality' – are not uncommon in electronics, as in other fields where large numbers of patents are concentrated in the hands of a few firms. (If given formal expression, they become cross-licences.) Unlike the patent pools, whose purpose was essentially to grant block licences to outsiders, such arrangements exist to permit mutual patent clearance by the parties – although they by no means preclude the parties from licensing outsiders independently, either for large blocks of patents or for individual patents.

### *Dominant patterns of licensing*

It is essential in discussing licensing in the electronics field to distinguish between straight patent licensing and agreements to provide either complete manufacturing rights, know-how, assistance, etc. or broader research information etc. in a defined field (or both). In the former licensing, the objective is merely to give patent clearance, and this may be done on either a broad or a narrow front, and on either a one-way or a reciprocal (cross-licensing) basis. In general, those on a broad front are normally cross-licences, whereas those on a narrow front are normally one-way, but there are exceptions. The sort of licensing undertaken by the patent pools was essentially straight patent licensing on a broad front. Also typical of this form of licensing was the procedure by which Western Electric (Bell) licensed its semi-conductor technology in the 1950s. The Bell basic patents were made available to all comers for a lump sum payment of $25,000, with in addition a fairly modest royalty on use of transistors under licence. At one time Western Electric had patent licence agreements with virtually all the large electronics firms in Europe. Where the latter had something to offer in exchange, the preferred arrangement was a cross-licence; by this means, a licensee might greatly reduce the royalties normally payable on the semi-conductor patents. In other cases, the licensing was one-way only.

In a 'manufacturing and know-how' agreement, the licensor, invariably a major research-based enterprise, provides the licensee (typically a component or equipment manufacturer who has not done basic research in the relevant area) with all necessary research results, designs and specifications, engineering know-how and patent clearance to manufacture a specified type of component or set of equipment. Typical of this sort of licensing are the arrangements under which National Cash Register licensed Elliott-Automation and R.C.A. licensed Marconi (whose main computer interests are now part of I.C.L.) to manufacture computers in the U.K.

Finally, 'information' agreements provide for the transfer between two parties of research results and other technical information, together with any relevant patent clearance. These are usually, but not always, reciprocal; virtually always at least one party is a research-based enterprise, and frequently both are.

Agreements in the electronic industry that contain substantial know-how are normally terminable after between five and seven years (depending on the life cycle of the equipment concerned), and for that reason the licensing situation in the industry is continually changing. However, the general picture is that most large British research-based firms nowadays have one or perhaps two broad information-sharing agreements in each of their main research fields. In almost all cases, such agreements are with foreign (usually American) firms. Most are cross-licences, and most involve fairly small annual balancing payments to reflect disparities in know-how flows or patent portfolios. In addition, some (but not all) major U.K. firms have one or two important manufacturing agreements with American firms (or perhaps with Philips or Telefunken), under which they manufacture components and equipment designed by the licensor. Finally, each large firms is likely to have up to several dozen patent licences; some will be field licences with other major firms – such as those on television receivers – but most will be licences taken or granted on specific components or assemblies, sometimes with quite small firms. Payments will be involved in possibly two-thirds of the latter, but they are usually very small (seldom more than a few thousand pounds annually). Payments on field licences, such as those on colour television receivers, can be much larger, but still fairly modest in relation to the R & D involved, and very small in relation to the value of output covered.[1]

B.   IMPACT OF THE PATENT SYSTEM

As reported in Chapter 9, the electronics companies that responded to our industrial inquiry were uniformly of the opinion that the size and direction of their R & D is not affected in any significant way by the existence of patents and that in general patents nowadays have very little impact on competition between major firms in the industry.[2] All large firms in the field take a fair amount of trouble to obtain patents and to suppress infringements, but in most cases they are seen as relatively incidental to the industry's operations. Their function is to facilitate licensing of technical information and to help secure royalties, which (except in important basic inventions) seldom amount to more than a very modest bonus to set against heavy R & D expenditures.

### Suspect validity

One explanation for the lack of impact is that an extremely high proportion of patents in the electronics field, as elsewhere in electrical engineering, is nowadays thought to be of very suspect validity. (Estimates as high as 90 per cent were cited to us.) The general level of doubtfulness appears to be very much higher here than in the chemical field, and may be taken to reflect broad differences in the nature of invention and technical progress in the two fields. Thus it is usually

---

[1] It is estimated that Western Electric received something over £3 million in total royalties from its transistor patents between 1952 and 1963 (Freeman, *Research and Development in Electronic Capital Goods*, p. 65 n.). By 1965, R & D costs on the transistor had reached over £20 million (Jewkes *et al.*, *The Sources of Innovation*, p. 215).

R.C.A.'s standard rate of royalties on its colour T.V. receiver patents is currently 1·0 per cent of the wholesale price of a complete set.

[2] There are of course exceptions and special cases. See pages 298–9 for discussion of an important licensing dispute involving colour T.V. that has recently come to the fore.

fairly clear whether a chemical compound or process is novel or obvious, although disputes about priority are of course possible; but there can often be considerable dispute about the novelty of obviousness of a particular arrangement or choice of electronic components and circuits, and even about the originality of component inventions themselves, especially where small improvements are involved. Moreover, quite a high degree of patent doubt can be present even where new components achieve a fundamental technical breakthrough. Even the transistor was not immune from challenge on the ground that some at least of the many patents which surrounded it were invalid.[1]

## *Limited commercial protection*

Furthermore, the extent of the monopoly offered by the great majority of patents in the electronics field is extremely limited. As observed earlier, the protection that can be obtained on sets of equipment is in many cases no more than marginal and this is *a fortiori* true of the more complex electronic systems, such as telephone exchanges and large computers, development work on which is not patentable except in so far as entirely new types of 'hardware' are involved, which is frequently not the case. Components and small assemblies can usually be patented in a more substantial way, but in many cases the value of the protection is minimised by the availability of a wide range of alternatives, or by the possibility of 'designing round' the patented features at minimal cost and inconvenience.

A further factor is that the life-cycle of many electronic products is extremely short. For example, the approximate span of a particular 'generation' of computers is said to be less than seven years.[2] Although equipment still continues to be sold after it has become technically obsolete, the market normally diminishes rapidly at that stage and any subsequent patent protection is immaterial. Since equipment life-cycles are to a large extent based on those of components, this factor applies equally in their case. Thus, the valves which were the basis of 'first generation' computers gave way to transistors around 1956 which in turn gave way to integrated circuits in 1962, and these in turn have been superseded since 1967 by complex arrays of circuits known as 'integrated equipment components' (I.E.C.s). In an industry where technical change is so rapid and where the 'lead time' on a new

---

[1] When Western Electric attempted to obtain retrospective royalties from U.K. firms on their use of transistors following the settlement of the anti-trust suit against it in the American Courts in 1956, and issued a writ for infringement against Pye, Pye responded by proposing *inter alia* to attack the basic transistor patents. The case was settled out of court for much less than the sums which Western was originally seeking.

[2] O.E.C.D., *Electronic Computers*, pp. 69–78.

component may be three to five years, the extra element of market protection available from even the strongest patent can seldom if ever be more than very marginal.

### Technical interdependence

Yet another factor tending to minimise the impact of patents in the electronics field is the degree of technical interdependence of the major manufacturers. As in basic chemicals, if perhaps not quite so much so, the principal firms in the various main product fields are engaged to a large extent in producing essentially similar ranges of items using similar methods, yet few can monopolise all inventions in a particular area, although some have occasionally come quite near to doing so. In these circumstances, 'give and take' is often seen to be in the best interests of research-based firms with a broad stake in the industry and, as in basic chemicals, patents are used as convenient bargaining counters and aids to licensing rather than monopoly devices.

### Secret know-how

Finally, in much pioneering work in the electronics field, as elsewhere in electrical engineering, the main obstacle to copying by outsiders is the existence of research results, technical expertise and to a lesser extent operating know-how, which do not enter into patent specifications, either because they are the sort of knowledge that is for legal or other reasons unpatentable, or because they arise well after patents have been applied for, or because firms choose to keep them secret. Although such details can seldom be kept completely secret for more than a few years, they can be usually suppressed sufficiently long to make them an effective barrier to 'painless' imitation in a field where technology is moving as rapidly as in electronics. Almost all the electronics firms in our inquiry stressed the importance of unpatented technical information, and stated that, by comparison, patents were usually a minor protective device, whereas secret technical expertise can sometimes be an important barrier to competition in new developments.

### Liberal attitude to patent licensing

For these reasons, the general policy of all except possibly smaller specialist firms in the electronics field is to grant clearance on the great majority of patents to virtually all *bona fide* applicants on reasonable commercial terms. (It should be stressed that this policy applies to granting patent clearance, but not necessarily know-how etc., as will be seen in due course.) Only in very occasional instances will patents not be licenced fairly readily. With the exception of the disputes over licensing of the P.A.L. system (see pp. 298–9), the few recent ones that came to our attention concerned specialised equipment developed essentially by a single firm for a limited market (in this case, scientific instruments), or related to a fairly minor design feature on a mass-produced product which for marketing reasons the patentee wished to retain as distinctively his own. (In the latter case, the item involved was a model of telephone receiver.) Exclusive patent licences are accordingly virtually unknown among large electronics firms, although small specialist firms sometimes insist on them.[1] Moreover, territorial restrictions on marketing do not appear to be a common feature of patent licensing in this field. As can be seen from Table 8.6, no specific licences granted in electronic components were confined to foreign rights only. Licences on equipment are inclined to be more selective in the territorial sense, but this is because agreements in the equipment field are more likely to contain know-how provisions.

The generally liberal attitude to patent licensing described above is not limited to minor electronics inventions; it has, at least in the post-war era, been equally adopted by patentees of basic inventions. As noted earlier, licences on Western Electric's basic transistor patents were made available at the time of the announcement of the invention to all comers for a relatively modest downpayment and a small royalty. Doubtless the pressure of American public opinion, together with the anti-trust action that was brought by the Department of Justice against Western in 1949, had an influence on this policy, but this merely demonstrates the limitations on patentees' freedom of action in such celebrated inventions, especially where there are provisions for official control of monopolies and restrictive practices.[2] Similarly, R.C.A.'s basic patents on the colour television receiver have been made readily available throughout Europe and elsewhere on payment of what are moderate royalties by usual standards.

Of course, there may be disagreement between licensor and licensees over the size of royalties, as occurred in the case of the transistor and more recently in colour television.[3] However, bearing in mind the

---

[1] It was pointed out to us that exclusive licensing cannot take place where the patents are involved in cross-licences – unless the latter are themselves exclusive, which is very rare in electronics, as in other fields.

[2] The well-known open licensing policy adopted by the Bell Telephone System antedates the Consent Decree of 1956, but the policy clearly owes much to that anti-trust action and to the fact that the Bell System is a regulated utility in the U.S.A. See Bode, *Synergy*, p. 48.

[3] British manufacturers of colour television sets initially objected to the royalty of $\frac{1}{2}$ per cent on the wholesale price of receivers asked by Telefunken for patent clearance on its P.A.L. system. (This royalty is in addition to the 1 per cent payable to R.C.A. for patent licences on the N.T.S.C. System, on which P.A.L. is based.) Although any U.K. manufacturer

generally modest rates of royalties in the electronics field, this probably indicates strength in the licensees' bargaining position rather than unreasonableness on the part of licensors. This seems especially so in circumstances where the licensor would find it hard to meet the market directly, and where prospective licensees can close ranks for purposes of negotiating terms for licences, as British manufacturers appear on some recent occasions to have done in taking licences from American firms (e.g., R.C.A. in colour television).

## *Conflict over licensing of P.A.L.*

Although we believe it to be broadly true that patent licensing policy in the radio and electronics field is nowadays generally liberal, some mention should be made of a current licensing conflict which, although not typical of the industry as a whole, could have implications for competition and prices in the field of colour T.V. receivers in the U.K. and elsewhere in Europe – namely, the disagreement which has occurred in 1972 between A.E.G.–Telefunken and leading Japanese manufacturers concerning licences on the P.A.L. system.

It is reported that negotiations between Telefunken and Sony over a P.A.L. licence for the latter to sell colour T.V. sets in West Germany and other European countries broke down in July 1972, and that Sony is now proceeding to supply the German market without a licence.[1] While Telefunken's terms for a licence in this case are not publicly known, it can be assumed that they are heavily restrictive, at least for sales by Sony in their principal European markets. Telefunken has subsequently taken steps in West Germany to sue Sony for infringement of its P.A.L. patents and Sony has responded by claiming that the proposed terms are unfair to consumers and contrary to Japanese Fair Trade and E.E.C. cartel regulations, and that in any case P.A.L. licences are not required for its sets, since they utilise Sony's own special circuitry which is alleged not to infringe the P.A.L. patents.

The general circumstances behind this case are of course by no means rare in the electronics field. The European equipment manufacturers, having witnessed the enormous competitive inroads made into their markets by Japanese exports of radios, monochrome T.V. receivers,

could obtain a licence at the stipulated rate from E.M.I., Telefunken's sole licensee in the U.K., many refused the licences offered, on the ground *inter alia* that German manufacturers pay only 0·3 per cent on sets for their home market. E.M.I. issued writs for infringement against the British manufacturers and all the cases have now (August 1972) been settled, the manufacturers agreeing to take licences at 0·5 per cent.

At the time of writing, the largest unlicensed British set manufacturer, Thorn, has yet to take a licence from R.C.A. R.C.A. is suing Thorn for infringement and this case is not yet settled.

[1] *Times Business News*, 1 and 10 August 1972.

high fidelity equipment, etc., are anxious to avoid similar competition in the colour T.V. field, which they fear could kill the European manufacturing industry. Seldom previously, however, have patents promised to provide a really significant measure of protection from Japanese competition, which hitherto has tended to emerge in fields where the basic patents have expired, or where patent coverage of finished products has been relatively minor. The P.A.L. patents have consequently been utilised in negotiations with Sony in what appears to be an unusually restrictive manner, bearing in mind the ready way in which they have been licensed to indigenous European manufacturers for manufacture in countries that have adopted the P.A.L. system.

It remains to be seen whether the P.A.L. patents alone will prove an effective device for restricting Japanese competition in Europe. We would doubt whether they will have more than a marginal impact, since so far as we can judge a compromise settlement of the dispute seems the most likely outcome; even if the P.A.L. patents are found to be infringed, which is by no means certain, the exclusion of Japanese firms from particular national markets by private licensing arrangements might well be held to be against E.E.C. rules on competition.[1] It seems more likely that Japanese firms like Sony will eventually be granted licences with fairly moderate royalties, and if European sales of Japanese colour sets build up rapidly from their present relatively low levels in German and U.K. markets, they will probably be dealt with through tighter official quotas as part of the general revision of quotas currently being negotiated between the Japanese and E.E.C. Governments. If so, the denial by Telefunken of its P.A.L. patents will prove to be little more than a minor card played in the course of resolving an economic problem that goes far beyond the question of patent protection.

### Lessons of the past

To some extent, the relatively liberal attitude towards patent licensing adopted by the modern electronics industry reflects the impact of some hard lessons learned in earlier years. Observers of the intensely patent-conscious period in both America and the U.K. immediately following the first world war have suggested that the attempt at restrictive control of basic patent holdings by opposing groups during this period resulted in a technical stalemate and a waste of energy on patent contests which harmed the industry's interests.[2] This was particularly a problem

---

[1] These were discussed in Chapter 7, pp. 135–6.

[2] W. R. Maclaurin, *Invention and Innovation in the Radio Industry* (Macmillan, New York, 1949) Ch. 6, and S. G. Sturmey, *The Economic Development of Radio* (Duckworth, London, 1958) Ch. 5.

in America after the first world war, when the electrical corporations, General Electric, A. T. & T. and Westinghouse, all had interests in radio patents and when Marconi also had an important holding. That problem was solved when General Electric set up the Radio Corporation of America in 1919 to purchase American Marconi and with it Marconi's American patents, as well as its extensive network of marine and long distance radio stations in the U.S.A. All three giants took shareholdings in R.C.A. and consolidated their patent holdings in radio through royalty-free cross-licensing agreements with the new company. Cross-licensing agreements were also signed with British Marconi, Telefunken and the leading French firm, C.S.F.

After a series of court decisions upholding the validity of its patents, R.C.A. established an unassailable patent position in the American radio industry and proceeded to offer licences on highly restrictive and expensive terms. (A royalty of $7\frac{1}{2}$ per cent of the net selling price of a receiver was demanded, with minimum annual payments of $100,000.)[1] These onerous conditions led to a series of bitter disputes with equipment manufacturers, culminating in a lengthy court action over royalty payments with R.C.A.'s principal licensee and competitor, Philco. Philco's claim that the royalties were too high was finally upheld by the U.S. courts and R.C.A. was compelled to reduce its charges to the entire industry and liberalise its licensing policy.[2] Keen competition in the manufacture of radio sets quickly followed, mainly from non-research-based firms concentrating on brand advertising, aggressive selling, low manufacturing costs from high volume production, and price competition.

In commenting on this period in the American industry's history, Maclaurin is critical of the exploitation of the patent system by the large corporations, but nevertheless feels that the security offered by patent protection was on the whole a necessary evil in the early stages of the industry's development and that 'the patent system, in spite of its weaknesses, did operate to encourage research and invention during the period under review'.[3]

The problem of conflicting patent holdings was also experienced in the U.K. around 1930, when rival patent pools on radio sets were operated by Marconi and S.T.C. Later the Marconi pool, with which the S.T.C. pool was amalgamated in 1931, was challenged successively by Hazelpat (set up to exploit the patents of the American Hazeltine Corporation) and by Mullard and Philips in combination. According to Sturmey: 'The squabbles among the giants of the industry over patents during the 1930s made life difficult for the ordinary set-maker and the necessity to choose between rival licences prevented him from

---

[1] Maclaurin, p. 131.    [2] *Ibid.*, pp. 135–9.    [3] *Ibid.*, p. 260.

constructing the best set which could have been built on the basis of existing knowledge'.[1] The difficulties were eventually resolved (but not before a long legal struggle between the Marconi pool and Mullard–Philips that reached the House of Lords) by a series of amalgamations of the pools, until by 1939 all the principal patent holders were members of a single pool.

These conflicts over patents appear to have left their mark on the major radio companies in Britain and America, and gave way in time to a much more liberal approach to patent licensing. Doubtless the passing of the era of basic and speculative discovery in radio to one of development and product improvement also had an important effect on relaxing licensing policies. After the war the British radio and T.V. pool, transformed with enlarged membership into the Broadcast Receiver Licensing Pool, pursued a decidedly non-restrictive licensing policy. It offered cheap licences to all equipment manufacturers who wanted them, and virtually all set-makers were included in the arrangements either as licensees or licensors.[2]

Although the rules formally precluded independent licensing by the pool grantors, this was not an onerous condition since any *bona fide* U.K. manufacturer could obtain a pool licence. No applicant could be refused a licence on standard terms (*viz.*, a royalty of 0·2 per cent on radios – later reduced when separate royalties become payable to Western Electric – and 0·4 per cent on televisions, with no minima specified). The only restriction of any significance was that no licensee should sell a set in the U.K. with import content higher than 10 per cent, but this never led to difficulties.[3]

As suggested earlier, the termination of the radio and T.V. pool can be attributed mainly to the expiry of E.M.I.'s basic television patents and the unwillingness of American patentees to put their patents into the pool. It would in our view be wrong to suggest that the demise of the pool betokens any change in the philosophy of non-restrictive patent licensing built up in the radio and television field since the 1920s; it reflects rather a shift in the centres of research away from the pattern established in the era of valve-based radio and monochrome television, when British-owned patents were the equal of, if not superior to, those owned by American firms.

---

[1] S. G. Sturmey, 'Patents and Progress in Radio', in *Manchester School of Economics and Social Studies*, Vol. xxviii, No. 1 (January 1960) p. 34.

[2] Monopolies and Restrictive Practices Commission, *Report on the Supply of Electronic Valves and Cathode Ray Tubes* (H.M.S.O., 1956), pp. 102–3. It should be noted that the pool licences covered circuit technique and configurations rather than components as such. Licences on components alone would not normally be needed by set-makers or users, since, under most standard conditions of sale, rights to use patented items are deemed to extend automatically to the purchaser.

[3] *Ibid.*, p. 103. This stipulation was dropped in later pool licences.

*Selectivity through know-how*

It must be emphasised that the policy of non-selectivity in patent licensing described above does not extend generally to the licensing of unpatented research results and other technical expertise in the electronics field. Where unpatented technical information is involved in a substantial way, as in 'manufacturing' and 'information' agreements, it is unlikely that any firm would license a close competitor without receiving some valuable information in return. In effect, this means that a large British electronics firm will seldom grant a manufacturing and know-how licence to another British manufacturer in one of its own principal product areas, while a foreign manufacturer will be licensed only for markets outside the U.K. and its major export territories. In turn, a British firm that has a complete manufacturing and know-how licence from an American firm would expect to be confined to selling in the U.K., Europe and the Commonwealth (perhaps excluding Canada). Similar conditions are likely to apply in technical information agreements, which are normally between companies of different nationalities unless exchange takes place in a very narrow field or involves small companies.

If pressed, most research-based firms admit to certain areas of advanced work in which they prefer to keep all research results and technical know-how entirely to themselves. (In some instances, this may mean that they also refrain from patenting key inventions, but more commonly patent applications are allowed to go forward on the ground that adequate protection is available through lead-times and expertise arising in the later development of the product.) For example, the latest work on manufacturing techniques for semiconductor microcircuitry tends to be closely guarded. In the telecommunications field, firms are inclined to keep their latest research on computerised telephone exchanges and advanced switching techniques to themselves. Similarly, computer firms are unlikely to divulge designs, know-how, etc. on their latest generation of computers until they have introduced it in their own markets. In general, no new technical innovation of real importance will be licensed in a manufacturing agreement until demonstrated and proved in the innovator's own operations – although in most cases patent clearance will be granted from the start to any reputable firm wishing to enter the same field.

The exercise of selectivity through unpatented know-how etc. may well have some effect on both the degree of competition and the rate of inventive activity in electronics, but it seems doubtful whether the R & D programmes of major electronics firms depend substantially on such security as is available from this source. The compulsion to undertake minimum 'threshold' R & D expenditures in order to survive is as strong (if not stronger) for firms committed to the electronics field as it is in basic chemicals; although economies can be made in research by opting to utilise advanced American designs and components under licence, as many European firms have done in recent years, no company can hope to stay long in an environment of such rapid technological change without a 'defensive' development effort, which in many products is very large in relation to the size of the U.K. and major export markets. The responsiveness of market shares to accumulations of relatively minor technical improvements and the speed and frequency with which these occur in electronic components, T.V. and audio equipment, etc., render it impossible for larger firms to rely entirely on manufacture under licence, because of the delays and costs of absorbing new information in this way. Furthermore, the influence of governments as financiers of R & D and customers for research-based products is strong in the capital goods sector of the industry, and any major shortfall in these R & D efforts below standards current among major trading and military powers would cause great official concern.[1] So too would any concerted attempt by a firm to monopolise technology developed at public expense or on the strength of large Government supply contracts.

### Public disclosure

It can finally be observed that the monopoly element in the patent system appears to have very little impact on the extent of disclosure of patentable inventions in this field. Firms in our inquiry were of the view that little would be kept secret under a thoroughgoing compulsory licence system that is not already closely guarded. They all stressed the strong tradition of technical publication in the electronics field and several component manufacturers pointed out that sales might well be adversely affected if supporting technical literature, giving all necessary details of circuits and layouts used, were not made readily available to all customers. All were inclined to minimise the general information value of patent specifications in comparison with technical journals and similar sources, and some said that, were greater secrecy required, this could be achieved by more intensive censorship of contributions to technical literature rather than by reducing patent filings.

[1] For example, U.K. Government support for advanced computer development is conditional upon specified levels and rates of growth of R & D (including that financed from other sources) being achieved. See *Industrial Investment: The Computers Merger Project, op. cit.*

*Conclusions*

It accordingly seems fairly safe to conclude that the impact of the patent system as we have defined it is nowadays relatively minor so far as the electronics industry is concerned. In cases where innovating firms exercise control over the spread of technical knowledge, they do so through selectivity in the communication of unpatented research expertise, manufacturing skill, etc., and only in rare and specific cases are patents nowadays used as a device for this purpose. The research-based firms of the industry seldom depart from their philosophy that any *bona fide* firm may obtain patent clearance for a fairly moderate charge, providing the facility is reciprocated. For these reasons respondents to our inquiry believed that their operations would in general be very little affected by compulsory patent licensing of the sort outlined. With a few exceptions, licensing would proceed very much as it has done under the present system. In virtually all important respects the size and direction of inventive activity, the public disclosure of R & D results and the transfer and technical information under licence would be unaffected. It is possible that compulsory licensing would lead to the avoidance of such conflicts over royalty rates as have emerged, for example, in connection with Western Electric's transistor patents in the 1950s and more recently over the P.A.L. colour T.V. system, but it is hard to believe that the impact would be very much more than that in today's world.

### C.    THE DEVELOPMENT OF TELEVISION

Owing to the technical ascendancy of American electronics firms since the war, it is not easy to find a major example of a basic electronics innovation for which a British firm has been responsible in recent years. We accordingly look back to E.M.I.'s pre-war contribution to the development of television as an illustration of the arguments of the preceding sections. While the general story of this development is fairly well known,[1] the role of patents in the exercise has not been fully explored, although at least one study examining the American picture has appeared.[2] Moreover, as an example of a major technical development undertaken almost entirely by three very large firms (R.C.A., E.M.I., and Telefunken), the television venture has a decidedly up-

---

[1] Jewkes *et al.*, *The Sources of Invention*, pp. 307–10. An extended account can be found in Sturmey, *The Economic Development of Radio*.
[2] W. R. Maclaurin, 'Patents and Technical Progress – A Study of Television', *Journal of Political Economy*, Vol. LVIII (Feb.–Dec. 1950) pp. 142–57.

to-date ring about it, and is therefore quite relevant to our present study.[1]

The principal original inventions in electronic television (so-called to distinguish it from the 'mechanical' systems of Ives and Baird) were made independently in the late 1920s by Vladimir Zworykin and Philo Farnsworth in the U.S.A.[2] Zworykin was a Russian electrical engineer who emigrated to America in 1919. He joined the research staff of Westinghouse, but his work on television was not encouraged until in 1928 he produced a revolutionary photo-electric tube which would transmit visual images. (Patents on the basic idea had been applied for in 1923.) This tube, which he called the 'iconoscope', so impressed D. Sarnoff, the vice-president of R.C.A., that Zworykin was assigned a number of assistants and encouraged to press ahead with his work on an all-electronic system.

Meanwhile Farnsworth, an independent inventor, had managed to interest a group of Californian bankers in the possibilities of television and, working independently in a laboratory in San Francisco, developed a camera tube which he called the 'Image Dissector', patents on which were applied for in 1927. He was able to demonstrate a crude working television system in his laboratory shortly afterwards.

After long patent interference proceedings to establish the priority of the inventions, Zworykin and Farnsworth each eventually obtained basic patents on their respective systems. However whereas R.C.A. committed large development resources to Zworykin's system in the early 1930s, Farnsworth failed to attract comparable backing for his, although for two years Philco financed his research in their own laboratories. In 1932, Philco abandoned their support in the belief that while Farnsworth was an ingenious inventor, it would take too long for him to develop an operating television system with commercial potentialities.[3] The American field was henceforward left primarily to R.C.A., whose research team under Zworykin proceeded to perfect the system to the stage at which American television broadcasting was commenced in 1940.

In the U.K., the Gramophone Company had taken an interest in television research before its merger with Columbia to form E.M.I. in 1931, but the work was stepped up when the Research Director of the

---

[1] For details of the part played by E.M.I. we have relied mainly on S. J. Preston, *The Birth of a High Definition Television System*, a paper read to the Television Society on 24 October 1952; and on conversations with the author and his successor as E.M.I.'s Patent Manager, Mr A. B. Logan.

[2] However, similar inventions were made slightly later by E.M.I.'s research team working independently in the U.K., as will be explained below.

[3] It seems generally agreed by experts in the field that, although Farnsworth had brilliant original ideas, the level of his technical achievement was very much lower than that of Zworykin.

new company, I. Shoenberg, recommended that a major research effort should be made in television. It was decided at this stage to abandon systems based on mechanical scanning and to concentrate on a fully electronic system. By 1932 a receiver using a 'hard' cathode ray rube (greatly superior to the gas-focused type used for oscillographs) had been devised, and the core of an electron pick-up (camera) tube (subsequently called the 'Emitron') had been invented. The principles by which picture signals could be derived from the pick-up tube were then rapidly mastered and the Emitron was developed by 1934 to the stage at which picture transmission became practical. In the course of the work considerable advances were made in special circuit techniques for the Emitron and effective solutions were found to other basic television problems such as the synchronisation of signal waveforms at the transmitter and receiver, suppression of secondary emission in the camera tube through 'cathode potential stabilisation' and the transmission of the D.C. component of picture signals, without which continuous adjustment of picture brightness by the viewer would be required. Important original contributions were made in a number of phases by A. D. Blumlein and P. W. Willans, and by W. F. Tedham and J. D. McGee on the tubes, but the work was essentially a team effort bringing together a wide variety of electronic expertise.[1] Basic patents on the Emitron and associated advances were applied for between 1933 and 1936, and subsequently granted.

By the end of 1934 it was clear that fully operational public television broadcasting based on the E.M.I. all-electronic system was a practical possibility, and the system was offered to the B.B.C. Despite pressure for the adoption of the 'all-British' system devised by Baird, which had been used in trial broadcasts since 1929 but which was clearly inferior to the E.M.I. system in picture quality and reliability, E.M.I. equipment was ordered for Alexandra Palace and regular broadcasting began in 1936.

Intensive R & D efforts on monochrome television continued at E.M.I. long after the adoption of their system by the B.B.C., although it was interrupted during the war when E.M.I. became a 'closed establishment' to work on radar. Among important advances after 1936 were the development of outside broadcasting equipment (first used for the Coronation in 1937), the introduction of the Super-Emitron (a camera with improved sensitivity particularly desirable for outside broadcasts) in 1938 and, post-war, the C.P.S. Emitron (incor-

---

[1] In addition, E.M.I. had the advantage of collaboration with Marconi in the development of transmitters. This arrangement led to the formation of the Marconi–E.M.I. Company to specialise in television transmission, in which Marconi took responsibility for radio transmitters and E.M.I. for the video side.

porating cathode potential stabilisation) and the Flying Spot film scanner, which raised the standard of B.B.C. film transmission above that in America. Important pioneering work was also done on the first large B.B.C. transmitters at Sutton Coldfield (1949) and Kirk o'Shotts. Owing to the post-war break-up of the Marconi–E.M.I. Company, this was a new venture for E.M.I. The transmitters were designed and manufactured almost entirely by E.M.I. and at the time of their introduction were the most powerful television transmitters in the world. In due course, patents were obtained on a number of inventions incorporated in these developments.

A remarkable feature of E.M.I.'s work in the development of television was the speed and economy with which it was carried out. Although starting on an all-electronic system some three years after R.C.A. (which in addition had the advantage of all Zworykin's earlier work), E.M.I. reached the stage of regular broadcasting more than three years before the corresponding stage in America. The following description is taken from Mr Preston's paper:

> In 1935, for example, only about 30 senior staff with about 120 assistants were working in the Laboratories. There was no time for mistakes. The correct decisions had to be made at each point to allow the practical results to be obtained in time with the limited effort available. In addition to all the work involved in developing the all-electronic television system, the Laboratory staff designed and made with some factory assistance all the 405-line video equipment and the associated sound equipment required for the opening of Alexandra Palace in 1936. This equipment, which came straight off the drawing board, has continued in operation to this day. They also brought the cathode-ray tube receiver to the stage at which it could be handed over to the factory for large scale production.[1]

By comparison, R.C.A.'s average annual R & D effort was probably somewhat smaller, but of course it extended over a considerably longer period. (Maclaurin mentions a research team of sixty in 1932, reduced to ten seniors in 1934.[2]) According to its evidence to the Federal Communications Commission, R.C.A. spent some $9\frac{1}{4}$ million on television between 1930 and 1939, of which $2\frac{3}{4}$ million was on 'research and advanced development', $2 million on patents and interference proceedings, and the rest on field tests, manufacturing costs, and preparation for programme transmission.[3] Very much less was spent by Farnsworth and his backers: just over $1 million between 1926 and 1938, of which about a sixth was on patent expenses and legal fees.[4]

---

[1] Preston, *The Birth of a High Definition Television System*, p. 7.
[2] Maclaurin, *Journal of Political Economy*, p. 147.
[3] *Ibid.*, p. 147.          [4] *Ibid.*, p. 149.

It is estimated that E.M.I. spent about half a million pounds on its R & D for television between 1932 and 1939.

It therefore appears that, at the exchange rates then current, R & D expenditure on television by R.C.A. and E.M.I. was about the same, although E.M.I. carried their programme out over a shorter period. The comparison would probably be more favourable to E.M.I. if other expenses were included. E.M.I. probably spent much less than R.C.A. on manufacturing equipment and testing the system, and E.M.I.'s patent and legal costs were undoubtedly much smaller than those of R.C.A. Much of the latter's enormous patent expenses were incurred in the course of extensive interference proceedings with Farnsworth and others, for which there was no counterpart on E.M.I.'s side.

E.M.I.'s television system has been quite unjustly termed a copy of R.C.A.'s system. This misunderstanding has perhaps arisen because of the existence of commercial links between the companies; in fact, although Sarnoff was a Director of E.M.I., R.C.A. exercised no control over E.M.I.'s policy at any stage, and there was no exchange of research or manufacturing information between the two companies until after the E.M.I. system was a proved success. The most that can be attributed to the link with R.C.A. was perhaps some influence on E.M.I.'s decision to opt for an all-electronic system, and 'rumours that Zworykin of R.C.A. had obtained picture signals from an electronic pick-up tube'.[1] These admittedly indicated to the E.M.I. team that they were on the right road, which was in itself an important piece of information, but nothing more than vague rumours, together with copies of R.C.A.'s patents to which everyone had access, were actually received. Furthermore, although Zworykin's basic ideas were patented in the 1920s, the Iconoscope was not fully developed until well after 1930. While the Emitron was a basically similar device, it was developed quite separately, and differed in important aspects, in some of which it was superior. Moreover, a number of basic E.M.I. inventions, notably in the transmission of the D.C. component and signal wave form synchronisation, were later adopted by the Americans, while R.C.A.'s Orthicon, introduced in 1939 and adopted as the basis of all American television, incorporated important features employed earlier in the Super-Emitron, as well as cathode potential stabilisation, patented by E.M.I. in 1934.

Although exchange of patent specifications took place between R.C.A. and E.M.I. throughout the period, these are said by those closely connected to have had very little impact on the work. R.C.A.'s patents gave very little away beyond the principles, which had been known for a number of years. The original patent licensing arrangement

[1] Preston, pp. 9–10.

between the companies was in the field of radio receivers, inherited from Marconi when E.M.I. purchased the Marconiphone Company in 1929 in order to enter the receiver field. Under this arrangement, technical publications and patent specifications in both radio and later television were exchanged and mutual patent clearance and sub-licensing rights in their respective territories were granted. Know-how, however, was not exchanged, although R.C.A., realising by 1932 that the E.M.I. team were making good progress, offered at that stage to supply information on the camera tube for payment. E.M.I. declined the offer because it was unwilling to pay, and only in 1937, when the E.M.I. system was in successful operation, was a know-how exchange – without payments – agreed to.[1]

The only real advantage to E.M.I. from the early patent exchanges with R.C.A., apart from patent clearance, was knowledge of R.C.A.'s new patents one year in advance of their general publication. Although this was useful, it was not a decisive factor in E.M.I.'s progress. Ultimately, R.C.A. probably got the better of the bargain, since it subsequently derived considerable income from sub-licensing E.M.I.'s patents in the U.S.A.

As it turned out, E.M.I.'s basic television patents proved to be relatively strong and capable of offering a valuable element of protection. By contrast, R.C.A. did not produce any patents of commercial significance in the early 1930s, and those obtained earlier by Zworykin on his work at Westinghouse were on principles, with little protective value. The Orthicon was strongly patented, but this did not appear until 1939.

In the licensing of television patents, a distinction must be made between patents on the receiver side, and those on camera and transmission equipment. From the earliest years, E.M.I. made patent licences on sets generally available to all manufacturers – through the radio and T.V. pool in the U.K., and by plain patent licences overseas. These licences were not accompanied by know-how or technical assistance. On cameras and transmission equipment, however, E.M.I. was initially reluctant to license other U.K. manufacturers and no British licences were granted in this field until after the war. A small number of patent cross-licences were concluded with overseas manufacturers, principally R.C.A. (referred to above) and Telefunken, which had developed its own electronic system and was on the verge of introducing regular public broadcasts in 1939. When television broadcasting restarted in the U.K. after the war E.M.I. licensed Pye to manufacture broadcasting equipment. (The latter had acquired know-how on camera and cathode ray tubes through collaboration with

[1] Preston, p. 9.

E M.I. scientists on wartime work, and through exchanges with R.C.A. after the war, and was proposing to manufacture, either by working under E.M.I.'s patents, or by carrying out independent research to avoid them.)[1]

It is estimated that by 1968 E.M.I. had received total royalties on its television patents of some £10 million, mainly from overseas manufacturers (principally in Germany and Japan). By then, the royalties had virtually ceased except for those from Japan.

In commenting on the part played by patents in the television development, E.M.I.'s patent specialists felt that prospective patent protection had not been a material factor in decisions to undertake the work. Patents were helpful at a later stage in securing royalties and mapping out the territory for know-how exchanges, but their absence would not have deterred E.M.I.'s management from going ahead with the venture. (Clearance under R.C.A.'s patents was an advantage, but the research would have proceeded even had such clearance not been available, because the stakes were so high.) The company's initial motive, as a leading manufacturer of radio receivers at that time, was to be a leader in a major new development in the radio field; subsequently, as the research bore fruit, it was possible to think in terms of winning the major orders for television broadcasting equipment which the B.B.C. was about to offer to British industry.

This view is very close to that of S. G. Sturmey, whose economic study of the British radio industry was cited earlier. Referring to E.M.I.'s work in his article on patents he comments:

> Would this work have taken place if patents had not been available for the inventions made? The answer is yes. The prize which was sought was the competitive advantage of being first in the field, of being able to secure contracts for the construction of B.B.C. Stations. In fact, in the manufacture of receiving sets, any radio manufacturer could secure a licence under the Marconi–E.M.I. patents on terms which were not at all onerous. E.M.I. was not the only enterprise seeking the same prize. A. C. Cossor Ltd. also developed an electronic television system in an attempt to capture the prize. Because they used a 'soft' tube they were unable to offer as high a standard as even the unsatisfactory Baird system.[2]

Although E.M.I.'s patents were in due course of considerable help in securing royalties on television (mainly from overseas), these advantages were not the outcome of a restrictive licensing policy. It seems inconceivable that either the television development, or the subsequent

---

[1] Discussion with Mr St. A. Crawshaw, Head of Patents Department, Pye of Cambridge Ltd.

[2] Sturmey, *The Manchester School of Economic and Social Studies* (Jan. 1960) p. 29.

spread of technology, would have been much different in a system of compulsory licensing with reasonable commercial royalties. In the field of receivers, E.M.I. did not attempt to exert licensing selectivity of any sort. Selectivity was successfully pursued on the camera and transmission side for a number of years, but the essential protective element here was secret know-how, not patents. Patents did not deter Pye in its plans to manufacture once it had obtained the know-how after the war, any more than they deterred E.M.I. from pressing ahead with its own development before the war. If anything, the patents acted as a spur to speed up research by Pye and others into alternatives which would not infringe them. There was certainly no question of R.C.A., E.M.I. or Telefunken attempting to hinder each other's pre-war development efforts through patent infringement actions, even though they were in strong competition for export markets and overseas technology sales. Finally, had any of these companies attempted to exert their early *de facto* monopolies in broadcasting equipment to charge excessive prices in their domestic markets, there seems little doubt that such a policy would have been overruled by their respective governments, who were either principal buyers of the equipment in question, or exercised close supervision over supply conditions, as for instance was done by the Federal Communications Commission in the U.S.A.

We would therefore conclude that patent protection had no appreciable impact on the efforts of companies like E.M.I. and R.C.A. to develop monochrome television. Similar arguments apply in the case of colour television, the development of which has been to an even larger extent concentrated in the hands of one or two giant corporations.

While it is hard to avoid the preceding conclusions when considering innovations made by large electronics companies, it is perhaps not quite so clear that the patent system has had a negligible impact on smaller development efforts. One example of these is provided by the work of Farnsworth on television. One observer, Maclaurin, has even gone so far as to suggest that patents were the principal moving factor in the financial backing provided for Farnsworth, and that such backing would not have been forthcoming under a system of compulsory licensing.[1] Although it appears from the available accounts that patents did play a more important role in Farnsworth's case than in Westinghouse and R.C.A.'s, especially when it became clear about 1938 that the Farnsworth companies would never be in a position to launch a working television system, it is hard to accept that Farnsworth's inventive efforts and the backing they received would have been very different in a world of compulsory licensing. As Maclaurin observes:

[1] Maclaurin, *Journal of Political Economy*, p. 153.

'Farnsworth had originally expected that he could create a commercial television system in a comparatively short time and with only modest funds at his disposal'.[1] He managed to convince both his early backers and, later, Philco of this, but when it became clear that his plans were hopelessly overoptimistic, his patents were seized upon as a 'second best'. By that time, the Californian backers had sunk too much money in Farnsworth to withdraw, and they naturally urged him to obtain the best price he could for his patents by offering them to one of the electronics giants. Although eventually both R.C.A. and A.T. & T. were persuaded to take licences, the royalties in the early years were far below the expenses incurred in the development, and the Farnsworth enterprise turned as a last resort to manufacturing as a supplement to licensing activity.

The most that can be claimed with confidence for patent protection in this case is that it was a factor in persuading Farnsworth's financiers to keep up their support when the primary object of the venture failed. But patents were by no means the only factor, and had the main object been achieved, the patents would have appeared as a minor adjunct of the work. In that event, it can hardly be doubted that Philco or some other large American radio firm would have seized the opportunity to destroy R.C.A.'s virtual monopoly of the television field, and would gladly have taken over the Farnsworth system, had it promised to be successful, with or without patent protection. Had this occurred, it would perhaps have been a case of patents helping to *promote* competition in the television field. As it was, the development was not taken up because Farnsworth, working largely on his own, failed to make sufficient progress with his system.

[1] *Ibid.*, p. 148.

# 13.  THE SMALL INVENTOR

This chapter discusses the impact of the patent system on the 'small man'. We include here not only the traditional small inventor, who works alone in his garden shed in his spare time, but also invention and innovation by small firms. In addition, we say a little about the employee inventor. This last topic relates to inventors employed by (generally large) firms, but it is convenient to discuss it in this chapter, since it does not fit naturally into any other part of the book.

The 'small inventor' is an ambiguous term, even when it is confined to the individual inventor working largely on his own. Many such inventors teach and undertake research in universities and technical colleges, in addition to pursuing their own inventive work. In this way they are likely to benefit from contact with colleagues and research students, and accordingly gain many of the advantages associated with team or group research. Some university teachers also act as consultants to companies, and it may depend merely on the type of arrangement made whether inventions arising from such work are patented by the individual or the company. In any event, some 'individual' inventions may result in part from cooperation by a number of people. Other individual inventors may operate as entirely independent industrial consultants, but here again such men may make their inventions in consultation with those employed by the firms they advise. There are many possible gradations, as Jewkes and his colleagues point out.[1]

On any reckoning, as Jewkes shows,[2] individual inventors have been, and still are, responsible for many notable inventions. What is more doubtful is how important the efforts of small inventors are nowadays compared with those of organisations set up for the purpose, bearing in mind the considerable sums spent on R & D by the Government and industry, the employment by them of large teams of research workers, and their provision of R & D 'overheads' (laboratories, expensive experimental equipment, computing facilities, testing and simulation facilities, etc.). Even greater doubt exists about the importance of small men as innovators.

---

[1] Jewkes *et al.*, *The Sources of Invention*, p. 83.
[2] *Ibid.*, Ch. v. This chapter discusses many aspects of the present subject very well, and it would be unnecessary duplication to repeat here much of what it says.

Equally debatable is the question which is of particular interest to us, namely the extent to which the activity of the small inventor depends on the prospect of being able to obtain a patent on a successful piece of work. For obvious reasons, this is difficult to assess in a systematic way, and the best we can do in what follows is offer our own tentative impressions based on discussions with those whose job it is to help the small man or negotiate with him for use of his inventions. We start, however, by seeing what can be learned from published data and similar information.

A.　EVIDENCE FROM PUBLISHED SOURCES

*Patent statistics*

There are several drawbacks to patent statistics as indicators of the importance of the small inventor.[1] The most obvious of these is that numbers of patents granted to particular classes of patentees bear no necessary relationship to the value of the patents, either to the patentee or to society. There is also the mechanical problem that it is not easy to tell, without careful study of individual patents (and not always even then), whether they were the result of corporate or individual research. What is more – and this difficulty may be especially serious in the case of individual inventors – not all inventions are patented. Nevertheless, the patent statistics are the main evidence that we have, especially over long periods, and the trend that they show seems indisputable. In the United States, the proportion of patents issued to corporations rose from 18 per cent at the beginning of the twentieth century to 58 per cent in 1936. The figure rose again to 64 per cent in 1946, although by 1955 it had fallen back to about 58 per cent.[2] In Britain, according to sample enquiries made by Jewkes, patent applications from companies were about 15 per cent of the total in 1913, 58 per cent in 1938 and 68 per cent in 1955.[3] We estimated earlier (page 56 above) that in 1968 some 30 per cent of *U.K.-originating* applications were attributable to private inventors.

It is interesting to note that these figures for the U.S.A. and Britain are considerably higher than those for Canada, where Professor Firestone has estimated that the independent inventor may now account for between 7 and 10 per cent of all patents granted.[4] Some 21 per cent of *Canadian-originating* patents, however, were from independent inventors, as compared with 5·4 per cent for those of U.S. origin and 9·4 per cent for those originating from other countries.[5]

[1] *Ibid.*, pp. 89–90.　　[2] *Ibid.*, pp. 88–9.　　[3] *Ibid.*, p. 89.
[4] O. J. Firestone, *Economic Implications of Patents*, p. 78.　　[5] *Ibid.*, p. 125.

All studies of patent statistics show that the percentage of patents issued to individual inventors varies greatly in different fields. Jewkes quotes figures for the United States and Britain.[1] In the U.S.A., patents issued to corporations in 'chemicals and related arts' rose from 34 per cent of the total in 1916 to 85 per cent in 1945. In 'radiant energy, signalling, sound and electricity', the figures were 39 per cent and 72 per cent in 1916 and 1945 respectively, but in 'aeronautics' the percentage to corporations was only 48 per cent in 1945, and in 'internal combustion engines' it was 49 per cent. Jewkes' inquiry for Britain in 1955 suggested that patents issued to companies in that year were 95 per cent of the total for 'electric discharge apparatus', 92 per cent for 'synthetic resins and cellulose', 95 per cent for 'general organic chemistry', 89 per cent for 'dyes and dyeing', 77 per cent for 'calculating etc. apparatus', 88 per cent for 'chemistry, inorganic, distillation oils and paints' and 97 per cent for 'electronic discharge-tube circuits'. In general, individual inventors do not now seem to be of much importance in chemicals, pharmaceuticals and some fields of electronics, but they continue to patent on a considerable scale in engineering and related fields.

Firestone reports (pages 125–32) the results of a sample survey of patents granted in Canada in 1957, 1960 and 1963. He found that individual inventors concentrate, in nine out of ten cases, on ideas that lead to new or improved products (as opposed to new processes). They are mainly preoccupied with consumer goods, less so with capital goods, and very little with industrial materials. In general, Firestone suggests, individual inventors are not in competition with big corporations in the type of things they try to invent, but supplement their research activities.

This sample also showed that 36 per cent of independent inventors hold one patent only, 39 per cent hold between two and ten, while 25 per cent hold over ten. In other words, assuming that the small man does not normally take out more than one or two patents on a particular piece of work, quite a high proportion of small inventors, in Canada at least, are 'repeat' inventors.

### R & D expenditure

Invention is of course only the first stage of the process of innovation. It must in most cases be followed by expenditure on development, which is likely to be much more expensive than the original invention, and then by innovatory investment, which is likely to be the most expensive of all. It therefore seems probable that the small inventor,

[1] Jewkes *et al.*, *The Sources of Invention*, pp. 88–9.

whether he be an isolated individual or a small firm, will very often wish to rely for the exploitation of his invention on the large firm. The role of the small man in the development of inventions is thus likely to be less important than his role in invention itself, and the evidence strongly suggests that this is so.[1] The figures for R & D expenditure are likely to reflect this, since they include expenditure on research and development as a whole, although they do not include much investment expenditure associated with innovation, because the bulk of this expenditure is on full-scale manufacturing, which is excluded for official survey purposes.

We estimated in Chapter 4 that very small firms (i.e. those employing less than 25 persons) may have spent at most some £34 million on R & D in the U.K. in 1967–8, or six per cent of the amount spent by larger manufacturing firms (page 56). It was also estimated (page 57) that expenditure on R & D by private inventors may have been about £60 million. Total expenditure was thus estimated at up to £100 million for both categories (or about £75 million, net of grants of £24 million), i.e., some seven per cent of total R & D expenditure in the U.K.

These estimates may well be on the high side. Figures for small firms as defined for the purposes of the Bolton Committee – i.e. firms with 200 employees or fewer – suggest that their share of total industrial R & D expenditure in 1968–9 amounted to four per cent only. Annual R & D expenditure per employee in small firms was about £9 per head in 1967–8 as compared with £65 for all firms.[2] Figures for Q.S.E.'s (qualified scientists and engineers) in relation to total employees also showed a lower ratio in small firms than in other firms: in 1967–8 the ratio in small firms was about one-half that in others. These figures are to some extent deceptive. The vast majority of small firms perform no organised R & D, but some are highly research-intensive; sometimes more research-intensive than large firms in the same industry.[3] Nevertheless it is clear that the small man is much less important as a spender on R & D than as an applicant for patents, which confirms what one would expect on *a priori* grounds.

Having said this, one can still argue that the importance of the small man in invention and innovation is underestimated by the R & D figures, even if it is overestimated by the patent figures (which may be swollen on account of a relatively high propensity to patent on the part of individual inventors and small firms). The Bolton committee's view

---

[1] See, for example, the Bolton report on *Small Firms*, Cmd. 4811 (H.M.S.O., 1971) p. 52.
[2] Bolton Report, p. 51.
[3] C. Freeman, *The Role of Small Firms in Innovation in the United Kingdom Since 1945*, Committee of Inquiry on Small Firms, Research Report No. 6 (H.M.S.O., 1971) p. 3.

(page 50) was that, as far as invention is concerned, individuals and small firms make a disproportionately large contribution, particularly in relation to their expenditure on R & D.

### Evidence on innovation

The contribution to innovation by small firms is only just beginning to be studied directly: most investigations utilise patent and R & D figures, which are much more easily obtainable, as a proxy. A few more penetrating studies have, however, been made for the United States, notably by Mansfield.[1] He has investigated the coal, petroleum and steel industries, and showed that, in the first two of these industries, the four largest firms accounted for a higher proportion of major innovations than their share in the total capacity of the industry. In steel, on the other hand, medium-sized firms were responsible for a larger proportion of the innovations.

In the U.K., the lack of evidence on innovation by size of firm led the Bolton committee to commission a special study by Professor Freeman.[2] Freeman and his colleagues drew up lists of U.K. innovations since the second world war, with the help of experts. They identified some 1,300 innovations in 50 industrial groups, arising from some 800 firms. Of 1,100 innovations that could be analysed, it was found that small firms accounted for some 10 per cent. This is more than double their contribution to R & D expenditure, although less than their share of scientific manpower, and less than half their share of employment and net output.[3] Although the share of small firms in output and employment has been falling, their share in innovation has been fairly steady, or rising slightly.[4]

Freeman found (pages 8–13) that there were big variations in the contributions of small firms to innovation in different industries. He identified two fairly clear-cut groups of industries: those in which small firms made little or no contribution to innovation, and those in which they made a significant contribution. Among the former were aerospace, motors, dyes, pharmaceuticals, cement, glass and steel, while among the latter were scientific instruments, timber and furniture, leather and footwear, textile machinery, machine tools, paper and board and general machinery. Small firms accounted for one per cent of the innovations in the first group and 17 per cent in the second. Freeman argued that, in general, industries where small firms contributed much less than their share of innovation were those of high capital

[1] E. Mansfield, *Industrial Research and Technological Innovation*, Ch. 5.
[2] Freeman, *The Role of Small Firms in Innovation, op. cit.*
[3] Bolton Report, pp. 53–4.          [4] Freeman, *The Role of Small Firms in Innovation*, p. 8.

intensity. In such industries, virtually all product and process innovations arose from large firms.

Some of the innovations made by small firms were very important ones. Freeman persuaded experts to 'weight' innovations in a number of industries for both technical and economic importance and the results suggested that weighting had little effect, but perhaps tended slightly to diminish the share of small (and medium-sized) firms in innovation.

In commenting on these findings, the Bolton committee (page 53) pointed out that it would be unwise to over-emphasise the role of small firms in innovation, since this would divert attention from a more important point, namely the complementary roles of small and large firms in the innovative process. A large number of innovations in large firms result from ideas originating outside, and it is suggested that possibly a majority of innovations may result from a movement of people from one firm to another: a movement which may take several different forms. In any event, the committee was clear that small firms continue to make an important contribution to both inventive and innovative activity.

Little quantitative evidence exists on innovation by individuals, as opposed to small firms. There is of course a good deal of qualitative evidence in Jewkes and elsewhere, and this seems to confirm that the inventions of individuals are often exploited (where they *are* exploited: see below) by firms unconnected with the inventor. Firestone also made some enquiries on this subject. He found that, when an invention owned by an independent inventor is worked in Canada, it is worked by one person or one firm in 73 per cent of the cases.[1] In 87 per cent of the instances where it is worked by one firm, this firm is 'unrelated' to the inventor, i.e. he holds less than 25 per cent of the shares of the firm. These figures tend to confirm the qualitative evidence.

Further confirmation is given in an interesting analysis of one hundred case histories of inventions produced by Lord Halsbury. He found that 19 inventions in his list were exploited by setting up a new company to work them with the inventor acting as a director, employee or consultant. Of these, five have survived but the rest were absorbed sooner or later by established firms as a result of licensing or take-over.[2]

---

[1] Firestone, *The Economic Implications of Patents*, p. 131.

[2] Lord Halsbury, 'Invention and Technological Progress', *The Inventor* (Journal of the Institute of Patentees and Inventors, June 1971) pp. 31–2. The article contains a number of other analyses, including one of the time lags between scientific discovery and invention – found to be 42 years on average, including 11 years' work by the inventor – and between the patent application and the subsequent innovation – 6 years for the product to be marketed or for the process to be operated (p. 23), leaving some 10 years only for the patent to run.

B. INSTITUTIONS CONCERNED WITH THE SMALL INVENTOR

A further perspective on the importance of the small inventor, and of the patent system in relation to him, can be gained by reference to the experience of institutions especially concerned with the promotion of his work. The most notable of these is the National Research Development Corporation, set up in 1948 by the *Development of Inventions Act* with loan finance provided by the Government. One of the principal statutory functions of the N.R.D.C. is to secure the development or exploitation 'where the public interest so requires' of inventions resulting from public research (i.e. research in Government establishments, universities, etc.), and of any other invention which it appears to the Corporation is not being sufficiently developed or exploited. The N.R.D.C. is thus empowered to help with the development of private inventions, but only if these are not being adequately exploited elsewhere and if their exploitation is in the public interest.

The N.R.D.C.'s usual practice, if it is interested in a particular invention (whether from public or private sources), is to acquire the rights in the invention from the patentee. In return for this, it provides the inventor with a share of the net revenue, if any, from the licensed use of his invention by industry. Financial help for development from the N.R.D.C. can take several forms, and may extend beyond the development stage to manufacture. Increasingly, as a matter of policy, the Corporation has involved itself in joint ventures with industry. In March 1971, out of a total of 404 current projects, 186 represented joint ventures with firms.[1]

By 1971 the N.R.D.C. had dealt with some 25,500 inventions submitted from all sources (of which some 5,360 had been accepted). From publicly supported sources had come a number of important inventions, subsequently backed by the Corporation, such as developments in electronic computers, cephalosporin antibiotics (by far the N.R.D.C.'s largest revenue earner) and the R.A.E. method of making carbon fibres. From private inventors had come notably the hovercraft and the hydrogen–oxygen fuel cell. In March 1971 the N.R.D.C. held directly 5,232 patents and patent applications, of which 3,788 were overseas. Its subsidiary development companies held 1,776, of which 1,542 were overseas. It had 560 licence agreements in force – 476 in the U.K. and 84 overseas. It only succeeded in breaking even on revenue account for the first time in 1968–9, and this was managed largely on the strength of royalty income from cephalosporin.

The N.R.D.C. handles a proportion of the civil inventions arising from defence expenditure, although contractors are also important

[1] N.R.D.C., *Annual Report and Accounts, 1970–71* (H.M.S.O., August 1971) p. 8.

here, and is the principal development channel for inventions from Government research establishments; it also deals with a substantial proportion of inventions from universities. Although it attempts to exploit as many inventions submitted from public sources as possible, its experience seems to be that such inventions tend on the whole to be comparable with those made in private industry and are seldom of great originality. Its experience with private inventors seems to be that only an extremely small number of private inventions submitted to it are worth exploiting, either on technical or economic grounds, although a very few do give rise to radically new developments. The hovercraft is the outstanding example.

The N.R.D.C.'s annual report for 1953–4 contained a famous statement, which still appears to be largely true: 'Our five years' experience requires us to report that . . . outside the field of light engineering and instrument manufacture, the isolated individual rarely appears to have any serious contribution to make to the advancement of technology. In the various fields of physics, chemistry, biology, medicine and the non-mechanical branches of the engineering science no meritorious proposals have reached us from such persons.' The N.R.D.C.'s experience had thus failed to confirm that 'a multitude of meritorious private inventors stand in need of public assistance' or that a spectacular increase in national wealth could be gained by supporting them. Of the 14,000 or so inventions from private sources submitted to it by March 1971, the N.R.D.C. had accepted less than 0·5 per cent. The conclusion appears inescapable: with some notable exceptions, most worthwhile inventions arising privately are supported by private industry. The widespread complaint of private inventors that industry ignores their meritorious inventions does not seem to be borne out by the experience of the N.R.D.C.

This is not of course meant to imply that the N.R.D.C., in standing ready to sponsor useful private inventions, does not have an important role to play. It seems desirable that some institution should be in a position to back private as well as public inventions with public funds. The N.R.D.C. fulfils this role in a serious and responsible manner, and the various complaints there have been levelled at it (e.g. an excess of commercial acumen) do not, as far as we can tell, seem well founded.

The experience of the N.R.D.C. in relation to private inventors appears to have been shared by other organisations concerned with individual inventive activity. Among the most interesting of these is the Institute of Patentees and Inventors, founded in 1919 in order (among other objects) to assist and advise inventors and research workers with regard to worthwhile inventions, and to examine and report on their subject matter, protection and exploitation. This Institute provides a wide range of services to its members on slender resources, including a (free) assessment service of the commercial viability of patented inventions. It has found that many interesting inventions have been submitted for appraisal, but that only a small proportion appear to have good commercial potential, often because they are not sufficiently distinct from existing products or processes or because similar inventions have been unsuccessful before. One of the main tasks of the Institute's assessment service is to suggest to inventors the best industrial application for their inventions. This is, not surprisingly, an area in which the small inventor, often without wide contacts, is normally at a maximum disadvantage. Even where he is helped to find the best application, however, very few private inventions manage in the end to find acceptance.

It is worth mentioning one other organisation concerned with the exploitation of commercially promising inventions (with no restriction as to sources). This is Technical Development Capital Limited, which was founded in 1962 by a group of insurance companies, merchant banks and other City institutions, including the Industrial and Commercial Finance Corporation. This body was modelled on the American Research and Development Corporation, founded in 1946. The object of T.D.C. is to provide risk capital for technical innovations, at the stage before profitable operation has been reached. It differs from the N.R.D.C. in that it is prepared to embrace any potentially profitable development in the private sector, and not only those 'where the public interest so requires' – however liberally this may be interpreted by the N.R.D.C. Its specific concern is with the stage of bringing a new product or process on to the market, and not just with the development stage (although the N.R.D.C. has increasingly concerned itself with these later stages). In 1966 T.D.C. became a wholly owned subsidiary of the I.C.F.C. One of the reasons given for this was the need to draw on the resources of a larger organisation to help with the task of dealing with a very large number of applications in almost every field of technology. The experience of T.D.C. confirms, once again, that there are a substantial number of inventions seeking support from non-private sources, and that comparatively few are worth backing. The few that are eventually successful are primarily in the fields of engineering, electronics and instrumentation.

A word should finally be said here about the reception given to the small inventor by large industrial firms. All spokesmen for research-based firms in our inquiry who were questioned on this subject stressed that approaches from the small man are taken very seriously and that great care is taken to see that he gets a fair hearing if this is merited. The larger and more patent-conscious companies generally have standing arrangements to deal with inventions submitted to them. The largest chemical and electrical groups each receive on average something like a dozen or more approaches per week and find it necessary to employ at least one technical graduate full-time to handle them (in consultation with the group's main R & D and engineering departments, who give specialist advice). The prevailing philosophy in these firms appeared to be that 'no stone should be left unturned' and that 'something may turn up one day, although it hasn't yet'.

Very few of those consulted could recall instances of inventions submitted from individuals or very small firms that had been accepted, although one or two isolated cases were mentioned to us, but all said they were ready to welcome promising cases. Most of the inventions submitted are relatively simple-minded, although some show genuine technical expertise or ingenuity, and the main reasons for refusing to take them up are either that the idea is an old one or that it is simply not a commercial proposition. So far as we could tell, there seems no substance at all to the claim that the small man receives scant attention from the large firm, much less that the large firm attempts to pirate the small man's inventions after showing him the door.

We were told that industrial firms will almost invariably insist on an outsider obtaining or at least applying for a patent on his invention before they will consider it seriously. The reason for this is not so much that firms are thinking of the possibilities for exploiting the invention, although this of course is often a consideration, as that a patent greatly reduces the scope for subsequent inaccurate claims by the inventor (particularly if disgruntled) as to what he submitted. For instance, where an alleged invention has a superficial resemblance to something on which the firm itself is working but is turned down as being of no value (as most are), the existence of a patent application makes it difficult for the inventor to make unwarranted claims that the firm has pirated his invention – a type of accusation that is not unknown to firms, and that can prove embarrassing to them, however unfounded.

#### C.    THE EMPLOYEE INVENTOR

The growth in the importance of corporate research, especially in the large company or nationalised industry, has raised the question of the position of those who make inventions as employees. Two main issues arise: the ownership of inventions made by employees who are not employed primarily to invent, do research, etc., and the ownership of inventions made by R & D staff. It seems clear that inventions in the first category are held by British common law to belong in most instances to the inventor himself, although there are problems in fringe cases. Inventions in the second category are normally held to belong to the firm, with no particular rights in the invention for the inventor. As a result of a recommendation of the Swan Committee, the 1949 Patents Act embodied a new provision (Section 56 (2)) giving the Court or the Comptroller power to apportion the benefit in cases coming between the two extremes. However, in the case of *Patchett and Stirling* (1955) the House of Lords rendered Section 56 (2) a dead letter, by holding that the basic position remained that an invention belonged absolutely either to the employer or the employee, unless there was a contract to the contrary. In 1965 the government introduced the Patents (Employees' Inventions) Bill to restore the position to what it was believed to be before *Patchett and Stirling*, but the bill met with difficulties and was finally withdrawn.

The controversy over the rights of the employee inventor was discussed at some length by the Banks Committee on the patent system (Banks Report, Chapter 16). The committee noted that most European countries have statutory provisions dealing with this matter and drew attention in particular to the complexity of the compensatory provisions under German law. It also noted the argument that the present system was not only inequitable to the employee but provided no encouragement to inventive employees. The committee found, on the other hand, that industrialists were against any change in the law. Among the reasons for this were the inhibiting effect that there might be on the organisation and effectiveness of an R & D department; for example there might be more secrecy than at present between members of staff. There was also the argument that able employee inventors could be rewarded by salary increases or promotion, and that this was not only equitable but also provided (it was implied) adequate incentive for invention. The conclusion of the Banks Committee was that it was not desirable to vary the common law position, although any contractual term in the employer's favour which went beyond the common law should be unenforceable, unless it was entered into after an invention had been made.

This conclusion of the Committee has not of course been universally welcomed, for obvious reasons. Our main concern here, however, is whether the legal position has any influence either on the propensity to invent or the propensity to patent. It is difficult to believe that its influence on the former is large: inventions of importance made by employees are likely to be made by those employed expressly to invent or do research, and such people know when they accept employment that they are in effect exchanging their rights in any invention they may make for a regular income from their employers.

Those who are particularly concerned to own their own inventions are likely to work on their own account, shouldering (as seems appropriate) the risks and hardships as well as any rewards associated with entrepreneurial ambitions in the inventive field. Many potential inventors are reluctant to take on such burdens, and welcome the security given by large companies, with their substantial resources. As far as propensity to patent is concerned, the present situation in Britain probably leads to fewer patents of a trivial nature being taken out by firms than would occur under a system where employees might be entitled to a share in the profits of inventions. It has been argued that in Germany, for example, there is a rush to the patent office as firms and their employees race to establish claims. This seems good neither for the quality of research done in firms nor for the efficient working of the patent system as a whole.

### D.  IMPACT OF PATENTS

We have seen that the proportion of patents issued to individual inventors is a good deal higher than their apparent share in R & D expenditure. Solid conclusions cannot be based on figures of this sort, but the evidence generally suggests that individuals, and also small firms, make a disproportionately large contribution where invention is concerned. Freeman's study of innovation by small firms in Britain since the second world war suggested that small firms make, in addition, a disproportionately large contribution to innovation when measured against their R & D, but not when measured against their employment and net output.

It seems clear from the experience of the N.R.D.C. and others that – apart from some outstanding exceptions – the vast majority of the inventive efforts of individual inventors prove to be worthless for technological or economic reasons, and thus never proceed to the stage of innovation. In this respect there may well be an important difference between individual inventors and small firms; but the difference must not be stressed too much, since many small firms which innovate successfully are founded by individual inventors: 'Route 128' in Massachusetts is perhaps the best example of this happening on a noticeable scale.

All the evidence suggests that individual inventors are much more important in some fields, notably mechanical engineering, than in others. They are of virtually no importance in such fields as chemicals and pharmaceuticals. Freeman came to much the same general conclusion for the small firms he studied. He stressed that they make little innovative contribution in industries of high capital intensity.

How does all this relate to the patent system? It is evident that individual inventors make great use of the patent system, and obviously regard patents as important to them. Almost all the companies and institutions with whom they deal also stress the need for small inventors to take out patents, although they do this partly for their own protection. The patent system obviously *protects* the small inventor, and gives him the opportunity to benefit from his invention, especially if someone else takes over its development and commercial implementation, as usually happens. But how far do patents actually induce him to invent? The answer to this is not so clear. Most inventors realise that there are some glittering financial prizes to be won, but that they are few in number. They must know that the statistical probability that they will make very much money from their inventions is not high. Perhaps there are inventors who are only prepared to invent because of the faint possibility of winning a large financial prize, but most seem equally if not more motivated by the chance of achieving 'recognition', if only of a minor sort. Such men (and they *are* men: Firestone found (page 127) that less than one-half of a per cent of all patents issued in Canada were to female inventors) probably do not need the incentive of the patent system to encourage them to invent. Nor do those who invent simply because it is in their blood to do so. In such cases, absence of patent protection would probably lead to a few (the 'successful' ones) being dramatically worse off, but there would probably be rather little overall reduction in their efforts to invent.

In so far as he does not need the incentive of patents to invent, the small inventor resembles the large company in most technically advanced industries. As we have seen, such a company needs to make technical advances, whether these consist of patentable inventions or not, simply in order to stay in the race. We have also seen that patent protection does sometimes encourage industrial innovation, if only in certain fields, of which pharmaceuticals is the outstanding one. While the individual inventor rarely manufactures or markets his invention, and consequently such encouragement as patents afford to these activities does not directly affect him, he has of course an indirect interest in these effects, since his returns derive from those obtained from the subsequent industrial working of his invention, and if this is inhibited his rewards will suffer correspondingly.

It seems significant that the industries found in our inquiry to be substantially affected by patent protection (in the sense defined in the inquiry) – primarily pharmaceuticals and some other areas of finished and specialty chemicals – are ones in which patented inventions by the small man are relatively few and far between. In the fields where the small man contributes with greatest frequency – namely mechanical engineering and related fields – patents were found to have a fairly marginal impact on innovation overall, although they do have a critical effect in a small minority of cases – for example, in the development of some types of specialised machinery. The assistance given by the patent system to the exploitation of the small man's inventions may be therefore something of an illusion on the whole, although it cannot be denied that the fortunes of the occasional 'small' invention can be crucially dependent on patent protection. Such protection is after all most likely to be an important consideration where developments are fundamentally new, and, as we have seen, the very few private inventions that do prove to be of real commercial value include a relatively high proportion of ones that are radically new and original, such as the hovercraft.

Thus even though it may well be broadly true that patent protection, as we defined it for purposes of our industrial inquiry (i.e., the element of monopoly protection that comes about through the operation of the present system, rather than a worldwide, thoroughgoing, compulsory licensing system), gives in practice rather little benefit or encouragement to most small inventors, this conclusion cannot be said to hold in all cases, including the *very* occasional one of outstanding economic importance. What is more, it is not generally thought to be true among small inventors and small research-based firms. If the protection given by the patent system were substantially reduced, it seems likely for this reason if no other that attempts at innovations by small firms of the more adventurous kind would be discouraged. Given the desirability of encouraging promising sources of initiative of the Route 128-type, this would be a real loss. It would also make it more difficult for the complementary activities of large and small firms in innovation, of the sort commended in the Bolton report, to take place.

It must not be forgotten on the other hand that the patent system does provide opportunities for large firms to stifle competition from their smaller rivals, even where the patents are widely recognised to be weak or relatively trivial. If faced with the prospect of infringement proceedings by a large firm, most small firms are likely to take a licence, or, if no licence is offered, submit to exclusion from the market (unless it is central to their operations), rather than undergo the expense and disruption of a patent dispute, however strong they believe their case. In most instances, we believe, large firms use their patents in a legitimate manner (i.e., in accordance with the spirit and intention of the Patents Act) and their approach to licensing is usually reasonable – even liberal for the most part nowadays in important fields like electronics; but there are doubtless some cases where large firms abuse the system at the expense of small, whereas abuse can very seldom operate in the reverse direction (although such cases do apparently arise[1]). On this account, admittedly, the weakening of the patent system might well be of some advantage to the small firm, but on balance this would probably be more than offset by the loss of patent protection for the small firm's own more notable innovations.

This conclusion holds more strongly, the greater the weakening that is imagined in the system: we think there is very little doubt that the small inventor would ultimately suffer quite heavily, and his activity diminish significantly in scale, if the patent system were *completely* dismantled.

Quite apart from any impact on the volume of activity, the question of the need for equity in dealing with the small inventor is clearly one of substance, although it is an issue on which we, as economists, venture only with great diffidence. The notion that individual inventors and small firms are unfairly exploited by large firms, and by large organisations such as the N.R.D.C., while completely unsubstantiated in our survey (which after all was answered mainly by large organisations, although we did try as well to hear the small man's point of view), appears to have wide public acceptance. Moreover, there has been some justification for it in the past and there must on occasion be justification for it today. The existence of patent protection is almost certainly of some help to the small inventor on such occasions, and it probably also gives him a greater feeling of security at all times. In any event, if the patent protection afforded to the small inventor were substantially weakened, there would certainly be an outcry on his behalf. It might even be joined by the large firms, since the problem of dealing with outside inventors is made much more manageable for them, and they are less open to accusations of unfair dealing, if the inventor has patent protection. If this occurred, a weakening of patent

[1] It is perhaps relevant to cite the well-known case of Killick v. Pye, in which Mrs Killick, a private inventor, sued Pye Limited for infringement of her patent on a universal stylus for gramophone records, the writ being issued in 1953. Pye, who manufactured and sold some 32,000 styli of this type in the years 1950–3 before it became obsolete, maintained that the patent was not infringed, but (in 1955) offered Mrs Killick a settlement based on 10 per cent of the price of the stylus (the latter being about 2 shillings). Mrs Killick refused to accept and in 1957 took her case to the High Court, where she won a favourable decision, which was later upheld in the Court of Appeal ((*1958*) R.P.C., pp. 23 and 366). Pye eventually settled in 1958 for some £4,000, which was paid to the Official Receiver, Mrs Killick having been declared bankrupt as a result of heavy overspending in anticipation of a large settlement.

This case is of interest here in that it shows that a small inventor can, if persistent, succeed in a full-scale patent action against a large firm, even where the case was and still is open to a considerable amount of legal doubt. (Certain aspects of the Killick v. Pye decision have been criticised by legal commentators. See Blanco-White, *Patents for Inventions*, pp. 52 and 127.) The fact that Mrs Killick was bankrupted during the action reflected her unwisdom in allowing the prospect of victory to go to her head and was not connected with her legal costs, for much of which she received legal aid.

protection might well lead to some other form of protection for the small man – and one which might be less in the public interest than the present system. Perhaps, in the light of this, we should look upon the Comptroller of the Patent Office less as the man who issues lottery tickets to the small inventor, and more as the chief constable of his professional police force.

# PART IV

---

## CONCLUSIONS

# 14. SURVEY OF RESULTS AND CONCLUSIONS

Basic to our assessment of the patent system has been the view that it should be judged by reference to an alternative (hypothetical, but not improbable) system differing in certain explicit and fairly fundamental respects from the existing one. The standard alternative chosen for intensive analysis was that of a thoroughgoing, worldwide, compulsory licensing system with 'commercially reasonable' royalties, and most of the arguments in preceding pages have been concerned with a comparison between this and the existing system. Furthermore, most of this concluding chapter will be devoted to a round-up of our findings resulting from this comparison.

It should be stressed again, however, that this is not the only alternative that could have been chosen, and that the results in some respects depend quite a lot on the exact choice of alternative system, as was indicated when the standard alternative was modified in Section F of Chapter 9. It is interesting, for example, to speculate on the consequences of a total abandonment of the patent system, far-fetched although we believe this to be, and hard though it is to assess. Accordingly, we shall try later in this chapter to say something, in outline at least, about other alternatives to the existing system, although this takes us somewhat beyond the bounds of our main study.

## A. THE STANDARD ALTERNATIVE

The essence of our standard alternative adopted as a yardstick for assessing the patent system is that no *bona fide* application for a patent licence can be refused and that royalties are set at reasonable commercial levels, determined if necessary by an official arbitrator. The system is imagined to exist overseas as well as in the U.K., and to apply to patents in all industrial fields. It may be summed up as a worldwide, thoroughgoing, compulsory licence system with 'fair' or 'correct' royalties, in the sense defined in Chapter 8 (pp. 171–2).

In comparing the existing patent system with the standard alternative case, three possible kinds of effects were distinguished and investigated, namely: effects on the rate and direction of inventive and innovative activity; effects on competition and prices; and effects on the disclosure and spread of technical information. The effects were investigated in a range of chemical and electrical and mechanical engineering industries and man-made fibres, which together comprise the industry groups which account for the bulk of patent activity in the U.K. (The sample covered roughly a third of all R & D done in these fields.) Some consideration was also given to the impact on the small inventor and the very small firm.

The findings for the principal industries examined were broadly as follows.

### Finished and specialty chemicals

This was the one group of industries in which we found unmistakable evidence that patent protection had a strong and pervasive influence on the willingness of firms to undertake R & D and apply the results. By far the most powerful impact appeared to be in pharmaceuticals, where about half of R & D and associated drug innovation is thought to be dependent on patents in the sense described. The impact on R & D in other fields in this group was much lower on average, but several areas stood out as being significantly affected, notably crop protection chemicals and, to a lesser extent, plastics materials and special-purpose industrial chemicals.

The essential characteristic of the branches of activity most affected is that they produce substances of the sort which embody or derive more or less uniquely from an invention or set of inventions for which 'strong' (valid) patents are obtainable. In addition, they tend to be activities that are heavily research-intensive, in the sense that the minimum amounts of R & D and associated expenditures thought necessary for long-term survival are large in relation to the value of sales, while other barriers to competition such as conventional economies of scale are not particularly important.[1] Above all, they are lines in which secret know-how, special engineering expertise, etc. cannot be relied on to delay the emergence of competition until after the 'pay off' period for protected innovations – perhaps because the essential inventive step is disclosed as soon as the product becomes publicly available.

The influence of patents in the finished chemical field should not be exaggerated. Although most are covered by patents of some sort, many types of chemical products are not affected by patent protection, includ-

[1] Trade marks and brand names undoubtedly provide an element of protection for many drugs and similar products, including many on which patents have expired, but they do not, we think, constitute as important a monopoly device as patents are capable of being in this field. For an assessment of the impact of brand names on the American pharmaceutical industry, see Walker, *Market Power and Price Levels in the Ethical Drug Industry*, especially Ch. 14.

ing many that involve R & D efforts which are large in an absolute sense. Thus, products sold in *mass* consumer markets are not in general patent-sensitive; this is the case for instance in synthetic detergents, although certain aspects of these (e.g., the use of fluorescent brightening agents) have been heavily patented, and certain new developments (for example the perfection of technology associated with the production of enzyme-containing detergents) have involved large R & D outlays.

It is hard to generalise about the impact of patents on prices and profits in the finished and specialty chemical field. The pharmaceutical industry is something of a special case in the U.K., in that it is subject to official price regulation which, although termed voluntary, appears to be both mandatory and reasonably effective for most participants – except in some cases of foreign-owned companies which have attempted to evade the official surveillance. While it would be unrealistic to assume that U.K. drug price control has been thoroughly effective in all respects, regulation seems to have been successful for the most part in dealing with the type of excessive pricing of patent-based drugs that has been observed in the past, backed as it is by Government's strengthened and much-feared reserve powers under Section 46 of the Patents Act. In these circumstances, research-based firms in the U.K. may rely on patent protection to secure a 'reasonable' return on their R & D, but they cannot exploit patent monopolies for profiteering purposes in ways that are still possible under some foreign patent systems.

In other branches of the finished and specialty chemical industries, we could find very little recent evidence of patent exploitation in the narrow profit-maximising sense. We were particularly impressed with the apparent rarity of unsatisfied demand for U.K. licences in important lines of chemical activity and, although recognising that this reflects among other things a fairly wide-spread 'keep off the grass' attitude, we also believe that it betokens moderation on the part of innovating firms in fixing profit margins and planning to meet the market at reasonable prices. There is furthermore some indication that royalties are not on the whole excessive in this field, at least among the firms in our sample. According to our calculations, using the admittedly rather crude method described in Section F of Chapter 8, actual royalty rates charged in pharmaceutical and other finished and specialty chemicals were on average slightly below the 'correct' rates applicable in these fields.

At the same time, it would be reading too much into our evidence to assert that patents nowadays have no significant effect on prices and profits in any of the areas covered – although to do so would not necessarily conflict with the finding that patents do have a significant impact on R & D in some areas. Several firms admitted that patents on drugs and other specialty chemicals often delay the fall in prices experienced ultimately by virtually all products in a rapidly-progressing technical field, but all insisted that the delay from this source could very seldom be more than a few years.

What we may conclude with some confidence is that the impact of patent protection on prices and profits seemed nowhere so large that it could be said, by any obvious standard, to outweigh the advantages to the economy as a whole from having access to products thought to be dependent on patent protection in the areas concerned. The point is simply that if the adoption of a (worldwide) compulsory licensing system would, as our inquiry suggests, result in the abandonment of a great deal of industrial R & D in pharmaceuticals, pesticides, sophisticated industrial chemicals and other special chemicals of that kind, it is of little comfort to know that the prices of some of these products, were they available, would perhaps be somewhat lower under a compulsory licensing system than they are under the present system.

Apart from the impact on the size and direction of R & D referred to above, patent protection has, so far as we can judge, a very appreciable effect on public disclosure (through patent specifications and other technical literature) of new technical information on finished and specialty chemicals, as elsewhere in the chemical field. Under a compulsory licensing system, there would probably be much more secrecy concerning the results of the R & D programmes that would survive, especially in the area of process improvements and other technical developments where implementation does not entail immediate disclosure. Such secrecy would probably detract somewhat, if not substantially, from the effectiveness of R & D and the efficiency of processes in the chemical field but, more seriously, it would make the formal exchange of technical knowledge between firms more difficult than under the present patent system. Reasons for this are dealt with in Section E of Chapter 9, but the general point briefly is that technical know-how can in many cases be transferred with much greater convenience and confidence when patents attach to the subject matter than when they are absent.

### Basic chemicals

In contrast to finished and specialty chemicals, it was found that patents have no more than a marginal impact (of the order of 5 per cent overall) on the R & D efforts of firms in the basic chemical field, and this seemed broadly true throughout the various branches of the industry covered.

Similarly, the impact on prices and profits in this group of industries was judged to be very minor.

To some extent, these findings can be attributed to the structure of the industries concerned. Mainly because of the economies of large chemical plant operation, stemming both from the existence of conventional economies of scale and from the fact that many basic chemicals are joint products of a relatively small number of highly integrated processes, the supply of most basic chemicals in the U.K. is accounted for by a few large firms, and it is almost inconceivable that small newcomers to the industry (attempting, in our context, to 'pirate' the latest technology of chemical processing from the established producers) could ever pose a serious competitive threat to the existing giants. Imports are a more serious threat in some branches of the industry, and competition from this source occurs from time to time; for that reason, patents can sometimes be a factor in adding security to R & D programmes in this field, and indeed important international licence agreements in basic chemicals usually restrain the licensee from selling – if not always from manufacturing *and* selling – in the licensor's major territories. But patents are typically a very minor factor in comparison with other restraints on competition. This is partly a reflection of the fact that 'conventional' barriers, such as large initial plant costs, transport costs, etc. are typically strong in this field, but it also reflects the relatively small size of R & D outlays in relation to the size of the market for the basic chemical 'building blocks'. Although the absolute sums spent on R & D in this field by I.C.I. and the other major chemical firms are very large, they are not so in relation to sales, so that the cost advantage obtainable by copying the technology of the 'majors' is potentially rather slight.

Apart from these considerations, two other points are relevant. It appears to be generally true that few, if any, important basic chemicals are nowadays capable of being wholly or substantially protected by patents. Technology in this field is too mature and too complex for this to happen, with the result that even 'basic' patents on key stages in a process can almost invariably be by-passed without undue cost or difficulty by skilled chemical engineers. Secondly, unpatented technical know-how presents in many cases a much more effective barrier to imitation than patented information. Chemical firms that develop process improvements can usually control the spread of these improvements far more effectively by refusing to supply know-how than by refusing patent rights, and not even the most thoroughgoing of compulsory licensing systems would change this.

Our evidence suggests that the principal impact of the patent system in this field is that it encourages the public disclosure of a great deal of technical information via patent specifications which would probably be kept secret in a world of compulsory licensing. The information chiefly concerned consists of key patentable improvements in chemical process technology – particularly the design and specification of parts of chemical plant, the use of special catalysts, solvents, etc., and the precise conditions under which they are most effective. By its nature, this type of information can be kept secret for quite long periods if the innovating firm wishes, and the inducement to do so rather than patent the results would be strong under a compulsory licensing system. As in finished and specialty chemicals, the greater secrecy would reduce the effectiveness of R & D and the general efficiency of technical processes elsewhere in the industry, but the impact would probably be more serious in this field than in most others, because an unusually high proportion of R & D and engineering effort in basic chemicals is devoted to improving process technology.

Something should perhaps be added about oil refining, since although it was not possible to obtain detailed figures for this activity in the inquiry, the impact of patents on this area of operations was discussed with the oil companies and enough was learned to justify the following broad conclusions. Spokesmen for the companies were generally of the view that patents have little if any influence on invention and innovation in oil refining, for reasons which are similar to those given already for basic chemicals. In particular, the absence in recent years of key patents on refinery processes was pointed out, and this was said to reflect the maturity of oil processing technology. The willingness of the major oil companies to license virtually all comers to use their patents (and in most cases, know-how) on the oil processing side of the business on reasonable terms without important restrictions was also pointed out. This appears to reflect both the mutual interdependence of the 'majors' in many areas of their oil business, and the inability of any one enterprise to meet more than a small fraction of what is in effect a fairly unified world market for petroleum products. There seems little doubt that the protection obtainable for petroleum products through brand names, advertising and above all systems of tied garages is valued by the industry much more highly than patent protection.

*Mechanical engineering*

Although patents are on average more numerous in relation to R & D expenditure in mechanical engineering than in any other group of industries, the impact of patent protection on invention and innovation in the branches of the industry examined was found to be relatively minor on the whole. We detected a number of cases in which developments of some significance were said to be fairly heavily dependent on patents, but these did not add up to very much in terms of R & D or production when measured against the overall magnitudes reported by mechanical engineering firms.

One feature helping to explain these exceptional cases is that, while mechanical engineering is not in general a research-intensive field in the way that pharmaceuticals or electronic equipment are, the R & D that is done tends to be concentrated in a rather narrow range of advanced products – which tend, of course, to be the ones that are patent-based. (Some indication of this is gained by comparing R & D/ Sales ratios for plant, machinery and equipment shown in Table 8.1 with those in Table 9.3.) Advanced types of plant and machinery tend to command markets of very limited size where patent protection can offer a useful competitive advantage, and although it is widely said to be difficult to obtain a strong patent on a basic feature of a machine in today's world, this is very occasionally possible, especially where the item is for use in a 'new' industry, like synthetic fibre manufacture or nuclear power generation.

By contrast, in the components and materials field – for example, automotive components – the essential object of technical effort is modification or adjustment of standard product design, linked with improvement of mass-production techniques so as to be capable of producing parts engineered to very high specifications in terms of precision and reliability. In this type of work there is usually little to patent, but often a great deal of engineering expertise and other technical know-how. The latter, rather than patents, is likely to be the main protective element in the component field. Nevertheless, exceptions are occasionally met with even here, although, as in machinery, they do not seem to be the sort that require a great deal of R & D expenditure for implementation. (Of the various industrial fields examined, components and mechanical equipment seemed the only ones where it is still occasionally possible for a firm to take the development of a fundamentally new invention to the stage of manufacture with an annual R & D budget measured in tens rather than hundreds of thousands of pounds.)

A relatively high degree of selectivity was found in licensing policy among mechanical engineering firms. Such firms are prone not to license their competitors in the U.K. in technical areas of importance to the licensor without a *quid pro quo* of similar value, and cross-licences between British firms in this field seem particularly rare. Virtually all licensing of any importance is with foreign firms, and is normally confined to markets outside the licensor's main spheres of interest, territorially or productwise.

It nevertheless appeared to us that selectivity in licensing has very little impact on prices and profits in mechanical engineering generally. We were impressed by the often-repeated view that machinery producers prefer to rely on products designed and researched by their own technical experts, and that the advantage obtainable through taking licences is typically slight; this is easily understood in a field where so much depends on engineering know-how resulting from familiarity with the product as it evolves through succeeding stages of development, and where patents seldom cover essential features of machinery or equipments. In the few cases where genuine monopolistic advantages follow from selectivity in licensing the vital protective feature is usually know-how rather than patents.

In the very few cases where patents could be identified as a definite factor affecting competition, there appeared to be little if any deliberate exercise of monopoly power over prices and profits by firms in the text-book sense. As far as we could tell, firms in this position refrained from fixing unduly higher profit margins on patent-dependent goods, preferring security and a 'quiet life' to the quick gains they might make from aggressive exploitation of their monopolies. A machinery producer is typically in business to supply a wide range of machines, etc. to a trade or industry, and is hardly ever in a position to exert patent monopolies over the whole range; he is usually subject to competition from two or three or more other producers over a large part of his range and therefore cannot afford to forfeit the goodwill of expert and knowledgeable clients built up possibly over decades for the sake of high profits on one or two patent-based models. In earlier years, some powerful (if benevolent) monopolies, such as that in shoe machinery discussed in Section B of Chapter 9 (pages 192–4), were built up in the machinery field with the help of tying clauses in licence agreements, but this practice is no longer operated by major firms so far as we could discover and we doubt whether it could ever again provide the basis for new monopolies in this or any other field.

While restrictive licensing policy seems to have very little overall effect on prices and profits in mechanical engineering, there is some evidence that it may have some slight indirect effect on prices via royalty rates, which by our calculations appeared on average to be on the high side compared with what could be expected on the basis of R & D expenditures. A compulsory licensing system with 'fair' royalties might well lead to reductions in some individual rates, although the impact would probably be extremely small, taking the field as a whole.

As in chemicals, the patent system clearly encourages the disclosure and publication of engineering inventions, and there seems little doubt that much more information would be kept secret in certain branches of mechanical engineering under compulsory licensing than happens at present. The area principally affected would probably be that of components, where secret know-how can frequently be relied on to give a useful element of protection, but where the disclosure of critical steps or features of an engineering process can be a great advantage to competitors. The impact would probably be much more moderate in machinery and equipment, where improvements in design and application are hard to conceal once the product in question is on the market.

### Electronics and allied industries

There appears to be fairly clear evidence that, although patents were probably a factor of some importance contributing to the early emergence of radio, they seldom nowadays have much impact on industrial R & D in this field or on prices, profits, etc. – except possibly among a small minority of very small specialist firms. Neither do they appear to have much impact on the disclosure and exchange of technical information in this area. (Of the few recent exceptions to this general conclusion that we can mention, by far the most important is that of the P.A.L. colour television system, where selectivity in licensing could help to delay the emergence in Europe of serious export competition from Japanese set manufacturers.) The essential reason is that patents are seldom capable of offering an appreciable element of protection in a field where the bulk of innovative effort (at least in industry) is devoted to the design and development of improved components and sets or systems of equipment, with relatively little devoted to basic patentable inventions with wide commercial application, except by a handful of very large firms (mainly centred in the U.S.A.).

Even where patents are obtained on 'basic' developments, firms in this field are likely to grant licences on them relatively freely, for several reasons. Thus, they are likely to be Government suppliers, and to rely heavily on the Government for R & D contracts or straight subsidisation of research, and the Government is unlikely to approve a restrictive licensing policy, at least towards domestic firms. There is likely to be a large technical overlap between the major research-based firms in the field because they work on more or less the same range of central technical problems, and there is therefore both scope and incentive for unfettered patent clearance in which virtually all participate. Above all, straight patent licences normally give very little of value away, since they are seldom of much positive use without a great deal of scientific and technical expertise to back them up. We did find that innovating firms in the electronics field sometimes exercise control over the spread of important new products and new technology developed by them, but this is done much more often by the selective communication of know-how and technical expertise to other major firms than by refusal or restriction of patent licences. In most cases in electronics, patents are a comparatively ineffective monopoly instrument, and the advent of a compulsory licensing system would affect neither the industry's technical effort nor its general degree of competitiveness to an appreciable extent.

### *Other electrical engineering*

The answers for other electrical machinery and apparatus are similar in many respects to those for the electronics and allied industries. Thus, the same points apply with regard to the insignificance of patent protection compared with unpatented technical information, etc. as a means of controlling the spread of new products and techniques, the technical overlap between leading research-based firms, the extreme rarity of valid 'basic' patents and, to a smaller extent, the importance of the Government as customer and provider of R & D funds to the electrical industry.

However, we did detect instances of selectivity in the granting of patent licences on certain types of electrical machinery and apparatus which were of a more than minor character and which were, as might be expected, more akin to the policies of mechanical engineering firms than those of electronics firms. As in mechanical engineering, these cases did not add up to very much in terms of R & D or sales, and they do not detract very much from our general impression that compulsory licensing would make very little overall difference to the R & D or the prices and profits of the firms concerned. Likewise, its impact on the publication of technical knowledge and the exchange of technology through licensing would probably be rather small, although of substantial importance in a very few instances.

### *Man-made fibres*

Of the various industries covered in our inquiry, man-made fibres (more specifically, the synthetic fibres branch[1]) is the one that we can discuss with least confidence. This is mainly because the nature of technical innovation in synthetic fibres has changed quite markedly in the last few years from what it was in the era that saw the development and introduction of the great synthetic fibres – nylon and Terylene.[2]

[1] Synthetic fibres are those produced from polymers synthesised from basic chemicals, and should be distinguished from the older 'cellulosics', based on rayon and protein fibres.
[2] 'Terylene' is the registered trade mark of I.C.I.'s polyester fibre.

Yet it is with fundamental innovations that a study of the patent system should be most concerned, and for that reason it seems appropriate to consider the basic developments of preceding years as well as our findings for the present day.

The evidence from our inquiry suggests that the patent system has currently very little impact on R & D in man-made fibres, and virtually none on the competitive state of the industry. The basic patents on nylon and Terylene, both in the U.K. and overseas, have now expired and no fundamentally new fibre has been discovered that approaches either of these in importance.[1] The principal technical achievement in the synthetic field in the last ten years has probably been the rapid development of yarn-processing techniques (mainly crimping and other forms of yarn texturising), which have effectively enabled the spinning process to be short-cut, and which have opened the way for the tremendous expansion in the use first of nylon and then Terylene in the knitting industry. At the present time, the tendency is for technical interest to move towards the search for new end-products which will reduce the fibre-makers' reliance on the traditional textile industry. Success in this area seems at the moment to be relatively limited, apart perhaps from the development of 'heterofils' – bi-component fibres bonded under heat and pressure to produce a new kind of 'matted' fabric – which are thought to have great potential for dress and knitwear.

While patents of some importance have been obtained on certain of these developments, notably I.C.I.'s master patents on Crimplene (a variety of textured Terylene which has become well established for dress and coat fabrics) and on the heterofils, they do not have the same unique protective value as the basic nylon and Terylene patents. The essence of technical advance in yarn texturising has been improvement in the speed and reliability of processes, and in particular a phenomenal increase in machinery running speeds. Much of this sort of work is not patentable, and where patent clearance has to be obtained it is usually of little positive use to the licensee without the very considerable know-how and operating experience of the licensor. The non-availability of this assistance would greatly hamper potential applicants in a world of compulsory licensing, and it seems hardly likely that there would be much relaxation of the industry's highly selective policy towards know-how licensing in such a world.

But in addition to this, the synthetic fibre industry presents a classic example of a technological revolution which, once started, cannot easily be stopped or retarded without great loss to the innovating firms,

---

[1] Acrylic fibres rival polyester in terms of total output, but their discovery and development (by Du Pont) antedate those of the polyesters.

whatever the competitive situation in which they later find themselves. Bearing in mind the large initial investments made in the 1950s by such firms as Du Pont and I.C.I. in nylon and polyester fibres, it seems unthinkable that the follow-up efforts they have made to improve processes and develop new markets would have been reduced in the face of greater copying or imitation in a world of compulsory licensing. (It could even be argued that such efforts would be redoubled in those circumstances, provided the initial investments had been made.) The most that can be said with confidence in favour of the patent system as it affects the present-day industry is that it probably encourages the publication of technical information, through patent specifications and other literature, which would be kept very much more secret under a compulsory licensing regime. In this respect, as in others, synthetic fibres resembles the basic chemical field, and the consequences for spread of technical information in these industries would probably be rather similar.

### Nylon and Terylene

We pause now to look back at the impact of patents on the invention and early development of the great synthetic fibres, which mainly took place in the 1950s.[1] There is some ground for believing that the basic patents did have an effect during their lifetime on prices and competition in these fibres.[2] It is well known, for instance, that these patents were licensed very selectively and that infringers were vigorously prosecuted. The general pattern was that manufacturing licences were confined to a few major international chemical or textile firms, each of which was granted exclusive or near-exclusive rights in their domestic markets. Thus, Du Pont, owners of the basic patents on nylon 66, granted exclusive U.K. rights to I.C.I. in the 1940s, and British Nylon Spinners was set up as a joint venture with Courtaulds to produce nylon 66 (Bri-Nylon) in the U.K. B.N.S. was taken over by I.C.I. and became part of I.C.I. Fibres Ltd. in 1964 and this company has remained the only producer of nylon 66 in the U.K.

In recent years, I.C.I.'s monopoly of nylon in the U.K. has been challenged by imports of nylon 6, and (since about 1967) nylon 66,[3] and by growing domestic production of nylon 6. (Nylon 6 is an alternative fibre manufactured using a different polymer from 66; its

---

[1] Case studies of the basic inventions can be found in Jewkes *et al.*, *The Sources of Invention*.
[2] See in particular D. P. O'Brien, 'Patent Protection and Competition in Polyamide and Polyester Fibre Manufacture', *Journal of Industrial Economics*, Vol. XII (March 1964) pp. 224–35. The following paragraphs draw heavily on this account.
[3] The last basic U.K. patent on the steam spinning of nylon 66 expired in 1964. Those in Germany and Switzerland expired in 1966, and in France and Canada in 1969.

manufacture did not infringe the nylon 66 patents[1].) Imports now account for a significant share (about one-fifth) of the U.K. market for nylon fibre. British production of nylon 6 remained on a small scale until after 1964, but there are now some four independent U.K. manufacturers – including principally Courtaulds (Celon) and British Enkalon (Enkalon). All are still relatively modest operations by I.C.I.'s standards, but that of Courtaulds is growing rapidly. It is said that, in its earlier years, nylon 6 was an imperfect substitute for nylon 66, especially in end-uses requiring bulked nylon, and was probably more costly to process,[2] but there is nowadays said to be little to choose between them economically, except that nylon 66 has a higher melting point and is stronger than nylon 6, and therefore still has slight advantages in some uses – e.g., in bonded fabrics and as tyre cord.

The picture in Terylene has been fairly similar, except that subsidiary patents continued in existence until 1970, while the basic patents are said to be less pre-emptive of other manufacturers' freedom than those for nylon.[3] The pattern of licensing resembled that of nylon in that the patentee, Calico Printers, confined rights strictly to I.C.I. and Du Pont.[4] I.C.I. established sole control over production of the main types of polyester fibre outside the U.S.A., either directly or through sub-licensing. (Some types fell outside the Terylene patents, and were manufactured by other firms, but they did not approach the commercial success of Terylene.) Large manufacturing operations were built up by I.C.I. in the U.K. (commencing in 1955), Australia and Canada, and other markets were met either by direct export or under licence from I.C.I., the latter being the preferred mode of exploitation on the Continent. Significantly, the proportion of U.K. output exported was and still is much higher in the case of Terylene than of nylon. I.C.I. has until recently remained the sole manufacturer in the U.K., but other British firms are now moving into the polyester field – notably Courtaulds (mid-1971); furthermore, imports of polyester commenced in 1971, principally from the E.E.C., Switzerland and Japan, and currently promise to reach sizeable proportions.

[1] Nylon 6 was developed by the German company I. G. Farben, which took out the basic patents in Germany just before the war and launched its fibre, Perlon, during the war. (Du Pont also did basic work on nylon 6 and obtained American patents somewhat later.) I. G. Farben did not obtain British patents because of the war, and nylon 6 has consequently not been protected by patents in the U.K.

[2] O'Brien, *Journal of Industrial Economics*, p. 232.

[3] The last basic U.K. patent on Terylene expired in 1964; that in Japan expired in 1968. Subsidiary U.K. patents on Terylene continued until 1970, but their protective significance is said to be relatively minor.

[4] The U.S. patent was assigned to Du Pont in 1949, while all others were licensed exclusively to I.C.I. C.P.A. did not itself manufacture, relying solely on royalties and payments for assignment.

It appears from these accounts that competition in both nylon and Terylene in the U.K. intensified quite sharply following the expiry of the patents. There is no doubt that prices of both fibres have fallen very substantially since the early 1960s, although this has of course been a feature of both since their first introduction on the market.[1]

It is not easy to judge how far these price reductions can be attributed to the expiry of patents and how far to other developments, such as productivity improvements in synthetic fibres that were not experienced in the cellulosic area, and the large increases in productive capacity built up by the major licensees in the 1960s. One commentator (O'Brien, in the article cited above) is of the view that patents had a fairly significant effect on pricing policy, although they were by no means the only, or the most important, factor. His conclusion for both nylon and Terylene is that the protected position in the home market afforded by international tariffs and patents enabled U.K. manufacturers to charge somewhat more at home than they otherwise would have done, and to subsidise their exports more heavily; he nevertheless observes that since a measure of differential pricing between home sales and exports is emphatically not peculiar to firms having patent protection, especially in industries subject to high tariffs, the influence was probably only a matter of degree.[2]

Our own conclusion would be that patents have been one of a number of factors tending to delay the impact of price competition in both fibres. In the case of nylon, they had the dual effect of helping to postpone nylon 66 imports until the late 1960s, and of helping to limit other

[1] U.K. prices quoted by the major British manufacturers to end-1969 have been reported as follows:

| *Nylon staple: 3 denier* | (Old pence per lb) |
|---|---|
| Prior to May 1950 | 180 |
| June 1950 – March 1954 | 135 |
| April 1954 – October 1955 | 123 |
| October 1955 – December 1961 | 117 |
| December 1961 – March 1964 | 109 |
| April 1964 – April 1965 | 103 |
| May 1965 – February 1966 | 96 |
| March 1966 – July 1967 | 92 |
| July 1967 onwards | 82 |

| *Terylene staple: 3 denier cotton type* | (Old pence per lb) |
|---|---|
| Prior to October 1955 | 144 |
| October 1955 – June 1961 | 120 |
| July 1961 – December 1963 | 110 |
| January 1964 – June 1965 | 90 |
| July 1965 – June 1967 | 80 |
| June 1967 – January 1968 | 59 |
| January 1968 onwards | 62 |

SOURCE: Commonwealth Secretariat, *Industrial Fibres* (London, 1970), p. 139.

[2] O'Brien, *Journal of Industrial Economics*, p. 229.

U.K. manufacturers to the development and production of nylon 6 rather than the initially more attractive nylon 66. In that of Terylene, patents have influenced U.K. prices mainly through their delaying effect on imports of polyester fibres. But it must also be said that I.C.I.'s monopoly over the manufacture of the polymers for nylon 66 and Terylene in the U.K., based on economies of scale in large plants, has probably been a more important factor.

It is even more difficult to assess the impact of patent protection on the basic discovery of nylon and Terylene, and on their subsequent development. Although he does not discuss this point at length, O'Brien states his belief that the large investment in R & D, market promotion and technical assistance to users would not have been justified at unprotected prices by the foreseeable scale of output (page 228). However, it is hard to accept that, if patents were only one of a number of factors helping to create the monopoly, and not the most important, the absence of patent protection would itself have deterred Du Pont and I.C.I. from these undertakings. The sheer size of I.C.I.'s initial investment in new plant for Terylene – £15 million by 1955, in addition to £4 million spent on development between 1941 and 1949[1] – was probably enough to deter others from competing before the success of the venture was established.

For these reasons, we are inclined to doubt that the absence of patent protection would in itself have dissuaded major international companies like Du Pont or I.C.I. from proceeding with the development of nylon or polyester fibres at more or less the pace that they did. Our tentative conclusion on this question is that patents contributed substantially to I.C.I.'s subsequent overseas sales of polyester fibre (and to a lesser extent, nylon), through both the protective element they offered for overseas production and the extra scope they gave for subsidisation of exports from home sales. On the debit side, both nylon and Terylene prices were somewhat (perhaps as much as 20 per cent) higher in the U.K. than they would otherwise have been, for a number of years (possibly between five and ten) following the commercial introduction of the fibres. We doubt, however, that the pace of invention or innovation in either nylon or Terylene would have been very much different in a world of compulsory licensing.

[1] Jewkes *et al.*, *The Sources of Invention*, pp. 214 and 310–12. This implies a capital cost of about £1 per lb of productive capacity, compared with an average selling price of about £0·3 per lb initially.

*Summary of effects*

At the risk of drastic oversimplification, our findings concerning the economic impact of the patent system in comparison with our standard alternative of worldwide compulsory licensing can be summarised as follows:

(*a*) *Industrial research and innovation.* The impact on the rate and direction of inventive and innovative activity undertaken by industry is extremely small on the whole in all areas examined except the 'secondary' (non-basic) chemical industries. There, pharmaceuticals stand out as an industry in which probably at least one-half of invention and innovation is heavily dependent on patent protection. A similar degree of dependence probably exists in crop chemicals and one or two other industries producing research-intensive chemicals for relatively limited markets. Certain other chemical product areas such as novel plastics materials and sophisticated industrial chemicals show a lower but still appreciable degree of patent-dependence. In contrast, R & D etc. in basic chemicals, including petroleum chemicals, is very little affected, and not at all in oil processing and refining.

(*b*) *Non-industrial invention and innovation.* Inventive and innovative activity outside large-scale industry appears on the whole to be very little affected. The small-scale efforts of the individual inventor and the very small firm do not seem to derive anything like as much stimulation from patent monopolies as has sometimes been thought. The profit motive is seldom a principal consideration for the dedicated private inventor, while the work of the very small research-based firm is often complementary to or derived from the operations of larger firms. It is noticeable that small inventors are not very active in the chemical fields found to be responsive to patent protection; they concentrate mainly on the mechanical and electrical field, where 'strong' patents are very few and far between. It should also be noted that the amount of resources devoted to small-scale invention and innovation is quite minor compared with amounts spent in industry.

On the other hand, it cannot be denied that small inventors are prolific generators of patentable inventions in relation to the resources used, and that the proportion of all valuable inventions that is attributable to the small man seems considerably higher than the proportion of resources used by them. Neither can it be denied that there have been cases – although apparently extremely few – in which prospective patent protection has been an important factor in inducing small inventors to persist for years with basic inventions which ultimately became major innovations (after industrial development). The patent system can therefore claim at least part of the credit for a very limited number of important innovations – possibly not many more than a small handful – resulting from the work of the small U.K. inventor in the last ten or so years.

Inventive activity in universities, technical colleges and government research institutions is essentially a subordinate activity deriving from scientific and technical research that owes virtually nothing to the profit motive. Inventions from these sources which have commercial potential are almost invariably transferred to industrial firms, most commonly nowadays through the agency of the National Research Development Corporation. Their development then becomes subject to the same considerations and arguments as apply to other R & D projects undertaken in private industry. For these reasons, the patent system can claim no credit in stimulating 'institutional' research which has not already been counted in relation either to industry or to the small inventor.

(c) *Prices and profits.* The impact of patents on the prices of manufactured goods sold in the U.K. appears on our evidence to be relatively minor in all but a few areas. The main one is in finished and specialty chemicals, where the prices of products dependent on patent protection are probably somewhat higher than they would be under compulsory licensing (assuming that they would be produced in those circumstances), but important instances of possible effects have also been referred to in synthetic fibres and colour television. Other instances of a much more minor nature were found in mechanical engineering and 'other' electrical machinery and apparatus; they were mainly cases oɪ individual patent-dependent products, but one or two were products which were not patent-dependent. In addition, royalties charged in the mechanical engineering field were found to be slightly on the high side, but the proportions of total mechanical engineering production involved were calculated to be very small.

There is some ground for thinking that U.K. prices of nylon and Terylene were appreciably higher for a period after their introduction than they would have been under a compulsory licensing system, but against this it must be remembered that patents were an important factor in assisting overseas sales of synthetic fibres by British manufacturers during the same period.

Traditionally, pharmaceutical firms have gained a reputation for earning high profits on the strength of patent protection, and evidence can be cited to suggest that the prices of leading drugs sold to the National Health Services in the 1950s were very much higher than those from unpatented sources. So far as the U.K. is concerned, this problem has been largely, if not wholly, dealt with by voluntary price regulation, backed up by the strengthened 'Crown Use' provisions of the Patents Act and supplemented latterly by the vigilance of the Monopolies Commission.

(*d*) *Spread of technical information.* There seems little doubt that patent protection has a considerable impact on the publication of technical information, both in the form of patent specifications and as technical literature relating to patented inventions. The main type of information affected is that relating to critical details of industrial processes, especially in the fields of basic chemicals and mass-produced mechanical components, where process technology absorbs a good deal of R & D effort.

The main consequence of the increased tendency to patent information in these fields (as compared with patenting under a compulsory licensing system) is that the formal exchange of technical information between firms through licensing is much facilitated. This is mainly because a patent constitutes a tangible and precise claim to an invention, whereas there may be considerable doubt as to the origin and status of information supplied in pure know-how agreements.

By comparison, the 'general information' benefits associated with the greater public availability of the information in question are probably fairly minor, although not negligible.

(*e*) *U.K. trade.* The special question of the impact of patent protection on U.K. trade would be difficult to resolve without a much more extensive study than the one we were able to undertake. So far as we can assess it, the main effect is that U.K. net exports of finished and specialty chemicals are somewhat higher than they would be under worldwide compulsory licensing; earnings from overseas investment (net of payments on inward investment) in the chemical field are also higher, as are net royalty receipts in this and other fields, but these effects are relatively small. The order of magnitude of the total impact on the current balance of payments in 1968 in comparison with the standard alternative was probably between £50 and £100 million. In other words, while the overall impact of patent protection is probably fairly small in relation to both total U.K. production and exports, it is by no means negligible when considered in relation to surpluses and deficits on the balance of payments.

(*f*) *Administrative costs.* We have throughout the preceding chapters refrained from a sustained consideration of the administrative cost of the patent system. However we cannot at this stage ignore the fact that the system involves an economic cost in that it requires not only a central administrative and judicial establishment involving patent officials, examiners and their supporting staff, but also many specialist or semi-specialist personnel in industry, as well as independent patent agents and semi-specialist legal and technical consultants.

The relevant point here is that the present patent system probably costs, if anything, less to run than would a practical, functioning, compulsory licencing system of the sort envisaged. The latter would probably not permit any reduction in the existing ranks of industrial patent and licensing personnel, for although the work of patenting might diminish under such a system, that of licensing might increase somewhat, and it is doubtful whether firms could cut down their patent or licensing departments to any measurable extent. Moreover, the size of the Patent Office would doubtless increase, in order to cope with the increase in compulsory licence decisions that would be required under a 'thoroughgoing' system. Conceivably a compulsory licence unit or office of some size would be needed, for, although the majority of applications would probably be dealt with routinely, a certain proportion would be referred to the Comptroller for arbitration, and the numbers requiring an extended hearing would probably be much greater than those under the limited compulsory licensing provisions of the existing system.

(g) *Summary*. The net outcome of these considerations may be summed up briefly as follows. The main advantage of a thoroughgoing compulsory licensing system in comparison with the existing patent system would be that U.K. prices of a range of finished and specialty chemicals (but probably few pharmaceuticals) and of certain special types of machinery and equipment in the mechanical and electrical engineering fields would be moderately lower than at present. There would in addition be somewhat less market security in general, mainly in the chemical and mechanical engineering fields, although the volume of patent licensing (including licensing under compulsory licence provisions or influenced by them) would probably not in the long run be very much greater than under the present system. Against that, the volume of R & D and innovation in finished and specialty chemicals would be significantly lower, and in pharmaceuticals and certain other areas very much lower, than at present. The volume of inventive activity by the small inventor would probably not be much affected, but small numbers of important basic inventions might be lost, and the small man in general would be worse off. The amount of patenting and other public disclosure of important process technology would be considerably reduced, as would transfer of technology under formal licence between research-based firms. The U.K. balance of payments would probably suffer to the extent of £50–100 million per annum (at 1968 prices). Finally, there would if anything be an increase rather than a saving in the administrative costs of the system.

If these broad findings are correct, the balance of economic advantage for the U.K. lies narrowly with the existing patent system rather than a compulsory licensing system of the sort outlined.


B.  SOME OTHER POSSIBLE ALTERNATIVES

We now consider how the preceding findings might be modified, were other alternatives adopted for the purpose of assessing effects. Firstly, it is of interest to speculate (and we can do little more than that) on the consequences of even more radical departures from the existing system – while retaining the notion of broadly parallel arrangements in the U.K. and most other western countries. Later, we look briefly at the implications of a 'unilateral' compulsory licensing system in the U.K.

### Compulsory licensing with 'conventional' royalties

One variation of the standard alternative would be a (worldwide) compulsory licensing system on the same general lines but with 'conventional' instead of 'commercially reasonable' royalties. This would differ from the flexible system we have imagined so far in that it would impose a relatively narrow and rigid pattern of royalties more or less mechanically, making only limited distinction between different licensing situations. Royalty rates in such a system would differentiate between the commoner types of licences (e.g., manufacturing, user and selling licences), they would probably make some allowance for scale of production under licence, and they might attempt to distinguish broadly between patents of differing economic importance, although this would clearly be hard to achieve properly using a set of near-automatic rules. An example of the sort of provision that might be made would be that patent royalties for manufacturing licences (not including payments for know-how) on a patent of 'moderate' value would be set at three per cent of the net selling value of output under licence where the latter is less than £250,000 per annum, the rate diminishing on a sliding scale thereafter; rates for user and selling licences would be lower, as would those for minor patents, while those for 'basic' patents would be higher. (The system might be supplemented by alternative 'lump sum' provisions that could, if preferred, be invoked by the licensor.)

The main advantage of this type of system as compared with our standard alternative is that it would be simpler and less costly for the authorities to operate – provided that the grounds for appeal were defined rather narrowly. (If this were not done, the system would become in practice little different from the standard alternative.) Its main disadvantage is that it would almost certainly be incapable of distinguishing adequately between patents of differing importance; in particular, it would tend to set payments for trivial or minor patents too high, and those on basic patents and patents with a high research content too low. The former tendency would encourage an unwarrantable amount of inventive activity in trivial subjects which would nevertheless pay well, if taken up by licensees. It would operate more especially against the interests of the small firm which seeks to avoid infringement actions and therefore takes licences because it is unable to afford the costs of designing sound numerous minor patented improvements. The tendency to underestimate the correct level of royalties for expensive and basic patents would in due course discourage the work on basic developments which depends to a substantial extent on royalty income – the bulk of which would (if our earlier findings are correct) survive under a genuinely flexible compulsory licensing system.

Apart from these considerations, there would probably not be a great deal of difference between a compulsory licensing system with conventional royalties and one with 'commercially reasonable' royalties. Outside the more highly patent-sensitive branches of chemicals and engineering identified in our industrial inquiry, the rate of invention and innovation by industrial firms would not be very much affected under either alternative – provided royalties were fixed at rates similar on average to those under the present system. As under our standard alternative, the extent of secrecy in many areas of process technology would probably increase as compared with the present situation, while prices of sophisticated chemical products and certain advanced kinds of machinery and equipment would probably be very slightly lower than under the present system.

### Compulsory licensing without royalties

A compulsory licensing system that totally or virtually eliminated payments for patent licences would represent a second radical step away from the patent system as we know it. Such a system could be operated by declaring all patents compulsorily subject to licences of right immediately or soon after grant. The result would be virtual abandonment of the present system, for a patent that is available to all (or almost all) applicants without charge has no economic value beyond any attaching to an official certificate of invention.

This alternative was not discussed with responding firms in detail because it was felt to be too unrealistic to merit much attention in our industrial inquiry, but general comments by industrialists to whom the idea was mentioned confirmed our impression that few if any firms would bother to take out patents in such circumstances. Some patenting activity would still take place, but it would be mainly by individuals seeking to establish priority over inventions for purposes other than a direct economic return.[1]

As serious as the drying up of patent applications from industrial sources, if not more so, would be the cessation of the bulk of associated publication of inventions, research results, industrial methods and processes, etc., in scientific and technical literature. It is probably no exaggeration to say that a tight curtain of security would descend over large areas of new industrial technology. Only the broadest indications of new processes, equipment, materials, etc., would be publicly disclosed; the details would be guarded with very much more care than is currently devoted to patented inventions and improvements. R & D departments of industrial firms would tend to become very much more security-conscious than they presently are.

It is extremely difficult to assess the impact of such an increase in industrial secrecy on the effectiveness of efforts to develop new technology and new products and on the transfer of technical information between firms. Our impression is that the impact would be largest in the chemical industry and in electronics, in both of which the publication and licensing of technical developments is often tied closely to patents. On the whole, engineering firms would probably be less heavily affected, partly because these firms have shown themselves better able to manage the formal exchange of information through pure know-how agreements (i.e., without patents), and partly because major new advances of a patentable kind are rarer in the engineering field.

Apart from greater secrecy, mentioned above, the main immediate consequence of switching to a compulsory licensing system with zero royalties, as compared with a similar system with 'fair' royalties, would of course be that *patent* royalties (i.e., royalties in payment for patent rights) would cease to be paid. Nevertheless a considerable portion of what are generally included as royalties under licence agreements would survive for, as we have seen, a sizeable element of these comprises payments for know-how etc., some of which – and perhaps the great bulk outside chemicals – would continue to be generated and licensed

---

[1] If small financial inducements were offered selectively under such a system – e.g., cash awards of up to (say) a thousand pounds on meritorious inventions, together with waiving of fees for successful applications – small inventors might respond in greater numbers than at present, whereas industrial firms would be unlikely to think the effort of patenting worthwhile.

even were the patent system substantially abandoned. Indeed, given the additional secrecy, payments of this particular type might well increase.

It was shown in Chapter 8 (see, in particular, Table 8.7, columns (4) and (5)), that total receipts from royalties and licence fees amount on average to approximately 12 per cent of domestic R & D expenditures by firms in our sample, the proportions in chemicals and mechanical engineering being, on the whole, much higher than in other fields (and the bulk of receipts being received from overseas). Our impression is that at least half in basic chemicals and probably over three-quarters in the engineering and electrical fields – not including electronics – are essentially payments for know-how,[1] and that the bulk of these would be unaffected under a compulsory licensing system with zero royalties. If so, the only industries in our sample that would suffer serious royalty losses in relation to their total R & D expenditure would (on the basis of Table 8.7) be pharmaceuticals and possibly basic chemicals. Losses might also be experienced elsewhere in the sample – e.g., by firms producing sophisticated materials or machinery – which although small in terms of other magnitudes might well be large in relation to the R & D in question. If this occurred it might cause them to cut back special R & D programmes. However, the total reduction in R & D effort as compared with the likely outcome under our standard alternative would probably be fairly small, except in finished and specialty chemicals, where it might be quite severe.

Finally it should be noted that the virtual cessation of industrial patenting activity envisaged here would have implications for the cost of administering the patent system which should not be overlooked in a comprehensive assessment. It seems reasonable to expect that national patent offices would survive, but on a considerably smaller scale, and that most of the expenditure by firms on their patent departments (but probably not on licensing) would be saved. Our guess would be that approximately two-thirds of the total cost to firms of protecting and licensing their British inventions at home and overseas might be saved, were industrial patenting virtually to cease. If the figures given in Chapter 6 (see Table 6.4) are roughly correct, this implies that firms in our sample might save amounts equivalent on average to about 2 per cent of their R & D expenditures, of which about one-third would represent a saving on expenditures on U.K. patents. For the economy as a whole, this implies a saving of highly qualified manpower valued at roughly £13 million in 1968 (i.e. rather over 2 per cent of £625 million[2]).

[1] In finished and specialty chemicals and electronics, the proportion relating essentially to patent clearance is probably relatively high.
[2] The figure of 2 per cent used here allows for the facts that, whereas over half of patent

*No patent system*

The switch from a compulsory licensing system with zero royalties to a world without patents would be a relatively minor step. In itself, it would have little impact on the behaviour of industrial firms which would, we believe, largely ignore patents in either case. The main result as compared with the previous alternative would be that individuals would no longer be able to take out patents, whereas many might to do under a zero royalty system (especially if token 'award to inventors' were offered under such a system). Small inventors, like firms in the previous section, would be obliged to negotiate in secret with prospective licensees and this would undoubtedly greatly weaken their bargaining position, and greatly hamper the transfer of inventions from smaller inventors to the industrial firms which largely develop and implement them. The effect would certainly be to discourage the inventive efforts of the individual and the very small firm, many of whom would survive under a compulsory licensing system with 'fair' royalties, or even much more modest financial awards.

Apart from this, the impact of having no patent system (as compared with our standard alternative) would be very similar to that of a compulsory licensing system with zero royalties.

For completeness, it should be pointed out that the entire costs of operating the patent system would be saved under this alternative. Assuming that industry accounts for roughly three-quarters of the cost of the system in the U.K., and that the estimate of £13 million for industry given above is broadly correct, this implies a total saving of highly qualified manpower valued at about £17 million in 1968.

*Float glass – an illustration*

As an illustration of the arguments in the preceding pages, it is useful to consider briefly one of the most important single innovations made in British industry since the war – the Float Glass process. This process was conceived by Sir Alastair Pilkington in 1952 and was developed by Pilkington Brothers to the stage of commercial production by 1959. The first U.K. patent was applied for in 1953 and granted in 1957. The process has almost completely superseded the plate glass process for manufacturing high quality flat glass, largely because it has eliminated the relatively costly and wasteful processes of grinding and

expenditure by U.K. firms is on obtaining overseas protection, much of the cost is incurred in the U.K., and that foreign firms utilise British patent agents and the facilities of the British Patent Office, in obtaining protection in the U.K. for their inventions. The figure of £625 million relates to domestic R & D performed by U.K. industry in 1967–8.

polishing entailed by that method.[1] Subsequent improvements have increased its capabilities in manufacturing different thicknesses of glass and it is now an economic alternative to the sheet process for ordinary window glass, while producing a higher quality product.

The float glass innovation involved both a brilliant and important basic idea which proved to be patentable – namely, the idea of forming a continuous ribbon of glass by a process in which hot glass from the melting furnace is floated along the surface of an enclosed bath of molten metal[2] – and years of expensive and pioneering development effort resulting in a succession of further important and patentable innovations and an accumulation of industrial know-how which were essential to enable the basic idea to be put into commercial practice.[3] In the period up to 1972 over 100 U.K. patent applications had been filed, with corresponding applications in some cases in over 50 other countries.

As was made clear by the Company to the Monopolies Commission, Pilkington at no stage intended to monopolise the float glass process. Had it attempted to do so, the major glass producers in the world would have retaliated by re-doubling their own R & D efforts and by suspending its access to their processes, some of which are utilised by Pilkington. Moreover, Pilkington was not in a position to meet world demand outside the U.K. and the territories of its overseas manufacturing subsidiaries, and fully foresaw that much overseas exploitation of the invention would have to be done via licensing. Licences are granted for manufacturing in the licensee's home territory and are non-exclusive, with export rights depending upon individual circumstances. They provide for the free exchange of know-how and patented improvements relating to the float process, although the licensee may license others to use his own patents associated with the technology if he wishes.

Licensing commenced in 1962 and by 1969 all the world's major plate glass manufacturers had taken licences. Pilkington's receipts from float glass licences totalled £17½ million by end-1969, all from overseas. Receipts include lump sum payments and a royalty on sales. Royalties in 1971–2 were running at over £9 million per annum. By

---

[1] For a technical description of the process, see the lecture by Dr L. A. B. Pilkington (now Sir Alastair Pilkington) to the Royal Society in *Proceedings of the Royal Society*, A, Vol. 314 (16 December 1969). Valuable accounts with commercial details can be found in Jewkes *et al.*, *The Sources of Invention*, pp. 334–7 and in the Monopolies Commission Report, *Flat Glass* (H.M.S.O., 7 Feb. 1968).

[2] Pilkington, *Proceedings of the Royal Society*, p. 8.

[3] It took Pilkington Brothers seven years and £4 million of development expenditure to make any saleable glass and a further £3 million of development expenditure before the process could achieve the set objective of replacing the plate glass process. The present day (1972) capital cost of a float glass plant of viable commercial size is very approximately £10 million.

mid-1972 float licences had been granted to 21 manufacturers in 12 countries (Canada, U.S.A., Mexico, Australia, Japan, U.S.S.R., Czechoslovakia, France, West Germany, Italy, Belgium and Spain). It can accordingly be seen that, in terms of licence receipts alone, the float glass project has turned out to be a profitable venture; in this as in other respects it is exceptional even among the more successful kind of patented industrial innovations.

There is in our view no question but that Pilkington would have undertaken the float glass innovation in a world of compulsory licensing, whether or not the system provided for patent royalties. The venture would have been justified solely on the basis of the very substantial savings it has brought about in the Company's own operating and capital costs; the prospect of such cost-savings has induced all major plate glass manufacturers to spend large sums in attempts to find a radical improvement for the plate glass process and Pilkington's management are firmly of the view that, if float glass had not been perfected, some other method would have been developed by a competitor, on which Pilkington would have had to take licences.

This argument turns, of course, on the assumption that the float glass or a similar kind of process, like much new process technology considered in our study, could be protected in a compulsory licensing world by keeping the essential information secret, at least for long enough to give the developing firm an adequate lead in applying the new technology. If this is (as we believe) true, no leading glass manufacturer could sit back safely in such a world in the expectation of obtaining the fruits of others' R & D at minimal cost. The pressure to carry through even a highly speculative type of project like float glass would not be greatly diminished in such a world.

The relevant point here is that whereas Pilkington would probably have wished to patent the float glass process in a compulsory licensing system with reasonable commercial royalties, it would probably have been very reluctant to do so under a system that allowed no patent royalties. In the former case, the company could anticipate receiving much the same patent royalties as were actually earned under its relatively liberal licensing policy, without sacrificing much genuine control over the spread of the process. Quite apart from the problem of know-how, it is hardly likely that a major competitor would have insisted on a licence to manufacture in the U.K. alongside Pilkington, since, if the latter's evidence to the Monopolies Commission (e.g., page 54) is to be believed, the U.K. market alone will not support more than one local flat glass manufacturer using the latest large-scale production and warehousing methods.

In the latter case, however, the Company might well have adopted a policy of complete secrecy and sought to conduct licensing without reference to patents. In doing so, it would have saved effort and expenditure on obtaining patents without sacrificing anything in the way of royalties (since patent royalties would be zero in this case, whether it patented or not) – while control over the spread of technical information would be greater without patent disclosure. Although licensing would in general be more difficult in the absence of patents and the published material linked with them, reasonably favourable licences could probably have been negotiated where an invention of such key importance was involved and where potential licensees were few in number, readily identifiable and long accustomed to licensing each other. Admittedly, it seems doubtful that, without patents, Pilkington could have earned quite as much in pure know-how payments as it actually received in royalties, or that it could have expected to exert as much bargaining power in such matters as the re-negotiation of agreements in this field. In these respects, Pilkington would probably be rather worse off under a compulsory licensing system with zero royalties (or, indeed, in a world without patents), than it would be under a system that provided for the payment of 'fair' royalties.

*Compulsory licensing in the U.K. only*

We finally consider briefly the consequences of a 'unilateral' compulsory licensing system in the U.K., foreign systems being essentially unaltered. More precisely, it is imagined that a thoroughgoing compulsory licensing system with commercially reasonable royalties operates in the U.K., other countries retaining the monopoly element in their patent systems as at present. In these circumstances British firms would be obliged to grant compulsory licences on patents in their domestic markets, without being able to insist on reciprocal treatment from foreign firms in the latters' main markets.

As suggested in Chapter 9, the principal implication of such arrangements, as compared with a *worldwide* regime of compulsory licensing, and considered from the viewpoint of the U.K. economy as a whole rather than that of individual firms, would be that the competitive position of British research-based firms in relation to their foreign counterparts would be considerably weaker – particularly in fields where R & D effort is sensitive to patent protection. This follows from our assumption that whereas much R & D by British-based firms in pharmaceuticals and other finished and specialty chemicals would be abandoned or heavily cut back if compulsory licences were available on British patents, R & D in similar fields by foreign-based firms would not be much affected by the weakening in the status of their British patents, since the latter would affect a minor part of their total market. The impact would show most clearly as a deterioration in the balance of U.K. external trade in the affected fields (see pages 223–5). The extent of the net deterioration in the U.K.'s chemical trade was estimated tentatively at some £110 million, as compared with the actual balance in 1968.

The implications of unilateral compulsory licensing are harder to assess in fields where the rate and direction of invention and innovation by British firms would not be much affected – i.e. fields other than the finished and specialty chemical industries. Two main kinds of effects seem likely in these fields. Firstly, since the bargaining position of British firms under unilateral compulsory licensing arrangements would be much weakened, the terms they would be able to secure in 'willing' licensing with foreign firms would probably be markedly less favourable than under the present system. Hence the volume of licensing between British and foreign research-based firms, which as we have seen constitutes the bulk of licensing activity involving British firms, might well be somewhat lower on this account as probably would net U.K. royalty income from overseas. Secondly, British firms' shares of their domestic markets might be affected in some cases. Thus, British firms (especially those without a substantial stake in R & D) would probably attempt to increase their market shares in areas dominated by foreign-based technology, while foreign firms would retaliate in areas where British technology is important. It is difficult to estimate the net effects of these developments, but they are not likely to be large, for several reasons: firstly, the areas (outside chemical specialties) where patent protection is instrumental in deterring competition are relatively minor, and innovating firms would probably cease to patent in these areas; and secondly, where patents are not a major consideration, the smaller non-research-based firms which are the main potential applicants for compulsory licences would find it no easier to overcome problems of secret know-how or scale economies than they do at present.

To the extent that compulsory licensing did expand, international royalty payments both by and to British firms would also increase, but this tendency would be counteracted by the damping effect on U.K. royalty income, mentioned above. And whereas imports of output under compulsory U.K. licence and profits payable to overseas companies might expand, there would be no corresponding increase in U.K. exports or overseas profits (because there would be no weakening of patent protection overseas). While we have rather little detailed evidence on these various effects, it seems safe to conclude that they would be significantly adverse on balance for the U.K. as a whole, and especially for the U.K. balance of payments in the affected fields.

It might perhaps be argued that the increase in competition in U.K. markets that would probably follow from a unilateral compulsory licensing system would benefit the U.K. consumer through reductions in the prices of patented items. However, it seems unlikely that the shifts in U.K. market shares attributable to this factor would be large enough to affect prices very much, although it might do in some exceptional cases, and we would guess that any benefit from this source would be heavily outweighed by the resource cost of correcting the U.K.'s balance of payments in the absence of any compensating improvement in the competitiveness of British manufacturers in foreign markets.

## C. CONCLUSIONS AND POLICY IMPLICATIONS

The main finding of our study, summarised in Section A above, is that the economic arguments in favour of the existing patent system, so far as we have been able to assess them, marginally outweigh those of a (worldwide) compulsory licensing system with 'commercially reasonable' royalties – considered by us as the most feasible of possible radical alternatives to the present system. In Section B we ventured beyond the central pre-occupation of our study to compare our standard alternative with a series of other possible alternatives. The conclusions, although based largely on rather tentative extensions of our main arguments, are thought to be sufficiently unambiguous to merit inclusion here, despite their relatively sketchy nature.

As far as we can judge, there would be rather little to choose between our standard alternative and a compulsory licensing system with conventional (rigid) royalties. The latter would permit some economy in the central administrative costs of a thoroughgoing compulsory licensing system – which would probably somewhat exceed those of the existing patent system – but would contain inflexibilities which would tend to encourage trivial invention and discourage worthwhile types of industrial R & D which would survive under a 'fair-royalty' system.

By contrast, a compulsory licensing system with zero royalties would represent virtual abandonment of the patent system as a stimulus to sustained industrial invention and innovation. Its main effect, as compared with our standard alternative, would be the disappearance of almost all patent activity by firms, and the plunging of industrial R & D and licensing into an atmosphere of even greater secrecy. This would tend to decrease further the effectiveness of R & D efforts and hamper licensing in certain fields (without causing it to cease altogether), while in others no marked reduction in any of these activities is likely. Some industries – notably chemicals and electronics – would experience quite appreciable losses of patent royalties, and this would tend to diminish their R & D, but outside these fields the general effect would not be very noticeable. The only solid advantage as compared with our standard alternative would be the saving of a high proportion of industrial expenditure on patent activity, including the costs of the central patent administration, so far as these are attributable to industry. Compared with losses to industry in other respects, however, these savings would be quite small.

It would be a short step to move from a compulsory licensing system with zero royalties to formal abandonment of the patent system. The main impact of this particular step would probably be felt by the small inventor, who might continue to patent under a zero-royalty system, especially if token cash awards to inventors were provided. Inventive activity by the small man would probably suffer considerably in a patentless world, for patents play an important part in negotiations between small inventors and the large firms to which they usually wish to assign or license their inventions. Again, the only definite advantage of having no patents as compared with our standard alternative would be the saving in the costs of operating the system, but these are a relatively minor factor in the total picture.

*Unilateral* adoption of a compulsory licensing system by the U.K. would be quite seriously disadvantageous on balance to the U.K. economy. The main disadvantages, as compared with our standard alternative, would be concentrated in the special fields where R & D is sensitive to patent protection, and would emerge mainly in the balance of external trade in these fields. Furthermore, industries where R & D is less sensitive to patent protection would probably suffer somewhat, essentially through a deterioration in the terms of licensing agreements with foreign firms, which would be reflected in a loss of international royalty earnings and some deterioration in the competitiveness of U.K.-based firms relative to foreign-based firms in British markets.

If these judgments are broadly correct, none of the various modifications considered above appears economically preferable to our standard alternative, and some are distinctly less preferable. It therefore seems reasonable to conclude that our central findings in favour (if only marginally so on the whole) of the existing patent system as compared with a worldwide compulsory licensing system with 'fair' royalties hold *a fortiori* with regard to other alternatives of a yet more radical or of a unilateral nature.

*Policy implications*

Since we have concluded that the existing patent system is preferable on balance in Britain, though in many fields only marginally, to any alternative system, it follows that we would not wish to recommend any root-and-branch changes in it. Nevertheless, within the present broad framework there is room for many possible modifications, as the recommendations of the Banks Committee show. Are there any changes which would seem to be desirable in the light of our conclusions?

It might be best to start by considering briefly some of the more important changes recommended by Banks, although since one of us was a member of that Committee it is scarcely surprising that we are in broad agreement with most of its recommendations. The main task of the Committee, it will be recalled, was to review the law in the light of the need for greater international collaboration and many of its conclusions derive from this (for example the separation of search from examination). Greater international collaboration was considered desirable, partly to secure greater uniformity between countries and partly to lighten the heavy administrative burdens increasingly associated with patenting. The attempt to secure greater uniformity, especially within Europe, had another effect, however: it led to suggestions for strengthening the patent system in several ways, for example by bringing 'absolute novelty' within the jurisdiction of the Patent Office. A further suggestion for strengthening patents that derived from European considerations was the recommendation that the patent term should be extended to twenty years. How do these suggestions for reinforcing the patent system look in the light of our research?

We have found no evidence that the present system is seriously defective in encouraging invention and innovation, so far as these activities are likely to be influenced by patent protection in today's industrial conditions – which we believe is, in most industries, not very far. This is the case even with such patent-dependent industries as pharmaceuticals, where the Government has weakened the patent monopoly in several ways.[1] It is true that we have been told by some industrialists that British patents are commonly so weak as to be of derisory value, although we are inclined to take with a pinch of salt their view that this produces widespread disrespect for the patent system among British manufacturers. (It seems to us that a company's

---

[1] However if, as we believe, activity under (or inspired by) Section 41 is now beginning to be more important, and continues to be so, the evidence of our inquiry suggests that there will in time be a serious and widespread check to fundamental R & D in the drug field. For that reason, we support the recommendation of the Banks Committee that Section 41 be repealed.

attitude to the patent system reflects very much the importance of its stake in patents; we encountered very few people in chemical firms who thought that the system could be taken lightly.) Accordingly, it is hardly surprising that we should have reached the rather milk-and-watery conclusions that we have. But while one can sympathise with those who want more certainty from the system – and we have no objection to the Banks Committee's suggestions aimed in this direction, provided that greater international collaboration yields economies in the work of granting patents – we doubt whether our conclusions would have been appreciably affected if the British patent system had been as strong, say, as the German one. In any event, while there may be good arguments for attempting to improve the general *validity* if British patents, we see no case for a substantial strengthening of the legal monopoly that goes with them. We think, for example, that a twenty-year patent would probably be less desirable than the present sixteen-year patent. Although this particular change is unlikely to make any appreciable difference to expenditure on R & D, because of the heavy discounting normally applied to distant years in major decisions on risky investment projects (as was seen in Chapter 2), it could unnecessarily prolong the period before which competition can bring down prices in the special areas (e.g. drugs and crop chemicals) where prices are thought to be sensitive to patent protection. The other 'strengthening' proposals made by Banks are not likely to have very much economic impact, at least so far as the principal economic criteria considered in our study are concerned. And from many other points of view we are strongly in favour of the recommendations made by Banks, which should clarify the patent law, lead to economies in its operation, and provide greater protection for small inventors and firms.

There is one subject which the Banks Committee looked firmly in the face, and then as firmly turned to look the other way. This is the relationship between patents and restrictive practices. As the Banks Report points out (paragraph 515) and as we said in Chapter 7 (pages 130–4), the absence of compulsion to register patent licences with the Patent Office means that very few licences are in fact registered and that public knowledge of restrictive practices in patent licences is very deficient. Similarly, the Restrictive Practices authorities have so far unearthed very little information about the nature of restrictions in patent licences, as we also pointed out in Chapter 7. One of the main findings of our inquiry is that certain types of restrictions, in particular ones relating to territorial markets for output under licence and to use of know-how, are fairly common in licence agreements in the chemical and engineering fields. Thus, for example, reciprocal restrictions affecting territorial use of know-how are not uncommon in cross-licences.

We recognise of course, as the Banks Committee did, that since monopoly is of the essence of patenting, one cannot apply ordinary restrictive practice criteria to such restrictions; and we agree with the Committee (paras. 516–17) that it is probably better not to burden the Comptroller with restrictive practice questions arising from patents, and that it would be desirable for public interest considerations arising from such restrictive conditions to be dealt with in restrictive practices legislation. There is no easy way in which this can be done, although something should in our view be attempted. Perhaps the simplest suggestion is that the scope of agreements liable for registration under the restrictive practices legislation should be widened to include licence agreements at present exempt. (This would not necessarily require the registration of an impossibly large number of licences; for one thing, many essentially one-way licences would not be registrable, since an agreement is only registrable where more than one party accepts restrictions.) We recognise that some such agreements come within the scope of these Acts already, but a more explicit treatment of them seems desirable than is at present provided for. This would probably entail some additional tests in the legislation – tests that would recognise the monopoly inherent in the patent situation – but these should not prove difficult to devise.

Apart from this, we think that the Registrar of Restrictive Practices should see whether anything more can be done within his powers under the Act as it stands to obtain rulings in the Restrictive Practices Court on the extent of exemptions for patent licences presently provided, especially in the case of agreements that contain a mixture of patent and know-how restrictions. We believe the question of official supervision of know-how restrictions in licence agreements (or rather the lack of it) under restrictive practices legislation to be particularly important, because our study found that whereas patent protection is in itself seldom nowadays an important barrier to competition except in specific fields, the same does not apply to secret manufacturing know-how, which probably constitutes an important protective barrier in a wider range of industries.

There is one matter on which we have reached a very definite conclusion: the lack of wisdom of any move to weaken the patent system in this country while other countries make no changes in the same direction. This would act quite heavily to our national disadvantage, not least as regards the balance of payments, and would have few countervailing advantages. It should be stressed that this conclusion applies to the U.K. but not necessarily to every other country. However unpalatable it may be to developed countries, it is necessary to recognise that countries which make little contribution to invention, and show few signs of doing so in the foreseeable future, may have something on balance to gain from weakening their own patent systems. This could apply particularly to poor countries, and more especially to large poor countries, where the problem of exporting 'pirated' products is not likely to be a serious one. Having done no research on the impact of patents in other countries, we are not in a position to reach any conclusions of our own on this point, but we must emphasise that conclusions drawn from British experience may not be valid elsewhere, especially where industrial conditions are very different.

Turning briefly now to a more specialised subject, our conclusion that patent protection is an important incentive for fundamental R & D in the pharmaceutical field raises some basic issues for public policy, which really go beyond the terms of reference of our study. While it is not within our scope here – or, for that matter, our competence – to evaluate the contribution to human welfare made by research in the pharmaceutical industry, several points can perhaps be made. It is a fact, as the Sainsbury Committee commented, that 'almost all the antibiotics except penicillin and streptomycin were discovered by scientists working in the laboratories of pharmaceutical firms, and this is true of most of the sulphonomides, of the steroids, and of the oral diuretics'. (Para. 211.) By comparison, the universities, government research establishments and other non-profit-making research institutions have been responsible for very few chemotherapeutic discoveries leading to new drugs, although they do virtually all pure research in microbiological and medical fields, and a fair amount of pharmacological research as well. (Cephalosporin is an important recent exception.)[1]

Secondly, it seems widely agreed by the medical profession that success in the field of basic drug research creates a need for further research. Many important drugs are not merely capable of being superseded: they *demand* to be improved upon, and the consequence of not doing so may in some cases (e.g., the early penicillins) be a return to ineffectual treatment, or worse. The use of antibiotics tends not merely to weaken natural resistance to disease: if intensive, it may also provoke the growth of resistant bacteria more powerful than before. Once the path of chemotherapeutic discovery has been embarked upon, highly beneficial as its results undoubtedly are, the consequences of failing to keep up the momentum of discovery are (it seems) likely to be extremely serious. Moreover, as progress is steadily made in the more

[1] Furthermore, we have been told that the record of State-controlled drug research in Communist countries is not good. For example, it is said that virtually no important drug discoveries have arisen in the Soviet Union.

tractable areas of drug research, the prospects for future progress in the less tractable areas are reduced. It was suggested by spokesmen for more than one pharmaceutical firm in our inquiry that the end of the first chemotherapeutic revolution is almost in sight; if so, much greater R & D expenditures will be required in future to produce advances comparable with those of the past. Yet the need for such advances will not diminish, for some extremely damaging diseases, such as cancer, have yet to be overcome.

We should end perhaps by trying to put patents into economic perspective. Important as they are in some industries, they provide on the whole only a very limited inducement for industrial invention and innovation. Where really big risks which involve large sums of money are concerned, the patent system may well not offer a sufficient inducement for public interest purposes. Here above all government intervention and assistance is needed, as for example in aircraft, atomic energy and space technology. The military aspect of these activities is one reason for government assistance, but not we believe the major one: it is the size of the commitment which makes government initiative and help so important. And once this help has been given, patents are of minimal importance, since more than adequate monopoly is provided by the sheet cost of private entry into these industries. Compared with *real* monopolies of this sort, the patent monopoly is small beer. What is more, where it has led to the possibility of abuse, as in pharmaceuticals, it has itself been subject to governmental intervention, and there is every reason to believe that further intervention of this kind would occur if it were found to be necessary. The patent system is essentially weak and vulnerable even in the more industrialised of modern societies, but it does confer some advantages, as we have shown, and it is an important protection for the small firm and the small man. On balance it is a valuable institution, but its economic value overall is quite modest, and it is desirable that extravagant claims should not be made on its behalf.

APPENDIX A. *R & D, net output, employment, fixed assets and*

| | | (1) | | | (2) | | | (3) | | (4) | |
|---|---|---|---|---|---|---|---|---|---|---|---|
| | | R & D (£m) | | | Net output (£m) | | | R & D/Net output (%) | | Index of real net output (1958 = 100) | |
| Industry | Minimum list heading | 1958–9 | 1964–5 | 1967–8 | 1958 | 1963 | 1968 | 1958–63 | 1963–8 | 1963 | 1968 |
| Food, drink, tobacco | 211–29, 231, 239, 240 | 5·5 | 15·0 | 19·6 | 917 | 1,300 | 2,002 | 0·9 | 1·0 | 115·0 | 132·1 |
| Chemicals and allied | 261, 263, 271–7 | 35·7 | 59·5 | 77·0 | 701 | 1,030 | 1,468 | 5·3 | 5·5 | 141·1 | 197·3 |
| Pharmaceuticals | 272 (1) & (2) | [8·0] | [13·3] | 17·2 | 99 | 186 | 287 | 7·2 | 6·4 | 148·0 | 229·4 |
| Plastics | 276 | [6·1] | [10·2] | 13·2 | 49 | 104 | 196 | 10·3 | 7·8 | 192·0 | 324·5 |
| Other | 261, 263, 271, 273–5, 277 | [21·6] | [36·0] | 46·6 | 533 | 740 | 985 | 4·4 | 4·8 | 134·7 | 178·1 |
| Petroleum products | 262 | 6·8 | 10·1 | 11·1 | 35 | 64 | 103 | 16·6 | 12·7 | [164·0] | [254·9] |
| Iron and steel | 311–13 | 5·1 | 12·5 | 14·2 | 549 | 629 | 793 | 1·4 | 1·9 | 111·3 | 123·8 |
| Non-ferrous metals | 321, 322 | 3·0 | 4·8 | 6·7 | 140 | 204 | 305 | 2·2 | 2·3 | 118·7 | 128·8 |
| Mechanical engineering | 331–349 | [24·8] | 40·2 | 62·3 | 1,015 | 1,273 | 2,064 | 2·7 | 3·1 | 121·7 | 153·5 |
| Metal goods, n.e.s. | 391–399 | [5·1] | 6·6 | 7·2 | 439 | 665 | 999 | 1·0 | 0·8 | 108·3 | 122·8 |
| Scientific instruments | 351–352 | [8·8] | 10·6 | 13·8 | 113 | 174 | 278 | 6·6 | 5·4 | [141·6] | [195·2] |
| Electrical engineering | 361–369 | 64·5 | 107·0 | 153·2 | 615 | 933 | 1,403 | 10·7 | 11·1 | 134·1 | 183·6 |
| Electronics and telecommunications | 363, 364 | 24·6 | 78·5 | 115·7 | 211 | 388 | 622 | 16·6 | 19·2 | [168·7] | [239·8] |
| Electrical machinery | 361 | [19·9] | 14·1 | 22·0 | 212 | 224 | 324 | 7·6 | 6·6 | [97·0] | [124·2] |
| Domestic appliances | 365 | [6·4] | 4·6 | 2·7 | 48 | 105 | 133 | 7·1 | 3·1 | [227·9] | [277·1] |
| Other | 362, 369 | [13·7] | 9·8 | 12·8 | 144 | 216 | 324 | 6·4 | 4·2 | [137·5] | [182·9] |
| Ships and marine | 370 (1) & (2) | [2·4] | 4·2 | 2·7 | 227 | 221 | 286 | 1·4 | 1·4 | 77·4 | 67·2 |
| Motor vehicles | 381, 382 | [16·4] | 33·1 | 45·6 | 439 | 794 | 1,091 | 3·9 | 4·2 | [166·0] | [197·2] |
| Railway equipment etc. | 384, 385, 389 | [0·7] | 1·8 | 1·8 | 95 | 68 | 57 | 1·5 | 2·9 | [65·7] | [47·6] |
| Aircraft and equipment | 383 | 100·0 | 138·6 | 163·6 | 285 | 325 | 490 | 38·0 | 37·1 | [104·6] | [136·4] |
| Textiles and man-made fibres | 411–23, 429 | [7·6] | 12·4 | 12·1 | 615 | 792 | 1,104 | 1·4 | 1·3 | 109·6 | 130·5 |
| Man-made fibres | 411 | 6·6 | [10·8] | [10·5] | 50 | 109 | 168 | 10·6 | 7·7 | 220·3 | 390·7 |
| Other | 412–23, 429 | [1·0] | [1·6] | [1·6] | 565 | 683 | 936 | 0·2 | 0·2 | 100·0 | 107·5 |
| Clothing and footwear | 431–3, 441–9, 450 | [1·0] | 1·4 | 1·3 | 352 | 444 | 601 | 0·3 | 0·3 | 117·5 | 120·2 |
| Bricks, pottery, glass etc. | 461–9 | 3·2 | 9·0 | 10·2 | 297 | 412 | 610 | 1·7 | 1·9 | 129·6 | 164·9 |
| Timber and furniture | 471–9 | [0·7] | 1·8 | [3·0] | 212 | 303 | 482 | 0·5 | 0·6 | 112·6 | 135·5 |
| Paper, printing, etc. | 481–9 | [1·3] | 3·5 | [5·9] | 577 | 847 | 1,253 | 0·3 | 0·4 | 127·8 | 151·2 |
| Rubber and products | 491 | [2·4] | 5·1 | 5·8 | 103 | 167 | 264 | 2·7 | 2·5 | [158·9] | [235·1] |
| Other manufactures | 492–9 | [1·7] | 3·2 | 3·4 | 125 | 204 | 359 | 1·4 | 1·2 | 125·8 | 170·0 |
| All manufacturing | | 296·7 | 480·4 | 620·6 | 7,851 | 10,848 | 16,012 | 4·0 | 4·1 | 120·0 | 145·4 |

For notes on these data, see page 368, and for further explanations, see Chapter 4, Section C.

*productivity in U.K. manufacturing industries, 1958–68*

| | (5) | | | (6) | | (7) | | | (8) | | (9) | (10) | |
|---|---|---|---|---|---|---|---|---|---|---|---|---|---|
| | | | | Index of | | Gross fixed assets | | | Index of gross fixed assets | | | Index of | |
| | Employment | | | employment | | (at 1963 replacement | | | (end- | | Share of | productivity | |
| | (thousands) | | | (1958 = 100) | | cost) (£m) | | | 1957 = 100) | | labour in | (1958 = 100) | |
| | | | | | | end- | end- | end- | end- | end- | net output, | | |
| 1958 | 1963 | 1968 | 1963 | 1968 | 1957 | 1962 | 1967 | 1962 | 1967 | 1963 (%) | 1963 | 1968 |
|---|---|---|---|---|---|---|---|---|---|---|---|---|---|
| 726 | 766 | 806 | 106 | 111 | 1,874 | 2,321 | 2,892 | 124 | 154 | 41·8 | 98·7 | 97·1 |
| 424 | 449 | 436 | 106 | 103 | 2,213 | 2,743 | 3,629 | 124 | 164 | 39·5 | 120·7 | 141·0 |
| 61 | 80 | 81 | 131 | 133 | [133] | [178] | [224] | 134 | 168 | 32·8 | 111·3 | 156·5 |
| 30 | 42 | 55 | 140 | 183 | [164] | [227] | [317] | 138 | 193 | 39·4 | 138·3 | 171·6 |
| 337 | 327 | 300 | 97 | 89 | 1,916 | 2,338 | 3,088 | 122 | 161 | 41·2 | 120·6 | 135·6 |
| 20 | 21 | 18 | 105 | 90 | 311 | 466 | 609 | 150 | 196 | 39·0 | 123·8 | 164·8 |
| 440 | 437 | 423 | 99 | 96 | 1,860 | 2,521 | 2,907 | 136 | 156 | 61·5 | 98·3 | 103·9 |
| 128 | 139 | 138 | 109 | 108 | 361 | 449 | 573 | 124 | 159 | 58·8 | 103·1 | 99·8 |
| 966 | 937 | 1,031 | 97 | 107 | 1,337 | 1,641 | 2,031 | 123 | 152 | 62·2 | 112·6 | 123·8 |
| 472 | 543 | 566 | 115 | 120 | 797 | 938 | 1,100 | 118 | 138 | 58·9 | 93·2 | 96·4 |
| 115 | 144 | 170 | 125 | 148 | [88] | [134] | [201] | 152 | 228 | 62·6 | 104·5 | 109·7 |
| 652 | 749 | 767 | 115 | 118 | 1,156 | 1,332 | 1,624 | 115 | 140 | 60·6 | 116·6 | 144·9 |
| 252 | 312 | 349 | 124 | 138 | [176] | [283] | [439] | 161 | 249 | 58·2 | 120·9 | 130·0 |
| 204 | 203 | 172 | 100 | 84 | } 980 | } 1,049 | } 1,185 | } 107 | } 121 | 73·2 | 95·2 | 132·3 |
| 46 | 72 | 72 | 157 | 157 | | | | | | 54·3 | 169·3 | 197·2 |
| 150 | 162 | 174 | 108 | 116 | | | | | | 54·6 | 127·9 | 154·6 |
| 275 | 204 | 180 | 74 | 65 | 566 | 636 | 669 | 112 | 118 | 75·6 | 92·9 | 86·2 |
| 377 | 485 | 511 | 129 | 136 | 835 | 1,101 | 1,353 | 132 | 162 | 58·1 | 127·4 | 134·2 |
| 130 | 77 | 49 | 59 | 38 | 307 | 329 | 330 | 107 | 107 | 88·2 | 101·6 | 103·2 |
| 275 | 255 | 228 | 93 | 83 | 451 | 549 | 616 | 122 | 137 | 71·4 | 103·3 | 138·6 |
| 850 | 749 | 701 | 88 | 83 | 2,276 | 2,296 | 2,430 | 101 | 107 | 57·1 | 117·1 | 139·9 |
| 36 | 37 | 43 | 103 | 119 | [186] | [244] | [313] | 131 | 168 | 32·1 | 180·6 | 256·5 |
| 814 | 712 | 658 | 87 | 81 | 2,090 | 2,052 | 2,117 | 98 | 101 | 61·1 | 109·5 | 121·0 |
| 583 | 554 | 525 | 95 | 90 | 583 | 601 | 650 | 103 | 111 | 64·4 | 120·1 | 123·3 |
| 304 | 304 | 307 | 100 | 101 | 560 | 713 | 985 | 127 | 176 | 58·0 | 116·4 | 124·5 |
| 254 | 263 | 271 | 104 | 107 | 257 | 296 | 362 | 115 | 141 | 63·4 | 104·2 | 113·4 |
| 542 | 585 | 614 | 108 | 113 | 1,273 | 1,520 | 1,840 | 119 | 145 | 57·7 | 113·4 | 119·5 |
| 108 | 116 | 127 | 107 | 118 | 244 | 283 | 375 | 116 | 154 | 56·9 | 143·3 | 176·1 |
| 140 | 176 | 209 | 126 | 149 | 174 | 226 | 319 | 130 | 183 | 55·4 | 98·4 | 103·6 |
| 7,781 | 7,952 | 8,077 | 102 | 104 | 17,506 | 21,212 | 25,679 | 121 | 147 | 56·5 | 108·8 | 118·5 |

NOTES ON THE DATA

This table contains the basic data used for the computation of R & D ratios and productivity growth, discussed in Chapter 4, Section C. The industry classification is that adopted by the Department of Trade and Industry in its periodic (recently, annual) survey of scientific research and development, published, along with other data, jointly by the Department of Education and Science and the Ministry of Technology. M.L.H. numbers refer to the Standard Industrial Classification (Revised 1963).

Although the requisite data were available for the majority of industries shown, some further estimation was needed in the case of certain industries which appear in the sources only in broader groupings, especially for the earlier of the years shown. Data for which an element of estimation by us was necessary are indicated by brackets in the table.

### (1) *Research and development*

Expenditure on research and development (at current prices) carried out within industry (including public corporations and research associations) or financed by it. The latter includes work done for industry by Government research establishments and universities.

The figures relate to firms employing 25 or more persons. Those for 1964–5 and 1967–8 are derived from a near-comprehensive survey of expenditure by large firms and a sample survey of smaller firms. Those for 1958–9 are probably somewhat less reliable, in that they derive from sample estimates of outlays per R & D employee covering about one-half of the field, in conjunction with a more comprehensive survey of R & D employment.

*Sources.* 1958–9: Department of Scientific and Industrial Research, *Industrial Research and Development Expenditure*, 1958, 1964–5 and 1967–8: Department of Education and Science/Ministry of Technology, *Statistics of Science and Technology* (1967 and 1970 editions).

Data in brackets are authors' estimates based on the distribution of R & D between industries in the nearest year for which published data were available. It should be noted that there was no official Inquiry in 1963–4, and the results of the Inquiry for 1968–9 were not available at the time of going to press.

### (2) *Net output*

Gross value added (at current prices) by firms employing 25 or more persons.

*Sources.* 1958: *Census of Production,* 1963, Summary Table 1. 1963: *Census of Production,* 1963 (revised), and preliminary results of the *Census of Production,* 1968, in *Board of Trade Journal,* 31 December 1969.

### (3)  *R & D/net output*

1958–63: sum of R & D in 1958–9 and 1964–5, after deflating the latter by 5 per cent as a rough adjustment to the 1963–4 level, divided by the sum of net output in 1958 and 1963.

1963–8: sum of R & D in 1964–5 and 1967–8, divided by the sum of net output in 1963 and 1968. The use of 1967–8 in place of 1968–9 is assumed to compensate roughly for the use of 1964–5 in place of 1963–4.

### (4)  *Index of real net output*

Index of industrial production (1958 = 100). Brackets indicate authors' estimates, obtained in most cases by deflating net output at current prices by an appropriate wholesale price index.

The figure for petroleum products is an index of refinery output.

### (5) and (6)  *Employment*

Average of employees on payrolls in census years, including part-time and 'proprietary' employees, and those employed on R & D.

*Sources.* Same as net output.

### (7) and (8)  *Fixed assets*

Gross fixed assets at year-end, valued at 1963 replacement cost.

*Source*: Estimates of the Cambridge Growth Project, kindly supplied from the Project's data bank by Mr V. H. Woodward.

Brackets indicate authors' estimates, made as follows. Published data on gross fixed capital formation for the five relevant industries were obtained for as many years as possible since 1945 from census reports, including minor as well as 'full-scale' censuses; figures for intervening years were then estimated by interpolation. The annual series of fixed investment extensions thus obtained were then deflated using the price index implicit in National Income Bluebook data on gross domestic fixed capital formation in manufacturing at current and at 1963 prices, and finally summed to yield estimates of capital stock values for the requisite years.

(9) *Share of labour in net output*

Wages, salaries and employees' contributions as per cent of net output in 1963.

Source for wages etc.: *Census of Production*, 1963, Summary Table 3.

(10) *Productivity index*

The index for 1963 is as follows:

$$\frac{(4)_{1963}}{(6)_{1963} \times \dfrac{(9)}{100 \cdot 0} + (8)_{1963} \times \dfrac{(100 \cdot 0 - (9))}{100 \cdot 0}}$$

The index for 1968 is obtained in corresponding fashion.

# APPENDIX B:
# THE CONDUCT OF THE INQUIRY

## THE SAMPLE OF COMPANIES

As explained in Chapter 5, five broad industry classes were chosen for investigation: chemicals (including pharmaceuticals and petrochemicals), oil refining, electrical engineering (including electronics), mechanical engineering and man-made fibres.[1] A selection was made of some 150 firms in these classes from a comprehensive list of U.K. quoted companies.[2] The selection included every seventh company from a tabulation in ascending order of net assets in 1960, except that all companies with assets in excess of £10 million were included. Some additions were made to take account of mergers and acquisitions and to include unquoted companies.

Letters were sent to senior officials of the selected companies outlining the purpose of the inquiry and inviting participation. Eventually, just over 100 replies were received, including ones from most of the larger firms, and of these 65 expressed interest in the study. However, some twenty of these indicated that patents were a very minor aspect of their operations and were firmly believed to have no significant impact on the business. These replies were subsequently checked with the aid of a brief mailed questionnaire, and verified in doubtful cases by telephone conversations with the officials concerned.

This left 44 firms which agreed to participate in the inquiry. (One or two of these were approached at a later stage in order to fill certain gaps in our coverage.) Our standard questionnaire forms were submitted to them and 30 were ultimately persuaded to undertake the task of completing the forms and take part in the accompanying interviews. These 30 comprise our 'main sample', data for which appear in the tables of Part II above.

The remaining 14 firms said that they could not tackle the job of completing the questionnaires, but were willing to supply information of a more limited sort, and all agreed to be interviewed. These comprise a 'supplementary sample' which was useful in providing extra material on particular questions thrown up by the main sample, as well as enabling us to check and extend broad assessments of 'effects' in key fields.

---

[1] In the event, it did not prove possible to include detailed information for oil refining in our tables, because of data problems.
[2] The list was obtained with the assistance of Dr Geoffrey Whittington from data on punched cards used for the Department's research on public companies.

The names of the responding companies are listed in Annex 1 of this appendix, and an indication is given there of the categories of production for which firms in the main sample reported detailed information.

An idea of the coverage of our inquiry can be obtained by comparing R & D expenditure reported by responding firms with the most recent official figures published by the Ministry of Technology, relating to all R & D carried out within private industry:

| Industry | (1)<br>R & D<br>expenditure of<br>30 main 'inquiry'<br>companies<br>(£m; 1967) | (2)<br>'Official'<br>R & D<br>expenditure<br>(£m; 1967) | (1) as proportion<br>of (2)<br>(%) |
|---|---|---|---|
| Pharmaceuticals | 6·7 | 16·4 | 41 |
| Other chemicals | 17·4 | 54·9 | 32 |
| Electronics and telecommunications | 37·0 | 105·6 | 35 |
| Other electrical engineering | 10·4 | 30·4 | 34 |
| Mechanical engineering | 6·9 | 51·3 | 13 |
| Textiles and man-made fibres | 9·2 | 10·8 | 85 |
| Total of above | 87·6 | 269·4 | 33 |

NOTE:

Expenditure reported in our inquiry (mainly for the calendar year 1968 or the nearest financial year) is here reduced by 6 per cent to make it comparable with the official figures.

It can be seen that our main sample accounted overall for one-third of all industrial R & D in the industries shown. Coverage in both chemicals and electrical engineering was slightly above this level, while the much lower coverage in mechanical engineering was offset to some extent by a very high figure in textiles and man-made fibres. High coverage depended of course on being able to include several major firms in a research field dominated by large firms. It is well known that R & D in mechanical engineering is for the most part dispersed among a large number of medium-sized firms, and accordingly our object there was to include a variety of fairly representative situations, rather than to aim for high coverage.

In addition to the above, the 14 companies in our supplementary sample together spent roughly £51 million on R & D in the U.K. in 1968 (£10 million in chemicals, £32 million in electrical engineering, £5 million in mechanical engineering and £4 million in other fields). Inclusion of these raises our total coverage of official R & D in column (2) to about 50 per cent.[1]

---

[1] Total R & D by our 44 responding firms, including their expenditure in other fields than those shown (e.g., that by the oil companies on petroleum products and that by the

Although an effort was made to include some smaller firms in the inquiry, the majority of those participating were inevitably large firms. Thus, of the 43 respondents, only nine had total U.K. sales (including exports) of less than £25 million in 1968 and of these, only three had sales of less than £12 million. Most of the smaller firms were in mechanical engineering. It should however be noted that some large firms reported quite modest sales in certain key divisions or categories of production.

QUESTIONNAIRE AND INTERVIEW PROCEDURE

The procedure adopted was to invite firms initially to supply fairly extensive data on patents, licences, royalties, R & D etc. by completing the first of two questionnaire forms (reproduced, together with their covering notes, in Annex 2 to this appendix). Form A was designed to collect data of a rather factual sort, such as could be supplied by patenting and licensing departments of the responding firms. It was stressed that a high level of accuracy was not necessarily required, and that reasonably realistic and consistent estimates based on expert knowledge or short-cuts would suffice if exact figures were not readily available.

The information thereby obtained was then used as the starting point for discussions on policy and 'effects' between the authors and officials of the responding firms. All firms were interviewed at least once and in the larger or more complicated cases several visits were arranged.[1] Although the patent or licensing manager (and sometimes both) frequently played a large part in these discussions, we were also anxious to talk to management on the research or engineering sides of the business, and firms were generally most cooperative in allowing us to consult senior personnel in these fields when we felt it desirable to do so.

In the course of such discussions, the returns on Form A could be clarified and elaborated, but the main purpose was to tackle the questions set out in Form B. Since these deal with judgments rather than facts, it was vital for us to be able to discuss them in detail with respondents if reliable results were to be obtained. The essential object was to arrive at mutually acceptable answers to key questions regarding the impact of patent protection on firms' R & D programmes (Section VI), patent-based production (Section VIII) and licensing and pricing

chemical companies on foods and beverages, etc.) was roughly £158 million in 1968, or about one-quarter of all R & D done by British industry in that year.

[1] In total, some eighty interviews were held in the course of the inquiry. In addition to those with participating firms, discussions were also held with the N.R.D.C. and the Institute of Patentees and Inventors.

policies (Sections VII and IX). In order to accomplish this, it was usually necessary to explain our 'alternative position' of a compulsory licensing system at some length and to consider estimates of the impact of such a system in the light of replies elsewhere on the forms, as well as of our general knowledge of the industry. Inevitably the success of such an unconventional exercise required a considerable measure of goodwill, imagination and frankness on the part of those to whom we talked. Such cooperation was forthcoming in the great majority of cases and we were on the whole impressed with the willingness of most patent, licensing and research managers to spend time to consider the issues in a constructive and dispassionate way.

The great majority of the 30 companies in our main sample were ultimately able to complete the whole (or virtually the whole) of both forms and one or two others supplied enough details to enable us to complete returns on their behalf. A few that were able to supply much of the basic information left one or two important parts blank (generally because of data or estimation problems) but were nevertheless included on the strength of more general information or rough assessments reached in the course of discussions. Certain gaps in our quantitative data are however unavoidable – hence the slight variation in the coverage of tables in Part II.

TECHNICAL POINTS

A number of technical problems arose in connection with the forms, but they were mostly of a minor character. (Thus, some companies reported numbers of patents *applied for* rather than granted in the specified years, and adjustments were made by us to make them comparable with the rest of the data. Various other minor adjustments of this type were occasionally required by us, as well as a certain amount of allocation of licensing information between categories, where broad indications only were given by respondents.) Two other sorts of problems are however of some importance in understanding the figures in Part II, and should perhaps be mentioned here. The first concerns the division of data between categories of production and the second the treatment of 'international' companies that do most of their R & D, as well as patenting and 'groupwide' licensing, overseas.

One problem in the division of data between categories of production was that not all companies were able to provide a suitable breakdown, although most did supply a division of some sort. In some cases, this did not matter greatly, for the companies concerned were sufficiently 'homogeneous' to warrant inclusion in their entirety in one or other category. In one or two other cases, respondents were classed in the category which they most nearly fitted, although this meant including a certain amount of sales, etc. which strictly should appear in a different category. The largest of the latter examples were the oil companies, whose reports for 'chemicals' did not distinguish between basic chemicals (bulk olefins etc.) and secondary products (plastics materials, agricultural chemicals, detergent materials, solvents etc.). Since the bulk of petrochemical output by value is in basic chemicals, it was decided to include information for these operations in that category, although strictly some should be included in finished and specialty chemicals. For this reason, the reader should bear in mind that the categories shown in the tables are essentially mixtures whose main component is as shown; they should not be thought of as highly refined divisions of data, although wherever possible extraneous categories (termed 'miscellaneous' or 'other' in many returns) were excluded from the detailed tables.

A further point of some note in connection with the breakdown of data is that a number of firms chose to report for their major product divisions or subsidiaries and tended to subdivide their data on R & D, patents, etc. accordingly. This means for instance that the patents arising from the work of a particular division are compared with the R & D expenditure of that division (or R & D expenditure on its behalf by a central R & D establishment), the licences granted and taken by that division, its sales and royalty income, etc. While this procedure was in general an ideal one from the viewpoint of our study, it did on occasion lead to anomalies – as, for example, when one part of a firm undertakes a substantial amount of R & D for use by another part without charging the latter, or produces a research-based component or material for use by another part without charge. In such cases, our figures tend to exaggerate the true R & D/sales ratio of the former part of the firm, and understate that of the latter. This kind of problem is frequently encountered when integrated firms are studied, and only partially disappears through 'swings and roundabouts' effects when numbers of returns are combined. Adjustments were made to allow for certain prominent cases in our data, but some tendency probably remains in our tables to overstate the true patent and R & D content of components and basic materials, and correspondingly to understate that of finished products and equipment.

The inclusion of U.K. subsidiaries of foreign companies in our sample posed certain special problems which arise partly from the fact that group patent and licensing records are typically kept at the group's central headquarters. Two types of problems may be mentioned. Firstly, it was necessary to decide whether to confine returns to patents and licences arising from a group's R & D in the U.K., or to seek data for, say, all its U.K. patents and licences, including those arising from foreign R & D. Since we were mainly concerned with the impact of the patent system on invention and innovation in this country, the former basis seemed preferable, and this was essentially the one adopted in our tables (unless otherwise stated). Moreover, this solution usually proved easiest for respondents, who could normally distinguish patents and licences associated with British R & D, although they might not have access to details for the foreign part of the group.[1] However, in considering other questions – such as the impact of licensing or competition in U.K. markets – it is useful to have information relating to *all* a group's U.K. patents and licences, including those arising from its foreign work, and there is therefore something to be said for having data for them as well. Where possible and relevant, rough indications were obtained of the volume of foreign-originating patents and associated licence agreements involving respondents, and this proved useful in discussing such questions as selectivity in licensing, which is more often a 'group' matter rather than one for the U.K. subsidiary alone.

Secondly, problems were encountered in the assessment of the *field* licensing activities of companies in our sample that were members of foreign groups. When large international companies license technology and patents in broad fields, they are prone to do so on a groupwide basis; i.e., patents arising from all a group's various research centres, including those of its subsidiaries in other countries, are typically included in a field agreement, without specifying the patents or subsidiaries involved.[2] Accordingly, some subsidiaries of foreign firms in our inquiry had difficulty in reporting detailed information on field agreements involving U.K.-originating patents, although they could usually give a general picture of how group licences affected them. No automatic solution was available for this problem. The guideline put to respondents was that group agreements involving British-originating patents *in a substantial way* should if possible be included in the returns, and where precise answers were not possible, rough numbers were estimated on the basis of discussions with those involved, assisted by knowledge of the industry gained elsewhere in the study. (See, for example, the notes to Table 8.6.) In our assessment of royalties etc., no allowance was made for receipts by foreign parents of responding companies attributable to their British-originating patents; similarly no allowance was made for payments by foreign parents for use of

---

[1] But see also below.

[2] While this appears to be common practice, it is by no means always done. In cases where a subsidiary of different nationality is exceptionally strong and independent, it may retain a large measure of control over its licensing policy, and conclude its own field agreements separately from the rest of the group.

others' patents by their U.K. subsidiaries. Such amounts should ideally be included for some purposes, but we believe for a variety of special reasons that those for firms in our sample were probably very small, except in the case of the oil companies, which are anyway not included in the relevant Table (8.7).

# ANNEX 1:
## LIST OF PARTICIPATING COMPANIES[1]

1. *The 'main sample'*

Chemicals and Allied:
  Albright and Wilson
  Bakelite-Xylonite
  B.P.
  Beecham (Pharmaceutical Division)
  British Oxygen
  I.C.I. (Pharmaceutical Division, Agricultural Division, Plant Protection Ltd., Dyestuffs Division)
  Procter and Gamble
  Shell
  Unilever
  Wellcome Foundation
Electrical Engineering:
  E.M.I.
  I.C.L.
  Joseph Lucas
  Laurence, Scott and Electromotors
  Mullard
  Plessey
  Pye
  S.T.C.
Mechanical Engineering:
  Armstrong Equipment
  Associated Engineering
  Babcock and Wilcox
  Baker Perkins
  British United Shoe Machinery

  G.K.N. Screws and Fasteners
  Morgan Crucible
  Sturtevant Engineering
  Westland Helicopters
Man-made Fibres:
  Carrington and Dewhurst
  Courtaulds
  I.C.I. Fibres

2. *The 'supplementary sample'*

Chemicals and Allied:
  Aspro-Nicholas
  Castrol
  Esso Engineering Services
  Fisons (Agrochemical Division)
  Glaxo Group
Electrical Engineering:
  B.I.C.C.
  Chloride Electrical Storage
  Ferranti
  G.E.C.–E.E.
Mechanical Engineering:
  Textile Machinery Makers (Research Division)
  International Harvester (G.B.)
  Vickers (Engineering Group)
Building Materials and Other:[2]
  Pilkington
  Turner and Newall

[1] Where a return was confined essentially to one or more parts of a company, the parts included are given in brackets.

[2] These firms were included for special reasons. Pilkingtons were consulted in connection with the Float Glass process, a major patented invention, while Turner and Newall have interests in a number of our fields, including man-made fibres and automotive components.

*Principal categories of production reported by thirty main sample companies*[a]

| Company | Chemicals | | | | | | | Electrical engineering | | | | Mechanical engineering | | | |
| | Finished and specialty | | | | Basic | | | | | | | | | | |
| | Pharmaceuticals | Plastics, dyestuffs, paints etc. | Cosmetic, food and crop chemicals | Soaps and detergents | Petrochemicals | Other basic chemicals | Electronic components | Electronic, radio, T.V. and ass. equipment | Telecommunication and broadcasting equipment | Other elect. machinery and equipment | Plant, machinery and equipment | Components and materials | Man-made fibres | Other |
|---|---|---|---|---|---|---|---|---|---|---|---|---|---|---|
| **Chemicals and allied:** | | | | | | | | | | | | | | |
| Albright & Wilson | . | X | X | . | . | X | . | . | . | . | . | . | . | . |
| B.P. | . | . | . | . | X | . | . | . | . | . | . | . | . | X |
| Bakelite-Xylonite | . | X | . | . | . | . | . | . | . | . | . | . | . | . |
| Beecham | X | . | . | . | . | . | . | . | . | . | . | . | . | . |
| British Oxygen | . | . | . | . | . | X | . | . | . | . | X | . | . | . |
| I.C.I. | X | X | X | . | . | X | . | . | . | . | . | . | . | . |
| Procter and Gamble | . | . | . | X | . | . | . | . | . | . | . | . | . | . |
| Shell | . | . | . | . | X | . | . | . | . | . | . | . | . | X |
| Unilever | . | . | X | X | . | . | . | . | . | . | . | . | . | X |
| Wellcome | X | . | . | . | . | . | . | . | . | . | X | . | . | X |
| **Electrical engineering:** | | | | | | | | | | | | | | |
| E.M.I. | . | . | . | . | . | . | . | X | . | . | . | . | . | X |
| I.C.L. | . | . | . | . | . | . | . | X | . | . | . | . | . | . |
| Joseph Lucas | . | . | . | . | . | . | . | . | . | X | . | . | . | . |
| Laurence Scott | . | . | . | . | . | . | . | . | . | X | . | . | . | . |
| Mullard | . | . | . | . | . | . | X | . | . | . | . | . | . | . |
| Plessey | . | . | . | . | . | . | X | X | X | . | X | . | . | . |
| Pye | . | . | . | . | . | . | . | X | X | . | . | . | . | X |
| S.T.C. | . | . | . | . | . | . | X | X | X | X | . | . | . | . |

*Principal categories of production—(cont.)*

| Company | Pharmaceuticals | Plastics, dyestuffs, paints etc. | Cosmetic, food and crop chemicals | Soaps and detergents | Petrochemicals | Other basic chemicals | Electronic components | Electronic, radio, T.V. and ass. equipment | Telecommunication and broadcasting equipment | Other elect. machinery and equipment | Plant, machinery and equipment | Components and materials | Man-made fibres | Other |
|---|---|---|---|---|---|---|---|---|---|---|---|---|---|---|
| **Mechanical engineering:** | | | | | | | | | | | | | | |
| Armstrong Equipment | . | . | . | . | . | . | . | . | . | . | . | X | . | . |
| Associated Engineering | . | . | . | . | . | . | . | . | . | . | . | X | . | . |
| Babcock and Wilcox | . | . | . | . | . | . | . | . | . | . | X | . | . | . |
| Baker Perkins | . | . | . | . | . | . | . | . | . | . | X | . | . | . |
| British United Shoe | . | . | . | . | . | . | . | . | . | . | X | X | . | . |
| G.K.N. Screws and Fasteners | . | . | . | . | . | . | . | . | . | . | . | X | . | . |
| Morgan Crucible | . | . | . | . | . | . | . | . | . | . | . | X | . | . |
| Sturtevant Engineering | . | . | . | . | . | . | . | . | . | . | X | . | . | . |
| Westland Helicopters | . | . | . | . | . | . | . | . | . | . | X[b] | . | . | . |
| **Man-made fibres:** | | | | | | | | | | | | | | |
| Carrington and Dewhurst | . | . | . | . | . | . | . | . | . | . | . | . | X | . |
| Courtaulds | . | X | . | . | . | . | . | . | . | . | X | . | X | X |
| I.C.I. Fibres | . | . | . | . | . | . | . | . | . | . | . | . | X | . |
| **Total companies** | 3 | 4 | 3 | 2 | 2 | 3 | 3 | 5 | 3 | 3 | 9 | 5 | 3 | 7 |

NOTES:

[a] In addition to general quantitative information about their patenting and licensing activities, the 30 companies in our main sample reported detailed information which could be classed in specific production categories, as shown.

[b] Although strictly an aircraft company, Westland Helicopter was included in this category as most of its innovative effort is in helicopter equipment. (Its principal helicopters are manufactured under licence.)

# ANNEX 2:
## THE QUESTIONNAIRE FORMS

---

The questionnaire forms and covering notes for our industrial inquiry
are reproduced in the following pages.

Department of Applied Economics, University of Cambridge

Impact of the Patent System on U.K. Industry

Introductory Note

## 1. Object of the Inquiry

An intensive inquiry into the Patent system is being undertaken by this Department with the help of selected companies in five industries - oil refining, chemicals, mechanical engineering, electrical engineering and textiles. The objective of the inquiry is to assess the economic impact of patenting and licensing on industrial activity in the U.K., with particular emphasis on research and development, innovation, patent-based production and competition. It is hoped that the results of the study, when published, will fill an important gap in knowledge about the U.K. economy, and will provide guidance for those concerned with public policy towards patents.

## 2. The Questionnaire Forms

You are invited to complete two questionnaire forms, A and B. Form A contains questions of a rather factual nature on research and development, patenting and licensing activities. A good deal of this information will, we hope, emerge fairly easily from your records and, where this is not so, approximations based on your knowledge of the situation should be adequate (see "Accuracy" below). We should like you to go ahead with the completion of Form A and return it to us as rapidly as you can.

Form B contains more fundamental questions on patenting and licensing policy, and the effects that follow from such policy. Some items call for the exercise of a large element of judgement - such as those which ask for comparisons between actual output and, "what output would have been in the absence of effective patent protection" (Section VIII, Form B) - and we are aware that these may cause difficulties. Accordingly, we suggest that Form B should not be completed until after the interview which we hope to have with an official of your company who is acquainted with policy in these areas. Naturally, progress at the interview will be greatly aided if Form B has been studied beforehand, and likely difficulties considered.

## 3. Coverage of the information

We assume that it will be most convenient for you to complete a single Form A and B for your company or group of companies, but if you prefer to report separately for individual divisions of your company or subsidiaries of your group we will gladly supply further blank copies on request. If you are reporting for a widely diversified company or group of companies you may prefer some parts of the organisation to be excluded if their patenting and licensing activities are relatively unimportant, but we hope that information given in the various sections will be consistent: for example, information on R & D and sales of production should be comparable with that relating to patenting and licensing.

Since our main concern is with British industry, information on patents and licences should be confined if possible to those stemming from British research and development. Companies with foreign subsidiaries or branches, or which are themselves subsidiaries of foreign parents, are accordingly requested to report for the U.K. members of their group only, if possible excluding patents etc. arising from work done overseas. Part IV of Form A does touch briefly on transactions with overseas members of the group, while elsewhere some questions relate to foreign patenting and licensing, but all necessary data should be available from your U.K. records.

## 4. Accuracy

We cannot stress too strongly that we seldom need absolutely exact answers and that in all cases where the information requested is not of a routine nature reasonable estimates will be adequate. Indeed in the vaguer questions it is deliberately made impossible for you to give exact answers. When a fairly straightforward allocation is requested (say, of R & D expenditure between major product

384

- 2 -

groups), accuracy to the nearest 10 per cent will be good enough.  As a general
rule, it would be better if all else fails to give a range within which the true
figures lies, rather than to leave an item blank.  In no case should an elaborate
exercise be necessary to get answers, although some brief calculations may be
required.

Blanks in the completed forms will normally be interpreted to mean "zero",
"negligible" or "not applicable".  If a particular item cannot be estimated but
may be fairly large, please write "N.A." (not available).

## 5. Categories of Production

Space is provided for you to report on up to four specific categories of
production plus a miscellaneous category ("Other") which could well be merely a
balancing item.  If your company's production is fairly uniform, you should report
for "total" only, but as the purpose of the breakdown is to discover whether the
patent system varies greatly in its impact between different types of production,
products of vastly differing R and D content should not if possible be grouped
together.

The choice of categories is left to you, but, as a guide, it may help you to
know that the two-digit product groups of the Standard Industrial Classification
(as listed for instance in the questionnaire of the Ministry of Technology's
annual Inquiry into Expenditure on Scientific Research and Development) would be
adequate for our purposes, although there is no need to follow that classification rigidly.  Any broad grouping adopted in your company's records would probably
be acceptable to us.

## 6. Confidentiality

All information reported in the inquiry will be treated as secret and will
not be seen by anyone other than the research team.  Information will not be
divulged or published in such a way that individual companies can be identified.
Confidentiality clearance will be sought from you in any cases of doubt.

## 7. Timetable

We should like completed Form As to be returned to the Department by the end
of June 1969.  If you wish to co-operate but foresee difficulties in meeting this
timetable a somewhat later date might be arranged, provided not too many companies
are involved.

## 8. Enquiries

If you have any problems in completing the form, please do not hesitate to
call Mr. C.T.Taylor on Cambridge 58944, Extension 270, who is the research officer
in charge of the project.

Department of Applied Economics, University of Cambridge

IMPACT OF THE PATENT SYSTEM ON U.K. INDUSTRY:

FORM A[1]

Name of reporting company or group ........................................................

I. Outline of Company's U.K. Operations
(For the most recent financial year available)

£'000

1. Capital employed (beginning of year)

......

2. Profits (after depreciation, before tax)

......

3. Sales of Production, by major category:*

£'000

| Category of Production | Home Market | Exports |
|---|---|---|
| (1) .......................................... | ............ | ......... |
| (2) .......................................... | ............ | ......... |
| (3) .......................................... | ............ | ......... |
| (4) .......................................... | ............ | ......... |
| (5) Other | ............ | ......... |
| Total | | |

* Exclude goods re-sold if possible.

4. Number of employees (mid-year, or nearest convenient date) .........

5. Research and Development

  (a) Total expenditure on Research and Development in the U.K. (£'000)

  (b) Of this, roughly what proportion was on "Research" (basic and applied)? (%)

  (c) Payments received from outsiders for R & D (£'000)

  (d) Number of employees engaged mainly on R & D (mid-year)

  (e) Of these, what proportion were qualified scientists and engineers (%)

6. Allocation of total R & D expenditure in the U.K. between major categories:

| Category of Production | % |
|---|---|
| (1) .......................................... | ......... |
| (2) .......................................... | ......... |
| (3) .......................................... | ......... |
| (4) .......................................... | ......... |
| (5) Other | ......... |
| (6) Unallocated | ......... |
| Total | 100 |

(7) Calendar year to which this information most nearly applies .............

[1] Before starting to complete the form please read the Introductory Note attached. Notes for guidance in answering individual questions are also attached.

13

FORM A

## II.  Patenting Activity

1. Number of employees engaged mainly on patent work, licensing and associated
   work in the U.K., excluding those engaged on R & D (mid-1968) ..............

2. Does your company have at least one separate department engaged mainly in
   this work?  (Please tick).

   Yes [ ]        No [ ]

3. Number of U.K. patents in force (end-1968):

   (a) with over 10 years to run          .............

   (b) with 5-10 years to run             .............

   (c) with less than 5 years to run      .............

   _____

   Total

4. Number of foreign patents in force (end-1968)   ...........

5. Number of new U.K. patents granted, by major category:

   | Category of Production | 1966 | 1967 | 1968 |
   |---|---|---|---|
   | (1) ............................................... | .... | .... | .... |
   | (2) ............................................... | .... | .... | .... |
   | (3) ............................................... | .... | .... | .... |
   | (4) ............................................... | .... | .... | .... |
   | (5) Other | | | |

   Total

6. Number of new foreign patents granted in 1968, by major category:

   | Category of Production | 1968 |
   |---|---|
   | (1) ...................................... | .... |
   | (2) ...................................... | .... |
   | (3) ...................................... | .... |
   | (4) ...................................... | .... |
   | (5) Other | .... |

   Total

7(a) Number of your U.K. patents for which renewal fees were payable for the first
     time in 1968                                    ..............

   (b) Of these, how many were actually renewed?     ..............

8. Estimated expenditure in the U.K. on patenting, licensing and associated work
   (not including R & D) in 1968:

                                                      £'000

   (a) Patent office fees                             .....

   (b) Payments to outside patent agents etc.         .....

   (c) Salaries of your employees engaged mainly
       on this work                                   .....

   (d) Other                                          .....

   _____

   Total

- 3 -                                        FORM A

9.  Approximately what proportion of the total of this expenditure was on taking out foreign patents and on granting licences on these (including licences to members of your own group)? (%)

    ..............................................................................

10(a) Number of provisional specifications filed with the U.K. Patent Office in 1966
                                                                ............

  (b) Of these, how many were completed?
                                                                ..........

  (c) Of those completed, how many were:

         (i) granted without opposition                         ..........

        (ii) opposed before grant                               ..........

  (d) Of those granted without opposition, how many have been subjected to 'belated opposition' before the Comptroller?
                                                                ..........

11. In cases of oppositions to your specifications before the Comptroller (before or after grant) that have been settled since the end of 1966, how many have resulted in:

  (a) withdrawal or rejection of the opposition without any substantial concession by you                           ............

  (b) withdrawal of the opposition in return for a licence    ............

  (c) substantial amendment of the specification              ............

  (d) withdrawal or refusal of the specification              ............

  (e) revocation of the patent                                ............

  (f) some other outcome                                      ............

12. How many Court actions has your company been engaged in since the end of 1966 for:

  (a) infringement of your patents                            ............

  (b) revocation of your patents                              ............

  (c) (a) and (b) combined                                    ............

13. Of such actions (Q.12) that have been concluded, how many have led to:

  (a) grant of licence(s) to your opponent                    ............

  (b) revocation of your patent(s)                            ............

  (c) suppression of infringements of your patent(s)          ............

  (d) some other outcome                                      ............

### III. Licensing Activity

(This section applies to licence agreements with <u>outsiders</u> i.e., organisations that are not members of your group.  Section IV deals with licensing <u>within</u> the group).

| | Category of Production ||||||
|---|---|---|---|---|---|---|
| | (1) | (2) | (3) | (4) | Other | Total |

A. "Specific" Agreements

   (i.e. agreements that specify individual patents.)

1. Number of such agreements in force, end-1968  ......  ......  ......  ......  ......  ......

2. Of 1, how many provided essentially for:

   (a) licensing of your patents to others  ......  ......  ......  ......  ......  ......

   (b) licensing of others' patents to you  ......  ......  ......  ......  ......  ......

   (c) reciprocal exchange of patents  ......  ......  ......  ......  ......  ......

3. Of 1, how many related essentially to:

   (a) U.K. patents only  ......  ......  ......  ......  ......  ......

   (b) foreign patents only  ......  ......  ......  ......  ......  ......

   (c) both U.K. and foreign patents  ......  ......  ......  ......  ......  ......

4. Of 1, how many involved payment of licence fees, royalties, etc., in 1968:  ......  ......  ......  ......  ......  ......

   (a) by your company  ......  ......  ......  ......  ......  ......

   (b) to your company  ......  ......  ......  ......  ......  ......

B. "Field" and "General" Agreements

   (i.e., agreements that relate to <u>groups</u> of patents - e.g., those in a particular technical field - without specifying them individually.)

5. Number of such agreements in force, end-1968  ......  ......  ......  ......  ......  ......

6. Of 5, how many provided essentially for:

   (a) licensing of your patents to others  ......  ......  ......  ......  ......  ......

   (b) licensing of others' patents to you  ......  ......  ......  ......  ......  ......

   (c) reciprocal exchange of patents  ......  ......  ......  ......  ......  ......

7. Of 5, how many were concluded with:

   (a) organisations operating mainly in U.K.  ......  ......  ......  ......  ......  ......

   (b) organisations operating mainly overseas  ......  ......  ......  ......  ......  ......

8. Of 5, how many involved payment of licence fees, royalties, etc., in 1968:

   (a) by your company  ......  ......  ......  ......  ......  ......

   (b) to your company  ......  ......  ......  ......  ......  ......

C. All types of Agreements

9. Total licence fees, royalties, etc. paid by your company in 1968 on:

   (a) U.K. patents (£'000)  ......  ......  ......  ......  ......  ......

   (b) foreign patents (£'000)  ......  ......  ......  ......  ......  ......

   Total          (£'000)

- 5 -

| | Category of Production | | | | | |
|---|---|---|---|---|---|---|
| | (1) | (2) | (3) | (4) | Other | Total |

10. Total licence fees, royalties, etc., received by your company in 1968 on:

   (a) U.K. patents (£'000)    ....... ....... ...... ...... ........ ......

   (b) foreign patents (£'000)   ....... ....... ...... ...... ........ ......

Total      (£'000)

11. (a) How many of your U.K. patents have you licensed on a 'sole' or 'exclusive' basis, end-1968? ....... ....... ...... ...... ........ ......

   (b) Royalties etc. received from these licences in 1968 (£'000) ....... ....... ...... ...... ........ ......

12. (a) How many 'sole' or 'exclusive' licences on U.K. patents have you obtained from others, end-1968? ....... ....... ...... ...... ........ ......

   (b) Royalties etc. paid on these licences in 1968 (£'000) ....... ....... ...... ...... ........ ......

   (c) Selling value of your production dependent on these licences in 1968 (£'000) (See notes toForm A) ....... ....... ...... ...... ........ ......

13. How many applications by your company for licences on U.K. patents have been refused since the end of 1966? ....... ....... ...... ...... ........ ......

14. (a) How many applications by others for licences on your U.K. patents have you refused since the end of 1966? ....... ....... ...... ...... ........ ......

   (b) Estimated selling value of your production in 1968 that was depend-end on these patents (£'000) (See notes to Form A) ....... ....... ...... ...... ........ ......

15. (a) How many applications for compulsory licences on U.K. patents have you made since the end of 1966? ....... ....... ...... ...... ........ ......

   (b) How many applications for compulsory licences on your U.K. patents have been made by others since the end of 1966? ....... ....... ...... ...... ........ ......

16. How many licence agreements relating to U.K. patents in force at the end of 1968 (Q.3(a) plus 7(a) above) were with:

   (a) companies in your own industry   .............

   (b) companies in other industries   .............

   (c) non-incorporated organisations   .............

   (d) individuals   .............

Total

17. Please indicate which of the following types of licence payments accounted for a substantial proportion (say, over one-third) of total royalties etc. received in 1968: (please tick appropriate item(s))

    (a) percentage of licensee's sales (or rate per unit of licensee's output):

        (i) with minimum annual sum guaranteed ☐

        (ii) without such guarantee ☐

    (b) percentage of licensee's profits:

        (i) with minimum annual sum guaranteed ☐

        (ii) without such guarantee ☐

    (c) single lump sum ☐

    (d) combination of lump sum and percentage of sales ☐

    (e) other ☐

18. Please indicate which of the following rates of royalty account for a substantial proportion (say, over one-third) of sales-related royalties received in 1968: (please tick appropriate item(s) )

    (a) less than 1% of sales ☐

    (b) 1 - $2\frac{1}{2}$% of sales ☐

    (c) $2\frac{1}{2}$ - 5% of sales ☐

    (d) 5 - 10% of sales ☐

    (e) over 10% of sales ☐

19. When your company grants licences to others to use its patents apart from 'licences of right', in what approximate proportion of cases does the agreement provide for the following: (please indicate to the nearest 10%*)

                                                             %

    (a) supply of know-how in the technical field of the patents:

        (i) by your company only .......

        (ii) by the licensee(s) only .......

        (iii) on a reciprocal basis (i.e., by both parties) .......

    (b) supply of know-how on a substantially broader basis:

        (i) by your company only .......

        (ii) by the licensee(s) only .......

        (iii) on a reciprocal basis .......

    (c) non-divulgence to a third party of know-how covered by the agreement:

        (i) by your company .......

        (ii) by the licensee(s) .......

    (d) observation by the licensee(s) of conditions relating to:

        (i) quantity of output produced under licence .......

        (ii) markets for output produced under licence .......

        (iii) price of output produced under licence .......

        (iv) quality of output produced under licence .......

---

* Alternatively, write 'most', 'few', 'none', etc. as seems appropriate.

20. Please consider whether you hold any patents that have been of outstanding importance in terms of licensing benefits secured for your company in recent years.  (Please tick)

Yes ☐     No ☐

21. If 'Yes', please indicate, for the principal cases:

| (a) Technical field covered | (b) Approximate royalties etc. received in 1968 from: | | (c) Whether any important licences have been obtained cheaply in direct exchange (Please write 'Yes' or 'No') |
|---|---|---|---|
| | (i) U.K. licensees | (ii) Licensees operating overseas | |
| | (£'000) | (£'000) | |
| ........................... | ................. | ................. | ............... |
| ........................... | ................. | ................. | ............... |
| ........................... | ................. | ................. | ............... |
| ........................... | ................. | ................. | ............... |
| ........................... | ................. | ................. | ............... |
| ........................... | ................. | ................. | ............... |
| ........................... | ................. | ................. | ............... |
| ........................... | ................. | ................. | ............... |

## IV.  Intra-group Licensing

(This section may apply where the questionnaire is completed on behalf of a _group_ of companies.  It relates to licensing activity _within_ the group only).

1. To what extent are patents owned by U.K. members of the group made accessible - (please tick appropriate answer) -

| | (a) to other members of the group operating mainly in the U.K. | (b) to other members of the group operating mainly overseas |
|---|---|---|
| (i) In all cases | ☐ | ☐ |
| (ii) In most cases | ☐ | ☐ |
| (iii) Sometimes | ☐ | ☐ |
| (iv) Rarely or never | ☐ | ☐ |

2. To the extent that patents are made accessible to the rest of the group, how far is this dealt with by means of formal licensing agreements (whether of a specific or general kind) between members?  (Please tick appropriate answer)

    (a) In most or all cases   ☐
    (b) Fairly commonly   ☐
    (c) Exceptionally   ☐
    (d) Not at all   ☐

3. Approximately how many licence agreements involving U.K. patents were in force between members of the group at the end of 1968? .............

4. Total of royalties etc. received by U.K. members of the group in 1968: (£'000)

    (a) from other members of the group operating in the U.K.   .........
    (b) from other members of the group operating overseas   .........

5. Total of royalties etc. paid in 1968 by U.K. members of the group to members of the group operating overseas (£'000)   .........

### V. Know-how Agreements

(This section relates to formal exchange of know-how etc. which is <u>not</u> linked to patents.)

1. Has your company entered into written agreements with outsiders (i.e. non-members of your group) to supply or exchange information on production, <u>without</u> reference to any patents?  (Please tick)

   Yes ☐      No ☐

2. If 'Yes', with how many companies did you have such agreements at the end of 1968?
   (a) companies operating mainly in the U.K.        ........
   (b) companies operating mainly overseas           ........

3. Which of your main categories of production were involved?  (Please tick)
   (1) ☐ ;    (2) ☐ ;    (3) ☐ ;    (4) ☐

4. How broad is the technical field most commonly covered in these agreements? (Please tick the appropriate answer)
   (a) A rather narrow field (e.g. a single process)           ☐
   (b) A rather broad field (e.g. a number of distinct processes)  ☐
   (c) A more general area of interest (e.g. a number of technical fields)  ☐

5. Total of know-how fees received from outsiders in 1968:
   (a) from companies operating mainly in the U.K. (£'000)    ........
   (b) from companies operating mainly overseas    "          ........

6. Total of know-how fees paid to outsiders, 1968:
   (a) to companies operating mainly in the U.K. (£'000)    ........
   (b) to companies operating mainly overseas    "          ........

Name of person to whom enquiries on this form should be addressed

.........................................................................................

Tel. No. ...........................
Extension ......................

- 9 -

## Notes on Particular Questions: Form A

### Section 1

The United Kingdom includes the Isle of Man and the Channel Isles, but not Eire.

Q.1. Total assets <u>less</u> current liabilities, as given in your annual accounts. Please exclude trade investments, if large.

Q.2. Profit for the year, net of depreciation but before deducting tax, interest etc., as given in the annual accounts. Please exclude income from trade investments, if the latter were excluded from item 1.

Q.3. For choice of production categories, see <u>Introductory Note</u>, page 2. Please enter the names of the categories you select in the blanks provided. Fill in less than four categories, if appropriate. Give more only if really necessary, using a second form. If goods re-sold are large but cannot be separated from total sales, please say so in a note on the form.

Q.4. Please adjust the figure if it is not 'typical' of the year as a whole.

Q.5. 'Research and Development' should be interpreted to comply as nearly as conveniently possible with the definitions used in the Ministry of Technology's <u>Statistics of Science and Technology</u> (H.M.S.O., 1968, page 6). Where there is doubt, our preference is for you to include as R & D the design, construction, testing and modification of the first prototypes of a new product, but to exclude work on getting the production process going smoothly, as well as routine design work associated with adapting products to the specifications of particular customers. But here and elsewhere, do not worry about fringe or doubtful items, unless they are very substantial.

Please include your company's expenditure on research done for you by research associations etc., as well as that done in your own establishments. Also include your expenditure on research done by you for outsiders (including the Government), adding a note in (c) to show re-imbursements from outsiders. Please do not include licence fees or other payments for research which is the property of outsiders.

Please do not include market research. Where expenditure is large, heavily rounded figures will be acceptable.

Q.6. The item 'unallocated' is intended to cover all R & D overheads which cannot really be assigned to particular categories of production (even if such an assignment is made in your accounts); naturally, it applies only if you report more than one category on the form.

### Section II

If numbers of patents, applications, etc., are fairly large, figures rounded to the nearest 10 will be quite acceptable. If possible, please include all patents arising from British work, even though these may be in a foreign subsidiary's name; and please exclude those arising from work done overseas, even though these may be in your company's name. But do not worry about the matter unless it is likely to be of importance.

Q.1. Do not include employees who engage only part-time or occasionally in these activities.

Q.5. If reporting figures for earlier years presents unreasonable problems, please report for 1968 only, if possible giving a rough indication of the corresponding figures for 1966.

Q.8. This question seeks to establish the full cost to your company of patenting, licensing and associated work done in the U.K., including work on foreign patents and licences and patents belonging to third parties. If possible, patents and licences that do not stem from R & D done in the U.K. should not be included.

Q:8(c).  Please include travelling expenses.

Q.8(d).  If possible, please include an allowance for part-time and occasional work done in this field. (For example, expenses of directors engaged on licence negotiations at home or overseas should ideally be included.)  A heavily rounded figure will be quite acceptable.

Q.10,11.  The year 1966 was chosen in view of the lapse in time between first application for a patent and possible development of opposition proceedings.

Section III

As noted on the form, this section applies to licence agreements with organisations that are not members of your group of companies (i.e. companies that are included in your consolidated accounts). Licensing of 'associated companies' (companies in which your company or group has an ownership interest which is less than a controlling one) should be included in this section.

Please include only licence agreements that involve U.K. members of your group. Where numbers are large, approximate figures will be satisfactory. Estimates of the numbers in different categories of production need only be approximate.

Q.1-4.  (Sub-section A) refer to 'specific agreements', by which we mean agreements that relate to specific patents licensed by or to your company. We expect that the majority of agreements entered into by most companies will be of this kind.

Q.5-8.  (Sub-section B) refer to 'field' and 'general' agreements, by which we mean agreements that relate to groups of patents licensed by or to your company, without specifying them individually. We expect that such agreements will be fairly common among larger companies in certain industries.

Q.4,8.  Here and elsewhere, 'licence fees, royalties, etc.' (sometimes abbreviated to 'royalties etc.').means all financial payments, whether lump sum or recurring, made in return for licences, including dividends on shares exchanged for licences, and payments for assignment of patents.

Q.7.  U.K. subsidiaries of foreign groups should be included in (a), while foreign subsidiaries of U.K. groups should be included in (b).

Q.9;10.  See note to Q.4, 8. It is probably reasonable to count royalties etc. paid to (or received from) organisations operating mainly in the U.K. as royalties on U.K. patents, while royalties etc. paid to (or received from) organisations operating mainly overseas can be counted as royalties on foreign patents.

Q.11(a), 12(a).  A 'sole' licence confers rights on the licensee to the exclusion of all other U.K. producers except the licensor. An 'exclusive' licence excludes the licensor as well.

Q.11(b), 12(b).  See note to Q.4,8.

Q.12(c).  A rapid way of estimating the selling value of output produced under sole or exclusive licences might be to divide the annual royalties etc. payable on these licences by an estimate of the usual rate of royalty on selling value applicable to them.

Q.14(b)  Please enter the estimated selling value of all goods produced by your company that depend substantially on patents for which you have refused outsiders a licence in the last three years. Please include goods which depend heavily on a component, material or process covered by such patents. Your best guess will probably suffice, heavily rounded if necessary.

Q.16(a).  We mean 'industry' here in the broad sense used in paragraph 1 of the Introductory Note.

Section IV

This section applies to licensing between companies of the same group, and is relevant therefore only where the form is being completed on behalf of a group of companies.

Q.4,5.   Amounts correct to the nearest £10,000 will normally be quite acceptable.

Section V

This section seeks information on the exchange between companies of know-how that is not linked to patents. Knowledge-sharing agreements and technical aid agreements should be included, but minor exchanges on a highly <u>ad hoc</u> or informal basis should not.

Q.2.     See note to Section III, Q.7.

Q.5,6.   Amounts correct to the nearest £10,000 will normally be quite acceptable. Please do not include licence fees, royalties, or other payments that relate to patents, either specifically or in a group. See also note to Section III, Q.7.

396

Department of Applied Economics, University of Cambridge

## IMPACT OF THE PATENT SYSTEM ON U.K. INDUSTRY: FORM B[1]

### VI. Patenting Policy

1. Would you say that your company has a definite policy with regard to the patenting of its discoveries? (please tick).

   Yes ☐   No ☐

2. If 'yes', which of the following best describes that policy? (please tick one).

   (a) Patent most things that are patentable ☐

   (b) Upon brief examination, patent most things that have a fore-seeable commercial use ☐

   (c) After critical scrutiny, patent only those discoveries that have a strong chance of commercial success, whether exploited by you or others ☐

   (d) Same as (c), except that you keep secret some/all* major/minor* discoveries relating to processes used by you.
   | *Delete as appropriate |

   (e) Patent only those discoveries that have a clear application to your own company's products or processes ☐

   (f) Patent only the occasional discovery of quite exceptional importance ☐

   (g) Do not patent anything (i.e. keep all discoveries secret) ☐

3. (a) Would you say that management in your company is actively alert to the possibility of patenting new discoveries? (please tick).

   Yes ☐   No ☐

   (b) If 'yes', are any written instructions on this point circulated to junior management or supervisory staff, either separately or as part of a larger document?

   Yes ☐   No ☐

   (c) Do routine appraisals of new discoveries automatically involve the assessment of their patentability?

   Yes ☐   No ☐

4. Is potential patentability a decisive criterion in deciding whether to go ahead with a particular research project? (Please tick the appropriate answer)

   (a) Never ☐          (c) In a significant pro-portion (say up to 10%) of cases ☐

   (b) In very few cases ☐   (d) In a relatively large proportion (say over 10%) of cases ☐

5. Does appraisal of research projects and plans for development of new products normally involve checking to see whether other companies' patents are likely to be infringed and, if so, what the cost of licences on those patents is likely to be? (Please tick)

   Yes ☐   No ☐

6. Approximately what proportion of your R & D in recent years would not have been carried out if you had not been able to patent any resulting discoveries?

   ....................%

---

(1) We hope to discuss this part of the Questionnaire at an interview with someone in your organisation. But notes for guidance in answering individual questions are attached, since interpretation will in some cases be crucial to the study.

### VII. Licensing Policy

1. Which of the following describe your company's policy with regard to licensing its patents? (Possibly tick more than one, deleting 'some' or 'any' as necessary.)

   (a) Grant any applicant a licence for some/any patents on a reasonable commercial basis ☐

   (b) Grant main competitors only a licence for some/any patents on a reasonable commercial basis ☐

   (c) Do not grant some/any competitors a licence ☐

   (d) Grant competitors a licence for some patents only if they agree to observe conditions regarding the quantity, price, or market for their production ☐

   (e) Grant a licence for some/any patents only if the licensee will supply his patents and/or know-how in exchange ☐

   (f) Licence nothing which is of key importance to your company's own products or processes ☐

2. (a) Please consider whether there were any patents in force at end-1968 for which you would refuse all conceivable licence applications. (Please tick.)

   Yes ☐     No ☐

   (b) If 'yes', which categories of production* were involved. (Please tick):

   (1) ☐ ;  (2) ☐ ;  (3) ☐ ;  (4) ☐ ;

   [*As reported in Form A.]

   | | Yes | No |
   |---|---|---|

3. Does your company

   (a) actively promote the sale of some/all* licences?  Yes ☐  No ☐

   (b) actively discourage the sale of some/all* licences?  Yes ☐  No ☐

   [*Delete as appropriate]

4. If 'yes' to 3(a), how soon in the life of an important patent does your company first take serious steps to sell licences? (Please tick appropriate answer)

   (a) Soon after the provisional/complete specification has been filed with the U.K. patent office ☐

   (b) Soon after the application has been accepted by the U.K. patent office ☐

   (c) At some later stage ☐

5. When you are deciding how much to charge for a licence, which of the following considerations, if any, typically has an important bearing on the decision:  Yes  No

   (a) An estimate of the cost of R & D associated with the patent, plus a reasonable margin for profit  ☐ ☐

   (b) The rate which is generally charged for that type of licence in the industry  ☐ ☐

   (c) The maximum that the potential licensee is likely to pay (if different from (a) and (b) )  ☐ ☐

398

FORM B

## VIII  Impact on Production and R & D

(Please consult the notes carefully when completing this section. Above all, please bear in mind that 'rough but honest' answers based on expert knowledge will usually be adequate for our purposes.)

Category of Production

| | (1) | (2) | (3) | (4) | Other | Total |
|---|---|---|---|---|---|---|
| 1. (a) Please estimate what proportion (by selling value) of your U.K. production in 1968 was 'patent-based' (i.e. effectively protected by patents) (%) | ...... | ...... | ...... | ...... | ...... | ...... |
| (b) Of that production (item 1(a) ), what proportion was based on <u>your own</u> patents? (% of 1(a) ) | ...... | ...... | ...... | ...... | ...... | ...... |

2. What percentage of the selling value of your patent-based production (item 1 (a)) was accounted for by:

| | (1) | (2) | (3) | (4) | Other | Total |
|---|---|---|---|---|---|---|
| (a) the R & D costs associated with that production (% of 1(a) ) | ...... | ...... | ...... | ...... | ...... | ...... |
| (b) the licence fees paid by you to outsiders (% of 1(a) ) | ...... | ...... | ...... | ...... | ...... | ...... |
| 3. Roughly what proportion of your total profits (Section I, item 2) in 1968 came from patent-based production? (%) | ...... | ...... | ...... | ...... | ...... | ...... |
| 4. Please estimate what proportion (by selling value) of your patent-based production in 1968 (item 1(a) ) would not have been produced, had effective patent protection not been available (% of 1(a)) | ...... | ...... | ...... | ...... | ...... | ...... |

5. In relation to the production 'not done' in 1968 in the absence of effective patent protection (item 4), what alternative action would in your judgment have been taken by your company? (Please tick)

|  | Yes | No |
|---|---|---|
| (a) Develop other lines of production based on 'secret' R & D | ☐ | ☐ |
| (b) Develop other lines of production not based on your R & D | ☐ | ☐ |
| (c) Develop no alternative lines; expand existing (non-patent-based) production | ☐ | ☐ |
| (d) Undertake no alternative production of any sort | ☐ | ☐ |

## IX  Impact on Pricing Policy, Competition etc.

1. When you are deciding what selling price to charge for patent-based products, which of the following considerations, if any, typically has an important bearing on the decision:  (Please tick)

|  | Yes | No |
|---|---|---|
| (a) Charge enough to cover relevant R & D costs in addition to costs of production, marketing, etc. | ☐ | ☐ |
| (b) Charge the maximum amount that the market will bear | ☐ | ☐ |
| (c) Avoid charging so high a price that competitors are encouraged to develop similar lines, notwithstanding your patents | ☐ | ☐ |

2. In your experience, is there a tendency for the prices of products based on your patents to fall:

|  | Yes | No |
|---|---|---|
| (a) as the date of expiry of the patent approaches | ☐ | ☐ |
| (b) as an increasing proportion of total U.K. supply of the product in question is produced by other companies? | ☐ | ☐ |

- 4 -                                     FORM B

3.  Please consider whether there were any important patents for which you tried but could not obtain a licence in the last 3 years?  (Please tick)

|                    | Yes | No |
|--------------------|-----|----|
| (a) U.K. patents   | ☐   | ☐  |
| (b) foreign patents| ☐   | ☐  |

4.  If 'yes', please state, for the principal cases:

| Technical field covered | Whether the reason was: | | | % Royalty | |
|---|---|---|---|---|---|
| | (a) 'No licence on any terms' | (b) Disagreement over (i) fees | (ii) some other factor | Asked | Offered |
| | (please tick appropriate column) | | | | |
| .................................... | ...... | ...... | ...... | ....... | ....... |
| .................................... | ...... | ...... | ...... | ....... | ....... |
| .................................... | ...... | ...... | ...... | ....... | ....... |
| .................................... | ...... | ...... | ...... | ....... | ....... |
| .................................... | ...... | ...... | ...... | ....... | ....... |
| .................................... | ...... | ...... | ...... | ....... | ....... |

5.  (a) Has your company successfully used the possibility of applying for a compulsory licence under Sections 37 or 41 of the Patents Act to obtain a licence in the last three years?  (Please tick)

Yes ☐    No ☐

(b) If 'yes', on how many occasions has this occurred during the period? ............

6.  In cases where you have been refused a licence (see item 3 above), what principal alternative action have you taken?  (Possibly tick more than one)

(a) Obtained broadly similar production rights from another source ☐

(b) Obtained broadly similar information through your own R & D ☐

(c) Developed unrelated lines of production based on your own R & D - or on patents, know-how, etc. obtained from another source ☐

(d) Developed unrelated lines of production with little R & D content ☐

(e) Undertook patent litigation for (i) revocation ☐

(ii) compulsory licence ☐

(f) Any other action (please specify) ............................
............................................................. ☐

(g) No particular action ☐

7.  How much expenditure on R & D in 1966-8 (annual average) would you have saved if you had been able to obtain all the licences you required?

(£'000) ............................

## X.  Impact on Technical Knowledge

1.  Broadly speaking, would you say that published patent specifications (apart from those to which you have gained access under licence) contribute to the spread of technical knowledge in your main fields of activity?  (Please tick appropriate answer)

    (a)  Very little          ☐

    (b)  Somewhat             ☐

    (c)  Substantially        ☐

2.  Does your company benefit from having access to published patent specifications in any of the following ways:  (Please tick appropriate box)

|  | Very little | Somewhat | Fairly Sub-stantially | Very Sub-stantially |
|---|---|---|---|---|
| (a) Provide guidance and stimulation for research staff on technical matters | ☐ | ☐ | ☐ | ☐ |
| (b) Provide management with a rather general 'feel' for new developments of a scientific sort | ☐ | ☐ | ☐ | ☐ |
| (c) Provide management with knowledge about the activities of competitors | ☐ | ☐ | ☐ | ☐ |
| (d) Assist patent staff with questions of 'prior art', 'infringement', etc. | ☐ | ☐ | ☐ | ☐ |

3.  Supposing an annual fee were charged for access to all new patent specifications, abridgements, etc. at the British Patent Office, what in your judgment would be the order of magnitude of the maximum sum that your company would have been prepared to pay for access to specifications published in 1968?  (Please tick the appropriate amount.)

    (a) Less than £1,000          ☐

    (b) £1,000 - 5,000            ☐

    (c) £5,000 - 20,000           ☐

    (d) £20,000 - 50,000          ☐

    (e) £50,000 - 100,000         ☐

    (f) Over £100,000             ☐

---

Name of person to whom enquiries on this form should be addressed          ...............................

Tel. No.          ...............................

Extension          ...............................

<u>Notes on Particular Questions: Form B</u>

<u>Section VI</u>

Q.6  An answer to the nearest 10 per cent would probably be adequate.

<u>Section VII</u>

Q.2(a)  Please state whether there were any patents held by your company that you would not licence to outsiders on any terms that could reasonably be offered.

Q.3  By 'active promotion' of licence sales we would understand that certain of your company's staff seek out prospective licencees as part of their routine work.

<u>Section VIII</u>

Questions in this section need particularly careful handling and are probably better explained through discussion than on paper.  In anticipation of such a discussion, we offer the following notes:

Q.1(a)  By 'patent-based' production we mean production that is heavily dependent on patent protection.  All goods produced by your company that you have patented, or that you produce under licence or that embody your patented or licensed processes, materials or components, are eligible for consideration under this heading, but we ask you to include only those for which your patents or licences are judged by management to be crucial.  For example, we would imagine that an ordinary motor vehicle which incorporates numerous patented components of a sort readily available from more than one supplier would not be judged to be patent-based.  On the other hand, a chemical whose production is restricted by licence to two or three manufacturers or a drug based on a material available only under licence from a single supplier would probably be 'patent-based' within the meaning of our term.

It is hard at this stage to give more explicit guidance than this, since much will depend on circumstances and on the nature of your principal product lines.  Inevitably, there will be room for some variation of opinion as to what should be included, but we believe it should be possible to arrive at a meaningful estimate for each main production category, if not a very precise one.  Please enter as accurate a percentage as you feel is possible for each category that you reported on Form A, resisting the temptation to exaggerate (in order to enhance the importance of the patent system) or to understate (so minimising the scope of protection).  Here, as elsewhere, your answers will be treated in the strictest confidence.

Q.2(a)  If available, the allocation for R & D costs appearing in your cost accounts for the relevant categories of production would be acceptable.  If not, please make the best estimate you can.

Q.2(b)  This figure might emerge as some average of rates for royalties on selling value specified in the relevant licence agreements.

Q.3  Please make the best estimate you can of the share of total profits (item 2 in Section I, Form A) accounted for by patent-based production in the various categories reported.

Q.4  This question invites your judgment as to how much of your patent-based production in 1968 would not have been undertaken, had effective patent protection not been available.  We should like you to tackle this question by considering what would have happened if the patent system confronting you in recent years had been substantially different from what it actually was.  The precise 'alternative situation' we have in mind is that there would be a system broadly resembling the actual one, with the exception that all patented goods and processes would be subject to <u>compulsory licence on reasonable commercial terms</u>.  In such a situation, no patentee would be able to refuse an application for a licence, or to grant licences on an exclusive or similarly restricted basis.  We cannot be very specific as to what 'reasonable commercial terms' would be, since they would vary from case to case; however it can be assumed that they would be the sort of terms likely to be recommended by an independent arbitrator, such as the Comptroller of Patents.

402

- 2 -

NOTES B   (Section VIII, Q.4 continued)

It seems plausible that there would be some  reduction in the scope and
volume of patent-based production as between the actual position and the
alternative situation outlined above.  In the extreme case, all patent-based
production might disappear under the modified system, perhaps to be replaced
by production of a type less heavily dependent on patents.  More realistically,
it is likely that some types of patent-based production would survive under
such a system, either because some production opportunities would be too
profitable to miss despite the threat of competition, or because the essential
technical information could be kept secret or transmitted in a controlled way
through agreements which do not involve patents, or because some reorganisation
might be forthcoming in the industry to overcome the worst threats of
competition.

We should like you to do your best, using this approach, to estimate the
proportion (by selling value) of your actual patent-based production in 1968
that would not be undertaken under the modified patent system described above.
Please note that we ask you to compare actual production in 1968 with what
it would have been in that year had the modified patent system been established
for a number of years.  Thus the essential comparison is between two long run
situations, rather than 'before and after', thereby avoiding effects associated
with the transition from one situation to the other.

We recognise that an exercise of this sort may present difficulties, and
we hope to discuss these at a meeting before the Form is completed.  We should
perhaps stress that the exercise is a device for assessing the impact of the
existing system, and in no sense reflects any pre-judgement of the system on
our part.

Q.5   This question extends the line of enquiry developed in Q.4.  You are invited to
state broadly what alternative action would have been taken under a modified
patent system to compensate for the loss of patent-based production referred
to in Q.4.

Section IX

Q.4   If space is short, please give details for the most important cases, adding a
note of the total number of cases that arose in the period.

Q.7   Here, as in Section X, we ask you to approach the question by considering an
alternative situation in which compulsory licences would be available for all
patents on reasonable commercial terms (supposing for the purposes of this
question that the scope of patented information were not affected).  A very
round figure would be quite adequate.

# SELECT BIBLIOGRAPHY

Details are given below of major published works on which we relied particularly heavily in the study. The list is not comprehensive. Other sources are noted in the text.

Blanco-White, T. A. *Patents for Inventions* (3rd edition, Stevens, 1962).

Boehm, K. in collaboration with Silberston, A. *The British Patent System: 1. Administration* (Cambridge University Press, 1967).

Brazell, D. E. *Manufacturing Under Licence* (Kenneth Mason, Havant, Hampshire, 1967).

Cooper, M. H. *Prices and Profits in the Pharmaceutical Industry* (Pergamon Press, 1966).

Firestone, O. J. *Economic Implications of Patents* (University of Ottawa Press, 1971).

Freeman, C. 'The Plastics Industry', *National Institute Economic Review* (Nov. 1963).

Freeman, C. 'Research and Development in Electronic Capital Goods', *N.I.E.R.*, (Nov. 1965).

Freeman, C. *The Role of Small Firms in Innovation in the United Kingdom Since 1945*, Research Report No. 6 for the Committee of Inquiry on Small Firms (H.M.S.O., 1971).

Jewkes, J., Sawers, D. and Stillerman, R. *The Sources of Invention* (2nd edition, Macmillan, 1969).

Kaysen, C. *United States v. United Shoe Machinery Corporation* (Harvard University Press, 1956).

Maclaurin, W. R. *Invention and Innovation in the Radio Industry* (Macmillan, New York, 1949).

Maclaurin, W. R. 'Patents and Technical Progress – A Study of Television', *Journal of Political Economy*, LVIII (Feb.–Dec. 1950).

Mansfield, E. *Industrial Research and Technical Innovation: An Econometric Analysis* (Longmans, 1969).

Mansfield, E. *The Economics of Technological Change* (Longmans, 1969).

National Bureau of Economic Research, *The Rate and Direction of Inventive Activity: Economic and Social Factors* (Princeton University Press, 1962).

Neale, A. D. *The Anti-trust Laws of the United States of America* (2nd edition, Cambridge University Press, 1970).

O'Brien, D. P. 'Patent Protection and Competition in Polyamide and Polyester Fibre Manufacture', *Journal of Industrial Economics*, XII (March 1964).

Patent, Trade Mark and Copyright Foundation, *IDEA: The Patent, Trade Mark and Copyright Journal of Research and Education* (By the Foundation: Washington D.C., quarterly).

Pratten, C. F. *Economies of Scale in Manufacturing Industry*, Department of Applied Economics Occasional Paper 28 (Cambridge University Press, 1971).

Salter, W. E. G., *Productivity and Technical Change* (Cambridge University Press, 1960).

Scherer, F. M. 'Firm Size, Market Structure, Opportunity, and the Output of Patented Inventions', *American Economic Review*, LV (1965), p. 1097.

Schmookler, J. *Invention and Economic Growth* (Harvard University Press, 1966).

404     **Selected bibliography**

Sturmey, S. G. *The Economic Development of Radio* (Duckworth, 1958).
Sturmey, S. G. 'Patents and Progress in Radio', *Manchester School of Economic and Social Studies*, xxviii, No. 1 (Jan. 1960).
Walker, H. D. *Market Power and Price Levels in the Ethical Drug Industry* (Indiana University Press, 1971).

*Official Reports*

(All published in London by H.M.S.O. unless otherwise stated. Reports are listed in chronological order.)

*Patents and Designs Acts*, Final Report of the Departmental Committee (Swan Committee) on the Patents and Designs Acts (Cmd. 7206), 1947. This Committee also produced First and Second Interim Reports (Cmd. 6618, 1945, and Cmd. 6789, 1946, respectively).
*Study of United States Patent System*, a series of studies of the U.S. Senate Subcommittee on Patents, Trademarks and Copyrights, 85th Congress, 1st and 2nd Sessions (U.S. Government Printing Office, 1957 and 1958).
*Administered Prices, Drugs*, Report of the Antitrust Subcommittee of the U.S. Senate Committee on the Judiciary (Kefauver Committee), (U.S. Government Printing Office, 1961).
*Patents, Designs and Trade Marks*, Annual Reports of the Comptroller-General of Patents, Designs and Trade Marks (1966–71).
*Report of the Committee of Enquiry into the Relationship of the Pharmaceutical Industry with the National Health Service, 1965–67* (Sainsbury Report), Cmd. 3410 (1967).
*Statistics of Science and Technology*, a periodic (recently, annual) survey by the Department of Education and Science/Ministry of Technology, 1967, 1968 and 1970.
*Gaps in Technology*, a series of reports by the Committee for Science Policy of the O.E.C.D. (by the O.E.C.D., Paris, 1969).
*The British Patent System*, Report of the Committee to Examine the Patent System (Banks Committee), Cmd. 4407 (July 1970).
*Small Firms*, Report of the Committee of Inquiry on Small Firms (Bolton Committee), Cmd. 4811 (November 1971).

# INDEX